NO WAY BACK HOME

The Unexpected Life of a Czech Family in India (1938 - 1977)

Miki
Hruska &
Evelyn
Ellerman

 FriesenPress

Suite 300 - 990 Fort St
Victoria, BC, V8V 3K2
Canada

www.friesenpress.com

Additional Contributer:
Evelyn Ellerman, PhD, Editor

ISBN
978-1-5255-6027-9 (Hardcover)
978-1-5255-6028-6 (Paperback)
978-1-5255-6029-3 (eBook)

1. BIOGRAPHY & AUTOBIOGRAPHY, PERSONAL MEMOIRS

Distributed to the trade by The Ingram Book Company

Dr. Pavel Jelen, Prof. (Emer.), PhD., P. Eng.
University of Alberta
and
Past President, Czechoslovak Society
of Arts and Sciences of Alberta (SVU)

A lively and occasionally gripping life story of an expatriate Czech family thrust into the often chaotic conditions of Indian society during the final years of British colonial rule. Seen through the eyes of the son of a self-made and occasionally authoritarian father, the family's story is intertwined with glimpses into Indian history, life in Calcutta, and interactions with other foreign newcomers and with Indians, both rich and poor. The book describes interactions with well-known personalities such as the Croatian born Mother Teresa and other European missionaries. Descriptions of family life include fascinating stories about the author's father trekking through Sikkim and Nepal and winning the downhill ski championship of India. The author's boarding school experiences connect with family memories of the Himalayas and visits to Kashmir, which are contrasted with precarious trips to see family in Communist Czechoslovakia. *No Way Back Home* is a page-turning book, containing many lessons for us all.

Dr. Klara Kolinska
Assistant Prof., Department of Anglophone
Literatures and Cultures,
Charles University, Prague

Miroslav ("Miki") Hruska's family saga *No Way Back Home* is a genial, refreshing, and illustrative example of the noticeably emergent genre of life writing, which combines a fascinating – and all-too-real – personal story with meticulously performed research of historical facts. Miki Hruska recounts his family narrative against the backdrop of some of the most fateful events that shaped the character of the twentieth century, not only for the Western world, but also for the East. Readers are offered a truly engaging insight into the circumstances that would bring an "average" young Czech family from their homeland to the whirl of Calcutta in the 1930s, what establishing a new existence in such a different world involved, and what eventually sent them on a new journey years later. The carefully documented story is told with enthusiasm, honesty and relish that make it a truly rewarding read – for fact, as well as for the simple joy of following a tale of another human being's life.

Asma Sayed, Ph.D.
Faculty, Department of English
President, CACLALS
Kwantlen Polytechnic University

Mike Hruska, a Czech-Indian-Australian-Canadian, has lived a truly global life. His book takes his readers on a unique and rare journey. The history of the Czechs in India, many of whom came to work at Bata Shoe Company during the prime days of the Raj, escaping the Second World War, forms the backdrop of Hruska's book. There is little known about India's relationship with the Czech Republic and the Czech families that lived in British India, and Hruska's book fills that void. Focusing on his family's life in Calcutta, Bengal, from the late '30s to the late '70s, Hruska brings out the contradictions that make India so complex: the joys of multiple religions, languages and tradition, and the chaos of it all. *No Way Back Home* is also a multilingual feast with words from Czech, Hindi, Bengali, and other languages, sprinkled throughout. Mike Hruska's book sheds a unique light on the experiences of migration and the shaping of a global identity.

Abhijit Gupta
Prof., Department of English
Director, Jadavpur University Press
Jadavpur University
Calcutta

Despite the storied history of Calcutta's cosmopolitan past, surprisingly little is known about the Czech presence in the city, especially in the years before the Second World War. Mirsolav Hruska's vivid account of a Calcutta childhood traces the travels of the Hruska family in the late 1930s from a Europe on the verge of catastrophe to faraway Calcutta. Thanks to the advice of his friend Tomik Bata, Hruska's father is able to secure employment in the famed Bata shoe factory in Batanagar, from where the family was soon to move to Calcutta. Through the eyes of the young Miki, we see a city which is endlessly fascinating and kaleidoscopic, but also precariously poised between change and chaos. Hruska mixes his reminiscences with a chronicle of the momentous times that he lived in, and the result is a work equally rooted in memory, history and geography.

A host of memorable characters intersperse Hruska's telling—Dandia the cleaner of floors who becomes a master of Czech cuisine, the eccentric dandyish Armenian, Coco Mackterich, who looks as if he has stepped out a Toulouse Lautrec painting, Suren Chatterjee, police commissioner turned family friend. And there is the tantalizing section on Czech cooking adapted for Calcutta, now entirely forgotten, but ripe for rediscovery.

For the Calcuttan, there is a wealth of riches in this book to linger over. Hruska's description of the shops and eateries of central Calcutta is a veritable delight—we learn, for example, that Trinca's was set up by one of the two Swiss families who owned Flury's. And who will not be charmed by the revelation that Josette Flury was young Miki's first serious infatuation? *No Way Back Home* is a work that will be a source of great interest to general and specialist readers alike, and a significant historical document in its own right.

DEDICATION

With love and gratitude to my dear wife, Evie

ACKNOWLEDGMENTS

My friend Mařus Bohman of Sydney, Australia, set me off on this journey. It was after reading Mařus' book on her family that I realised there was an important story to tell about my own. Thanks, Mařus, for your generosity and assistance!

This book was written over a period of many years and bears the imprint of many people; I have accumulated several personal debts of gratitude. First and foremost, I would like to express my love and thanks to my wife, Dr. Evelyn (Evie) Ellerman, for her invaluable and unfailing encouragement, guidance, and advice. She inspired me to pursue this dream. Drawing on her extensive knowledge of literature and oral history, she was my sounding board when the "little grey cells" were asleep and problems needed to be solved. She read and edited the manuscript many times and I consider this book as much hers as mine.

Part of the preparation for writing this book was developing the ability to speak Czech well enough to interview my relatives about family history. In addition to improving my spoken Czech, I wanted to be able to read historical material in that language. A series of wonderful teachers has helped me accomplish both of these linguistic goals, starting in 2006, in Prague, with Dr. Ilona Starý Kořánová. Ilona showed great patience in getting me past the simple "kitchen Czech" that I had acquired at home as a child. She also generously gave me many of the books on Bata that I used in writing this memoir. The fact that I could read and understand such valuable resources is a testimony to her skill as a Czech teacher. Děkuji Ilona!

Once I was able to ask intelligent questions in Czech and understand the answers, I went to Czech Republic to formally interview my relatives. This was such a rewarding experience; I still re-play the tapes made during these sessions. They are filled with laughter and many loud accusations that the other person had it all wrong! I would like to thank my uncles Ota and Karel Krobath for their enthusiastic assistance in telling their stories, as well as my treasured cousin Dr. Karel Krobath, for his support and guidance.

In Edmonton, Jana Marešová taught me still more about the Czech language and provided the breakthrough moment when I became truly confident in reading Czech. She had to put up with some stubborn resistance on the grammar front, but I am glad she brushed this aside. Děkuji Jana!

In recent years, there have been several Czech teachers here in Edmonton who helped me to progress further in my ability to speak and read the language of my parents; in particular, I would like to mention Dr. Stanislav Štěpánik, Dr. Ondřej Haváč, and Dr. Lida Lambeinova. And I would also like to acknowledge the Wirth Institute at the University of Alberta, which brought these scholars to Edmonton. Without this program, I would never have been able to further my skills in Czech. Another institutional boon has been the friendship and support provided by the SVU (the Czecho-Slovak association) in Edmonton, where I regularly have the opportunity to practice my Czech.

My sister, Martina, and brother-in-law, Ivan, encouraged me and were willing to correct errors in dates or events and make suggestions for content related to family history. I would also like to acknowledge the support of my brother, Charley, and my daughter, Toni.

Finally, I cannot forget all the encouragement from my Canadian family and friends for their comments and active support over the years it took me to complete this book. In this regard, I want especially to mention Dr. Noémi Nagy, who pushed me, asking *when* the book would be ready.

HOW I CAME TO
WRITE THIS BOOK

Life is not what one lived,
But what one remembers
And how one remembers it
In order to recount it.

Gabriel Garcia Marquez[1]

The New Market

Early in a beautiful Canadian autumn in 2005, my wife, Evie, and I were sitting on our patio when she casually mentioned that a regional SHARP (Society for the History of Authorship, Reading & Publishing) conference had been scheduled for Calcutta in January 2006. She added that she would like to attend but only if I would accompany her. Being a Calcutta boy at heart, I couldn't ignore this chance to return to the city of my birth. So, in early 2006, we found ourselves in Calcutta, staying at the Fairlawn Hotel,

---

1   This passage is taken from the opening words in Gabriel Garcia Marquez' work, *Living to Tell the Tale*.

a 200-year-old landmark centrally located near the New Market (also known as Hogg Market). The Fairlawn had a "faded charm" generated in part by the memorabilia of a lifetime collected by its octogenarian owner, Mrs. Violet Smith; once we had settled in, we met with Violet for tea in the courtyard, where I soon discovered that she had known my Dad quite well in the 40s, 50s, and 60s, when my parents were living and working in Calcutta.

In the years since the family had left Calcutta, I had visited the city sporadically, mostly on business. But, on this trip for my wife's academic conference, I had time to kill and so began to revisit spots that I remembered from my youth and childhood. By chance, it happened that a former high school friend, Edward (Tiny) Gonsalves from Stonyhurst College in Lancashire, England, whom I had not met physically in 50 years, was then in India building roads near Patna, Bihar. We had been in sporadic touch via email and so arranged to meet in Calcutta. While Evie attended her conference at Jadavpur University, I went for a stroll to the New Market with Tiny.

We had barely made our way into the car park area, directly in front of the market building, when we heard a voice calling out "*Sahib, Sahib!*" I stopped momentarily but walked on and then noticed a short, wiry old man carrying a cane basket under his arm. He wore the red armband of an official porter working at the Market. As he approached, he addressed me in Hindi: "*Mera nam Baswant hai, Memsahib Hruska's coolie*" ("My name is Baswant, Mrs. Hruska's porter"). I stopped dead in my tracks, utterly dumbfounded. He knew my mother's name! I was overwhelmed as I pondered his greeting. He had actually recognized me and remembered Mum by name after more than 45 years. I wondered how such a simple man would recognize *me* at all, let alone remember my mother's name after all this time. Clearly, over the decades that she had shopped at the Market, Mum had developed a friendship with him; I was touched by his spirit. But, as I thought more about it over the coming days, he seemed to represent the best part of this wonderful city that had been such a big part of her life and my own.

This surprising and wonderful encounter at the New Market was the last of a series of emotional events that led me to reconstruct the unique narrative of my parents' journey from Czechoslovakia, to India, and finally, Australia.

The "Dark Side" of the Family and the Hungarian Connection

It had all started in early 1990 with my mother's furtive revelation of a family secret. Our family had by then migrated to Australia from Calcutta. Most Sundays in Sydney, around 4 pm, I would visit my mother, who lived close to me. On these visits, we chatted on various matters over a cup of coffee and her home-made Czech pastry. She liked to talk about current affairs and politics, which suited me just fine. This particular Sunday, I was expecting that we would talk about Prime Minister Bob Hawke, who had won the recent election. I knew that she had never quite got over Hawke's silly 1987 election promise that, by 1990, "no Australian child would be living in poverty." What actually happened during our visit was quite different; but, as I reflected on it later, my mother had increasingly started to reminisce on our Sunday visits about her past life in both Czechoslovakia and India.

Mum met me at the door. The normal welcoming procedure was set aside: there were no embraces, no pleasantries. She immediately took my hand and led me into her living room with an unusual determination. I sat down on the couch next to her, sensing her urgency to tell me something important. Looking at me with quiet intensity, she said, "Mikusko (her pet name for me), I feel that I must tell you about the 'dark side' of the family."

Being somewhat surprised and having no idea what her concern might be, I am afraid that I responded in a light-hearted manner, "Of course, Mum, why don't you tell me of this 'dark side.'"

She paused momentarily, looked at me directly for a moment, quickly turned away in shame and said, "Miki, I have to tell you that Babička (my grandmother, 'Babi') was illegitimate!"

I could see that this revelation was a serious thing for her, so I responded slowly, "No! Are you sure? How do you know?" in a tone that reassured her of my concern about the terrible thing that she had just exposed. Mum replied, "I have kept Babi's birth certificate away from you. It is around here somewhere; but the section that records the father's name has been left blank."

In western society, at the time we had this conversation, illegitimacy no longer made any difference to the ways in which people viewed themselves or were treated by their family members. But, for my mother's generation, illegitimacy was still a terrible thing. In her youth, the shame of it had the power to rip families apart: pregnant girls could be shunned and abandoned to poverty, or death. No one spoke of it. So, for my mother, this was indeed a deep, dark secret. It turned out that my great grandmother (on my mother's side), Mathilda Vesely,[2] was in service at a nobleman's estate in Hungary working as domestic help, possibly in the kitchen, during 1894 or 1895. She was very young, about 14, at the time.

Mum believed that her grandmother worked on the estate of Count Esterházy just south of Vienna at a place called Eisenstadt. Furthermore, Mum had reason to believe that one of the younger members of the Esterházy family had taken advantage of the girl with the result that she had fallen pregnant. Before the baby was born, my great grandmother left the Esterházy estate to return to her village, where a marriage was eventually arranged. However, her new husband would not lend his name to the birth certificate when the baby, Marie, was born.

As family stories go, this was mildly interesting to me, but not earth-shattering. It might or might not be true; after all, what proof was there that the Esterházys were involved in any way. But, what came next truly surprised me. My mother continued with her story. "You know Miki, this Hungarian may have had some remorse about what he had done; for, when your great grandmother left the household, she was given some money, three valuable violins and some library books as compensation. She was told that, if she ever needed to raise some money, all she had to do was sell a violin or a book."

The story got better in the telling; I shifted forward on the couch and listened more intently. Mum went on. "Apparently much later, she sold one of these violins to help her husband establish his first business as a metal worker in Třebíč (a small town in Southern Moravia). Eventually, she left the two remaining violins to her daughter, our Babi."

Mum believed that a second violin was later sold when Babi married Děda (my grandfather); apparently, they used the cash to establish his own

2   In the nineteenth and early twentieth centuries, birth certificates could have variant spellings for the family name. My great grandmother's birth certificate has "Vesely," while her daughter's birth certificate has "Vesela."

4

business as a locksmith, general repair, handy man in Uničov (a very small town in upper central Moravia).

After my mother related this piece of family history to me, I had two reactions. On the one hand, the story had overtones of a 19th century historical romance, where the immoral nobleman corrupts the innocent country girl. On the other, if this account were true, then I had some noble Hungarian blood coursing through my veins, not something that a true Czech could be entirely happy about. Bob Hawke never even got a mention on this amazing Sunday.

Being a music lover and knowing that the Esterházys at Eisenstadt engaged Haydn as their court composer for many years and that the estate had a resident orchestra of professional musicians, I was most intrigued by the violin story. If there were any noble establishment in that part of Hungary that would have had a few violins to spare, it would have been at Eisenstadt. Many years later, when I met my cousin Karel Krobath in Vienna after an interval of over 40 years, I related the violin story to him. He stood up, left the room and returned with a violin on which he proceeded to play a few bars. Inside the instrument, stamped quite plainly, was the word "Esterházy." This was the remaining violin, which had been passed on to Karel as the only violin player among my great grandmother's descendants.

A few years later, Evie and I visited Eisenstadt, where we learned that the Esterházys had a reputation of being very generous to their pensioned servants, sending them off to their villages with money and goods. It was beginning to look as though the story of the pregnant serving girl sent home with money, violins and books might be true.

After seeing the violin in Vienna and hearing from other members of the family that the story was accurate, I realized how ignorant I was about our family history and wondered what other information, or even "secrets," there might be. Certainly, our immediate family history of disruption and migration due to the Second World War and subsequent imposition of an Iron Curtain over Czechoslovakia after the War's end meant that there were a lot of gaps for me to fill in. My parents had been separated from the land of their birth for many decades; but, I had been separated from my parents from the age of six for twenty years at ever more remote boarding schools and, finally, university. There was a lot I didn't know about my parents, simply because I had spent so much of my life away from them. As I approached retirement, I began to think about identity: my own, and that of my parents. I asked myself what were the touchstones of geography, culture and family circumstance that make us who we are?

Visit to Prague in 2002

The next moment leading to the writing of this book occurred in 2002. The Czech Republic, as it is now known, had not really been on my mind prior to retirement. I had lived and worked for over four decades in Germany and then Australia and had retired in October of 2001. Evie and I had met earlier when she came to attend the wedding of a mutual friend; subsequently, she took a year-long sabbatical leave in Sydney. During her year there, we married, but chose to live in Canada where she still worked. Our honeymoon trip back to Canada in July and August of 2002 would take us through Asia and then Europe, including a visit to Prague.

By 2002, Prague had really started to come alive after years of suffocation under Communism. We arrived just after massive flooding had devastated many historic areas near the river. But the old city was still magical. The narrow and irregular streets; the diverse architectural styles of the churches, monasteries and convents, many of which are highly ornamented; the gentle hillsides covered with tiers of pastel houses decorated with painted emblems: all these features totally enchanted us. The copper-and amber-coloured rooftops of the *Staré Město* (Old Town) shimmered and came alive with the glow of each evening's sunset.

We loved being in this city. There was so much to see and do that we knew we needed to spend more time there. I wanted to know more about the art, history, architecture, people, language and culture. For the first time, I realized a strong impulse to explore my Czech identity. From my childhood exposure to the language in my parents' home, I had enough conversational Czech to speak with people in Prague, even though my grammar was weak and words occasionally failed me. To my surprise, I found myself wrapping this new feeling of "Czechishness" around me and enjoying every minute of it. An inner voice kept saying, "Miki, this is a significant part of your heritage and of who you are!" I began to reflect more and more about the circumstances of my parents' departure from Czechoslovakia to India and eventually Australia.

I suggested to Evie that we return to Prague for three or four months, perhaps during her next sabbatical year; my thinking was that she could attend conferences and pursue her research from a base in Europe while I tried to track down my extended family. She told me that her next sabbatical would be in 2006. It would take a few years to settle in to my new life in Canada before I started to plan for our sojourn in Prague. But, finally, I was ready. I decided to begin by renewing my connections with those surviving members of the family with whom I had had irregular contact. This could be a starting point to finding others. But how to do this? Who could I write to? Who could I call? I told Evie that I had a first cousin, Karel Krobath, who was a physician in Vienna but that I had no idea how to reach him. My wife worked for a distance education university and was more than familiar with online searches. She rolled her eyes and said: "Miki. He is a doctor. He will be on the internet." Within 15 minutes, she had found my cousin and given me his email address.

The e-mail message that I sent to Karel was quite formal in tone. I informed him of our plans to visit and stay for some time in Prague and asked, in a tentative way, whether we could perhaps meet somewhere convenient in the Czech Republic or in Vienna. I had no great expectations as I felt like a total stranger at this point. Imagine my joy when I received the most welcoming and happy response, as he introduced me to his own family and filled in our personal "family contact gap." It seemed to me that the long years under Communist rule had caused many of my Czech relatives to hang onto their memories of family; whereas, I, who had grown up and lived in democracies, had been absorbed in everything *but* maintaining family connections. I remember quite clearly that my first thoughts on reading his email were, "I have a family…"

On the first day of our three-month stay in Prague in 2006, it was ironic that my initial meeting with Karel (before we even picked up our door key) was at a bank near our apartment in the Vinohrady district. Right at the bank's front entrance, who should be entering at the same time? None other than Karel, only I did not recognize him immediately. We both stopped and looked at each other furtively and slowly recognition dawned on us. I said, "Karel, is that you? And he responded, "Miki, is that you? Ah, good. Just a second, I have a printer for your wife's computer here in my car." The omens looked good for making family connections in Prague.

My Daughter's Wedding in Sydney, 2007

Throughout 2006 and 2007, I discovered and visited several times my two remaining maternal uncles and their families in various, small Moravian towns. Then, in Sydney, November 2007, I attended my daughter Toni's wedding. On this trip, my sister Martina gave me the proverbial "shoebox" full of personal material belonging to my parents: newspaper clippings, photos, and other mementoes. There were photographs with early images of my maternal grandparents. I was amazed to actually see a photo of my maternal grandfather for the first time. In addition, there was a surprising and unexpected set of early photographs and news clippings relating mainly to Dad, especially to his exploits as a nationally recognized athlete. I knew that he had been a champion skier and ski jumper. The clippings portrayed Dad participating in ski jumping competitions in Czechoslovakia. However, I had had absolutely no idea that he was also such an accomplished runner and that his name was well known in Czech athletic circles.

The papers in this personal archive contained all sorts of correspondence that helped to fill gaps in the story of my parents' early years in Batanagar, the Bata shoe factory town on the outskirts of Calcutta, which was their first home in India. It also contained information about their subsequent move to Calcutta after Dad left Bata. One shock was to find documentation that Dad had been fired from his job with Bata. The reason appears to have been intransigence towards some of the Czechs in the management hierarchy of the Indian operation. Dad had always led us to believe that he left Bata of his own volition and then moved to Calcutta to another job. I remember his words clearly, "Miki, I left because I wanted to get away from Bata, which was the closest thing you could find to a modern form of slavery." Perhaps pride had led him to alter the story, but this was not the first time I was to find information that didn't match what I thought I knew about my parents.

Gradually, more questions welled up in my mind. Did my father's experience at Bata mirror that of other displaced Czechs? Was the experience of those who had come to India earlier in the 1930s to start the factory different from that of my father's generation, who left as war became an imminent threat to the company? I was able to find answers to some of these questions over the coming years of research.

Mařus Bohman

Prior to my 2007 visit to Sydney to attend Toni's wedding, I had absolutely no plans to write a book. I was just trying to learn more about my family while poring over a growing number of photographs, scanning them digitally, and restoring them. I planned to prepare some sort of organized pictorial record and leave a digital copy for my children and grandchildren, my brother and sister, and their respective families. I viewed this as my retirement project. However, while I was in Sydney for the wedding, my sister gave me a book written by an acquaintance of my own generation, Mařus Bohman. Her book outlined the lives of her parents and her brothers and painted a portrait of her parents' Bata years working in Mokameh in Eastern India. She had also written about their social life there. I was quite encouraged by this story; it made me feel that I might be able to gather my own information into a book about my parents' time in India. But, I wanted to focus on the social and political context that affected them as well. It seemed to me that my family and other readers might be interested in having a personal window into the lives of Czechs living at a time of great change, at the end of empire in India.

The Isabel Allende Factor

Ideas about writing a book began to occupy my thoughts more consistently. In early spring of 2007, Evie and I had to drive for six hours from Edmonton to Southern Alberta to visit some friends. On such long car trips, we often listen to music or an audiobook. This time, the audiobook was Isabel Allende's *My Invented Country*. Well, right from the very beginning, her story captivated me. She recounted her memories of Chile, memories that captured the essence of Chile's striking geography, its engaging history and how those elements had sculpted its social landscape. She included numerous colourful accounts of her family and friends, with all their eccentricities and foibles. Allende also explored the personal consequences to her and her family of the tragic coup against her uncle, the democratically elected President Allende, by the CIA-supported General Pinochet. Isabel Allende had been forced to leave the country.

Allende's conception of "nostalgia" engendered in me the notion that I also had a paintbrush and canvas. My painting could express the memories, the nuances and moods of family histories and relations, the changing historical times, the geography of the land and the spaces that we had lived in. What a challenge! I started to think about my parents differently - not about what they did as a simple sequence of events, but how their lives intersected with their geographic, social and political space over time. No matter how much research I did, there would always be gaps in their story - thoughts, acts, and feelings that I would not be able to recover. But I was fascinated about exploring the possibility of what *could* be recovered.

What prompts a person to write about their family? A difficult question, indeed! For me, the impetus came from a sense of loss, dislocation, and confusion. My parents were Czech, but historical circumstances took them to Calcutta in a British colony half-way around the world. They were not refugees at first; they were simply taking advantage of an exotic job opportunity. Once in Calcutta, the Second World War and then subsequent Communist rule in Czechoslovakia made them stateless people for a time. They could not go home. Thankfully, India granted them citizenship, so they decided to make their lives there. But, then, political events in Bengal led all of the Czechs to leave, most of them for Sydney, Australia, in the 1950s and 60s. Essentially, the Bata-men and their families were always strangers in a strange land.

Unlike my parents, for whom Moravia in Czechoslovakia would always be home, I was born in India. India *was* my cultural reality in a way it never could be for my parents. To begin with, I spent the first 20 years of my life in as diverse a culture as one could imagine. The accident of my Czech background was of little interest to me as a child. I spoke English, some Hindi in the broader community, and some Czech, but only at home. Increasingly, as I grew older and went away to boarding school and university, I was submerged in other languages and cultures, first English and then German. In some ways, I became a sort of cultural chameleon, fitting in wherever I happened to be. My wife jokes that I adopt whichever national identity will win me an argument.

For the greater part of my life, this shifting cultural ground did not bother me. In fact, it gave me a cultural fluidity that I enjoyed. So, for 60 years, I just got on with living - boarding school, university, work, marriage, children, travel, friends. But, like so many other people, as I approached retirement, I began to take an interest in lives other than my own. Since I had lived so much of my own life separated from my parents, I began to wonder who they really were. My father had a large presence in every room he entered; it struck me that I had never actually known him. My mother had spent much of her life in the shadows; who was she? How did their experiences shape their lives? They had been displaced and had lived most of their lives on the margins of other cultures. How had that shaped them and could I capture some of these experiences in a book?

My Love Affair with India

Another important driver for me in writing this book is my lifelong love affair with the city of my birth and the country that is my spiritual home. Although I have always said that India gave me my values, whenever I return to Calcutta or indeed to other parts of India, my emotions range from joy in the face of its humanity and the colossal sweep of its languages, religions, and cultures, to utter despair when confronted with the cruelties of life - the poverty, the contradictions, and the monumental political and social problems. So, one of the things I wanted to try and untangle in my mind by writing this book was the incredible enigma that is Calcutta and Bengal, because they provided the daily backdrop for my family's life.

In particular, I wanted to write about Calcutta which, to a large extent, *is* my India. The famous Indian satirist Jag Suraiya wrote in his book, *Calcutta: A City Remembered*, the following: "Anyone who has ever been there has his own Calcutta. All you have to do is listen to it, as I have listened to mine."[3] How true. I definitely have my own Calcutta, not the modern one, but a Calcutta from the late 40s to the early 70s. I have not

---

3   Jag Suraiya, *Rickshaw Ragtime: Calcutta Remembered*, 5.

only listened to it, I have viewed it through what I hope is an observant and enquiring eye; I have felt it, smelt, and touched it.

Conclusion

There were, therefore, several emotional moments over a period of years that led me to think that I had a story to tell: my mother's story about the "dark side" of the family; the visit to Prague and my growing sense of affinity to my Czech roots; the unexpected "shoe box of family information"; efforts to find and get re-acquainted with Czech family members; inspiration from Isabel Allende's own story; reading Mařus Bohman's book about her parents and, finally, the poignant meeting with Baswant, the porter, at the New Market. In the process of writing, I came to know fresh, and sometimes disturbing, details of my parents' lives. I was able to correct many impressions that were just plain wrong and fill in memories that were sketchy at best. More importantly, I think I got to know my parents in a way that was not possible during a childhood and youth spent so far away from home. Equally important for me was the opportunity to forge vibrant connections with my mother's family;[4] these strengthened ties have provided me with a touchstone that gives shape and meaning to my personal and cultural identity.

As I was collecting stories and organizing information, I began to realize for the first time that our family's life was inextricably linked to a much larger story - the historical context and geo-political reality of Europe at the end of the Depression and on the brink of the Second World War, the last days of the British Raj, and the early years of India's Independence. We were present for and profoundly affected by some of the great turning points of twentieth century world history. I have therefore tried to situate our family's story within the context of major historical events in Czechoslovakia and India, but in particular Bengal.

4   It must be clear by now that this is book is rooted only in stories from my mother's side of the family for the sole reason that I have no documents or stories from my father's side, except for one or two anecdotes that I have included and identified as such. Saddest of all for me is that, as a result of World War II, I have no connection with the Hruska family; we simply don't know where they are.

I am not a trained scholar of Indian History (my history degree is in Ancient History), but I have a keen interest in the history of India and particularly Calcutta. I have tried to read as widely as possible, both from my personal library and from public and university libraries. I have consulted as well with those academic friends who are Indians with an interest in the subject matter. I have therefore re-created a history for the Czech and Indian phases of my parents' lives based on lived experience, family stories, research, interviews, and personal documents, as well as the advice and guidance of many friends and scholars. All the historical events and facts can be verified. Any errors this book contains in presentation or interpretation are my own responsibility.

Although this book is a true story, some of my narrative is a reconstruction, using dialogue, location, and a personal point of view. I have also used the techniques of creative non-fiction to re-create scenes and situations in order to draw word pictures or illuminate facts. I hope this device brings parts of the story to life and provides readers with better insight into the lives of the people and the country.

A note on street names. Many Calcutta street names have been changed over the years, both to erase colonial associations and to honour the lives and achievements of notable Indians. The unfortunate result is that some of these new street names have no resonance with the local inhabitants. Others do. For instance, in the past, you might travel down Chowringhee Rd. and turn into Park Street. Today you would be travelling down Jawaharlal Nehru Road and turning into Mother Teresa Sarani. Both are very notable and recognizable figures and the change has been more easily accommodated. But, if you wanted to turn into Free School Street on the left from Mother Teresa Sarani, today you would be turning into Mirza Ghalib Street. Who was Mirza Ghalib? His name does not resonate with most Calcuttans and so, if you were to ask for directions today, you would still ask for Free School Street. Some name changes still confuse people. For instance, the former Elgin Road was renamed for a much beloved Prime Minister Lal Bahadur Shastri after his death in 1965. But today, this road has mysteriously acquired the name Lala Lajpat Rai Sarani and no one can tell you when this name change occurred or for what reason. Some streets have been named after Ho Chi Minh, Lenin, Karl Marx,

Friedrich Engels, Hare Krishna, William Jones, Picasso, Charlie Chaplin, Shakespeare, Helen Keller, William Carey (missionary) and James Hickey (newspaperman). Even the British were guilty of ambivalence over street names. For instance, Chittaranjan Avenue was renamed Central Avenue but then changed back to Chittaranjan Avenue after Indian Independence.[5] For clarity in this book, I have decided to use street names as they existed during my parents' lives to avoid confusing myself, if no one else.

Name changes extended to the city itself. Calcutta was an anglicized name given to the city by the British. Prior to 2000 there was a move to rename Calcutta. On 23 December 2000, the name change was approved and Calcutta officially became Kolkata, probably for patriotic rather than linguistic reasons. In addition, the province of Bengal was re-named Bangla, which means Bengali. Again, as these name changes occurred well after my parents left India, I refer to present day Kolkata and Bangla as Calcutta and Bengal. Mention is also made of Ootacamund, which is an anglicized reference. The original Indian name is Udhagamandalam, but for the purposes of this book and for the reasons listed above, I refer to it as Ooty - interestingly, this name is still commonly used in tourist and marketing brochures, likely because it is easy to say. No offence is meant.

In writing this book, I have used various languages that are germane to the context. These include Bengali, Hindi, Sikkimese, Czech, French, German, Hungarian and Spanish. I have assembled them into a Glossary under each language heading. For the Hindi references, I have made my own interpretation of the sound(s) and transcribed them into a representation of the English equivalent in written form. As I am not a native Hindi speaker, but have heard and spoken Hindi over many years, I have used the colloquial language as I know it and transcribed the words accordingly. I make no apologies for correctness of grammar or proper vocabulary usage.

And thus I decided to become the camel that put its nose under the vast tent of the family narrative and invite you to join me ......

5   The reference for the new street names is www.calcutta.web.com under Street Name Change.

CHAPTER 1

Czech Origins

Even though my parents came from Czechoslovakia, I knew very little about that country while growing up in India. It was all very far away from my reality. My parents and their friends spoke a language totally unlike anything I heard on the streets of Calcutta. At that point in my life, I could speak a sort of "kitchen Czech," aside from the more usual English and Hindi. And, I basically knew nothing of Czech history or culture. But there were moments during the year when I was aware that my family came from a place with its own traditions. At Christmas, our family would go to celebrate midnight mass in Batanagar, a Bata factory town close to Calcutta. We would sit in the little church filled to bursting with mothers and children, while the men spilled out through the front entrance onto the surrounding lawn. There was a collective sense of joy and pride when the Czech community prayed in its own language and, especially at the end of the service, when they sang the Czech national anthem, "*Kde domov můj?*" ("*Where is My Country?*"). Many members of this little expatriate community shed a tear as they heard the beautiful words. Their singing was an outlet for their emotions and a focus for their collective sense of identity and loss. For these people, my parents and their friends, it was increasingly obvious that there was no way back home. As a child, I had no notion of who these people were or how they had come to be half-way around the world from their homeland. It would take me several decades to begin linking such memories with historical fact in order to understand something about their lives and my own identity.

Getting Started

My family's earliest stories about itself come from the last decades of the Austro-Hungarian Empire, when the Habsburgs controlled the region from which the family came. But, although we know the birth and death dates for some of those people, the real stories about my mother's family date from the birth of that illegitimate baby girl, my grandmother - affectionately known as Babi - who was born on 10 January, 1895, in Třebíč and christened Marie Anna Vesela.

Babi's future husband, Rudolf Krobath, was born on 11 April, 1889, in Padochov to Karel Krobath, a locksmith, and Apolonia Rysava. The Krobaths, had moved to the Brno region from their home in Marburg (*Maribor* in Czech) in the then Duchy of Styria.[6] My grandfather Rudolf started his working life at a vehicle repair workshop in Třebíč. This early apprenticeship defined his later career in mechanical repair workshops for all kinds of cars, motorcycles, farm equipment, and bicycles. His son, my Uncle Karel, recounts that his father had a very good relationship with his clients in Třebíč. We have an interesting document about my grandfather, an *Arbeitszeugnis* ("Certificate of Work"), that is very complimentary. There is some uncertainty as to how and when Babi and Rudolf Krobath met, but it was likely in Třebíč or even at Eisenstadt where they both worked. According to my Uncle Ota, my grandmother had gone to work at the very same estate where her own mother had come to grief some years earlier.

---

6   The Duchy of Styria was located in a part of modern-day southeastern Austria and northern Slovenia. It remained part of the crown lands of the Austro-Hungarian Empire until its dissolution in 1918. For some reason, the Krobath family decided to move from Styria to the Brno region in the north, a region that later fell within the boundaries of the present-day Czech Republic. Eventually, the family moved again and settled in Třebíč, a small town some 35 miles to the west of Brno.

This information surprised me. But it was probably emblematic of the times that people followed *any* opportunity for work. The money the young people earned by working for the Esterházy family would have been used to support their own families in Třebíč. At some point during this employment, the First World War broke out. I do not know when Babi and Rudolf left their jobs with the Esterházys, but I suspect that they decided to return to Třebíč in hopes of avoiding the emerging troubles brought by war. Babi became pregnant and the next important event in their lives was their marriage on 7 October, 1916 at the respective ages of 22 and 27. A mere 3 months after their marriage, my mother, Marta, was born on 3 January, 1917. At this time, the family was Catholic, so they must have felt considerable pressure to get married in order to avoid any social stigma.

With the end of the War, the Austro-Hungarian Empire dissolved and Czechoslovakia emerged as an independent country on 28 October, 1918.[7] The region known as Moravia, where my grandparents lived, formed part of the new nation. At first, the country could barely feed itself, but a turning point in the rejuvenation of the Czech economy took place around 1920.[8] By 1929, the Czech economy had become quite strong. It was blessed with many entrepreneurs who exhibited great vision and very progressive management ideas and systems.

However, despite this emerging period of prosperity in Czechoslovakia after the end of the War, the Krobaths struggled financially. By the mid 1920s, their family had grown to five children; making ends meet was proving to be a challenge. They lived in a house (which no longer exists) that was adjacent to the river that runs through Třebíč. I have visited the spot and it has a lovely direct outlook onto the river. My grandfather continued to work in the centre of Třebíč as a mechanic; his pride and joy during these years was his Harley Davidson.

The Great Harley Davidson Affair

And, so, we come to a Sunday in Třebíč. It is not important which Sunday, but for readers who care about such things, it is the third Sunday. Much of

---

7   Hugh Agnew, *The Czechs and the Lands of the Bohemian Crown*, 170.
8   By 1920, a new Constitution was in place, as well as a legal system, and an organized state administration.

the small town has been astir for many hours. As the church bells peal loud and far, people start to make their way to church for mass. At the *Kostel Svatého Martina* (Church of the Holy Martin), Father Janda prepares to say mass for his congregation. The Church is slowly filling up as grandfather Rudolf, Babi and their children take their places in their accustomed pew at the back of the church. As is the custom in these parts, Rudolf doffs his hat to friends and acquaintances and greetings are acknowledged.

The mass passes uneventfully: the incense burner swirls about to great effect and soon the altar is shrouded in fragrant smoke that drifts up to the ceiling. Not all the candles on the altar have been lit as these are austere times and the Church has to set an example. On this particular Sunday, there is no especially inspired singing from the choir, the sermon is delivered in a monotone and the theme hardly seems relevant or uplifting. The collection plate is passed up and down the pews for the faithful to make their humble offerings in silence. It has been a typical Sunday mass: the congregation, not quite engaged, has gone through the motions. Many people are consulting their watches, mentally counting down the remaining time until they can get home for lunch. The Krobath family is no exception. Then, the organist plays a rousing liturgical piece to herald the celebrants departing for the sacristy. Fr. Janda acknowledges his congregation with a small nod of the head as he passes by. His flock slowly empties out of the church.

But on this particular Sunday, grandfather Rudolf waits inside the church door at the end of the mass. He tells Marie to take the children outside and wait for him there. When Fr. Janda re-appears from the sacristy, he has changed out of his liturgical vestments into his lay clothes. Rudolf approaches slowly to talk to him.

"*Nazdar důstojný pane* (Greetings, Reverend Father) *Janda.*"

"*Nazdar, Rudolfe.* How is the family? I was pleased to see you all at church today."

"I hope that I am not holding you back from anything important. I just wanted to ask whether you have been happy with the test ride that you made on my Harley Davidson. If you are satisfied, please make arrangements to pay for it at the agreed price. If you are not happy, then please return the Harley to my workshop tomorrow," replies Rudolf.

"Oh! That is a good idea. I will see you tomorrow."

In the morning, Rudolf goes to the workshop and awaits the arrival of Fr. Janda. He also takes the opportunity to prepare the papers that are required to complete the sale and transfer of the motorbike. At about 10 o'clock, the priest arrives on the Harley Davidson and indicates to Rudolf that he has indeed been very happy with the Harley and wants to keep it.

"Well, Fr. Janda, we agreed on a price of 6,000 crowns. How do you wish to settle this amount?" asks Rudolf.

"I'm sorry. I know that a price was mentioned but I didn't realize that you actually wanted me to *pay* for the Harley," replies the priest.

"Fr. Janda, if you are happy with the motorcycle and you want to keep it, then you can pay me for it. I have expenses to meet. I have already spent money for minor parts and materials to get the bike up to scratch and I have paid my mechanic. I do not run a charity. This workshop is my livelihood and I am a decent, honest worker in this community. If you cannot pay me at this moment, I can wait a few days until you make your financial arrangements."

"But Rudolf, I think that you should reconsider. By this generous act of making the Harley available to me, you are doing a good deed. And I am sure that this offering will not go unnoticed in the eyes of the Holy Mother Church and Jesus. You can be assured that you will be rewarded in heaven."

"Fr. Janda. Good deeds are all well and good, but these are tough times. I have a family to look after *now* and I cannot afford to wait for my reward in heaven. Jesus is not going to pay the bills or put food on the table *today*. This is not the first time that you have tried to pressure me to be charitable. In the past, you have asked me to forget an invoice for other work that I have done for you. On those occasions I *was* charitable: I ignored small amounts. But the Harley is worth much more to me than a minor repair bill. So, either pay me the agreed price or return the Harley. I must say… you always seem to have an excuse to avoid paying or delaying the payment and I am utterly fed up!" replies an increasingly agitated Rudolf.

"That may be so," says the priest. "But I know that you are a decent, God-fearing Catholic and I personally will not forget this gesture of donating the Harley to Holy Mother Church. I am sure you know that the Church has very limited financial resources. Paying for this motorcycle will put a great strain on our church funds. It would impede our pastoral work, which is meant to bring comfort and solace to all our congregation."

"Father, I do not give a damn for your spiritual welfare problems. We are both in the same boat: you have to look after your congregation and I have to look after my family. I care first about my family and my workers. If you had no intention to pay the agreed amount, then why did you indicate that you were interested in buying the Harley from me in the first place? I could have saved myself the cost of preparing it for sale! And if finding money locally was an issue, why have you not looked elsewhere for funds?"

"But that would have meant going to Brno to obtain funds and that would have been very difficult for me and jeopardized my doing the Church's work," replies Fr. Janda.

"So, are you going to pay me or not?"

"Rudolf, be reasonable. Why can't you look at the wonderful offer of the Harley to the Church as a contribution to God's good work here on earth? I am absolutely sure that you will be rewarded a thousand times when you are in heaven enjoying eternal happiness in God's bosom."

"I'll give you God's bosom! If you don't get out of this driveway immediately, I may arrange for *you* to have an early appointment with God's bosom yourself!" shouts Rudolf. "*Už té mám až po krk* (I've had it up to here with you), *zatracený katolický zloději* (bloody Catholic thieves)! If you have no intention of paying for the Harley, get out of my workshop right now, or I'll use your dog collar to throw you out."

The story goes that Rudolf then took the Harley and secured it in his workshop. As Fr. Janda was leaving, Rudolf, vibrating with rage and disappointment, muttered, "*Katolický odpadky a paraziti (Catholic rubbish and parasites)*. You can take your hypocritical religion and shove it you know where!" As the priest left, Rudolf told him to take his future repair business to Brno.

Still angry, Rudolf stopped work, grabbed his coat, went home and collected the birth certificates of his wife and all his children. From there, he went straight to the public notary's office in Třebíč, where he demanded that the notary officially record on all the birth certificates that Rudolf had withdrawn himself and his family from the Catholic Church.

This lively tale, told to me by both my surviving uncles, explains the Public Notary's attestation that I found on the birth certificate of my grandmother Marie - small and handwritten on the left-hand side; it affirms that the whole family left the Catholic Church effective Sunday, 18 June, 1922. According to my Uncle Karel, there had been a Rudolf Krobathian explosion of monumental proportions when his father got home from the interview with the priest. In his father's eyes, the Church should have been ashamed for trying this form of pastoral blackmail in such difficult economic times. The result was that, with this incident, there was no further relationship between Mum's family and the Catholic Church.

The story of the family's departure from the Church has become part of Krobath lore. I have re-created it with great pride, as today all Krobaths view this decision by grandfather Rudolf as a "badge of honour." I must admit that, when I heard the story, I also felt a sense of pride to be associated by blood with a man of such strong principles. Later on, apparently, grandfather Rudolf did manage to sell the Harley, but the buyer's name remains unknown. I like to think of him roaring around to this day somewhere on the misty country roads of the Czech countryside.

The Depression Years in Třebíč and the Move to Uničov

The Depression years had a delayed economic impact in Czechoslovakia.[9] Nevertheless, getting work in the early 1930s became increasingly difficult. Farm machinery repair and maintenance and serving other needs in the agricultural sector had been a prime source of work for my grandfather. However, such steady work gradually dried up. With a family of children now numbering ten, he decided to re-settle his family in an area where the living costs were lower and where he could perhaps eke out a living in a different farming community. As it happened, his son Honza had been living and working near Uničov. Therefore, and as an interim measure, in 1930 or 1931, the family moved from Třebíč to Uničov, which is approximately 14 miles north of the major town of Olomouc. Here another part of the story unfolded. My grandmother still had two violins and some of the valuable books left to her by her mother. The proceeds of the sale of

---

9   Jaroslav Pánek, Oldřich Tůma, et al., *A History of the Czech Lands*, 416.

one of these violins (let's call it Violin #2) helped my grandfather establish a modest mechanical workshop, possibly in Uničov but more likely near Šternberk (a small neighbouring town with a greater population than Uničov), and where most of his customers would likely have come from.

The move to Uničov improved the family's financial situation to a certain extent. There, they were closer to the land than in a city or town and they had better access to the farmers and local food markets. Some work trickled into the workshop from repairs to farm equipment and bicycles. The family struggled. My Uncle Karel said that their existence during these times was very much hand to mouth. They had little money and the younger children wore the clothes that their elder siblings had outgrown. He added that my grandmother, Babi, cooked mainly potatoes and cabbage; meat (usually a rabbit) was included only very occasionally. The boys made regular forays into the neighbouring forests to find mushrooms to add to the daily meals. This was how the rural poor ate at this time in Czechoslovakia. Uncle Karel added that, when they could afford flour, it was used to make dumplings which, at the very least, filled their stomachs. On days when there was no food, he remembers that the children were sent out into the surrounding countryside up to a radius of 6 miles to find or beg food. But, despite all these hardships, the family stayed together.

I asked my Uncle Karel about my grandfather; in particular, I was interested to know if he had any recollection about him as a person. From the only surviving photographs, I thought I saw a man whose face reflected a hard life. The way he looked straight ahead in one photograph made me think of someone asking, "What is next for my family?" Karel thought about his response very carefully and noted that his father had been a very good and capable tradesman. Over the years he had acquired woodworking skills and he had built all the furniture for their home. But he excelled as an auto mechanic and had a reputation in the district as the go-to person who could repair practically anything. This reputation helped him to keep solvent. What really tickled my fancy was the fact that he loved motorcycles, especially his Harley Davidson. I often wondered if he went on trips into the countryside with Babi on the back seat. They would have presented quite a sight together. But he also loved the violin and could play it competently.

Karel was particular in mentioning that his father was a very honourable man and that he had made every effort to instill this quality in his children, as well as the need to value work and fair dealing with people. This probably explains in part his falling out with the Catholic priest of Třebíč who stubbornly refused to honour a deal. I think that would have been quite a brave step for someone to take at the time. He also apparently had a large circle of friends and nurtured these friendships throughout his life. And no doubt a lot of this nurturing took place in the *hospoda* (tavern). Karel added that he never saw his father roaring drunk, although that may also have meant that he could hold his beer and slivovitz.

In the first picture I encountered of my maternal grandfather, I see a man, very simply dressed, likely wearing his one and only suit, but who appears to have a mischievous grin on his face. I remember being quite surprised because the photograph did not match my own expectations. I had imagined a slightly smaller, but stocky man, judging by the appearance of other members of his family. In another photo, he is sitting with his friends in the *hospoda* enjoying a beer in what appears to be an animated discussion that had drawn a laugh.

When I go through my memory of talks with Mum about her parents, the only verbal image of him that came to mind was when she recounted that he loved to play the violin and that he had an interest in medicine. He actually had aspirations for Mum to become a doctor and that *she* learn to play the violin as well. Mum mentioned that on occasions he would become quite impatient with her when he believed that she was not taking her violin lessons seriously. She related that, on one memorable occasion, his on-going frustration with her led him to hit her on the head with the violin, which damaged the bridge of the instrument. Nursing a small bump on her head, she yelled at her father and decided not to speak to him until further notice. The tragedy for Mum was that he died from tuberculosis soon after this incident; Mum told me that she regretted all her life that her last words with her father had been uttered in anger.

In the early 1930s, several of the older children, my mother included, moved to the Otrakovice area for employment with the Bata shoe factory which, by that time, was well established in Zlin. It was a very successful company that was known throughout the country. Otrokovice, only about

6 miles away, could be considered a dormitory suburb to Zlin: it offered affordable housing and easy access to the Bata factories. The Krobath family had grown considerably and had already started to disperse. Obviously, finding a position at the Bata shoe factory at Zlin was paramount in much of their thinking. During these Depression years, the eldest children had to put their individual dreams on hold. The two eldest, Mum and her brother Noris, went to Otrokovice to find work as teenagers. Despite the difficult times, Bata was still hiring. Details are quite sketchy but it appears that one of Mum's brothers, probably Bořivoj, was already working at Bata and living as a boarder with one of the distant relatives of Tomáš Baťa. According to my Uncle Ota, it was Bořivoj who helped Mum and Noris get work at the Bata factory. I believe that Mum started with Bata soon after her 16th birthday in about 1933. She told me that she and Noris continued to provide her mother with financial support for the family.

As soon as they were of age, other members of the family started to work at the Bata plant as well. By 1936, Mum, Noris, Bořivoj, and their sister Marketa had found work there; all but Bořivoj lived with an architect in Zlin. They were followed by my aunt Hanka, and later by uncles Jan, Ota, and Jura. Jura later left and joined a construction company; his work took him to all parts of Czechoslovakia. With the older children sending money home, Babi no longer had to send the younger ones out to forage in the forest for food.

Bata and Zlin

Since the Bata shoe company forms such an important part of my family's history, I think I should provide some context here. Tomáš Baťa,[10] born 3 April, 1876 and died 12 July, 1932 in a plane crash, founded his company in Zlin. "Why Zlin?" you might ask. The little Moravian town of Zlin was his birthplace. It is located close to the eastern border with Slovakia. At the turn of the 20th century, Zlin was not very economically advanced. Its economy was based primarily on agriculture and single-family, craft-based enterprises. But it is quite beautifully situated in a small valley, surrounded

---

10   The Czech family name is spelled Baťa; but as his business grew, the spelling "Bata" was used. This is the spelling that I will use throughout this book.

by gentle rolling hills. This is the town where Tomáš Bata's father, Antonin Bata, established his small cobbler's workshop. In 1894, Antonin's three children from his first marriage, Anna, Antonin and 18-year-old Tomáš, asked for an advance on their mother's inheritance and started their own shoe-making enterprise.

In 1895, the affordability of leather in shoemaking seemed out of reach and so Bata looked at what was available, namely a low-cost alternative: canvas. This is typical of the innovative thinking that led to the success of Bata. Why not make canvas shoes with leather soles instead? He started to produce this hybrid shoe and called them "*batovky*." Soon, he built his first factory.

Tomáš Bata was a visionary who was quite committed to new ideas in management and production. He travelled to Germany and the United States, so that he could absorb the most forward-thinking practices into his shoe manufacturing business in Czechoslovakia. He noted, in particular, progressive methods in organising the workforce so that there would be a harmonious relationship between management and workers. Bata was especially influenced by people such as Ebenezer Howard,[11] a journalist who had developed an interest in town planning. Howard's goal was to have towns free of slums, where people could enjoy the benefits of stable work, education, and recreation in a "country" environment - a blend of city and nature. For Bata, Zlin satisfied most elements in this vision and so it became the focus of his ideas for a planned community.

At first, the company expanded gradually but, with the advent of WW I and the attendant military requirement for boots and other footwear, the company soon experienced rapid growth. By the end of World War I, Bata had become a leader in the era of mass-produced shoes, exporting shoes throughout Europe and the Middle East. And Zlin benefited from this rapid growth. The town was transformed through its association with Bata. By 1917, the year my mother was born, Bata employed over 5,000 people.

Tomáš Bata proved to be an extraordinary entrepreneur. In the economic slump that followed the War, Bata kept his company going by cutting

11   Karel Kouba, "Bata's Zlin in Czechoslovakia 1918-1938: A Model of a High Modernist City."

the price of shoes in half and asking his workers to take a 40% cut in wages. He buffered this request by supplying his workforce with food and clothing at drastically reduced prices. In addition, Bata modernized his production equipment and started profit-sharing schemes for his workforce. Early on, Tomáš Bata developed a system of identifying and training people like my father to acquire managerial skills. His goal was to provide the company with the necessary management and leadership skills for the future. And, it was after WW I that the company began its aggressive global expansion into many countries. By 1931, this list included India. So, in an economically depressed region of Czechoslovakia, during a worldwide depression, the Bata shoe factory grew and provided employment opportunities for thousands of people, including my mother and most of her siblings.

Events Leading up to the Second World War

At this point, I need to insert another bit of context that had a significant effect on my mother's family. After World War I, Czechoslovakian politicians were confronted with the issue of the Sudeten Germans and their desire for autonomy. After 28 October, 1918, the new state of Czechoslovakia found itself comprising a mix of three dominant peoples: the Czechs, the Slovaks (hence the name Czechoslovakia) and more than three million ethnic Germans - with German as their main language - living in Czechoslovakia. The region was loosely known as the Sudetenland.[12]

12 At the end of WWI the treaties of Versailles, St Germain and Trianon broke up the Austro-Hungarian Empire and took land from Germany, Austria and Hungary to give to other countries. The Sudeten (referred to the northern, southwest, and western areas of Czechoslovakia) was taken away from Germany and the Austro-Hungarian Empire and given to Czechoslovakia. After WWI, the English name "Sudetenland" (specifically the border districts of Bohemia, Moravia, and those parts of Silesia located within Czechoslovakia) was coined and was used to define the areas that had large ethnic German populations. The region also included Czechs, Slovaks, Hungarians, Poles and Ruthenians. It should be noted that the term "Sudetenland" encompassed areas well beyond the Sudeten Mountains, namely parts of Karlovy Vary, Liberec, Olomouc, Moravia-Silesia, and Ústí nad Labem. In 1934, the entire Czechoslovak population numbered approx. 14.73m, of which 22% were German speakers (approx. 3.23 m). During the inter-war years, the term "Sudetendeutsche" (Sudeten Germans) was used to refer to ALL indigenous ethnic Germans.

The Germans who lived in this area referred to themselves as Sudeten Germans. They enjoyed quite generous benefits but were not considered to be part of the mainstream Czech peoples and their German language was not officially recognized by the Czechoslovak state.

This refusal to recognize German as a language of the newly-formed country occurred in 1919. They resigned themselves to living in Czechoslovakia as an ethnic minority, but resented the situation, as they believed that they had no stake in the Czech constitution. They felt their rights were being ignored and that they were discriminated against as individuals. In the 1918 census, they comprised roughly 24% of the total Czech population.[13] With the worldwide Depression in the 1930s and with their underprivileged status in the new Czechoslovakia, they listened quite sympathetically to the propaganda of Adolf Hitler in Germany. Once Austria had been annexed to Germany in early 1938 (the "Anschluss"), Hitler began to enthusiastically support and encourage Sudeten German ideas of joining his Third Reich to escape the perceived oppression by the ruling Czech majority. They were especially interested in the economic measures he instituted to improve job opportunities in Germany. As a result, the Sudeten Germans started to agitate for autonomy from Czechoslovakia, even the right to align with Nazi Germany.[14] The problem that would shortly arise for my mother's family was that they were Czechs living amongst the Sudeten Germans in the disputed region.

Tensions were running high in Europe. Hitler had been able to exert considerable pressure leading up to the 1938 Treaty of Munich.[15] In late September 1938, Great Britain, France and Italy met with Hitler in Munich to resolve the issue of the Sudetenland. Hitler's demands remained unshakeable, namely, that the Sudeten lands would be annexed by Germany. The Allies were desperate to avoid another war, so a policy of appeasement was adopted, the main thrust of which was to pressure the Czechs, under President Beneš, to accede to Hitler's demands. Britain and France made it very clear to the Czech government that they would be on their own if they did not comply. The Czechs now realized that their 1925

---

13   Agnew, 168.
14   Ibid., 192-193.
15   Ibid., 204-206.

treaty with France meant nothing.[16] And so, in a last-ditch attempt to avoid a second world war, the sell-out of the Czechoslovak nation was inevitable: the lands where the Sudeten Germans lived would be ceded to Germany in 1938. In one fell swoop, Bohemia and Moravia lost approximately 38% of their combined land, together with the German population and approximately 500,000 Czechs.[17] Even after this agreement, Hitler made further demands that the Czechs cede to Polish and Hungarian claims on Czech sovereign lands. The Czech army was mobilized on the country's relevant borders. On 29 September, 1938 in Munich, the English prime minister, Chamberlain, and French president, Daladier, formally capitulated to Hitler's demands; the Czechs were not allowed to take any part in the conference. Britain offered some vague guarantees to the Czechs regarding border security. With armed resistance deemed pointless, the Czechs finally accepted the terms of Munich on 30 September. President Beneš resigned and went into exile on 5 October, 1938.

The carving-up of approximately one third of Czech territory went ahead. Czechs who lived in these German-speaking areas were forced out. The Czech economy did not have the capacity to absorb all these displaced people, so unemployment increased dramatically. During the intervening period between October 1938 and March 1939, there was a great deal of political manoeuvering between the Czechs and the Slovaks, the Germans and the Czechs, and finally between the Germans and the Slovaks. It soon became obvious that Hitler didn't just want the Sudetenland, he wanted all of Czechoslovakia. In the final resolution of these negotiations, on

---

16   In 1925, Germany proposed that France, Germany, and Belgium recognize as permanent the frontiers that had been agreed at Versailles. This included the promise not to send German troops into the Rhineland and Alsace-Lorraine. France and the UK agreed. Germany, however, refused to guarantee its eastern frontiers. France signed separate treaties with Poland and Czechoslovakia to assure their security concerns. This treaty is known as the "Treaty of Mutual Guarantee Between France and Czechoslovakia," signed at Locarno, 16 October, 1925.

17   *K otázce vysídlení občanů ČSR ze Sudet, Těšínska, Podkarpatské Rusi a Slovenské republiky v letech 1938/1939* (para 1). (On the question of the displacement of citizens of Czechoslovakia from the Sudeten, Těšín, Sub-Carpathian and Slovak republics in 1938/1939). See Bruntal.net http://www.bruntal.net/2007072602-k-otazce-vysidleni-obcanu-csr-ze-sudet-tesinska-podkarpatske-rusi-a-slovenske-republiky-v-letech-1938-1939

15 March, 1939,[18] the Czechs agreed to place the country under Hitler's authority. The Third Reich then created the Protectorate of Bohemia and Moravia under German governors and the protection of the German army. Germans living in the Sudetenland were offered German citizenship. Unfortunately, the Czechs, who had been living in this area for generations, had very little choice but to leave the area, as they knew they would feel the wrath of the Sudeten Germans.

Uničov and Šternberk were located within this newly delineated region of Sudetenland after the Munich Agreement. And, after 1938, the Sudeten Germans started to exact their revenge on the Czech minority. It started with a general boycott of Czech businesses. Then, in early October 1939, the remaining Czechs, together with a few Jewish families living in these annexed lands, were given an ultimatum. They had either to cease their loyalty to the Czechoslovak government and remain in Sudetenland or leave everything behind and move out of the area.[19] The Krobath family livelihood worsened day by day. My grandfather Rudolf found it was becoming increasingly difficult to secure work for his repair shop. According to Uncle Karel, the Nazi officials informed my grandfather that, if he threw in his lot with the Germans, they would guarantee that his situation would improve. Grandfather turned the German offer down and made the hard decision to abandon everything and move the family to Otrokovice, where he believed he could get some work. He left everything behind, his workshop and all its equipment, with no chance of selling it or receiving compensation. He was a proud Czech man and could not bring himself to live in these German annexed territories. He was about 50 years old and in poor health, having recently been diagnosed with tuberculosis.

Uncle Karel remembers that, when the family made their move from Uničov to Otrokovice, they were allowed to take 33 pounds, or the equivalent of 1 suitcase each. In Otrokovice, they found it extremely difficult to find a place to stay and, according to my Uncle Ota, they found shelter in a small room at an abandoned dairy plant, where they lived in extremely cold, cramped and difficult conditions. Uncle Ota, the youngest surviving

---

18   Agnew, 207.
19   *K otázce vysídlení občanů ČSR ze Sudet, Těšínska, Podkarpatské Rusi a Slovenské republiky v letech 1938/1939* (paras 5-7).

child in the family, is unclear on this situation but it appears that there may have been seven or eight family members living in this one room. They lived there for quite some time until their plight became known to a social worker. As there were no other alternatives to accommodate the whole family in a more suitable living arrangement, the authorities decided to split them up and place the children with foster parents. Uncle Ota told me how extremely difficult this was on the family; but they finally agreed and so the younger children went to foster parents in Otrokovice. Mum and uncles Noris and Rudolf all helped with whatever financial support they could afford. However, Mum and Dad had married in 1937 and would soon be leaving Czechoslovakia.

With war now an inevitability, all Czechs - whether intellectuals, business people, or workers - began to prepare for what was coming. Some, like the Bata family, made private arrangements to move their liquid assets out of the country and to leave their lives in Czechoslovakia behind. It was during this time that Tomik Bata, son of the factory owner and a personal friend of my father's, advised him to leave Czechoslovakia, in fact offered him a place in the company's Indian operation.

The Rest of the Family:
Babička (Babi) My Maternal Grandmother

Before we get to the adventure of going to India, I would like now to introduce in more detail some of the people in my mother's family. In the process of writing this book, I came to realize that, as a child, I actually got to know my grandmother Babi reasonably well. She was quite a personality in her own right, a very real person to me. So, I started to sift through my memories and have tried here to portray my grandmother and some aspects of her life.

After her husband, Rudolf's death in 1946 at the relatively young age of 57, Babi moved her family to the village of Loučka (pronounced "Loadj-ka"). I first met my grandmother in Czechoslovakia two years later, in late January 1948, when I was seven years old. After arriving in Czechoslovakia from India, Mum and I made our way to Dolní Dlouhá Loučka (hereafter referred to as Loučka) by train and bus. Loučka is a small village midway between Uničov and Šternberk in the Olomouc region of

Northern Moravia. It is home to a very small rural community even now; but in the 1940s the population had peaked at around 300 people. It is a quaint village and its character has not changed much. Entering from the north, the road leads to a small central square with a well, the village's main water source. The earliest image I have of this particular spot were the few long benches where Babi and other grannies would sit, catching up on all the local news and village gossip. Even in the late 1940s, many of these grannies still wore the national dress of their district with rich, hand-embroidered blouses and stiff, starched, colourfully-pleated dresses riding over a petticoat. They all wore the obligatory headscarf. It was here in the village square that I got my first sight of Babi, as Mum and I got off the bus, recovered our luggage, and greeted her. Babi and Mum had a very emotional meeting after an absence of some ten years. So, this was it. I was seven years old and had finally met my grandmother. She was in her 50s, a largish, thickset woman, her body reflecting the reality of having had 13 children in a very short time.

Many of the details are unclear but I remember that, after we left the well, we walked down a narrow road with trees lining the right-hand side. We soon came to a small hidden pathway in the trees. All I could see was a little stream. In Czech, such a watercourse is called *potok* (little stream) and we always just referred to it as the *potok*. Laden with our luggage and with Babi leading the way, we followed the path and crossed a little bridge and soon stood in the small courtyard in front of her house. Babi's home was very old, small, and quite charming. At one end of the tiny footbridge, a short flight of steps led directly down to the *potok*. Most cottages were accessed by footbridges over the *potok* and presented a truly picturesque rural image. A small barn with a hayloft flanked one side of the house. Chickens and rabbits occupied the ground floor of this barn.

Babi's little house had been home to several of my uncles and aunts, many of whom now worked in Zlin and lived in Otrokovice, close by. My aunt Marketa had married a local man and lived in a house that shared a common boundary with Babi's. Aunt Hanka lived in Loučka with Babi. Hanka commuted to a neighbouring factory that produced tractors and farm equipment. Uncle Jura lived intermittently in Loučka, since his job as a construction worker took him all over the country. The youngest surviving son, my Uncle Ota, would later live directly across the road with his wife, Boženka. He became the village's handyman and, over time, was totally self-sufficient, with a backyard full of vegetable gardens, fruit trees, and pens for rabbits, chickens, and pigeons. They were a close-knit family and supported each other; to this day they form my abiding memory of Loučka.

Babi's U-shaped house wrapped around the courtyard. It had an entrance located on the right wing that led directly into her famous kitchen. In many ways, her house resembled a miniature doll's house with small interior doorways, low ceilings and tiny rooms. But all life revolved around the kitchen, which was in many ways reminiscent of a Dutch family kitchen scene in a Brueghel painting. A magnificent ceramic stove with a large cooking surface and beautiful porcelain-tiled chimney dominated one wall. The cooking surface had a solid iron grate, perhaps a half inch thick, heated by wood and coal, burning directly underneath. Babi always seemed tired and she did not spend much time on her feet. A well-used, day bed graced the opposite wall, and she immediately retired there when we arrived, took off her slippers and reclined like a noble Roman lady of leisure into the sagging contours of her divan.

In fact, the kitchen divan was Babi's throne; from here she directed the activities of her household and neighbouring family. Her children helped with cleaning the house and the outside chores. They made daily trips to the well to draw water for her. They obtained firewood from the nearby forest to keep the kitchen stove going, which also warmed the house. She cooked here, but the kitchen also served as the family room, the dining room and lounge area. The kitchen was where any discussion about important "Krobath" matters occurred. And the family often gathered there just to socialize. All the day-to-day life of Loučka was exposed and analyzed in Babi's kitchen. In a village as small as Loučka, all the comings and goings were noted. It was in the kitchen that Babi dispensed advice to her daughters on everything from relationships, to raising children, to dealing with the baker, or with the communist officials who ran the village. She had no time for the local communist apparatchiks. And it was in the kitchen that I experienced her legendary sharp turn of phrase whenever she assailed them directly. Even at the tender age of seven, and despite not knowing the language very well, I noticed the occasional flashes of anger and the tart tongue. Indeed, many of the colourful words, phrases, and occasional swear words that became part of my "kitchen Czech" originated with dear old Babi. I think in particular of "*trouba hloupá*" (stupid nitwit).

Over the years, I discovered that Babi was not above poking a bit of fun at her "city boy" grandson. In 1959, after I had left Stonyhurst College in Lancashire, England to return to Australia, I decided to make a stopover in Czechoslovakia to visit my grandmother and other relatives. I made my way to Loučka and soon settled into my old room upstairs above the kitchen. I enjoyed seeing the Loučka family again and, after having been force-fed, like a goose being prepared for foie gras, with pork, mountains of cabbage and dumplings, all swimming in a veritable ocean of gravy, and later washed down with the obligatory slivovitz, I soon retired to bed.

Next morning, I took my 19-year-old self down to the kitchen to Babi's throne and sheepishly asked her where I could get some hot water to have a shave. Well, Babi got up off her divan, pursed her lips, put on her *papuče* (slippers), straightened her tracksuit pants, grabbed my hand and said, "Come with me." We went out to the courtyard and thence to the little bridge that straddled the *potok*; she pointed to the short flight of stone stairs leading directly into the stream. Then she told me in a cocky manner, "We still don't have running water but I am sure that the flowing water in the *potok* will do." It was early autumn and the water was bloody cold. So, I took my inaugural morning ablution and cold-water shave standing in the middle of this freezing stream in my boxer short pyjamas. This cold shave every morning did not improve with time, but my grandmother never let me in on the joke. I actually believed that all the village men were out in that stream, every day, shaving (even though I never saw one of them there)! She had made her point about the difference between city and village life, but she couldn't resist driving that point home every day of my visit. Despite this cruel joke, I do remember with fondness and affection this strong-willed, sharp-tongued woman, who had endured so much for the sake of her family. Little did I know that it would be decades before I would see her one last time, when she came to visit us in Sydney and stayed with us for six months.

Uncles Karel and Bořivoj Krobath

Some members of the family did not end up at the Bata shoe factory. My Uncle Karel, who now lives in Otrokovice, had decided early on that he wanted to train as a machinist; eventually he became well-versed in all sorts of tool-making machinery, including lathes, and turning and drilling machines. As a young man, he had served an apprenticeship with his father in his workshop and was familiar with a wide variety of mechanical repairs, including automobiles. When the War started and the Germans marched into Czechoslovakia, they forcibly took many Czechs to work in their factories near the German-Czechoslovak northern border as cheap labour. For many people, this was a death sentence, as they succumbed to a continual onslaught of enforced heavy work, under poor living conditions and deprivation. They were dispensable parts in the German factory system: the Germans made absolutely no effort to look after this workforce, because they could get additional labour south of the German-Czech border whenever they wanted to.

It became common knowledge that those who had been forcibly removed to work in Germany would likely never return. However, my Uncle Karel had a skill that the Germans needed, namely, experience as a skilled lathe operator and machinist; and he knew about automobiles. The Germans sent him to work in the armament factories at Eisenach, making military vehicles. Eisenach is located to the west of Czechoslovakia and situated in the state of Thuringia. An infant, pre-war, auto industry had existed there that produced the Dixi brand of vehicles. These car-making facilities were later acquired by BMW in 1928. With the outbreak of war, this BMW plant had been converted to produce not only armaments, but also aircraft engines, and automobile and motorcycle spare parts.

In 1944, the allies bombed this plant and it sustained heavy damage. While at Eisenach, Uncle Karel learnt that his father's tuberculosis and general health had deteriorated. The family was extremely concerned about him. Rudolf was the breadwinner and the family's livelihood appeared to be threatened. All production work had ceased at Eisenach as a result of the bombing, so my uncle took the opportunity to slip away in the general confusion and managed to make his way back to Plzen in Czechoslovakia. However, the Czech militia captured him and put him in prison until the

Czech security police decided what to do with him. During this intern-ment, he endured multiple beatings and theft of all his property by the Czech security police before he was allowed to return to Otrokovice on the condition that he went back to slave labour at Eisenach once he had seen his father. And, after some time, Karel did return to Eisenach to assist with the rebuilding of the workshop where he had worked previously.

His memory of his detention by the Czechs filled him with much disgust, as he recounted to me his mistreatment at the hands of his own countrymen. He remembered quite clearly that, at Eisenach, he had worked with a German technician who had been quite kind and helpful to him. This German not only helped him with food and clothing but took great pains to ensure that he did not get into any trouble because of his absence. Fortunately for Uncle Karel, the knowledge that his father was dying of tuberculosis had been taken into account. Anyway, after a second bombing in 1945, the plant where he worked was in a shambles and there was nothing more that could be done at Eisenach. In any case, Germany now lay in tatters; amid the great confusion all over the country, Karel took the opportunity to leave for good. This time, he managed to get back to Otrokovice without being caught and soon was helping his family in the workshop.

The War took its toll on my grandfather. In 1946, shortly after the War ended, he succumbed to the ravages of tuberculosis. After his death, Uncle Karel and one of his brothers took over the workshop in order to support the family, which was suffering from extreme poverty. But Uncle Karel had married Marie by this point and had his own family to look out for. His wife had been assigned to work in Germany as forced labour. However, her family managed to get one of their doctor friends to issue her with a medical certificate saying that she had tuberculosis; this prevented any extradition to a German factory and likely saved her life.

At the end of the War, the Beneš government nationalized numerous Czech companies, probably because of the dominant influence of the Communists in the new interim government.[20] As famous entrepreneurs, Tomáš and Jan A. Bata, were now personae non-gratae in their own

20   Derek Sayer, *The Coasts of Bohemia*, 244.

country. In February 1948, the Communists came to power and, as part of the process of creating a communist state, erased any reminders about Bata and his legacy. The Batas were portrayed as ruthless capitalists by the Communists; they even renamed the town of Zlin, "Gottwaldov." Of course, after the fall of Communism in Czechoslovakia, the Bata name and the name of Zlin were restored.

My Uncle Bořivoj, who had been employed at Bata prior to the War, was directed by management to work at the "Svit" factory located near Loučka. My grandmother had found it very difficult to make ends meet in Otrokovice. So, shortly after grandfather Rudolf's death in 1946, the family decided that it would in the best interests of all that they also move to Loučka. They bought a small house there, the same one that I came to know when I visited Czechoslovakia with my parents a couple of years later.

Uncle Karel did not move there because, after the Communists appropriated the family's workshop, he was forced to find alternate work in a factory that used the machinery he had become familiar with. He worked there until he retired. Today he lives in Otrokovice in a modest fifth-floor apartment with Aunt Marie. At the time they moved into it, the apartment was on the fringes of town by the river; it still has a very nice view to an open field and a forest beyond. It is in a charming location.

Karel and Marie are a warm and hospitable couple; every visit to them is most enjoyable. My Aunt Marie is a very good cook; the highlight for me is the opportunity to taste her wonderful Czech cooking. Aunt Marie enjoys *detektivky* (detective books) very much. Evie also reads detective stories; and it is the one area where she can connect with Aunt Marie, given that neither of them speaks the other's language. Each time we visit the Czech Republic, we make a stop in Prague at *Palác Knih* (Palace of Books) *Luxor* bookstore on *Václavské náměstí* (Wenceslas Square) to buy Aunt Marie detective stories that have been translated into Czech. Uncle Karel, not being very mobile, listens to the radio. His son Karel has given him as many electronic toys as possible and Uncle Karel, when he is in command of the TV, is surrounded by a bevy of remote-control devices. Cousin Karel also bought him a car some time back and, when he could still drive, my uncle made the trip to Vienna to celebrate birthdays and Christmas with his son. Other times, he would visit his brother in Loučka and daughter in Vrbno, which is located to the north of Olomouc. With his wartime experiences in Germany, Uncle Karel learnt to speak German. While my Czech was passable when Evie and I first started to visit my uncle, it was, for some years, easier for me to communicate with Uncle Karel in German whenever a Czech word or expression failed me. These days, after having taken many Czech classes, I find that we can visit only in Czech.

Whenever we visit Karel and Marie, we also visit my other Aunt Marie who was married to my Uncle Rudolf (named for my grandfather). Unfortunately, I missed getting to know Uncle Rudolf, as he died in July 2006, just when we had come to Prague during Evie's sabbatical year. Uncle Rudolf was affectionately nicknamed *bratr filozof* (Brother Philosopher) by Mum, probably because he was considered to be the intellectual in the family. I was told that he joined the Communist Party as a young man. One view amongst family members was that joining the Party was an economic decision rather than a true ideological commitment; however, some have a contrary view.

To Join the Communist Party or Not

After the Communists took over, considerable pressure was put on people to join the Party. When you became a Communist Party member, you got quicker access to better apartments (whenever they became available), and the waiting time to buy a car was reduced from five-eight years to approximately three years. But, most importantly, you got access to the better-paid jobs. My uncles Noris, Bořivoj, Rudolf and Ota all joined the Communist Party; but the opinion in the family was that, in the case of Noris, Ota and Bořivoj, joining the Party was simply a passport to a better job and a possible jump ahead in the queue for an apartment. Uncle Noris, for example, never spoke in any positive way about Communism or its effect on their lives.

However, I think my Uncle Rudolf and his wife were dedicated Communist Party members. I remember always being warned when we visited them to be very careful about offering any political views, since no one could be sure where such idle talk would lead. And this rule also applied to their children. I can't speak to the conditions that led these relatives to join the Party, but I admire the brave convictions of my Uncle

Karel. He held true to his beliefs and never did join the Communist Party; consequently, he suffered. He ended up working in a machinery shop in Otrokovice and waited patiently in line for his apartment. But he is a person who is comfortable with his lot in life and happy with his decision. I couldn't possibly pass judgment on anyone for their actions during the Communist era. On balance, I believe the system forced them to make choices that were more about survival than anything else. In Bengal, India, my family experienced a short period under a "Communist Party"; but the Bengali version of Communism resembled more a benign socialist government with no secret police, or oppressive living conditions. Comparing these two "Communisms" is like comparing chalk and cheese.

I want to include here a vignette of my parents' struggles to support their Czech families during the Communist era. It was always dangerous for my parents to go to Czechoslovakia because the Communist regime was unpredictable. In late February 1953, Mum visited Europe to spend some time with the family. She arrived in late February and went straight to Loučka. On 5 March, 1953, near the end of her visit, news came through that Joseph Stalin had died. This news, with its accompanying, somber, martial music, was broadcast on the many street loudspeakers scattered throughout the village on lamp poles. Despite the fact that Czechoslovakia had turned well and truly communist by 1953, Mum had no real appreciation about the true nature of Joseph Stalin, or about what he had done to millions of people in Ukraine and elsewhere. All she knew was that she had to keep a low profile.

Two days later, a telegram came from Dad in Calcutta telling her to leave Czechoslovakia immediately. My Uncle Noris also strongly urged Mum to leave, as the political situation was deteriorating. Both Dad and Uncle Noris feared that, if she delayed, she would not be allowed to leave the country at all; they were worried that the borders could be clamped shut at short notice. So, she packed her suitcase in a hurry and left for Prague, where she went directly to the airport. For a while, it looked as though she were too late. She had to argue with government emigration officers about her desire to leave for India. Luckily, she had an Indian passport. After much debate and showing them her passport, she requested help from the Indian embassy; soon afterward, she got the green light to leave. Later, she learnt that many foreigners who had been visiting Czechoslovakia at the time had difficulty leaving, and some had had to stay behind. She was lucky indeed; but for her Indian passport, Mum might have had to spend the rest of her life in Communist Czechoslovakia.

Uncles Ota and Jura Krobath, Aunts Boženka, Hanka and Marketa

Ota is my youngest surviving uncle. He still lives in Loučka with his wife Boženka. They have an impressive orchard and vegetable garden in their back yard that provides them with much of their food. In his retirement, and when he is not working in the garden and orchard, Ota seems to be involved in a never-ending building program on his house with his sons. Every time I see him, another addition has appeared on his house. His sons, Milan and Petr, live with him and both work in the area near the village. They are a closely-knit family and help each other out. Yes, Ota still has his chickens and rabbits.

During the Communist era, I remember that, somewhere hidden in the garden, was a "still" where he brewed his own brand of *pálenka* or *slivovitz* (a fairly potent, transparent, alcoholic liquid with a slightly oily texture, but with the kick of a mule; Evie thinks it could double as paint stripper). But, today, the illicit still is passé; if you pay the state taxes, you may brew it legally. The romance of the illegal brew appears to have disappeared. Nevertheless, wherever it comes from these days, when I visit Uncle Ota, there is the obligatory *Frťan,* or snort of Slivovitz. He serves it with a glint in his eye, asking that the offered little snort should be demolished without protest. To be polite, I know I must get this firewater down in one hit, locked eye-to-eye. Then while I catch my breath and balance, the small glass is always magically replenished and, before I know it, there is another toast to someone or other, and on it goes. For his part, Uncle Ota sits calmly and knocks back this "paint stripper" as if it were mother's milk. This rural Czech tradition has become part of our personal tradition whenever we see one another.

Today, when I visit Uncle Ota and his delightful wife Boženka at their home in Loučka, I am reminded of how beautiful it is to be self-sufficient on a small property. It is a simple life, but they lack nothing when it comes to the real necessities. Ota's long narrow back yard is a gardener's treasure trove. Scattered about are fruit trees yielding cherries, apples, plums and pears. Ota knows the value of plums, a vital ingredient in the production of slivovitz. These are small, but important, joys. Directly behind their house, he has a huge rabbit pen and a hen house. Smart thinking on their part as rabbits are fast breeders and a chicken or rabbit dish regularly graces their Sunday table. The rest of the garden is given over to vegetables of every sort and the bushes are replete with raspberries and black currants; there are even little strips of strawberries growing down one side. Ota and Boženka are happy and have a wonderful generosity, both in kind and spirit.

Unfortunately, I only got to know my aunts Hanka, Marketa and my Uncle Jura in passing. I probably saw more of Hanka, as Mum and Hanka had a close relationship. Hanka's life was in many ways quite tragic. Like her siblings, she grew up very poor and went to work at an early age; the drudgery and physical demands of her work took their toll on her. She worked in an assembly plant for agricultural machinery, located quite close to Loučka, and accessible by the local bus. The work was hard and soon affected not only her general appearance but also her health, in particular her legs. She suffered chronically from varicose veins. In addition, Loučka did not offer any outlet at all for a young attractive woman, so she had no personal life. She worked basically to support her family. She was also a woman in a man's world of heavy industry; any relationships that she developed at work were fleeting. One of these led to a pregnancy and the birth of her son Mirek. This event ended any prospects for her of a marriage in such a traditional community. Hanka devoted her life to her son and the rest of her family. She lived with Babi; the revolving routine between house and factory became her norm. Her son Mirek suffered from severe depression and later, in his teen years, he committed suicide. Hanka died quite young, a broken soul, and a victim of the harsh reality of life under the Communists.

From the few times that I met Marketa, she seemed to me to have achieved her life's ambition by marrying a local man and starting a family. I am not sure if she also worked, but I don't believe so. My memory of Marketa has always been of the aunt who lived next door to Babi. Their houses were connected via a back lane and, every day, Marketa would hop over her fence and make her way to Babi to help out, catch up, and pass on the village news. A simple life indeed: no great cares or worries and with no great ambitions involved. But it suited Marketa totally. I never really got to know her well and know very little of her life.

My Uncle Jura presented a formidable appearance. He was tall, athletic in build and good-looking, with a wonderful shock of hair. The baldness gene in my mother's branch of the family obviously passed him by. He became a construction worker and his job took him all around the Republic. However, in between jobs, he lived in Uničov and visited Babi irregularly. He also found time between all his travels to get married and have a son. This relationship did not last very long; Jura committed suicide at a very young age. I do not have very much more to add about him, but I feel that constantly having to work away from home in the demeaning Communist system played a part in his depression and eventual suicide.

Uncle Noris and Aunt Boženka

The eldest brother in the Krobath family was Noris. My Uncle Noris and his wife, Boženka, were two important members of the family who, over time, become the central focus of our family in Czechoslovakia. They were the prime contact point between my parents and the rest of the family. Noris was an intelligent man who had lost his opportunity to improve himself through further education because of the family's economic circumstances. He went to work at the Bata plant in Zlin as a mechanic and Boženka worked in the administration of the *obchodní dům* (Department Store) in Zlin. Noris and Boženka were unable to have children; as a result, the extended Krobath family became their de facto "children" and the object of their attention.

Despite the strictures of Communism, Uncle Noris, who held the firm conviction that "thoughts are free," immersed himself in the world of books. The breadth of his reading was astonishing. His knowledge ranged from history to archaeology to science; you could hold a discussion with Noris on any subject. They lived in a small flat in Otrokovice, where their lives revolved around family and friends, their little vegetable garden, and his rather quaint hobby of building model airplanes.

I got to know Uncle Noris quite well, and still remember his low voice in our many interesting conversations over so many subjects. Since they had the transport (my father had bought Noris a car), Noris and Boženka took me to see the surrounding Moravian countryside. They also stayed in touch with Dad's family during these difficult years. Unfortunately, Noris is no longer alive and my Aunt Boženka died in March 2006, just before I came to Prague in the summer, so I did not get to meet her again. Noris continually kept Mum informed through letters about the family, their comings and goings and all their needs.

During the communist regime, the country had a shortage of readily available foreign currency. The Communists devised a scheme whereby those people who lived outside Czechoslovakia and who had been sending money to their relatives could arrange to have the foreign currency amount that they wished to transfer exchanged into Tuzex certificates. I believe that Tuzex could be obtained from a Czech bank only by using foreign currency. These certificates could then be redeemed at specially desig-nated Tuzex stores located all around the country. In these stores, a person who had Tuzex could exchange them for western goods that ranged from houses, to cars, clothing, medicines, and food. Tuzex certificates were sold at a healthy premium; in this way, the Communist government earned foreign exchange from those people supporting their families from abroad. Tuzex could also be transferred. The Tuzex store became the Communist version of a Sears catalogue but with an added currency exchange gouge for those who bought the certificates.

Mum and Noris were close, so, Noris took on the role of Tuzex "Czar" for our family; he did all the shopping, according to my parents' wishes. Dad bought him two Simca cars over the years with these Tuzex certifi-cates to enable him to move more freely in the country and support the family. One of these cars was a 1956 Simca Aronde 1300 and the second, a 1963 Simca 1300. Today, the latter Simca sits in my Uncle Karel's garage in Otrokovice under wraps and awaits restoration by my cousin Karel's son, Mathias. Sometimes the help my parents sent was financial, sometimes a parcel of clothing and, very often, medicine. I remember sending Noris model aircraft kits from Revell, courtesy of the Tuzex certificates. When he completed them, he would display them in his small apartment; but they eventually found their way to the younger members of the family.

Noris was a kind man and we all loved him. Even though Dad's family was scattered throughout Slovakia, Noris made a point of visiting them regularly. Years later when we lived in Sydney, Australia, and after Noris had retired from work, my parents brought him and his wife to visit us in Sydney and he stayed for six months. We took the opportunity to show him as much of the country as possible.

Complete Krobath Family.

In all, there were thirteen siblings in the Krobath Family: Marta (Mum), Noris, Rudolf, Karel, Boris (Bořivoj), Marketa & Honza (twins), Hanka, Jura, Ota, Miloš (died of TB), Pinda (incinerated on a truck carrying old films), Mirka (died of meningitis). I have only touched on a few of them, as some I never met or knew.

Buchlovice (Dad's birthplace) and his Mother, Antoinette

One of my very first memories of Buchlovice, which is situated in Moravia, came when my Uncle Noris drove us one day to visit my paternal grand-mother. We traveled south to Uherské Hradiště and took the turn-off to Buchlovice. Just before entering the little village, there is a wonderful sweep on a fairly flat road that leads directly into the centre of town. Buchlov castle is located on a small hill and the village seems to be spread out around most of its base. According to Dad, Count Leopold von Berchtold, whose castle this was, had been one of the main architects of the First World War.[21] But what I remember most of the entry road was

---

21   Between 1906 and 1911, von Berchtold served as Ambassador for the Austro-Hungarian Empire to the Russian court in St. Petersburg and later joined the court of the Emperor Franz Joseph in Vienna, where he was appointed the Foreign Minister of Austria-Hungary. During his time in Russia, both Russia and the Austro-Hungarian Empire wished to control the Balkans; the situation was complicated by a strong Serbian separatist movement, which was supported by the Russians. The result was the Balkan Wars of 1912-1913. Von Berchtold, was not decisive enough to handle the situation and the crisis escalated into the First World War. He resigned in January 1915, retiring to his residence in Vienna and moving between his estates in Hungary and Buchlov. He eventually died in November 1942 in Hungary. His tomb lies in the family crypt near Buchlov castle. See Christopher Clark, *The Sleepwalkers: How Europe Went to War in 1914*, 61, 85, 110-13, 469-70.

that it resembled a grande allée with cherry trees on each side of the road. On this particular trip, the cherries all seemed to be ripe for the picking. So, what does a young boy do? Naturally, he pesters his uncle to stop the car so that he can pick the cherries. At the time, I thought that this was absolutely sensational. Cherries, totally free, and anyone could pick them! We filled a few containers and entered the village. I have a few oil paintings of village life painted by the Czech artists Bezdek and TVDK (both unknown to us) and I am struck by the similarity in appearance and rustic character between the actual houses and those in the paintings.

Buchlovice is indeed a charming place although today, with the increasing affluence of the Czechs, it has become gentrified and modernized to such an extent that the older houses are being torn down and replaced. On that first visit to Buchlovice, Dad told me a story about the forest that covers the hillside between the village and the castle. He pointed out to me two noticeably different heights in the trees: the trees on the lower portion of the hill being generally shorter than the rest. Apparently, what happened was this: in the absence of Count von Berchtold, and while World War I raged across Europe, Dad was just a little boy who liked to play in the forest. One day, he happened to have some matches with him and accidentally set the forest on fire. By the time the fire was extinguished, most of the trees on the bottom half of the hillside had burned down. So, what we see today is the re-growth of that part of the forest and hence the two different levels of the tree line. Dad told me this story with a chuckle, even though he got quite a thrashing at the time from his father.

I am sorry to say that I know almost nothing about my father's early years. Apart from his mother, I know little of his grandparents or his father. He was born to Christian and Antoinette Hruska in Buchlovice on 28 July, 1911. I cannot recall a single occasion when Dad talked about his father. I have often wondered why. But he took every opportunity to tell me about his mother, Antoinette. I am also aware of his brothers Ludwig, Kristian, Othmar and František but can say little about them. I did meet Ludwig and František on one trip to Czechoslovakia. I believe that his family spent most of their early lives in Buchlovice, although I know that some of his brothers moved to other parts of Czechoslovakia. His brother Ludwig settled in Rožnov and there is evidence that his brother Kristian moved to Roque Sáenz Peña, Chaco, Argentina, whether temporarily or permanently, I don't know. But let us concentrate on Buchlovice.

Dad obviously had a deep love for his mother. He spoke of her affectionately and told us of the brave role that she played in the Second World War in the partisan movement. Grandmother Antoinette had chosen to be responsible for keeping one section of the escape route from Nazi Germany open for those people who were fleeing its oppression. She was recognized by Czechoslovakia and France for her bravery. My father often described to me how his mother, in her old age, would hold court in her kitchen in Buchlovice (much as my Krobath grandmother had in Loučka), a rustic kitchen with its large porcelain stove. The family used to gather around her to talk about their lives, the events of their community and their nation and to listen to her views and opinions, which had been shaped by her interesting life and experiences during the War. I remember Dad showing us a picture of this kitchen "court" and the assembled family, sitting around a frail old woman, everyone leaning forward so as not to miss a single word she uttered. It is clear that they all loved our Babička. Dad could never look at that picture without a tear coming to his eye. I had the privilege of meeting her only once as a boy. I can't remember much except that this charming woman's life inspired me to the point where I proudly gave her name – Antoinette - to my only daughter. Australians have a habit of abbreviating everything and today she is known as Toni, but any mention of Toni always reminds me of my grandmother, Antoinette.

While at Buchlovice, I met a cousin of Dad's named František, who was a dwarf. František often invited me to go mushroom picking with him. We went to the nearby forests where, because of his stature, he was closer to the ground than I was, and saw the mushrooms earlier and much better than I ever could. As a result, for every mushroom that I found, he already had four or five in his basket.

Dad's Brother František

Dad's eldest brother was also called František. When I first met him, František lived in Piešťany (which is now located in Slovakia), where he had become a successful businessman. František, eldest of the five brothers, was actually a half-brother to Dad, but I don't know the details. Before the Communist takeover, František had established a successful liquor distribution company. The only other faint recollection that I have is that he may have had an equity interest in a well-known brewery in the Piešťany district. František and Dad were very close and my father often spoke about him.

Piešťany is a famous spa town. The mineral springs and their medicinal properties were well known in the Middle Ages; European royalty, the nobility, the wealthy and even Ludwig van Beethoven came there to "take the waters" regularly.[22] The mineral springs are now enclosed in a building that dates from 1820 and is called the Napoleon Spa.

When the Communists took control of Czechoslovakia in February 1948, people like my Uncle František were labelled "greedy capitalists" and "enemies of the people" and had their properties and business assets confiscated. As a further humiliation, the Communists expropriated his home and sub-let the various rooms in it to other people. František and his wife were then forced to become the live-in janitors to service the rest of the residents in their own house. As further punishment, he received a pittance of a pension from the government. Dad helped them to make ends meet for over twenty years. Despite this humiliation, František and his wife never lost their spirit and never complained or showed their bitterness. František's wife was a great cook, especially when it came to all those small, traditional, baked goods that are the mainstay of a Czech Christmas. On one early visit to their humble apartment, we were confronted with a huge table near the front door absolutely covered with every conceivable sort of baking; this unexpected bounty struck my boyish heart and remains a cherished memory. It seemed we were in a bakery shop and, of course, very gentle and subtle pressure was applied to ensure that we sampled at least one item from the many varieties spread out. Saying "No" was not an option!

---

22   http://www.englishmaninslovakia.co.uk/2016/07/13/piestany-in-the-footsteps
-of-beethoven/

Dad's Early Years

After I emigrated to Canada in 2002, I still visited friends and family in Australia on a yearly basis. When in Sydney in November 2010, I would meet up with many Czechs of my generation for lunch and a chat. Once, I met Rudy Sicha, who showed me some photographs, obviously taken in Czechoslovakia, that showed his father and Dad together in uniform. I have since verified that the photo depicted Dad doing his national military service in 1931/32 as a 20- or 21-year old. I knew that Dad had been a close friend of Rudy Sicha's father, but what Rudy said surprised me. Apparently, these were photographs of our respective fathers doing their national service in the Czechoslovak *Marine*! I was quite stunned, as Czechoslovakia is a landlocked country: it has no access to the sea at all. And, as for bodies of water, it has only a few major rivers running through it, including a small section of the Danube on the Slovakian border with Hungary. Perhaps they completed their national service as part of some river patrol group. It's a mystery.

Mum and Dad as Young People

There is a huge gap in the family record, both in memory and in written documents. When my parents met, Mum had left school and was already working at Bata. I am not quite sure what she did there, though she probably worked in the Bata office, performing administrative duties. The reason I think she was in administration is because that is where my father worked. So, how does a young man from Buchlov meet a girl from Loučka? The answer is buried in the main office corridors or factory floor at the Bata Shoe factory in Zlin. Dad was employed in the Office Machinery Department, most probably in the servicing and maintenance section for all the office machines in the company. He often mentioned that this work helped him understand the fundamentals of moving parts machinery.

They had a small circle of friends and there are numerous photographs of them all together, laughing and obviously enjoying the summer and winter outdoor life. Mum and Dad loved to ski and they passed this passion on to their children later on. Dad was a natural athlete: he represented the Bata Sports Club in alpine, cross-country skiing, and ski jumping. His specialty events were slalom and downhill skiing, and the

Nordic combination - basically a cross-country skiing event that incorporated a 10-mile cross-country ski race coupled with ski-jumping. Their interest in winter sports did not seem to confine them to visiting only nearby locations; in fact, it took them to other major recreational ski areas in Moravia and Slovakia. Many years later, when I visited Czechoslovakia with my parents, I remember well a visit to Štrbské Pleso in the Tatras, a place that they had visited often; I was pleasantly surprised to be regaled with all their experiences in this beautiful spot.

Dad had a great love of mountains and he referred to the Tatra Mountains with almost reverential awe. The Tatras are a border mountain range that separates Poland from Slovakia. He could name every peak, every geographical detail, their height, their snow cover, and could even pass judgment as to their degree of difficulty for prospective climbers or skiers. Sometimes, he would point out the best ascent route for climbers. Obviously, his love of the outdoors and the mountains started here and later shifted to a much larger stage, namely the Himalayas in India. By contrast, Mum viewed these visits to the Tatras more for the grand scenery, the fresh air and above all for being with her boyfriend and skiing with him.

The photographs taken in summer attest that this same close group of friends enjoyed their hikes in the surrounding countryside and, if a lake happened to be in the way, they stopped and had a swim. Swimming was the one passion that Mum enjoyed most of all when we were living in Calcutta.

I would like to think that these happy outings in Moravia brought my parents close together; and they were clearly the glue for a lifelong love affair with mountains and water. Many years later, as a family, we always spent our holidays somewhere in the mountains, either in India or in Europe. Their happy time together in Zlin led to a growing love between Mum and Dad that culminated in their marriage on 9 May, 1937. They were 20 and 26 years old respectively. After their marriage, they rented a small apartment in Zlin located within walking distance of the Bata factory. I have visited this apartment; it is located on a hill that overlooks the town of Zlin, the factory, and the valley beyond.

Prior to 1920, there appear to have been no organized athletics in Zlin. But in June 1924, an athletics club under the name of SK (Sokol)

Zlin[23] was registered with the Czech Athletics Union in Prague. This club became the sporting outlet for Bata workforce, with predominantly male athletes. In 1927, the athletics club acquired a cinder running track, changing rooms and a covered grandstand. These facilities, as well as the active encouragement of Bata, attracted many promising athletes. Dad was part of this sporting trend. The club expanded rapidly. It had produced its first Czech athletics representative in 1928. The club had already turned out an early champion in Ludvík Komanak, who won the Czech National title in triple jump.

I have numerous newspaper clippings from this period that testify to the incredible athletic prowess of my father. He was a gifted 100m, 400m, 800m and 1,000m runner in athletics and was part of an elite group of sportsmen then competing for Bata in athletic meets throughout the country and even internationally. In 1934, three athletes from the Zlin athletics club, including Dad, took part in the first European Athletics Championships held in Turin, Italy. Dad took part in the 400m track event, but without success; the event was won by a German.

Dad was then selected to go to the Berlin Olympics in 1936, but an injury caused him to miss this unique opportunity. However, this setback did not stop him from asking one of his friends to get the autograph of a very special athlete, the one and only Jesse Owens; this autograph is now one of my prized possessions.

Dad also became an elite winter sportsman. Many newspaper clippings indicate that he excelled in both Alpine and Nordic ski events. During his time at Bata, he jumped a distance of approximately 150 feet, a distance right up there with the world's best at the time. I remember him showing me the style that he used, namely the "lean forward" method over the skis where you placed your arms well out in front of you for equilibrium and balance. He added that this technique had been overtaken with the advent of Birger Ruud, the great Norwegian ski jumper, who changed the jumping style radically by placing his hands at his side, thereby improving the aerodynamics; after Ruud, ski jumps lengthened dramatically. But the jumping hills in Europe at that time were few and far between and not designed

---

23   Zdeněk Pokluda, *Zlin*, 83-84.

to cope with the new distances that the Scandinavians could achieve. My father's love for the sport sustained him so much that, whenever we visited Czechoslovakia, we always made a pilgrimage to some of the ski hills that he knew and I would listen to him recounting his glory days and telling me of all the great jumpers of that era.

How Did Mum and Dad Get to Calcutta?

It all started with Dad's friendship with Tomik Bata, son of the founder of the Bata company. They came to know one another because they were both amateur pilots. Contained within the letters and other records left to me by my parents, I found Dad's pilot licence. To my surprise, he not only knew how to fly, he was good enough to have taken part in aerobatic competitions and won some minor awards in competition. It was within his circle of pilot friends that Dad became friendly with Tomáš Bata Jr. He used to refer to him as Tomik when speaking Czech and Tommy when speaking English. He spoke about this relationship often when we lived in Calcutta; according to Dad, Tomik Bata was the main reason why he and Mum eventually moved to India in 1938.

It happened this way. Tomik had already been speaking to my father in 1937. By May 1938,[24] there was a partial mobilization of the army in Czechoslovakia in response to the stated intentions of the Nazis to annex the territories of the Sudeten Germans. Even though there had been no overtly hostile reactions on the Czech/German border area, tensions ran especially high and this fact was not lost on Mum and Dad. They also probably had some inkling that war would break out in Europe. The Munich Conference in September 1938 had basically sacrificed Czechoslovakia and ceded all of the German-speaking territories to Hitler and the Nazis. It must be said that President Beneš had been dealt a poisoned hand by the Allies and had no other option but to agree to the terms. In his memoirs *Mnichovské Dny. Paměti*, President Beneš wrote, "War - a great European war - will come, with great upheavals and revolutions…."[25] German occupation appeared to be imminent.

24   Agnew, 197.
25   Edvard Beneš. *Mnichovské Dny. Pameti*, 342.

Mum and Dad had no direct experience of any sort of major conflict and their schooling probably did not even touch on the many aspects of politics and war. But I do know that Dad acted on the advice of his friend Tomik Bata in Zlin. After all, the Bata family, as leaders not only in their local community but also in the wider national Czech community, had a much better informed and clearer insight into the regional and global politics that were unfolding in Europe. Indeed, the Bata family itself was preparing its own personal plans to leave Europe. So, Dad heeded the advice of Tomik Bata to leave Czechoslovakia prior to any outbreak of war. Tomik suggested a move to India, saying that the Bata organization in Calcutta could open up opportunities for a newly married couple and a competitive employee like Dad.

President Beneš resigned and his subsequent exile[26] would have added gravitas to the seriousness of Tomik's warnings and brought them more into focus. Czechoslovakia was going to lose one-third of its land to the Nazis and the question had to be asked: "Would it end there?" Dad was already married; within 15 months both he and Mum had acquired Czech passports, visas for France and Great Britain, money export permits from the Czech authorities and, with these preparations, they got ready to finally move from Zlin to India. And, so, on 20 December, 1938, Mum and Dad left Czechoslovakia with no notion that this break would separate them from their families for a very long time. They traveled by train through the German border at Lundenburg and on to Marseille in France where they caught a boat that took them to India; the ship finally berthed in Bombay in January of 1939. From there, they made their way across India by train to Calcutta. On 15 March, 1939,[27] the Germans occupied the rest of pre-war Czechoslovakia. World War II would erupt in a few months.

When he left for India in late 1938, Dad had a letter with him from Bata Zlin that set out the terms of his possible employment at Bata in Calcutta. Dad had agreed to a 2-year initial work period. What is interesting in this letter is that the terms and conditions of his position were not spelled out at all. The letter basically stated that Bata India would be responsible for

---

26   Agnew, 206.
27   Ibid., 207.

employing him and outlined the terms and conditions of his remuneration. The only concession by the company was that it would be responsible for their medical and pharmaceutical costs.

The letter also includes a short paragraph saying that, if Dad completed his 2-year term and wanted to return to Czechoslovakia, then Bata India would be responsible for his repatriation costs. The letter is dated December 1938. I find the tone of the letter extremely stark. However, it appears to have been put together in a hurry with the minimum of commitment by Bata Czechoslovakia, which was itself on the verge of crisis at the time. War was looming.

After the German invasion, Czechoslovakia became a Nazi occupied country until the end of the War in 1945; the Prague uprising occurred on 5 May of that year[28] quickly followed by liberation by the Soviets and the Americans. Hardly had the war ended and amid the aftermath of its devastation, when the Communist Party emerged as the dominant political power. It confirmed its ascendancy with a coup d'état in February 1948[29]; this event introduced a totalitarian communist regime to Czechoslovakia. These two major historical events were of great importance to our family: the first was instrumental in my parents' decision to leave for India and pursue their subsequent life there; the second was instrumental in their remaining in India after the War.

28   Derek Sayer, 235.
29   Ibid., 245-246.

CHAPTER 2

The Early Years in India

Setting Foot in India

Mum and Dad finally arrived on Indian soil at Bombay on 5 January, 1939. Their life in India had begun. Their final destination was Batanagar, near Calcutta, where Dad would start work at the Bata Shoe Factory. He didn't know it at the time, but Dad would come to realize that the Bata company played an important role in the economic development of India, establishing several plants across the sub-continent. The Bata vision had created a large shoe manufacturing industry that mentored Indians and provided significant job opportunities to thousands of people, training a sizeable cadre of managers, and establishing many company-based institutions.

Even though my father's work with Bata in India would be of short duration, there is no doubt that Bata had an important influence on my parents' lives. Bata was already well established in India when they arrived, which provided them with an extremely soft landing. The turmoil in Europe was far behind; but, for a young Czech couple newly come to a foreign country, impending war was an important reminder of how tenuous their situation was. One of their first challenges was not so much that they had arrived at a time of war, but at the height of the British Raj. With that one boat trip to

Bombay, Mum and Dad had become part of a minority community, "foreigners" in a British colony. As non-British Europeans, they were treated as second-class citizens in colonial society. After Independence, this would change. In the meantime, Batanagar provided a buffer to the worst of the exclusions and snobbery endemic in British India: at Batanagar, they had a safe space to start their lives together, to participate in society and to grow and prosper. Their first task was to learn English!

I have often wondered what it was like for my parents to arrive in a totally different cultural environment from the one at home. In India, they had their first encounter with a sea of humanity, the like of which they had never before experienced. They had to confront and absorb so many new contrasts. What did they feel after they had left behind the quiet charm of the small, ordered, company town of Zlin and set foot in the major metropolis of Bombay, with its skyline of multi-storeyed buildings; the chaotic street congestion replete with all types of two- and four-wheeled transport, some motorized, but the rest pulled by men and bullocks; and the endless crowds of people carrying all shapes and sizes of loads on their heads as they trod the fine line between overbalancing and maintaining a steady pace? What was their reaction to the heat, the humidity, and the dust? How did they come to grips with the noises and smells of an Asian city festooned with garish billboard advertising in both Hindi and English for the latest movies, hair oil, saris, toothpaste, shaving cream and biscuits? How did they react to the ever-present street vendors? And all this chaos in languages they couldn't even understand! Many aspects of this Indian experience have hardly changed; so, I can imagine that their 1939 stop-over in Bombay would have been little different from my own experience returning to India forty or fifty years later; the big difference between us was that I had been born in India and could speak English and passable Hindi.

A Letter Home

Dear Maminko and Bedek:

Finally, we are in India.[30] *It has been some time since we said goodbye to you in Zlin, and we wondered what lay ahead of us. But at least I had Mirek with me to cope with all this uncertainty and to face up to the trip. We have just arrived in Calcutta and this is the first chance I have had to write to you and Bedek* (Mum's pet name for her eldest brother, Noris). *In Marseille, a week after we left Zlin by train, we boarded a ship of the British India Steam Navigation Company.*

The trip from Marseille across the Mediterranean was uninteresting until we reached the coast of Egypt and the Suez Canal. I had never heard of the Suez Canal before; all we were told was that it was the shortest way to India. At the entrance to Port Saïd harbour, the ship's captain pointed out the statue of Ferdinand de Lesseps to us; he was the Frenchman responsible for the Canal. The statue is quite imposing; his right hand is outstretched and seems to be pointing towards the East. Sand, sand everywhere as far as the eye can see. We saw a caravan of camels here, fully laden with goods and bobbing up and down as they walked in a line behind each other. Quite a funny sight. What a world we live in! A week before, we had walked in beautiful green forests and countryside and in Egypt all we could see was endless sand.

Even on the ship, the heat was unbearable. We were not prepared for this type of heat in January; it was extremely unpleasant and very dry, so much so that at times I felt I was gasping for air to breathe. We slept with our cabin windows open to get some relief from the cool night air. The English passengers promenaded on the

---

30 I have taken the liberty of inventing this "letter" based on my mother's memories and my knowledge of what their first days in India were like.

deck in their lightest summer clothing. They obviously knew something about the tropics that we did not! At least in the evening,
we did not have to wear formal dress like the English people when
they came to the dining room. We had none. But, I believe that we
were more comfortable.

At Aden, the ship stopped for about two days to take on coal,
enough to last the rest of the trip. Mirek and I made a short visit
to the city but the terrible heat outside drove us back to the ship.
The trip from there to India was uneventful; we spent a lot of time
on the deck, walking around the ship, sitting in the deck chairs
and enjoying the sea breezes. One evening, our captain told us at
dinner that we would be landing in Bombay early the next day on
Thursday, 5 January.

We were still sleeping in our cabin when the sound of the engines
changed as the ship slowed down and we awoke wondering if
anything bad had happened. Then, we heard the incessant "caaw,
caaw, caaw" of sea gulls. Mirek looked out of the porthole in the
early morning light to find a line of triangular sails of fishing boats
as they returned to land. In the distance, he could make out a
skyline with tall buildings that appeared to be much taller than
anything we have in Zlin. The ship found its berth, moving ever
so gingerly into its allocated place. This was the signal for us to
get up, get dressed, prepare our luggage and all our papers, and
disembark. Out on deck, we got our first smell of the East.

The ship's crew led us directly into a large building. There were
many, many people inside, all talking loudly in languages that we
could not recognize. At first, we were a little bit confused because
we did not know where to go. No one spoke Czech and so we moved
with the wave of passengers; soon, we were standing in front of
an official, whom we guessed was with Indian Immigration and
Customs. Without asking anything, he handed us four copies of
some form, with many carbon papers in between and indicated

that we were supposed to fill them out. I looked blankly at Mirek, who was equally perplexed about what to do with all these forms. But, then, some of our fellow passengers kindly helped us to fill them out. My first impression was that Indian officials had a liking for paper, because all we got was a stamp here and another stamp there as we passed from one table to the next. Sometimes after giving us the stamp, someone in starched white shorts would write over the stamp before drying the writing with a roll blotter. Once, when the officer's ink well had run dry, there was a moment of panic. His arm shot up in the air and he called out somebody's name without even looking around. An assistant soon materialized and filled the inkwell. He then had to reassure himself by dipping his pen into the inkwell many times, before scribbling something in our passports.

Well, maminko, I must say that my first experience of India seemed to be officials - all types of officials - moving around in white uniforms or blue uniforms, with stiffly creased trousers. They did not appear to be in any great hurry. They hugged all sorts of things to themselves, like folders and loose papers. Behind some of the seated officials stood men dressed in khaki uniforms; some wore turbans, and they all carried some sort of large stick. People opened and closed doors all the time and greeted everybody. They all appeared to have a job to do but it was a mystery to me. I said to Mirek "Welcome to India. Our new home. It should be interesting."

All of this moving from one table to the other, trying to understand what was going on, was very time-consuming, confusing and tiring. We finally got to the end of the paper shuffling and went to an area to claim our bags. We had no idea if someone would be there to meet us and we kept looking over the heads of all these people to see if there was a sign or anything that said "Hruska" or "Bata."

As we waited to see if someone had been sent to meet us, we had more time to look around. Mamo, (endearment term for mother), the heat and humidity inside these buildings was absolutely unbearable, totally unlike anything in Otrokovice or Zlin. At times, it felt that the heat could melt the glass off my sunglasses. I could feel and taste the humidity in the air. We started to sweat and our clothes became drippy and clung to us. They had a few ceiling fans scattered here and there that were meant to provide some relief. All they did was re-circulate the hot air even more. I now know why most of the men wore wide, short pants, with big pockets. Those shorts probably gave some ventilation from below! They reached down to just above the knee. But Mirek and I had to laugh, as the bottom of the short pants appeared to be twice as wide as they were around the waistline. Even so, as baggy as they were, all these shorts had a razor-sharp crease running down the front. Even the policemen wore these shorts and the whole picture was finished off with their scarlet turbans.

Just as we were starting to wonder what we would do if nobody appeared, this small man with a sign held high above his head with "Bata" splashed across it, came into view; we waded through the crowd towards him and introduced ourselves. We hardly understood him. All we knew were single words that we had memorized like "hotel," "train," and "buy tickets." We managed to understand that we would spend a day in Bombay and that we would be picked up and taken to the railway station to board a train to Calcutta. The man gave Mirek all the hotel and travel documents that we would need, including instructions about finding the right platform and the reserved sleeper carriage for our trip. Finally, we relaxed.

What an introduction to India and Bombay!

Saturday morning, 7 January, we left our hotel for the Victoria Terminus Railway Station. Mamo, I have never seen such a beautiful railway station building anywhere. There was a large concourse inside full of people pushing their way here and there as they tried to find their trains. We showed our ticket to a train inspector and he kindly directed us to the right platform and reserved carriage; otherwise, we would probably have missed our train in the chaos on the platforms. Our compartment was small and private. It contained two basic bunks, one above the other: there was also a small overhead fan. While we waited for the train to pull out, the train attendant brought in a large ice block, covered in sawdust, in a waterproof container to help us keep cool: but this was only a temporary relief, as it melted quite rapidly. Oh well. It might be replaced at the next stop. Finally, the train slowly jerked forward out of the station. It moved really slowly and it felt like ages before it gathered speed and we left the city behind. Mirek and I sat glued to the window as we watched the change from city to country. The countryside appeared quite dry. The land, houses, and trees seemed to be covered in a layer of dust. We began to pass small villages, scattered here and there, with very simple houses, probably made from mud or some other basic materials. The train trip was long, very long. The open carriage window gave us our only relief from the heat as the wind streamed in; any part of the compartment that was not protected from the direct sun became too hot to touch.

The passing countryside was so flat and so vast. It had a yellowish, sandy colour that stretched right to the horizon. At times we saw a farmer with a tall white turban working in a field holding a sickle in his hand; at other times we saw people working their cattle. We particularly enjoyed watching the women, sometimes six, seven or eight in a line, walking beautifully erect on a well-worn mud path, balancing clay water pots on their heads.

Every now and again, we stopped at a train station. Some of these stops lasted a long time, unlike the trains at home where we would be on a platform for no more than 10 minutes. We never left our carriage at these stops. The platform was full of people, most of them dressed in white loin cloths, pushing and shoving each other as they tried to board the train with all their bundles of luggage. Some even had chickens, with their legs tied together and held upside down. Some tried to make last minute purchases from food vendors strolling along the platform. At our open carriage window, they tried to sell us something to drink or eat. At times, many hands reached up to our open window, each holding something to sell to us. They all gestured beggingly at us to buy something. They all talked over each other with a pained look that said "Please buy from me." One word stuck in my ears. It was "Chai, Chai," and we soon understood that it meant tea. I mentioned to Mirek that it was identical to our own Czech word for tea. I now had learnt my very first Hindustani word. Then the food sellers were pushed aside by the miscellaneous junk vendors who sold things like home-made food, cold drinks, glass wrist bangles, combs, and hair oil. Every now and then, a beggar would thrust his hand up towards us with a melancholic look on his face asking for money while, at the same time, his other hand rubbed his belly to show his hunger. This was quite hard for us to experience for the first time and I honestly did not know how to respond to them. There was also one person selling what looked like small tree twigs and, while we observed him, we noticed that people bought quite a lot of these twigs from him. We had no idea what they were. Perhaps it was something that people ate or chewed on. I did not know. The train journey, via Kanpur and Nagpur, lasted another two days. After we arrived in Calcutta, the mystery of the twigs was cleared up when someone told us that poorer Indians used the ends of these twigs as toothbrushes to clean their teeth.

It was on the train that we experienced our first Indian sunset. It was beautiful to see, Mámo - a large red ball sinking below the horizon. As we prepared for the night, we prayed that the ceiling fan would continue to work. We got up early. The pale greys of the night sky slowly gave way to light pink, then a darker shade *of pink until the great ball of the sun arose again over the horizon and slowly, the many features of the countryside were highlighted. This landscape is quite unlike anything that we know in Czechoslovakia. But it is fascinating, nevertheless.*

Anyway, I must stop now. I hope that I have given you some idea of what we have experienced since we left Marseille. I am excited about what lies ahead and feel fortunate that I am starting this wonderful adventure with Mirek by my side. He often wonders what is waiting for him in Calcutta and Batanagar. I hope that all is well in Otrokovice and I shall write again soon when we are settled. Give my love to all the family.

Love Marta

It is interesting that this trip still takes about three days today, just as it did in 1939, and a visit to any Indian railway station is still quite an overwhelming experience. Back in 1939, the British Raj was the ruling authority in India. One enduring legacy of their colonial presence was an extensive and efficient railroad system that was managed by the colonial administration. However, even the British could never have imagined the problems of controlling daily life within the halls of an Indian railway station. Imagine the impressions that a newly arrived young Czech couple would have had when they confronted Bombay's Victoria Railway Station. Even today, the façade of this building is truly magnificent. The exterior looks like a Victorian gothic cathedral mixed with hints of Indian architecture. Exquisite woodcarvings decorate the surfaces. As Mum and Dad passed through the bright red, brick arches into the cavernous interior of this station, they would have experienced a full onslaught to their senses: the sights, the sounds, and smells. They would have walked straight into a maelstrom of humanity with driving waves of people, many confused or lost, moving in chaotic patterns, some pushing here, some jostling there, others standing still while trying to make sense of the various overhead signs, others just giving up and sitting down and, in doing so, presenting yet another type of human barrier for travelers to deal with in the station.

They would have seen women in beautiful *saris* and *cholis* (a type of blouse) of the brightest colours, some barefoot, others in dainty sandals. Many women wore their wealth on their bodies, in intricate gold necklaces and earrings, with bangles on their arms, feet, and wrists. My mother told me she was fascinated by the elaborate, bejewelled nose rings. Men wore everything from shorts to western style pants and open-necked shirts to *dhotis* (loincloths) and others appeared to be wearing straight-cut *kurtas* (a loose shirt falling either just above or below the knees of the wearer). The sound of a chant or the tinkle of bells would signal the presence of a few scantily attired *sadhus* (holy men), bare-breasted and wearing a flimsy, dirty bolt of material wrapped around their waists. Sadhus all had their markings, be it ash, long matted hair, painted foreheads or grains of rice stuck to their foreheads; others displayed Lord Vishnu's white chalk or paint mark. It was in this train station that my parents would also have encountered for the first time a few Sikhs, strong and upright in stature, elegant and resplendent in their colourful turbans.

Mum and Dad would definitely have confronted up close, and not protected by a train window, the many pushy hawkers selling every conceivable item from food, drinks, toys, newspapers and magazines, to a wide array of totally useless consumer articles. Beggars mingled with the throng of people, many with deformities and showing signs of disease. My parents would have seen the haggard and ubiquitous children begging, pressing and touching them for *baksheesh* (loose change). If they had given in to this plea, they would have been instantly besieged by other beggars and would likely have missed their train. They probably would have tried to push a path through them or turn away or ignore them, but ignoring beggars is always difficult and never very successful in India.

They would also probably have encountered incessant noise, as hundreds of people talked and shouted at all and sundry. As they sought their way to the trains, they would have had to weave their way through a slalom course of suitcases, tin boxes, jute and clothing bundles, gunny sacks, bed rolls, portable kitchens, and pots and pans scattered throughout the station. They would have smelt the food being cooked with all sorts of exotic spices. These mobile cooks may also have taken great delight in thrusting their homemade delicacies in the faces of this young European couple. What they would not have understood at the time was that many of the groups of people squatting on the platform around their possessions, could be there for days, while they waited for their trains to depart. After all, this was not the age of electronic screens displaying information on the movement of trains; and most people were illiterate in any event. So, they just turned up at the station, asked someone when their train was due to depart and waited, even if it meant sleeping on the platform for several nights. Mum and Dad would have seen many families camped out like that on the platform, making breakfast or brewing some tea while they waited for a train. Finally, Mum and Dad would have felt relief as they found their first-class carriage and stored their luggage away, shutting this other, totally foreign, world out… at least until the train pulled into the next station. They had had a relatively, civilised introduction to India at the Bombay Harbour Port Authority; but, with the train station, they had been introduced to another face of India altogether.

After travelling for days across the central part of India, the train would have begun to slow as they neared the environs of Calcutta, finally crawling to a halt in Howrah Station. As they alighted from the train, they would have encountered a similar scene to the organized chaos of Bombay, except that Howrah Station in Calcutta was even more chaotic and a much poorer contrast.

The New Family Home: Calcutta

What do we know about Calcutta? By 1939 it had become the nation's largest, metropolitan city by area. The main part of the city lies on the eastern side of the River Hooghly, a tributary of the mighty Ganges River, and approximately 90 miles from the mouth of the Bay of Bengal. The Hooghly is navigable and Calcutta had, at that time, well-developed port facilities. However, the Hooghly is also prone to a build-up of silt, which influences not only navigation, but the size of ships that can reach Calcutta to pick up cargo.

Calcutta's layout was originally planned to be on a rectangular grid, oriented on a north-south axis. But this grand plan gathered dust on a shelf somewhere long enough for the more affluent and desirable, central residential area to evolve to one plan, while the rest of the city grew around it in a haphazard fashion. The commercial and administrative centres lay more to the north of the city, for instance, in the Burrabazar district. Here the streets are narrow and random in direction. And, like all cities built on the banks of large rivers, Calcutta was very much affected by the lack of adequate bridges.

What made Calcutta unique in India was the imperial factor. Calcutta was, for years, the imperial capital of British India and so the influence of Victorian England can still be seen in its architecture and some of its streets. In 1939, when my parents arrived, these buildings would have been impressive in their size and design and immaculate in their upkeep. The *Maidan* (a large park that contains Fort William), provided the city with its main lung. It offered all Calcuttans a large, open, recreational area filled with trees and grassy areas and included what was then one of the city's architectural jewels, namely the Victoria Memorial. The *Maidan* faces the central part of the city where most of the British and Europeans lived. Hotels, restaurants, cinemas, the shopping areas and the wider avenues of the city were located here. Moving away from this central area, the city spread out to no particular plan, as evidenced by the Howrah district, on the western side of the River Hooghly, where the city's main railway station is located. Apart from the ordered, central core of the city, the rest of the road network resembles randomly tossed spaghetti, partly accounted for by Calcutta's numerous *nullahs* (watercourses) and canals.

Early History and Origins of the Name Calcutta

Since Calcutta is the city of my birth and my heart and the place our family called home for several decades, I would like, at this point, to include a little of its history. Calcutta was the child of British imperial trading interests in India and was first established by the British East India Company (or the Company). It was "founded" by the merchant trader, Job Charnock, in 1690. However, use of the word "founded" needs to be qualified. Calcutta was not founded in the sense of a new, greenfields settlement. The original site was chosen as a suitable landing-place for the Company, as it offered good navigational opportunities for vessels. Three small rural settlements (Sutanuti, Gobindapur, and Kalikata), were already in existence, but grew in importance through the activities of the Company.

The origin of the name "Calcutta" is a matter of ongoing conjecture. Calcutta may have derived its name from the Bengali "Kalikata," the name of one of three villages that the *zamindar* (landlord) Sabarna Ray Chaudhury leased to the Company in November 1698. Calcutta is not an ancient Indian city. On the other hand, some religious devotees have attributed its name to the worship of the goddess Kali. Pilgrims still flock to the Kalighat, a temple on the banks of the river Hooghly. There are several other scholarly opinions about Calcutta's name origins, some less fanciful than others. Kalikata may have also been derived from *kali* (lime) produced in a *kata* (kiln). Others believe that it may have been derived from the Bengali word *Khal* (ditch) that has been *kata* (cut or excavated). Still others believe that the name has its origins in the Bengali word, *Kilkila*, referenced in old literature; it apparently means "flat area."[31]

One of the many fanciful explanations for the origin of the name Calcutta derives from a Hindu myth and its association with the goddess *Kali.* Calcutta is primarily a city of Hindus. One version of the ancient origin myth has it that a resident Hindu god-king was angered that his daughter Kali (the goddess of death) married the god Shiva. He insulted Shiva by not inviting him to an important religious sacrifice. Kali was enraged and sacrificed herself by leaping into a searing fire. When Shiva found the charred remains of his wife, he grasped what was left of her and started a fatal dance of cosmic destruction. The other gods, alarmed by Shiva's action, pleaded with the god Vishnu to deal with Shiva; Vishnu responded by stopping Shiva in his tracks with a *chakra* (a thunderbolt). Vishnu then removed Kali's body from Shiva by cutting her up into 51 pieces and flinging them far and wide. The spots where these body parts landed became places of pilgrimage for Hindus. Kali's little toe fell at Kalighat (now a part of "Kolkata") and hence the evolution from the original name from Kalishetra (the place of Kali) to Calcutta and then to Kalikata and finally Kolkata, which is its current name.[32] One has to admit that there is a romance to these myths, especially when they are tied to the origin of names.

---

31   Sukanta Chaudhuri, ed., *Calcutta, the Living City. Volume 1: The Past*, 1.

32   Geoffrey Moorhouse, *Calcutta*, 19-20.

British tenure at the river landing that would eventually become the city of Calcutta was a bit shaky at first. Job Charnock was, at one point, temporarily driven away from the Company trading post by the resident Muslim ruler.[33] Charnock went as far as Madras (now called Chennai), but later returned, leasing land from the Armenians, the Portuguese and the Emperor Aurangzeb. Slowly, Calcutta evolved into a permanent settlement. But there is a romantic twist to this story. Charnock, who became the first governor of Calcutta, is reputed to have married an Indian woman whom he rescued from committing *suttee*;[34] however, evidence for this union is hard to find.[35]

Calcutta's British Imperial History

The central importance of the Maidan is not restricted to the health and well-being of Calcutta's residents. There was originally a military purpose for this park. Fort William is one of those Calcutta landmarks that one cannot actually visit. It is situated on the east side of the River Hooghly and has an interesting history. During the early British occupation in India, the British East India Company had three major footholds on the sub-continent: Fort William in Calcutta, Fort St. George in Madras and Bombay Castle in Bombay. The Company sought mutually beneficial alliances and treaties with the various *Nawabs*[36] and princes who ruled in their own areas of interest. It had a tenuous relationship with the Nawab of Bengal, Alivardi Khan. However, his grandson, Siraj-ud-Daula, who succeeded on Alivardi Khan's death, decided to tear up the treaty and confront the British in Bengal.

As the last independent ruler of Bengal, Siraj-ud-Daula had witnessed the takeover of Bengal by the Company, something he resented. In particular, he took issue with both the Company's attempt to oust him from power and its rejection of his claim that the Company had abused the trading privileges given them by the Mughal rulers of India. In retaliation

---

33   Chaudhuri, ed., *Calcutta, the Living City. Volume 1: The Past*, 1.

34   *Suttee* is a traditional practice in which a Hindu widow cremates herself on her husband's funeral pyre in order to fulfill her true role as wife.

35   Ibid., 7.

36   A *Nawab* is a semi-independent Muslim ruler of an Indian state.

for what he saw as an alien occupation, he attacked and captured the garrison situated at Fort William[37] on 20 June, 1756. The story goes that, subsequent to the attack, 146 British people - a number that is open to historical scrutiny - were imprisoned in a reputed 20 ft. by 20 ft. room with no ventilation. This was subsequently called the "Black Hole of Calcutta." Apparently 23 people survived the ordeal. One of the stories about this episode was recounted by survivor, John Zephaniah Holwell; however, conflicting accounts from other survivors cast doubt on Holwell's story.[38] Nevertheless, it was his version that took on a life of its own in Britain, as an example of British determination and bravery contrasted with the cruel, barbaric behaviour of the *Nawab* and his followers.[39] An indignant British public was outraged to the point that, after this incident, the British East India Company was effectively given "carte blanche" to do whatever it deemed necessary to bring order to the region. The Company's response was to send a military force headed by Robert Clive, whose 3,000 troops were heavily outnumbered by a 50,000 strong army of Indians who had artillery assistance from the French. Surprisingly, after experiencing an initial onslaught from Clive's artillery, most of the Nawab's men fled, leaving Clive to claim a famous victory on 23 June, 1757.[40] This definitive Battle of Plassey started a decline in what had been a predominantly French trading presence in that part of India and ultimately led to the British conquest of India.

37 There were two forts. The first one was built in 1696. The second one was built after the Battle of Plassey in 1758. This is the fort that borders the *Maidan* today. https://en.wikipedia.org/wiki/Fort_William,_India

38 The account by Holwell, a surgeon in the employ of the British East India Company, is now accepted as a gross exaggeration, since the prison was much too small for this number of people and also had a small window opening onto a verandah.

39 In recent times, Indians have responded to the ongoing cultural hysteria about the "Black Hole" by quietly obliterating the site (which I actually saw before they destroyed it), so that no one is quite sure now just where the "Black Hole of Calcutta" was and no monument can be raised there to the British "martyrs." Subsequent scholarship suggests that only about 60 people were captured and placed in a room designed for six or seven. As many as 40 people may not have survived their ordeal because of the sweltering heat, and lack of food and water. Whatever the actual numbers, it was a cruel thing to do and remains a shocking event in the city's history.

40 Ibid., 12.

The British East India Company's experience with Suraj-ud-Daula led the Company to rethink the way that it protected its investment. A new fort was built, but a guiding principle for it was that it had to be defendable. After deciding where this new fort was to be located, the British required a large, cleared, open space that would provide a "clear line of fire" in all directions. This was the genesis for the *Maidan*, which survives as a complete entity to this day despite all sorts of pressure for commercial development around its perimeter. Ironically, the Fort's guns were never again fired in anger. Today, the Fort is still in use by the military and remains an imposing structure. Over the years, under successive British administrations, trees were planted in the *Maidan* as part of its "beautification."

In 1772, after Clive's victory at the Battle of Plassey, Calcutta was named the Imperial Capital and became the central hub for the expansion of trade and British influence in greater India. Over the next 100 years, it developed into *the* dominant centre for imperial commerce and political power in India. With this rapid growth, came a growing level of economic exploitation and increased pressure for Indians to assimilate to Western culture. The Company acquired the power to levy taxes on Mughal lands and also to exercise control over the Mughal armies. In fact, the Company evolved from being solely a trading and commercial firm to the de facto government in India. This transformation in the Company's role promoted significant change to the city's architecture. Many great imperial buildings were constructed, such as the Writer's Building (ca 1780), Government House (ca 1800), and St. Paul's Cathedral (ca 1820). This cathedral still stands and is located directly opposite our former home at 53 Chowringhee Rd. The gardens of St. Paul's were our playground when my sister and I were toddlers.

Despite all this prosperity for the Company, the seeds of resentment were well and truly sown with the imposition of taxes[41] meant to support its administration and its private army. This army was split into three sections, one of which was located in Bengal. Most of its rank and file soldiers were either from high caste Hindu or well-to-do Muslim

---

41   There is an excellent discussion on this subject in Shashi Tharoor, *Inglorious Empire: What the British Did to India*, 9-16.

families. Status was important to them. So, they were all horrified when, in a monumental, military purchasing blunder, the British asked them to use new rifle cartridges that were wrapped in paper greased with cow and pig fat, and which had to be opened by mouth. This religious insult appears to have been a tipping point. The cartridges offended *everyone's* sensibilities: Hindus considered cows sacred and Muslims felt pig fat to be ritually unclean.[42] The Great Indian Mutiny of 1857 occurred all across the Indian sub-continent: thousands of people were killed; entire settlements were razed to the ground. The Mutiny was soon quashed by troops loyal to the Company, but Indians had accomplished some important goals. After peace was restored, the Company's monopoly of power in India was eliminated through the institution of a colonial government overseen by London; and, just as importantly, the Mutiny made the British think twice about their relationship with Indian peoples.[43]

By the time of the Great Mutiny, Calcutta was well established as a colonial city. Long known for its intellectual culture, Calcutta was host to hundreds of newspapers, printers, publishers and book shops in many languages, including Bengali, Hindi, and English.[44] It had a thriving manufacturing sector, especially in textiles and jute. The Governor's House was built in 1804, followed by the Town Hall, the Hindu College and the Ochterlony Monument. Shortly before the Mutiny, the first railway line in Bengal was opened on 15 August, 1854; it ran from Calcutta to Hooghly. Also, in the year of the Mutiny, the University of Calcutta was established, followed by the construction of a General Post Office and the Indian Museum. Calcutta witnessed its first horse-drawn tram car in 1873[45] and its first telephone call (between Calcutta and Howrah) in 1882 or 1883.[46] And throughout it all, Calcutta grew and grew into a city of opulent homes juxtaposed to tanks (a large, artificial source of water) and the chaos of

----

42   Pyarelal, *Mahatma Gandhi. Volume I: The Early Phase*, 48-49.
43   Amaury de Riencourt, *The Soul of India*, 215.
44   This tradition of a vibrant book culture remains today. Calcutta plays host each year to the world's largest public book fair and boasts entire streets given over to bookshops and printers.
45   Chaudhuri, *Calcutta, the Living City. Volume 1: The Past*, 234.
46   Ibid., 236.

tiny, cramped dwellings. As Rudyard Kipling observes in his poem, "A Tale of Two Cities."[47]

Once, two hundred years ago, the trader came
Meek and tame.
Where his timid foot first halted, there he stayed,
Till mere trade
Grew to Empire, and he sent his armies forth
South and North,
Till the country from Peshawar to Ceylon
Was his own.
Thus the midday halt of Charnock - mores the pity
Grew a city
As the fungus sprouts chaotic from its bed
So it spread
Chance-directed, chance-erected, laid and built
On the silt
Palace, byre, hovel-poverty and pride
Side by side.

Though my parents could not know it when they arrived, Calcutta - with all its chequered past - would become their inheritance and ours. In Mum and Dad's time, Calcutta still looked like an imperial city. Yet, amongst all these magnificent, imperial, architectural symbols, it was also a Bengali city. Bengali architecture is an exquisite blend of oriental and European styles; the city still boasts numerous gorgeous, historical homes.

The 20th century was an important period in Calcutta's history; it marked the peak of its rise in importance, as well as its eventual decline. Lord Curzon, Viceroy of India, partitioned Bengal on 7 July, 1905,[48] into East and West Bengal. Prior to 1911, Calcutta's role as the capital led to an enormous amount of dissension and a growing opposition to British rule that included much agitation and protest. The solution came with the

47   Rudyard Kipling, "A Tale of Two Cities," *Verse Inclusive Edition, 1885-1918*, 86-88.
48   Chaudhuri, *Calcutta, the Living City. Volume 1: The Past*, 37.

transfer of the seat of government from Calcutta to Delhi in 1911;[49] social and political calm ensued for a time.

Throughout the colonial era, Calcutta often reflected the worst elements of British rule. The assumed absolute power of colonial rule bred an air of "superiority" which pervaded the whole Indian sub-continent; it led many British colonials to demonstrate racial antipathy towards India's peoples and others. In Calcutta, this racialism was obvious in the way the British treated both Indians and non-British Europeans. Slavs like my parents were simply ignored socially or excluded from British clubs. Derogatory language towards Indians intensified over time. Physical violence became the norm, whether it was in the household towards servants, or in public to anyone deemed to have infringed on British rights. This arrogant behaviour created and sustained an enduring image of the British Raj as an odious imposition on India as a whole.

Arrival in Batanagar

It was into this highly charged racial and historically-conflicted environment that my unsuspecting parents arrived. Mum and Dad made their way directly to the Czech expatriate "colony" at Batanagar after arriving in Calcutta. Dad started his work at Bata on 21 January, 1939, after barely two weeks in the country. He presented his introductory letter from Bata Zlin that set out the terms of his employment with Bata India. The fact that he had arrived in India so soon after the letter was written, together with its vague phrasing, indicates to me, at least, that Dad had had no real opportunity to negotiate any terms and conditions. His acceptance of this stark and somewhat detached letter says a lot about the urgency of his decision to leave Czechoslovakia and about the confusion and uncertainty that must have existed amongst Bata's management at the time. Nevertheless, what I keep coming back to is that all of Dad's children have been the beneficiaries of this lucky opportunity and the obviously difficult decision to leave everything known and comfortable behind.

There were a few occasions when I asked my father about his working life at Bata, but he was always rather reticent to talk about his experiences.

49   Ibid., 31.

He often remarked that, while Bata India provided him some job security, working there felt like a form of modern servitude completely unlike the vision of caring for workers which was prevalent at Bata headquarters in Zlin. I remember my father saying to me, "Working at Bata was a little bit like working on a modern slave plantation. You got the opportunity to work, you were provided a shelter, you had to live by all the company rules, whether they made sense or not, and if you were a good boy they patted you on the head and looked after you. Heaven help you, however, if you wanted to show them any innovative ways of doing something because, if it clashed with the normal way of doing things, it created bitterness and resentment."

Dad's Job at Batanagar

Dad's prime responsibility was for the technical maintenance and operations of the shoe-making production machinery. In addition, he had the responsibility for ensuring that the internal company telephone exchange and the administration's office machinery worked. There is no doubt that his work at Batanagar mirrored his previous experience at Bata Zlin. I have wondered whether Batanagar management had previously identified a need for a maintenance and operations specialist to senior company management in Zlin. Since he fitted the requirement and also, with the possible influence and advice of his friend Tomik Bata, this might have been the reason that he was encouraged to go to Calcutta and why it was a relatively easy decision for him to make. In any event, his skills and experience were a good match for the need and, after a short time, Dad also became responsible for the maintenance and operation of Bata's printing press.

Bata Calcutta had at least two waves of Czech ex-patriates before the War: the original "Batmen" and those who followed later. Many of the early "Batmen" behaved as an elite. This group kept to themselves socially and could be overbearing in their attitudes to the latter-day group in the workplace. Partially inspired by the influence of the British Raj, the original "Batmen," many in senior management, had developed levels of bureaucracy that were a nightmare for latter-day arrivals, who were used to the flatter, more democratic, organizational structure of Bata Zlin. Over the years, tensions developed between Sales and Production, and

Sales and Maintenance. For instance, Sales complained that they could not meet their sales targets due to the unavailability of product caused by production difficulties. Many things could have caused these production difficulties: for instance, raw material shortages, equipment breakdown, or even labour "go-slows." Naturally, the production people would then turn inward and lay their own blame game at the feet of the material supply or maintenance people.

After he had left Bata, Dad related several stories of these "tribal differences" between the two groups of Czech employees. Knowing many of the personalities involved in these various disputes, I understood his frustrations.[50] Dad often recounted that he had persistent problems with some of the Czechs working in Sales, and that these frustrations eventually led to his dismissal from Bata. After he left the company, Dad kept in contact with other Czechs who had also left Bata; ironically, these men related to him similar experiences about their frustrations with the old guard. He frequently said to me how unfortunate it was that this clique stuck to and protected themselves against the latter-day arrivals, irrespective of who was right or wrong. However, for some men in this second group, being fired or leaving of their own volition was a blessing in disguise. Many of them, like my father, went on to establish extremely successful businesses. For others, leaving Batanagar was treated as a "badge of honour"; and there was certainly no love lost for those of the old guard who remained. But there was an insidious side to the situation, too. In later years, I came to know that this elite group had carefully looked after its own interests when the time came to retire, garnering particularly beneficial pension entitlements from the company.

After their arrival in Batanagar, Mum and Dad were allocated a modest two-storey house in the southeast corner at the furthest extremity of the colony. The living area consisted of two similar sized rooms on each floor: a lounge, kitchen and pantry on the ground level and two bedrooms and a toilet on the second floor. The house came furnished with the bare essentials, two small beds nestled within a wooden frame to which a mosquito

---

50 In fact, these divisions persisted amongst the children of the various Batamen who eventually emigrated to Sydney, Australia. Although it was seldom mentioned, we all knew which group of Batamen our fathers had belonged to.

net could be attached, a small wardrobe, a heavily varnished dining room table and sideboard, and a few chairs. The sitting room was equipped with a two-seater sofa, with springs that squeaked out that their "use-by date" had well and truly passed, and a coffee table. Any invited guests could choose between the sofa and the kitchen chairs. The house had no carpet or curtains, something that Mum soon rectified. When Mum opened the windows, her new flying and crawling house guests moved in to escape the heat of the day. Mum and Dad learned to cope with some of the more necessary of these unannounced guests; lizards, for example, darted up and down the walls with complete freedom. Some scurried across the ceiling upside down. As startling and unappealing as the lizards were, my parents soon became friends with them because they feasted on the great variety of insect life, especially mosquitoes. In short, they kept the insect population in check.

A small pathway led from the road right into a semi-enclosed terrace by the main house entrance. On either side of this access path were two tiny flowerbeds populated by drooping flowers thirsting for water. A little strip of grass surrounded the rest of the house. This was the best place to sit outside and enjoy the evening air. After my father left Bata, I remember him showing me this first home, which had one redeeming feature: one side looked onto a large, open, grassy area and another side was adjacent to the river Hooghly. My parents used to enjoy the cooling winds blowing off the river. In the hot and humid season, this was an added bonus to their creature comforts. During their early weeks and months at Batanagar, they went for long walks through the colony and enjoyed the relatively pleasant, balmy evenings, especially in winter.

The new work environment at Bata was unlike anything that Dad had experienced before. I have often wondered, as I reflected on his early months working here, how he coped with this situation. First, how did he communicate with anyone? Dad's knowledge of English was practically non-existent. How did he pass on his instructions to his new Indian colleagues? Did the Indian workers know any Czech? Did my father have the assistance of a translator for Czech to English and for Czech to Bengali or Hindi? Did the company provide any language classes for the newer Czech arrivals to Batanagar? I do not know. All I have been able to ascertain is that Bata sent Indian managers to Zlin to learn Czech and the Bata method in 1933. On their return to Batanagar, they would have been able to serve as intermediaries for the Czechs until the Czech managers had learned enough English, Hindi, or Bengali to be able to communicate on the factory floor.

With such a close-knit community at Batanagar, my parents found themselves socializing with other Czechs defined by the provenance of their arrival in Calcutta, by whether or not they were part of the management elite, or perhaps by other factors. Mum and Dad made friends with many of their colleagues; these were friendships that lasted long after many of them had left Bata. I think, in particular of their friendships with the Spindlers, the Krizkas, Bobals, Gottliebs, Surys, and Valentas. In the case of the Valentas, my sister Martina eventually married their eldest son Ivan, a direct result, I believe, of the friendship formed by our two families during their early days at Batanagar and which endured even after Dad's departure from Bata.

Germany Invades Czechoslovakia

Dad hardly had any time to settle into the new job and new environment of Bengal when global events proved that his decision to leave Czechoslovakia had been correct; war broke out soon after in Europe. The heavy tread of studded German boots had started their relentless goose-step across national boundaries, including Moravia, from which many of the Czech expatriates in Batanagar came. Naturally, they feared for their families and friends. The news from home, whether from family letters or fellow workmen returning from Zlin, painted an extremely grim picture of an ever-lengthening Nazi shadow over their beloved homeland. Mum and Dad could only imagine the personal tragedy unfolding in Europe and were grateful that they had left this turmoil behind. Slowly, they began to realize that their stay in India would be much longer than anticipated.

In Batanagar, the implications of war were becoming painfully obvious. The company would have to rely on Zlin less and less for support. Stories started to filter out of Zlin that Bata had already been making provisions for war by sending raw materials, machinery for leather preparation and shoe manufacture, and shoe inventory to many Bata outposts around the world. Not so obvious at first was the loss of intangible links to Zlin, namely access to production experts, scientists, chemists and other researchers. Batanagar had a limited investment in these skills and relied heavily on Zlin for them. The loss of Bata Zlin's management direction in Calcutta was an even more serious issue. In the vacuum that now existed, Batanagar become increasingly independent of Zlin. As the situation in Czechoslovakia deteriorated even further, inter-company communication slowed, became a trickle and soon ceased altogether. During the time that Dad was settling into his job at Batanagar, getting to know his new colleagues, and learning a new language, reports from Europe had become quite disheartening. To him and many of his colleagues, all-out warfare appeared inevitable.

Outbreak of World War II in Europe

On Sunday, 3 September, 1939, the BBC in London interrupted a peaceful day with the news that Britain had declared war on Germany after the latter's invasion of Poland. Like all Europeans, the ex-patriate Czechs in Batanagar were apprehensive about the future. Even though everyone feared another war, no one had actually believed it was possible. It was just too terrible to contemplate. This denial of the inevitable might explain why little planning had been done at Bata India for what war would mean for their operation. Nevertheless, even though the Batamen had taken little time to think about it, they now realized that their traditional role as employees of Bata would change. Production of shoes for the civilian market would be curtailed and the existing production capability would be switched over to the production of military footwear and other associated goods. I believe that this move to support the war effort with an emphasis on military footwear production would become a contributing factor to Bata's post-war commercial success. But, in 1939, it meant that the Bata colony was now effectively engaged in the war effort in India.

With the outbreak of war in Europe, Lord Linlithgow, the Indian Viceroy, took it on himself to declare war on Germany on India's behalf without consulting any of the Indian leaders, nor clarifying why India should participate in the War at all.[51] Many provincial ministers resigned in protest. In contrast, the Muslim League supported the British war effort.[52] I have often wondered if they ever imagined that, as a result of their support for Britain, they might be unfairly treated in any future independent India dominated by the Congress Party.

In Batanagar, during the early months of the War, many of the Czechs would meet after work, or on weekends to talk about the situation. They wondered how their families were coping. News from home had slowly begun to dry up. Many realized that they probably had had their last communication with their loved ones and friends for quite some time. In many ways the not-knowing was worse than the knowing. These were indeed very trying times for many Batanagar families.

By early 1940, many Czechs openly wondered what the impact of the War would be on Czechoslovakia. They knew that Joseph Stalin and Adolf Hitler had signed a neutral, non-aggression pact.[53] The questions were numerous. Some openly asked, "On which side and when will the Russian bear jump?" a reference to the possibility of Russia joining Germany in the War. Others, realizing there was nothing they could do, were thankful to be in Calcutta far away from the European theatre of war; they immersed themselves in their wartime work.

In late June 1941, Mum and Dad were sitting out on the verandah enjoying the cool evening air and the relief of a brief monsoon squall that had passed through Batanagar. The passage of the rain had left the garden covered in a heavy mist as the rain water evaporated from the heated land. Other adjacent houses in the colony were barely visible, as was the night sky. No moon could be seen, just a few scattered stars. An eerie silence enveloped them. As night fell, the silence was broken by the continuous, buzzing of cicadas. Inside the house, the telephone started to ring. Mum answered and listened with heightened interest as Mr. Spindler said, "Have you heard the news? I just heard on the radio that Germany has invaded

---

51 Nisid Hajari, *Midnight's Furies: The Deadly Legacy of India's Partition*, 35-36.

52 Madhusree Mukerjee, *Churchill's Secret War: The British Empire and the Ravaging of India during World War II*, 7-8.

53 Tad Szulc, *Czechoslovakia Since World War II*, 17.

Russia!" There was a short silence, then Mum replied, "So, this will mean that Russia will be fighting with Britain and its allies, won't it?"

When Mum hung up the receiver, she told Dad the news; they were both relieved. Later, many would speculate whether Hitler would crush the Russians in a short period of time and celebrate Christmas in Moscow. But other older and wiser heads drew on their knowledge of Franco-Russian history and reminded everybody about Napoleon and his disastrous campaign in Russia. Many Czechs relished this divergence of opinion and a few wagers were laid that day on the outcome of Hitler's invasion of Russia.

Early Years in Batanagar

In early 1940, Mum became pregnant, which meant they could look forward to something other than news of the War. Mum had to carry me during the monsoon months, an unpleasant, extremely hot and humid period in Bengal. This must have been a very uncomfortable time for her. Dad, being the sort of creative, "hands-on" person he was, decided to start planning for the birth, which was expected in mid-November. What could be more normal for a new Dad than to build a pram from scratch? Soon a very elaborate pram with a woven cane exterior and chrome supports started to take shape; he decided to paint it a cream colour. Whether the baby would be a boy or a girl, cream was viewed as neutral. When I saw this pram later in photographs and on film, I realised that the design incorporated many of the mechanical characteristics that one found in a car. It even came with a spring suspension system and air-filled tyres. I have absolutely no recollection of the "ride," but no doubt it afforded its new occupant comfort; it was altogether a suitable "perambulatory conveyance."

The local hospital in Batanagar did not have proper facilities to handle a birth and was definitely not recommended. Dad made arrangements for Mum to deliver at the Elgin Nursing Home in Calcutta. So, when the time came, and after the obligatory warnings of an imminent birth had been given and heeded, Dad and Mum went to Calcutta either in a friend's car or a taxi. At the time, the trip to Calcutta took about an hour, so Mum must have given adequate warning to everybody. She checked in and soon went into labour. On 14 November, 1940, at about 4 pm, I entered the world weighing between seven and eight pounds. Now, we Czechs may sometimes be accused of having a singular lack of imagination. This was confirmed in the naming of the new baby: Miroslav. Same name as Dad. No middle name, nada, nothing. Not a very creative appellation, but Dad assured me later that it was a Czech custom to name the first boy after the father, so I could do nothing about it. Why could not some more creative thought have gone into the choice? There were many exciting names around. Why not "Sergio" (in my next incarnation I know that I am coming back as a conductor called "Sergio Café"), or "Boris," or even "Oscar?" Instead I got Miroslav. In an English colony. In India. It made my early life interesting, to say the least. Only the Czechs at Batanagar could pronounce it. But, Mum, bless her imaginative heart, called me Miki from the start and today I have to admit that I rather like Miki. So, the real name, Miroslav, is domiciled in my passports, driver's licence and other bits of ID, but to my friends and family, I am Miki. The important thing was that, by the end of 1940, the Hruska family had grown to three.

The summer months of 1941 rolled by; for my parents, life in the Batanagar compound was broken by frequent visits to Calcutta to see the Victoria Memorial, the Botanical Gardens, and the Zoo with their newborn son. They slowly became more familiar with Indian culture and life, especially the various Hindu and Muslim festivals in late September/ early October. In particular, they wanted to experience the popular Bengali festival of *Durga Puja* (*Puja* means festival). This is an important event in Bengal. Probably originating in the 17th century, it takes place before the full moon in late September. In Bengal, *Durga Puja* lasts for about two weeks, 10 days of fasting, feasting and worship and the last four days of pure fun and gaiety, music, dance and some theatre celebrating the dramatic events associated with the goddess Durga's legend. The multi-armed goddess Durga is worshipped with great passion and devotion.

In Calcutta, all the government offices, educational establishments, and law courts shut down for this period. For Bengalis, *Durga Puja* was and is much more than a festival. It is a carnival and an emotion that marks happy times. Families enfold themselves in good food. During this particular *Puja*, the straw and clay image of the goddess Durga with her many arms and three eyes sits astride her "vehicle," usually the back of a rickshaw; these images are on every street. She is worshipped throughout the city. During this colourful and unique festival, Bengalis erect massive, elaborate *pandals*, which are structures made from bamboo and cloth to house an image of the goddess. Prayers are recited at various times. When I was a boy, the city was awash with the sounds of Indian music and devotional songs mixed in with the latest popular Hindi film (later known as Bollywood) songs, blaring out from loudspeakers. On the last remaining days of the festival, the city is overrun with numerous processions of Durga on rickshaws or carts (if the owner has money), heading for the *ghats* on the river and other convenient venues along the river's edge. Devotees tip the goddess into the river, where she soon disintegrates and sinks. If some remaining debris from a *pandal* remains, they are gathered up and taken away to make next year's "vehicle." For Calcuttans, *Durga Puja* is an occasion full of colour and spectacle. In later years, Dad knew that I enjoyed *Durga Puja*, so he would take me down to the area known as *Kumartuli* (or *Kumortuli*), in northern Calcutta, near Chitpur Road, where the most beautiful images of Durga are assembled. Sometimes we drove to more affluent parts of the city to see the extravagant two- and three-storey *pandals* that housed Durga.

In November, when the cool weather begins, Bengalis celebrate *Divali*, the Hindu festival of lights. This is another occasion for much good-natured fun, enjoyment and happiness amongst families and friends.

While life went on in Calcutta, only sporadic, abbreviated news about the War in Europe filtered through to Batanagar. Information about the major theatres of conflict were reported in some detail by both the newspapers, *The Statesman* and *Amrita Bazaar Patrika*. However, news of how the War was going in Czechoslovakia hardly existed on any news reporting radar. For example, Mum had no idea that her brother Karel had been taken to work at a factory in Germany.

The small colony of Czechs at Batanagar was by now totally isolated from Zlin. The Bata factory had learned to adapt to the new reality of obtaining all their raw materials, new equipment, maintenance and repairs from local sources. Dad also had to accede to this reality, namely, being self-sufficient and adaptable. This would later prove to be a valuable experience for him when in business for himself.

Early in the War, the call went out from Czech President Edvard Beneš, now living in exile, to expatriate Czechs, asking them to enlist and join the war effort in exile.[54] Some of Dad's single colleagues in Batanagar took up the call and shipped out to France to join the Free Czech Army that had been assembled there. Dad chose to remain in Batanagar, primarily because he didn't want to leave his wife and young son alone in a foreign country, with no income or official status. But, he also felt that he could contribute to the war effort much better in Calcutta, where he had responsibilities at the Bata factory to produce military boots. Keeping all these production facilities functional was important work for the War.

The Indians established a Civil Defence Force throughout the country in which Dad enrolled. I have no idea what the Batanagar unit of the Defence Force did, but I suspect that they prepared to deal with such emergencies and evacuations that could possibly arise. Until Japan entered the War, India was not under any direct threat. Afterwards, it was another story. Calcutta was very close to Burma and was bombed by Japanese airplanes. At some point, the BBC Far East Radio Service began to provide the colony with all the latest news and developments of the War in Europe. The early news from the battlefront was depressing, as Hitler and the Nazis swept aside everything that stood in their path. By 1941, the situation in Europe continued to deteriorate. Many in Batanagar surmised that it was only a matter of time before the War would touch them in India.

India's Aspirations for Independence and Japan's Entry into the War

During 1940 and early 1941, most of the Czechs at Batanagar continued working in a company geared to the War effort. On a personal level, during these early years, it was the evacuation and air raid drills that reminded them that the country was at war. But, in India, there were undercurrents at play. Since the 1920s, there had been a growing political movement with one important goal: securing independence from British rule. Ironically, the movements driving this objective came from diverse political fronts. The Communist Party of India, founded in 1925, belonged on one side of

---

54   Hugh Agnew, *The Czechs and the Lands of the Bohemian Crown*, 208.

the spectrum. The Congress Party of India, originally formed in 1885, and now under the leadership of Gandhi, Nehru and others, represented the other end. One of their goals was to use the period of wartime stress and chaos to push the drive to eventual Independence further. All these parties attracted numerous radicals, including Indian expatriates living in Britain and other places. Many had been influenced by the Communist movement in Europe and by the British Labour Party. Their common bond was an English education; but they differentiated themselves in approach and were often at odds with each other. The Congress party was committed to non-violence, but other groups wanted a war against British imperialism and their associated Indian collaborators.[55]

During the early years of WWII, India was directly involved, providing both troops and resources for the Allies in Europe. But back home in India, colonial officials were fighting on two fronts: they had not only to assist Britain in fighting the European War, but also to deal with the aspirations of "pro-independence" political groups, a struggle that had not been helped by the British treatment of Indians in numerous events leading up to the War.

In Batanagar, these political undercurrents were not invisible to the Czechs and their Bengali workforce. But the Czechs realized that it was prudent to be seen as supporting the Indian war effort in Bengal and stay out of local politics. Thus, Bata produced shoes to support the troops and individual Czechs showed their support by joining community and civil defence groups.

Despite the War (or perhaps because of it), many Czechs at Batanagar still tried to maintain some normalcy in their lives by keeping up their traditional ties to Czechoslovakia through the celebration of various Czech festivals. Some of the Czechs in Batanagar, especially the women, had brought their national costumes from their districts and, whenever

55   My abbreviated commentary on India's aspirations for Independence is based on my readings of various sources. I recommend the reader to these works in particular: Nirad C. Chaudhuri. *Thy Hand, Great Anarch! India: 1921-1952*; Amaury de Reincourt, *The Soul of India*; Nisid Hajari, *Midnight's Furies: The Deadly Legacy of India's Partition*; Sukanta Chaudhuri, ed., *Calcutta, the Living City. Volume 2: The Present and the Future*.

the occasion arose, they wore them proudly. However, on a more informal level, friends used to meet over dinner or other social gatherings; these were occasions for preparing Czech food and singing traditional Czech folk songs. Many of the Czechs in Batanagar had brought with them an intimate knowledge of their traditional dances and music. Music was never far away; it was part of their psyche. There was a common saying: "*Co Čech, to muzikant*" ("Every Czech is a musician"). The musical styles ranged from folk songs to polkas to hymns and they loved to perform in a choir or group setting irrespective of their musical taste. Not all of these songs are known only to Czechs. Few people know, for example, that one of the most famous Czech polkas is called *Škoda lásky* ("Wasted Love"); but most non-Czechs know it as the "Beer Barrel Polka," or by its opening lines ("Roll out the barrel… we'll have a barrel of fun…").

As 1941 progressed, families started to make their arrangements for Christmas. But, in early December 1941, came news of the Japanese surprise attack on the American naval fleet based in Pearl Harbor. This attack finally provoked the Americans to enter the War.

During this troubling period and in a general atmosphere of uncertainty about what Japanese involvement would mean for India, Dad suddenly left Bata on 11 February, 1942. The Czechs at Batanagar would very quickly find out that Japan's aggression would bring the War to Calcutta's doorstep. But, for my father personally, the great adventure of bringing his new bride halfway around the world and becoming a father, was now in peril. In very short order, he would have to vacate their house in Batanagar, move his family to accommodation somewhere in Calcutta, and find another job.

Dad's Dismissal from Bata

It was 11 o'clock on Friday, 11 February, 1942. Mum was getting ready to feed me and lay me down for my mid-day nap. She looked forward to sitting down and taking a break from attending to my needs. So far it had been a stiflingly hot day, with absolutely no relieving breeze from the river to cool the house down. All the fans had been set on high but to little avail. Mum went into the kitchen to make a glass of fresh lime and water. She barely heard the sound of the door opening: Dad had come home unexpectedly. He appeared strangely subdued. He was normally a very outgoing person and had always taken an interest in the goings on at home and much more so now that there was a baby around. But today he seemed completely disinterested in his surroundings. Mum asked him, "*Mirku* (this was her nickname for him), is anything wrong? You don't seem yourself today. Are you sick?"

He put his briefcase down near the door, went into the kitchen, looked momentarily at what was on offer in the fridge, and then poured himself a glass of iced water. He went into the lounge and sat down. Mum joined him on the couch, turned slightly and looked at him directly. Finally, after a long pause, he said in a very low voice, "I have been sacked from my job. I just could not continue working with some of these absolutely stupid people in such a poisoned environment. I've had constant problems with some of the Czechs working in the Sales Department. They never stop complaining that their work is compromised by my department. They claim that they cannot get certain brands of shoe from the production department, mainly because of the inoperability of the machinery. They are completely unreasonable and don't want to understand that it's not always possible to get production machinery back into operation quickly after it has broken down. They don't seem to even realize that there is a war going on; some materials are scarce or are being sequestered by the military. When breakdowns occur, we simply can't get our hands-on spare parts readily. Some of the parts have to be made in the workshop and this doesn't occur overnight. All these idiots see is that their sales figures suffer when production has been interrupted."

Mum asked him, "Is this something that happened over the last few days or has it been going on for some time?"

Dad thought a while and replied in a frustrated voice, "It's been going on for some time now. I've been getting increasingly fed up with some of the Czechs who have their own selfish expectations and are quick to place all the blame on other departments, especially mine. Most of them are glorified paper pushers with big mouths; I've lost my patience with these *hňupy* (half-wits!)"

"But *Mirku*, can't you at least explain the situation to the senior managers? Surely, they understand the circumstances about operating in wartime and the shortages of spare parts," Mum asked.

"Most of them have been here longer than we have; the managers they blame are the newcomers. I simply cannot continue with their negative attitudes towards the operations and maintenance people. Today, I had simply had it. I got very angry and went straight to my boss and told him that I was not prepared to work with these people and I left the room. After about an hour, he came in to my office and told me that, after discussions with the people in Sales, he had decided to let me go. I was quite shocked at how quickly this decision was made, but I went to my office, gathered all my things and came home."

Mum was momentarily silenced as she took in what he had just said. They were now a young couple cut off from family and home, in a new country. The only thread of comfort during this time had been their small circle of friends in Batanagar and the relative security of work. Now all of this seemed lost. Their future looked bleak.

She asked, "*Mirku*, what does this mean for us?"

"I'm not sure exactly, but we will have to leave Batanagar in a short while and move to Calcutta. I will have to find accommodation for us and look for a new job. The one concern that I have right now is how easy it will be to find work. On the other hand, with the war effort here in India and the need for people, I'm sure that something will turn up. Right now, I don't know what more I can say," he said, trying to offer some hope to Mum. Many years later, he told me that he had been extremely worried.

They sat there silently and reflected on their new reality. There were no tears, no more questions asked. There was an unspoken acceptance of the fact that the first chapter of their life together had closed. As if to remind themselves that life would go on, they both went into the kitchen, poured themselves more water, and carried on through the afternoon with their own little routines. Later that evening, some of their closest friends came around to find out how they were and to offer any support they could. The Gottliebs and the Spindlers brought some cakes and Mrs. Gottlieb helped Mum with dinner.

Over the coming week, Dad was a busy man. He settled his financial affairs with Bata. There was a disagreement over a small amount of money that Dad felt was owed him. He must have had some savings for, within a relatively short space of time, he managed to find an apartment in Calcutta, paid a deposit and three month's rent in advance. Meanwhile, in Batanagar, Mum had been making arrangements to pack up their personal items and have them removed to the new flat at 53, Chowringhee Road, which was to be their home for the rest of their time in Calcutta. In fact, Chowringhee Road was going to be instrumental in shaping their future lives.

Rudolf Krobath (my grandfather, Děda)
in Třebíč

Děda in Loučka

Děda with some of his family in Třebíč

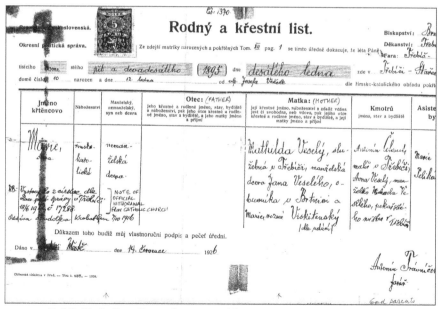

Babi's Birth Certificate showing Public Notary Stamp about leaving Catholic Church

Babi's Wedding Day

*Babi with Mum (standing)
and Brother Noris*

Uncle Noris, Babi, Děda

Babi on her way to Sydney

Babi in Loučka

Mum 16 working at Bata

Dad's Mum (left) with Mum's Mum

Dad's Mum, Antoinette (90th Birthday)

Dad aged 15

Dad aged 7

Dad running 400m at Pardubice (1933 Czech Athletics Championships)

*Dad ski-jumping at 1934 Czech Ski
Jump Championships*

*Dad cross-country skiing at 1934 Czech
Skiing Championships*

Bata Ski Team (Tomik Bata and Dad far left)

Jesse Owens 1936 Signed Card

Mum and Dad's Wedding Day

Mum and Dad's Mum, Antoinette

Krobath family home, Loučka

Me, early morning in the Potok

Mum and Dad at Otrokovice Air Show

CHAPTER 3

Calcutta During the Second World War and Dad's Work at Metal Box

Calcutta in the Early 1940s

Mum and Dad did not find the transition from Batanagar to Calcutta in 1942 easy. They had been sheltered from the actual life of Calcutta while they lived in Batanagar; now, for the first time in their lives, they were alone in a big city and not just any big city. Calcutta was a great Indian capital: it was crowded, noisy, contentious, disorganized, dirty, and completely unlike any urban centre they had ever seen in Europe.

Prior to 1940, Calcutta had enjoyed a reputation for continual political unrest and agitation. At times, this agitation was intensely targeted on specific local issues; at other times, it was indicative of a general unrest. It might, for instance, zero in on the numerous issues that existed between Hindus and Muslims, or it might play a part in the country's nationalist aspirations. Hindu-Muslim relations had become contentious due to the shameful decision by Lord Curzon, Governor of Bengal, to partition Bengal into East Bengal (predominantly Muslim) and West Bengal (predominantly Hindu) in 1905.[56] This "wedge politics" approach by the British caused political and religious tensions to simmer from the 1910s to the 1930s, notwithstanding the policy reversal in 1912,[57] when the British re-united the two parts of Bengal. Feelings ran high in spite of the best efforts of Muhammad Ali Jinnah, the effective leader of the All-India Muslim League from 1913, and Gandhi, the "father" of the Indian Independence movement, to calm the two communities.

Undeterred by the rising ferment, the British pushed the partition idea forward as well as the transfer of the capital from Calcutta to Delhi in 1911 (Delhi was formally inaugurated as the capital of India in 1931).[58] Their plan was to diminish the growing Bengali influence in colonial politics and to dampen emerging nationalism in Bengal and across the colony. However, the communal distrust between Hindus and Muslims never really died in Calcutta, or in other parts of India. In the 1920s, the antagonism between Hindus and Muslims surfaced sporadically and led to scattered riots that reached right down to the village level for reasons that, on the surface, appeared rather trivial. There were, however, serious and deadly riots in Nagpur and Lahore in 1927. The geographic reach of these confrontations ranged from Calcutta in the east, to the Central and United Provinces, and even to the Bombay Presidency in the west.

In 1928, Britain established the insensitive and offensive Simon Commission and dispatched it to India to review the political situation and the Indian form of government. It did not include a single Indian member. This Commission was regarded by Indians as an affront and an unnecessary interference in their political aspirations. [59] It instigated a boycott by the Indian National Congress and further ignited intense, Indian nationalist agitation, by way of a nation-wide *hartal* (strike) where, against a backdrop of waving black flags, loud chants invited Sir John Simon to

---

56   Sukanta Chaudhuri, ed., *Calcutta, the Living City. Volume I: The Past*, 37.
57   Sukanta Chaudhuri, ed., *Calcutta, the Living City. Volume II: The Present and the Future*, 15.
58   Ibid., 15.
59   Nirad C. Chaudhuri, *Thy Hand, Great Anarch! India: 1921-1952*, 260 ff.

return to the United Kingdom.[60] Most of the Indian leaders opposed the Commission's recommendations and its mission failed accordingly. This period also witnessed the rise of Congress leaders like Jawaharlal Nehru who, for the first time, encouraged the establishment of an independent India. In May 1930, after the culmination of his famous salt march, Gandhi was imprisoned for his role as leader of the civil disobedience movement. In June, Nehru was arrested at the Indian National headquarters, leading to even more agitation. It is a measure of how concerned the British were over rising civil unrest that they passed the Government of India Act in 1935 to protect Muslim minorities.[61]

Calcutta already had a long history of labour unrest through seemingly endless strike activity and never-ending protest processions that coursed regularly through its streets. Through ingenious tactics, strikers could paralyze the city. These early years spawned the Communist Party of India (at first, within the aegis of the Congress Party), which immediately started to exert its own considerable influence over the labour movement. Eventually, its activities would migrate to the political arena. The Communists achieved political power by differentiating themselves from the Bengali *bhadralok*.[62] This group had been exposed to western, liberal, democratic values and had an affinity with the moneyed classes: they knew how to use and exploit capital. After the 1937 elections in which no party achieved an absolute majority, a Muslim-Hindu coalition ran the governing legislature in Calcutta and so the city reverted to a state of relative calm leading up to the Second World War.[63] The Communist Party had been declared illegal by the British in the early 1930s and went underground from about 1934 to 1938.[64] Instability and unrest simmered for many years. After the British nominated Delhi as capital in 1931, it allowed all the provinces in India to establish and run independent

60 Sukanta Chaudhuri, ed., *Calcutta, the Living City. Volume II: The Present and the Future*, 20.
61 Geoffrey Moorhouse, *India Britannica*, 240-241.
62 The *Bhadralok* were drawn from upper Bengali castes who formed an economic middle-class, delineated by wealth or education.
63 Chaudhuri, ed., *Calcutta, the Living City, Volume II: The Present and Future*, 23.
64 Geoffrey Moorhouse, *Calcutta*, 308.

legislative assemblies in 1937, but these assemblies were all relatively fragile until the late 1940s because of the conditions created by WWII, the Quit India movement, and the Bengal famine.

Like all colonies, India was full of contradictions. Despite Delhi now being the capital of India, Calcutta remained the economic engine; this was the city where great fortunes were still being made. By the mid 20th century, Calcutta had achieved the status of a key port city. The presence of numerous well-known British companies and banks in Calcutta high-lighted where the real strength and importance of the British colony lay. The hinterland behind Calcutta, which produced coal, tea, and jute (at the time Calcutta was the world's largest supplier of jute), became the financial and industrial hub for British commercial and imperial interests.

Manifestations of the British Raj were everywhere. The city had many English-style clubs supporting the large expatriate (predominantly British) population. Many of these clubs had strict membership rules that rein-forced the colonial notion of an exclusively British enclave. By the late 1930s, a few clubs had relaxed their membership rules for non-British foreigners but some maintained financial barriers that precluded the non-British from joining. Overt racism and a cult of superiority towards Indians was quite evident. Nevertheless, between the wars, Calcutta demonstrated a subtle blend of western and eastern cultures and was justifiably considered to be the cultural capital of India. Indeed, along with Shanghai and Hanoi, it was often called the "Paris of the East."

This was the Calcutta that my parents moved to as they started their new life away from Bata and the walled Czech enclave of Batanagar. They were now part of a city with a spirited tradition of political and labour protest, a city of factional politics, a city very prepared to confront its colonial master in the cause of nationalism, and a city that had already given birth to a communist party movement. I doubt that, even in 1942, my parents had any inkling of what Communism meant, especially this Indian variant, but the reality of the later communist putsch in Czechoslovakia and the emergence of a powerful, ruling Bengali communist party in Calcutta would have an enormous impact on them.

53 Chowringhee Road

Very soon after leaving Batanagar, Dad found the Chowringhee Road apartment;[65] this was on a thoroughfare that was closely associated with Calcutta's early history. Chowringhee Road is not very far from the river Hooghly and thus close to the economic heartland of British India. Its first historical mention is not as a road but as a small village very close to Govindpore, one of the original settlement sites that the British East India Company occupied in 1680.[66] After the Battle of Plassey, Calcutta started to grow and take on all the trappings of an administrative centre, namely, fine buildings, infrastructure, residential areas, large mansions, parks, and roads. Chowringhee Road was one of the principal streets in this young town and became a very desirable residential address. Among its first noted early residents were Justice Stephen Caesar le Maestre (Judge of the Supreme Court of Fort William) and the Irish journalist, James Augustus Hicky (founder of *Hicky's Bengal Gazette* in January 1780, the first printed newspaper in India).[67]

As commercial activity grew further and expanded, some of the prominent business houses also established their offices on Chowringhee road. In Mum and Dad's time, many corporate headquarters were already based there, including Imperial Tobacco (established in 1910), the Bank of India, the ANZ Grindlay's Bank, Imperial Chemical Industries, the Standard Chartered Bank, the Geological Survey of India, the Indian Museum, Firpo's restaurant and night club, the Grand Hotel, and the Metro Cinema in the north. At the further end, Chowringhee merged with Dharamtallah Street.

Chowringhee Road was a broad thoroughfare with an extremely busy tramline running along one side all the way to the junction with Dharamtallah. A large tram terminus was situated at this junction with tram turning circles to point the trams in different directions of the city. Chowringhee Road was home to some truly majestic buildings of imperial architecture. In Mum and Dad's time, at the intersection of Chowringhee Road and S.N. Banerjee Road, a magnificently ornate building, the

65   Another version of the word *Chowringhee* is *Chourangi*.
66   Chaudhuri, ed., *Calcutta, the Living City. Volume 1: The Past*, 11.
67   Ibid., 18.

Whiteway Laidlaw Department Store, stood on the corner. This store, with its elaborate "wedding cake" structure, its imposing size and façade, was the emporium of choice for Calcutta's expatriate colonial population. In the mid 20th century, even though the exterior of the building was covered with grime from prolonged exposure to the heat, rainfall and humidity, it was still possible to discern some of the grand architectural features of this wonderful building. At No. 12 Chowringhee Road, the Old Continental Hotel, one of Calcutta's oldest hotels, has an entry in its guest book, dated 18 February, 1896, where Mark Twain, the American humourist and author, wrote some complimentary things about the hotel during his very short stay in Calcutta.

To this day, Chowringhee Road remains one of the main arteries of the city. It extends from a pleasant, middle class, residential area to the downtown areas of Park Street and Lindsay Street, where the shopping venues, hotels and entertainment areas are located. We lived on a relatively quiet and congestion-free section of the road. Our apartment building was directly across from St. Paul's Cathedral, the major Anglican Cathedral in Calcutta. St. Paul's was built in the neo-Gothic style much admired by the Victorians. It was surrounded by beautifully landscaped gardens with two, large, rectangular water ponds, or "tanks." These gardens were a blessing for any young mother and Mum made use of them often. As a young child, my playground was the gardens of St Paul's Cathedral. Naturally, the *amahs* (nannies) who took their charges for daily outings to the Cathedral used the opportunity to meet and discuss their concerns and their employers while the children played on the lawn.

My sister, Martina, had her own *amah* when she was a toddler; her life included a daily visit to the park at St. Paul's, where her *amah* would guide the pram into a circle formed by other prams – rather like the circling of the wagons in western movies – and then join the other *amahs*. This would maximize their chat time. Martina's *amah* would try to coax her to sleep with the endless chant of "*Nini, Baba, Nini; Roti, Makkhan, Chini*" ("Sleep, Baby, Sleep; Bread, Butter, Sugar"). This was a banner song from the *amah's* hit parade that I believe most white toddlers heard when they went to the park. By the time Martina came along, I was already beyond the *amah* stage, but I would still go with Martina to St. Paul's and meet up with my friends, many of whom were little Indian boys. We played various games in our short pants and we were well-armed with sticks. The stick was a weapon of honour; you could not participate in any adventures without it. There were trees to be climbed, extravagantly choreographed stick fights, large bushes to hide in and be explored, and water tanks to be closely prodded and inspected for marine life. When Martina returned home, I went along and was ready for my bath, casually tossing my pants and shirt into the *dhobi* (laundry man) bundle.

Our apartment was accessed from the main thoroughfare of Chowringhee by turning off the road under a small overhead bridge cum terrace which connected the three-storey apartment building to the separate garage area enclosures opposite. We first passed through a largish, gravel-covered courtyard with free/guest parking for three or four cars. On one side of the courtyard, facing the apartment building, were six or seven lockup garages. The living quarters for the servants that worked in this apartment building were situated above these garages. Although the garages were intended to house cars, most of them served as additional living areas for poor Indian families like our servants; the owners of the building collected the rent.

Dandia, Kalu, and Paidya - Our Servants

I look back with deep affection at the people who worked for us in the apartment. In Calcutta, in the established residential areas, households generally had the means to hire a veritable beehive of servants, many of whom had developed the colonial skill of looking "busy," when they had but a single function to perform. When Dandia joined our family, he was employed as a cleaner/sweeper; but he was the total antithesis of the "colonial servant." He worked hard and went about his job energetically. He wielded his natural, jute-stringed broom in broad, scything movements to get rid of the surface floor dirt, before he moved onto his "wetted cloth" routine. Dandia appeared to glide slowly across the floor while squatting on his haunches and without ever being noticed or interfering with anybody's space. He kept low to the floor and he hardly ever looked up at us as he shifted his position intermittently. All we could see was him pushing out one foot to another spot and moving in a sideways motion to the next spot as he covered the room. Dandia had a younger brother, Kalu, whom we also hired as a cleaner, but Dandia was the senior servant in our household. We soon referred to him as *Burra* (Big) Dandia, an appellation that pleased him, as he felt that it gave him status.

Dandia was a *harijan*, and came from Orissa, a neighbouring state to Bengal. *Harijans* belonged to the lowest social stratum in India's caste system. Collectively, they were also commonly referred to as the "untouchables," since their designated work incorporated the filthiest, unhealthiest, most undesirable tasks that could be performed. No one else would do it. Mahatma Gandhi - who strove to improve their status and lives - coined the name *harijans* to refer to these "untouchables."[68] Within the Indian caste system, *harijans* were differentiated from and kept separate from other social categories. They lived on the fringes of society and their lives were generally filled with prescriptions and proscriptions as to what they could and could not do. For instance, they could not enter the houses of the higher castes, and they were not allowed to draw water from wells frequented by the higher castes. They were denied entry to any Hindu temple. Interestingly, further social stratifications occurred within the *harijan* class. For instance, the *dhobis* (people who washed clothes) and the *nai* (barbers, hairdressers, beauty parlour workers) considered themselves to be superior to the lowest orders such as the *Bhangis* (the sweepers and scavengers, who were outcasts even amongst outcasts).

Within the caste system, a common understanding existed for what the rules were that governed work activities and all the minutiae in the specialties of that work. Dandia understood that he cleaned the floors and did nothing else. He understood that he did not clean up the table or wash the dishes, even if this needed doing. And for his work, he earned a living wage. Most people like Dandia accepted these rules; this was their dharma,

---

68   Gandhi founded a weekly called *Harijan* to give voice to his political, social, and cultural views. In the very first edition, in response to a question by the Rev. S. Jones on the caste system, Gandhi responded: "Untouchability as it is practised in Hinduism today is, in my opinion, a lie against God and man and is therefore, like a poison slowly eating into the very vitals of Hinduism." See Gandhi Heritage Portal, *Harijan*, 1.1 (11 Feb. 1933) https://www.gandhiheritageportal.org/journals-by-gandhiji/harijan.

which is an important tenet of Indian religious beliefs and philosophy.[69] In its simplest form, *dharma* means an acceptance of your station in life, by submitting and conforming honestly and completely to the rules of prescribed behaviour. If the *harijans* diligently performed their work, they could accumulate good *karma* (a belief that anything said or done has a cause and effect). A good deed performed, or the intent to do a good dead, will earn a future good deed, and vice versa for bad deeds. *Karma* is like an accounting balance sheet that keeps track of all rewards and punishments earned from your current and past lives. If you have good *karma*, or assets, you can be released from your current station to another in your reincarnation after death. Dandia hoped and believed that, if he managed to accumulate a lot of good *karma*, he could look forward to a better life in his next reincarnation.

Dandia was a man of mettle. He was intelligent and wanted to learn and keep on learning to improve his situation in this life. So, under Mum's mentorship, he slowly progressed from being a sweeper to a cook for the simple dishes. For a while, Mum still took responsibility for cooking all the Czech dishes that Dad loved. But Dandia learned quickly and soon could cook both the Czech and Indian dishes. Indeed, he became so proficient in this job that Mum entrusted all the cooking to him. But it did not end there. Dandia began to do all the grocery shopping for the family; this was a source of great self-esteem for him, as he was now entrusted with sums of money that sometimes exceeded his monthly wage. Dandia took great pleasure in accounting for every anna. We delighted in seeing him grow as a human being. My fondest memories of Dandia were when Mum spoke to him about the Czech dishes for the evening's menu. Dandia noted all of this down in his notebook: yes, he had started to learn to write, a substantial achievement for an individual wanting to better himself. It would be interesting to know what this did to his own personal *dharma* and *karma* balance sheet. The final act of triumph was when Dandia came to "rule"

---

69   The concept of *dharma* is addressed extensively in the *Bhagavad Gita* (*Lord God's Song*), the great Hindu texts embedded in the Hindu epic the *Mahabharata*, the longest epic poem in the world. It is a foundational text for Indian culture; large parts of it are known or memorized by Indians to this day.

the kitchen. What was even more remarkable was Mum's own admission to us that he cooked Czech food better than she could.

The household arrangements for our servants deserve a mention here. Imagine a garage living space where the doors are thrown open during the day. Families of between four to six people live in this small structure. All the families share one external water tap and they cook in the open outside. Paid work provided this benefit: a garage to live in, a place of one's own. Many servants had notions that this was going to be their whole life. Our driver, Phul Mohammed, as well as our cook, Dandia, lived in one of these garages. As a young boy, I remember visiting them and drinking a cup of tea with them; I noticed early on that these poor people had an enormous generosity of spirit and a sense of sharing, something I believe they had in common with poor people everywhere. But they had work, which was important, for they supported their extended families living in small villages in the rural hinterland. Our driver supported his whole family even though they lived in a village over 350 miles away in Bihar; he saw them once a year when he went on his *chhuti* (holidays) for about four weeks. This idea of family separation had very little resonance with me when I was young, but I started to understand it much more once I had my own family. It must have been very, very difficult for those who found work in the city yet had families in the countryside. But it was an accepted part of the cycle of life in Bengal, probably in other parts of India as well, for it meant life for their family.

What an irony, indeed, that this type of long-distance family support now exists amongst even the highest educated Indians. It is quite common for one spouse to pursue university studies or work in some foreign country, while the other spouse stays at home or pursues their own work ambitions. I know of many examples of this kind of arrangement. But the maxim in India at the time amongst the poorer classes was that, when you had work, you hung on to it because, for everyone who had work, there were hundreds waiting in line if you lost your job.

Besides Dandia and Kalu, we had a part-time helper who had special skills that came in handy from time to time. His name was Paidya and he worked in my father's factory. He was a toolmaker by trade but, somewhere along the way, he had learnt how to polish silver and ornamental cut glass, in addition to laying out a dining table with plates and cutlery. Paidya certainly knew how to decorate a dinner table and the crowning glory was his ability to create all sorts of interesting animal and geometric shapes with the table napkins, a sort of napkin origami. His creations drew many comments that naturally reflected well on Mum.

The Apartment

Mum and Dad's small apartment was on the second floor.[70] It contained a separate dining room, lounge room, a large bedroom, kitchen, and bathroom. Since the lounge had very large windows, we referred to it as the "verandah"; this was where I slept on one of the sofas when I came home from boarding school and where my sister also slept once she became a day-boarder in Calcutta. Neither of us had our own space. I was hardly at home from the age of six, so "my own space" did not mean much to me. The solitary bathroom contained a large stand-alone enamel tub served by an antique, hot water heating system. The apartment had high ceilings and each room had a fan.

The livable area was cramped but it served as a storehouse for our treasures, including my collection of comics, Mum's *Saturday Evening Post*, Dad's *Popular Mechanics* magazines, my Harry Belafonte and Kingston Trio records and, eventually, the wonderful, boxed, vinyl set of Beethoven symphonies conducted by Herbert von Karajan, given to me by my mother on my 16th birthday and which was my introduction to the world of classical music. These long-playing records were absolute treasures, as they had been smuggled into the country. Calcutta had no record store of note where we could buy any current or classical music. As a teenager, my sister immersed herself in the world of Pat Boone and other clean-cut, white-hosed and shod performers. If I remember correctly, she started the local chapter of the Pat Boone fan club and his paraphernalia filled her cupboard and her world. We had a low, round coffee table in the verandah and this doubled as the utility work surface whenever I built my balsawood model planes or "infrastructure" with my Meccano set.

70   I am using the Canadian practice here of nominating the first floor up from street level as the second floor.

Books were not part of our upbringing and our meagre library reflected this reality. Mum read a bit. Initially, when her English language skills were developing, her reading encompassed the *Readers Digest*, sometimes the *Saturday Evening Post*, or *Colliers*; old copies were bought from the roadside booksellers. Later on, our family doctor, Dr. Ronald, introduced her to books written by Somerset Maugham, Pearl Buck and others. Somerset Maugham became her favourite author; whenever she went to the Swimming Club, she spent much time in the outdoor area reading in the shade of an umbrella. I cannot recall her ever reading any of the classics. What a pity, but this way of life probably reflected my parents' education and rural background. The charm of good books came from outside the family circle, from friends who introduced us to the writers they loved. As children, this opened our eyes to a different world, even if it came later rather than earlier. For his part, Dad devoured *Time*, *Newsweek*, *Life*, and *Popular Mechanics* magazines and I believe that much of his *Weltanschauung* (worldview) was formed by their slanted content. My parents' time in Calcutta coincided with the era of Stalin, Khrushchev, the "Cold War," and Communism in Czechoslovakia. Dad was vocal in his hatred for anything associated with Communism and for that matter anything associated with the colour "red." So, his reading was definitely right-wing. I have often thought that it was unfortunate that my parents missed out on the wider pleasures of reading.

Shortly after they settled in at Chowringhee Road, Mum and Dad began their introduction to and fascination with India and its rich heritage and culture. With this growing awareness and with the support of some of our Indian friends, we learnt - in our own way - to understand and appreciate many aspects of Indian cultural life and the values of the country where we now lived. I remember one occasion very vividly. I had returned home for the holidays. While my sister Martina's *amah* was preparing her for a visit to the park at St. Paul's Cathedral, I was quite rude and disrespectful. Mum found out what I had done and asked me to apologize, but I boorishly ignored Mum's request. Mum then rang Dad at the factory; he dropped everything and rushed home. Slowly, I began to understand the gravity of the situation. Dad again asked me to apologize to the amah and I stupidly refused. I knew that this brinksmanship would lead to punishment and, being a blockhead, my initial reaction telegraphed to Dad a "catch me if you can" message; so, we started to race around the dining room table, where every move he made was matched by an equal and opposite move on my part.

With a looming stalemate, Dad changed tactics and reached for a dinner plate in the china cabinet and hurled it my direction. It missed me but this simple action brought about an instantaneous behavioural change. In shock, I stopped running. The next plate flew across the dining room table and hit me in the chest, fell to the floor, and shattered. He reached for another plate. I surrendered immediately. Subsequently, I received the worst thrashing from Dad that I had ever had. Finally, he took hold of me, looked me squarely in the eyes and said, "Just because you think that you are superior and privileged, it is absolutely no reason to be disrespectful or rude to anyone else, no matter what their station in life or the work that they do. They are all doing honest work and that *must* be respected. All work is honourable, no matter who is doing it." And then he added, "Remember, Mikushko, you might be in the same situation one day, doing work that others consider to be of low value but that you hope others will respect. So, go now and apologise to Martina's *amah*." His message was simple and profound. I followed his command and I have never forgotten what he said. I believe that Dad and Mum's views on the universal quality of respect and tolerance for all people was partly shaped by their own humble beginnings, but also by their daily experience of the caste system and racial divide in Calcutta. It was a profound and salutary lesson; thankfully, I received it at an early age.

Ours was a simple household and we had plain, practical furniture. However, I remember that both my parents, once they began to make some money from the business, started to collect Persian carpets. These beautiful carpets soon covered the floors around the apartment. They definitely made it much warmer in tone. Mum was the expert here and she knew her regional designs and knots. Her favourite carpets were from Tabriz, Kashan, Nain and, in particular, the Turkmen carpets with the Bukhara designs. Mum and Dad also had some exquisite prayer carpets from Qum and Isfahan in Persia/Iran. From an early age, I was surrounded by these beautiful objects and started to gain an appreciation and knowledge of the intricate craftsmanship - the weaving techniques, the designs and the materials including the natural dyes - involved in their making. This early exposure influenced me so much that, today, I can't imagine living without such wonderful, hand-crafted masterpieces. Mum and Dad also started to collect other art and surrounded themselves with many beautiful things, like carved Chinese ivory figurines (even today I am enthralled at the detail and warmth of these pieces). They enjoyed the fact that they chose them together. Over the years, when my parents made the occasional trip to Czechoslovakia, they brought back some delightful Czech oil paintings, many of which adorn my own walls here in Canada. Some of these paintings were given to my parents by Czech artists who did not want their work to be displayed anywhere on walls in communist Czechoslovakia.

Our verandah had a window that overlooked another house, a side alley, a terrace, and a garden. There was no shade and little respite from the searing heat of summer. During Mum and Dad's early years in Calcutta, there was no air-conditioning either; any relief to be had from wave after wave of rippling heat entering the house was provided by the overhead fan and by shuttering the house completely. On really hot evenings, we threw the windows open so that we could catch the cool evening air circulated by the verandah ceiling fan. Welcome to air conditioning, Indian style! Often, when we looked out of these large windows, we could observe aspects of Calcutta life in our immediate neighbourhood. From this high vantage point we could see the family in the next house sitting on their manicured lawn enjoying high tea. Probably a wealthy family, as all their servants wore immaculate white uniforms with a sort of napkinned turban perched on their heads. A slight glance towards the mansions on our left brought a cleric into focus parading up and down a shaded colonnade reading a book with a tassel attached, probably the Holy Book itself. This verandah window was also an important communication medium. When we required water in the bathroom, one of us would go to the window and shout out, *"Muni-ma, pani pampa kholem"* ("Muni, open up the water pump"). Muni-ma was the self-appointed caretaker of the building and lived in a small room under our verandah window; it was she who turned on the pump that sent water up into our bathroom.

Each year, we celebrated our version of Czech Christmas in the verandah and, after Christmas dinner, all our dinner guests assembled there around the tree to partake in the warm, friendly tradition of gift-giving. Dad always managed to get a real Christmas tree sent to him by his good friend Bobal, who lived in Pathankhot in northern Punjab, right on the Jammu-Kashmir border. Bobal was a friend from Dad's Bata days. Like Dad, Bobal had left the shoe factory to start his own business; he manufactured wooden boxes and crates. Bobal's business was situated near the foothills leading up to the Himalayan mountains and close to the forests in the province of Himachal Pradesh (located in Northern India and bordered by Jammu, Kashmir, Punjab, Uttarakhand and Tibet). Pathankot was the last major city on the highway that linked Jammu and Kashmir with the rest of India and had become an important hub for the region. Bobal had also established a lumber plant for the trees harvested in the local forests.[71]

From our early childhood, Mum and Dad encouraged us to become involved in family festivities and gatherings whenever we had friends or visitors drop by. I remember quite clearly that we never had the feeling that we were children who had to disappear. Perhaps the small area of the apartment contributed to this desire for inclusion. It also meant that we were often part of boisterous dinner parties with much verbal jousting, singing, joke-telling, laughter, and adult conversation.

The verandah had another important purpose: it doubled as our own in-house cinema. Dad owned a 16mm Paillard Bolex movie camera, which he used extensively, especially when he went trekking. I lost count over the years of the numerous times we saw all his Himalayan mountaineering movies, his expeditions to Nepal and Sikkim, and other family movies. When friends came over, invariably after dinner we retired to the verandah and watched these movies. I am sure that, between my brother and myself, we can still reconstruct the commentary provided by Dad on any film shown, for it hardly ever varied. We got to know intimately many of the images of the great Himalayan peaks like Jannu, Kabru, Kangchenjunga,

---

71 After Dad established his own business manufacturing hurricane lanterns, he shipped the lanterns around the country in wooden crates made from timber processed at Bobal's plant.

Chombu, Pandim, Sharikidanechung (my personal favourite, as the name has such a wonderful lilt to it) and many more through these commentaries. Dad had found his element. His obvious love of the mountains came through strongly and his audiences felt that they were there with him as he made his way up the Lachung Valley in Sikkim to another pass and valley beyond. These evenings were never dull or boring and I never tired of watching the movies over and over again.

The dining room was small but, if the walls could have spoken, they would have yielded up stories of numerous wonderful evenings shared with family friends over food or even casual meetings with coffee and Mum's cookies. In addition, the dining room table was the main "Operations Centre" for the family; here, the daily activities of our household were planned or coordinated by Mum. In many ways, it resembled the old kitchen in the farmhouse where my grandmother lived and where she held court, dispensed advice, kept warm, managed her family, listened to their travails, and cooked for them all. Mum displayed her prized collection of Czech cut glass here in a chiffonier. In one corner, near the kitchen entrance, I had my own little cupboard, where I could store my books, music, Meccano set, comics, and the miscellaneous treasures of a young boy. It is true to say that the dining room was the undisputed domain of Mum and Dandia. The rest of us moved quickly through this nerve centre on our way to the kitchen fridge for a drink or a snack.

Every second day in the morning, Mum and Dandia conducted their management meeting about household matters. Dandia would prepare the shopping list and, on cue, just like a repeated message on a closed loop cassette, Mum would ask Dandia why there was a need for more sugar, rice and potatoes. Like clockwork Dandia would respond, "Memsahib, you know that *burra* (big) *sahib* (Dad) eats a lot, *chota* (small) *sahib* (yours truly) eats a lot, and feeding of many foreign visiting people to house, all the *khana* (food) goes quickly." Mum listened to this explanation every time very politely and patiently, but never lost her cool as she knew that some of the sugar, rice, potatoes and other food was diverted elsewhere to feed not only Dandia's family but also our driver, Phul Mohammed. She never made an issue of this. When I was older, and finally understood this whole process, I came to admire her attitude. She told me that she knew what transpired but never objected because Dandia never abused this little privilege. Mum viewed it as a small recompense for the many long hours of sterling work that he did at our place. There was another ritual argument, this time relating to the cost of food and how Dandia managed the money when he went shopping.

The servants received their pay once a week when Mum would count off the rupee notes to pay them. Keeping in mind that Dandia came from the lowest caste and had advanced in status from sweeper to cook, I always admired the way that he accepted his salary. Yes, I call it a salary, for he had made something of himself and he always accepted his money with his hands cupped and outstretched, head bowed, eyes looking down to the ground. He would then raise his hands, still holding his money, to his forehead in an expression of thanks and backed away into the kitchen. He never once stopped to count his money, as he trusted Mum completely. Mum asked him repeatedly to stop performing this ritual because it made her uncomfortable, but he always made this gesture of gratitude. I loved the wonderful relationship that Mum and Dandia enjoyed and she inspired a tremendous loyalty from him in return. And yet they were worlds apart. Years later, when I reflected on this, I understood what trust can truly mean, what humility can truly mean and how it became possible to have such a human friendship between such vastly different people.

Our home life was uncomplicated. In the early and war years in Calcutta, we were mostly concerned with supporting each other. We were not a family of readers. The opportunity to attend a musical concert was practically non-existent. My parents could not avail themselves of any amateur theatrical groups performing in the city because of the language barrier. They had to find a different way of indulging their interests. So, they entertained their friends at home and they were known as good hosts. Everything else was a luxury.

Mum and Dad had their own little rituals that persisted throughout the years. Sunday mornings was one. It would be late morning, about 10 a.m. Dad's Sunday ritual involved sleeping in. His low frequency snores cascaded through the house, echoing off the tall ceilings. We definitely knew that Dad was still asleep in the apartment's only bedroom. While he was sleeping, Mum would enjoy relative peace seated at the dining room table, an overhead fan slowly circulating whatever cool morning breeze remained at this time of day. Dandia had already prepared some tea for her and she liked browsing through the morning edition of the local newspaper, the *Sunday Statesman*. Mum mainly scanned the headlines and, if a headline touched her sense of humour, she would chuckle and read the full report. These were stories of no great import. On this particular Sunday, the newspaper carried reports of a Bengal government minister addressing a crowd in the *Maidan*, and a few columns at the bottom reported on accidents in the city. Her interest was drawn to the following small headline, "Rickshaw hit by overloaded bus. Rickshaw *wallah* (the man pulling the rickshaw) in critical condition and passengers hanging on outside of bus being treated for bruising when they fell off after the collision." Further on, there was a short news item headed, "Calcutta CID Police Chief asking for arms!" which caught her fancy. On page 3 of the paper, she found the following headline, "Calcutta Municipal Corporation wondering why the sewers are smelling so strong," and she read on, wryly amused. Of course, everyone knew why the sewers smelt. What was there to wonder about!

When my parents first moved to Calcutta, Dad had a bicycle that he used for general transportation and later for getting to work. He often went for cycle rides on the road that meandered past the Victoria Memorial, the Calcutta Race Course, and Alipore Zoo. Mum either walked to the markets, usually in the winter months, or used a rickshaw to get the family groceries home from the New Market, where everything that she needed was available under one very large roof.

Daphne Ross Kindergarten

After my fourth birthday, Mum and Dad decided that I needed to start school. British parents, during the Raj, did not blink an eyelid with the decision to start a child's school life quite early. For most children, that meant attending a boarding school at some stage. It had not been lost on my parents that the ex-patriate community was quite comfortable with the idea of their children, aged four and upwards, attending boarding school. Daphne Ross Kindergarten, where my parents sent me daily, although not a boarding school, offered more than just a normal kindergarten with sand-pits and swings for play. Daphne Ross Kindergarten pursued a learning agenda, something of which I am reminded as I read my old report cards.

My very earliest recollection of school and especially Daphne Ross Kindergarten was going at age four with my *amah* by rickshaw. The school was located on Theatre Road, not far from where we lived. I remember the rickshaw ride well as I enjoyed my own open convertible experience. I wore my uniform and my own little brown *topee* (a pith helmet to protect the wearer from the sun) and chinstrap. Rain sometimes spoilt the trip, becoming unpleasant as the rickshaw-*wallah* would fold down a dirty, heavy, tarpaulin drape that limited visibility. He negotiated all the traffic and "played chicken" with the cars. When we disembarked, the fare was about four annas. He would give us such an impoverished look with an outstretched hand holding the money, asking my *amah* whether this was adequate compensation for his effort. How could a miserly four annas help to feed his family? On the days when my *amah* paid with a rupee note, the rickshaw-*wallah* invariably never had any change: so, my amah would have to go to the nearest *paan* or soft drink shop to get some change. [72] Practically every day during my kindergarten years, we experienced the same rickshaw theatrics with the disgruntled look; but, every school day, that same rickshaw-*wallah* waited at the corner for us to go to kindergarten.

I have absolutely no recollection of what went on at the kindergarten but the report cards remind me of my time there. Can you believe that a child of four had assessments for each term! Obviously, somebody believed that these riveting documents would interest my parents. No doubt the kindergarten also had its own rules for behaviour that could lead to my expulsion. My report cards described how I recited my ABCs, played, sang or carved creative sculptures in the sand pit. The cards also had a learning component, namely reading and drawing. No examples of my masterpieces survive. Seventy-five years ago, these assessments served as measures of childhood success for Mum and Dad. I wonder if they felt any pride (or concern) knowing, "Little Miki sang like an angel" or "Miki

---

72   *Paan* is a dry betel leaf which is folded into a triangular shape and filled with finely crushed areca nut, cardamom, grated coconut, and small amounts of crushed candy and held together with slaked lime paste; it is chewed by many with much relish.

was a good boy for most of the term," or "Miki played well in the sand and swung on the swing carefully," or "Miki was a naughty boy because he did not finish his tiffin[73] on Thursday last week.

But how strange is this? Move forward a half-century. When Evie and I visited Delhi in 2002, I remember how concerned friends of mine were that their four-year-old daughter had not been studying sufficiently to pass an entrance examination for a highly recommended convent school. It seems that four-year-olds still have not escaped being assessed, but the degree of difficulty has changed significantly. Our friends recounted that their child would have to pass an oral exam. I came away from that trip grateful that I had been raised at a time when only my capacity to sing and play was of any interest to my teachers and parents. On reflection, I believe that my attendance at Daphne Ross indicated how much Mum and Dad had assimilated, at least in part, to some aspects of colonial life.

Metal Box (23 March, 1942 - 24 August, 1945)

After Dad left Bata, he needed to find work as soon as possible and he had very few options available to him. Because of the language barrier, working for an Indian company would have been difficult, even without any consideration of the cultural issues. His only immediate option was to find work with a British company. Indian industry had already started on the path of supporting the war effort and Dad had skills that were in demand in those difficult times. So, after a single month's job search, he found work with the Metal Box Corporation on 23 March, 1942. Dad's previous technical training and background, as well as the experience gained at Bata in the Operations and Maintenance departments, were appropriate assets. So, Metal Box hired him in the same capacity to work in their Munitions Production, Supply, Medical, Food, Ordinance, RAF support, and Gun and Shell divisions. He started on a salary of Rs 700 per month, with a rental subsidy of Rs 160 per month.

Metal Box Corporation was incorporated as an engineering company in Calcutta in 1933. Initially, the company's main line of business was

---

73   In India, tiffin refers to a light lunch; it originated in British India and became very much part of common English parlance there.

to manufacture a diverse range of metal containers with closures (for processed food stuffs and related uses), flexible packaging and injection molding components, paper products, domestic hardware, industrial components, and a wide range of engineering hardware and products.

The company had a large shop floor with machines for drilling, sheet metal extraction, lathing, welding, seaming and reaming, as well as electrolytic baths for galvanizing metals. This pot-pourri of machinery was totally different from that required in the production of shoes. Thus, during the early war years, Dad started to gather a formidable breadth of knowledge and mastery in the operation and maintenance of metal-working machinery.

It was the hands-on diversity of his experience at Metal Box that would provide Dad with the technical foundation to start his own manufacturing business three years later. At Metal Box, he became familiar with the operations and maintenance of the various types of machinery that would become an integral part of his later business. Here he also came to understand the capabilities and limitations of punch and extrusion machines. On his own, he took an interest in and became familiar with the technology for galvanizing metal, which he introduced to Metal Box. It was at this company that he also learned about dry soldering, painting metals, and packaging technology.

Political Developments in India during World War II

In March 1942, the British Government, through the initiative of Sir Stafford Cripps, tried to obtain the support and cooperation of various Indian political leaders. Cripps wanted this support to be a tangible one with actual plans to recruit Indians to form a British Indian Army and fight in both the European and Southeast Asian theatres of war. Cripps' plan was doomed to failure, however; Lord Linlithgow's unilateral declaration of war on behalf of India had been a catalyst for public anger, revolt, and disorder that produced a surge in nationalism and a strong desire to seek Independence. It was becoming apparent that Britain was not prepared to make any further political concessions towards Indian self-government; indeed, Britain hoped to reverse powers already granted by restricting civil liberties and provoking the Indian National Congress as much as possible.

On the other hand, the widely divergent ways in which each group planned to achieve Independence caused serious divisions amongst them.[74]

The underground push for Indian Independence continued during the War. "Free India" movements existed overseas in Germany and the USA; these were movements that actively campaigned against the British throughout the War. In August 1942, Gandhi started his "Quit India" movement. Once again, the British imprisoned Gandhi, along with other Congress Party leaders, and this led to numerous outbreaks of civil disobedience in many parts of India, including Bengal, which the British repulsed. Outright revolt at a time of worldwide warfare was not viable.[75] Gandhi was opposed to active Indian participation in the war effort, probably because of his own moral convictions as a pacifist, but also because he had no faith in British promises about future Independence. Eventually the Congress Party and influential Indians, including Pandit Nehru, agreed to offer full support for the British war effort. Even the leader of the Muslim League, Muhammed Ali Jinnah, supported this decision but his motivation disguised his desire to obtain a separate Muslim state.[76]

The early setbacks in the War in Europe encouraged some Bengalis to seek alliances with the Axis powers, in particular Germany. One of these movements had morphed into an offshoot of the Congress Party under the leadership of the Bengali Netaji Subhas Chandra Bose, (Congress President from 1938 to 1939). Subhas Chandra Bose, sought alliances with the Axis powers to resist the British, thereby hoping to gain India's liberation and

74 Cripps tried to achieve his agenda against a backdrop of news headlines reporting on Allied setbacks, speculation about an Allied defeat in Europe, and a general apathy for cooperation with the British. Furthermore, he had not done his homework: he engaged with the wrong politicians, and there was no great clarity in what he was trying to achieve. See Yasmin Khan, *The Raj at War: A People's History of India's Second World War,* 132-4, 139-140.

75 The Japanese threat forced other Indians to put the "Quit India" aspiration on hold. Congress agreed to set it in abeyance and Gandhi was imprisoned for his troubles. But the flame had not been extinguished. See Hajari, *Midnight's Furies: The Deadly Legacy of India's Partition,* 39-41. In Bengal, the impetus of a "Quit India" movement manifested itself in many interesting ways with women and in some cultural circles. See Chaudhuri, ed., *Calcutta, the Living City. Volume 11: The Present and the Future,* 24, 38.

76 Khan, 138-139.

NO WAY BACK HOME

Independence.[77] He formed an army, the Indian National Army, with Indian soldiers who had been captured during the fall of Singapore. The Japanese had later released them as part of their support for splinter groups opposed to the British. However, with the allied war effort against the Japanese becoming increasingly successful by 1945, Bose's insurrection was short-lived.[78]

After the Japanese made their surprise attack on the US Naval Base at Pearl Harbor in December 1941, the Japanese imperial forces embarked on a rapacious military push into Southeast Asia. They won victory after victory and moved from Wake Island in the Pacific to Malaysia and eventually Singapore. In mid-January 1942, two Japanese divisions advanced into Burma. The rapid advance of the Japanese Army and the fall of Rangoon, the capital of Burma, on 7 March, 1942, sent shockwaves throughout the expatriate community in Calcutta and, indeed, the rest of India. Various supply routes from India to China, where the United States had troops, were either threatened or cut off. By early May, the Japanese were knocking at India's door. On 1 May, 1942,[79] they captured Mandalay, forcing the British troops under General Alexander to complete a general retreat into India later that month.

The unfolding events in the Far East, the strong Japanese advance into Burma and the potential ramifications if India fell to the Japanese brought the British and Americans together in a strangely conflicted alliance. Britain's strategic thinking focused on the defence of India and its

---

77 Subhas Chandra Bose was born on 23 January, 1897. He was first and foremost a nationalist and revolutionary and eschewed anything to do with British colonial rule, even employment. See Chaudhuri, ed., *Calcutta, the Living City. Volume II: The Present and the Future*, 19. Bose was of one mind with Nehru and Gandhi in this aspiration. However, in 1939, he had a falling out with Gandhi at the Congress Party meeting at Tripuri over the latter's ideas about non-violence. See Durga Das, *India From Curzon to Nehru & After*, 192.

78 Bose took over leadership of the Indian National Party (INA), which had been established in Singapore after its fall to the Japanese. The INA was now a fighting force that worked with the Japanese Army. In October 1943, the INA and the Japanese advanced into India, occupying Kohima. They were defeated by the Allied 14th Army. Bose fled to Japan from the battlefields of S.E. Asia, subsequently dying in a plane crash. See Khan, 118, 245-246, 172.

79 Khan, 99.

continued colonial domination there, while the Americans were more interested in prosecuting a war against the Japanese. The situation in Burma had become critical. Despite their very different objectives, both the British and American military leaders realized that Calcutta was conveniently located to become an important centre for managing the logistics of their armed forces. Putting a halt to the Japanese advance in Burma was now their joint objective. If this could be achieved, the Americans would be able to secure their logistical supply lines. As for the British, halting the Japanese advance through Burma would prevent Japan from attacking India through the port city of Calcutta.

1942 was a pivotal year in the prosecution of the War in the East. Calcutta experienced a large military buildup. At the same time, refugees were streaming into the city: many came by sea after the fall of Malaysia and Singapore; others arrived on foot from Burma. Still others managed to come from the north into Bengal via Assam and were assisted in making their way to Calcutta by the tea planters in the region.

In the interim, the presence of both British and American troops ensured that the simmering independence movement stayed on the back burner. The British showed no inclination whatsoever to engage with the issue. Demands from Indian dissidents that the British "Quit India" continued. The British suppressed these movements ruthlessly, imprisoning Gandhi and Nehru as well as other party functionaries. At the local level, demonstrations, riots, and sabotage in the colony during 1942[80] distracted British authorities from plans to invade Burma to the extent that, by early October, they had a long list of reasons why they could not mount a spring offensive on Burma: chief among them were supply problems, the monsoon, the state of the troops, and the lack of naval and air power.

The Americans had previously opened up a theatre of operations against the Japanese in Chungking, China, under the command of General Stillwell; they drew most of their supplies from India via the overland route from India to China, which went through the north-western part of Burma. However, the continued Japanese occupation of major strategic locations in Burma essentially closed this 620-mile, overland, dirt supply

80   Chaudhuri, ed., *Calcutta, the Living City. Volume II: The Present and the Future*, 23.

road to necessary war resources such as teak, rubber, and rice. It was imperative that this supply route be re-opened.[81]

It wasn't that the British had made no preparation in India for the War; it was just that preparation had been late in starting. As part of the frenzy to stop the Japanese, the Allies' supply services expanded the port capacity of Karachi to the west and Calcutta to the east. Improvements in maintenance and scheduling to India's antiquated railroad system allowed it to support Chinese and American forces in the rugged terrain of North Burma. Strategically, Bengal was now extremely important to the Allies in India; it was not only the natural bridgehead from India into Burma, but also an important location for the possible defence of India. Calcutta was a mere 124 miles from the Burmese border, so the city became a focal point in the planning and implementation of this objective.

When Dad started at Metal Box in 1942, the company's production had become very much geared to supporting the war effort: in particular, the supply of munitions to the British army fighting in nearby Burma, Malaysia, and Singapore. Metal Box requested from the military authorities in Calcutta that Dad be exempted from military service because of his engineering skills. This exemption was granted. However, it was while at Metal Box that Dad joined the City's Civil Defence group, since the threat of a Japanese invasion was becoming increasingly real.

Calcutta, July to December, 1942

During the latter half of 1942, the situation in Calcutta remained quite tense; the population swelled up with starving and displaced people from the fall of Burma, Malaya and Singapore, along with the criminals and prostitutes that are typically attracted to a large military presence.[82] Soldiers were everywhere. The Sonagachi district in Calcutta gained

81   Khan, 259-264.
82   Calcutta witnessed a huge influx of prostitutes that were fleeing the various war zones in the region. They posed a significant threat to the Allied forces, who could not control or manage the significant increase in venereal disease. Local politicians were alarmed; they saw this social change as an attack on their perceived ideas of Indian moral purity. The issue also fuelled anti-colonial rhetoric in Indian society. Ibid., 239-244.

notoriety as a "red light" district; the taxi drivers and rickshaw-*wallahs* knew all the best addresses and American GIs soon found an outlet for their dollars, chewing gum, and Chesterfield cigarettes. However, American soldiers did not have a very good reputation for behaviour during this period. The contrast with other armies was also apparent when it came to material goods. American soldiers and all their associated logistic support groups started to appear in Calcutta in large numbers. For most of these soldiers, World War II would provide their first and lasting impression of Calcutta.[83] It soon became very obvious to locals which troops had access to money and supplies, including medicines, alcohol, and cigarettes. Although there were many British clubs, bars, and restaurants flourishing in Calcutta, Indians and British expatriates were shocked at the conspicuous consumption and sumptuous living arrangements of the Americans. They engaged many servants, whom they overpaid. By contrast, their partners-in-arms, the British, had less money and lived in more austere conditions. This disparity in disposable income led to some resentment and even hostility between the two groups.

The Chinese had supplied the Allies with two battalions which were meant to provide the initial resistance to the Japanese in Burma.[84] The Americans, in the early buildup phases of the War, took over the role of logistic support, as they wished to retain their communication links to China through Burma. The British, on the other hand, were responsible for the operation and maintenance of the air bases to the west of Calcutta. Billeting became a problem for the arriving British and American troops; as a result, many were billeted in Calcutta's numerous social clubs.

The British had set up a camp city at Barrackpore Golf Course. Many of the resident expatriate women organized Ladies Auxiliaries to provide services for the war effort. Some women helped out in the hospitals. But, for the existing expatriate community, life was relatively unchanged. Clubs like the Calcutta Swimming Club, the Tollygunge Club and the Saturday Club were well frequented and tea, bridge and mahjong parties continued as always. There developed two distinct tiers of life amongst the non-Indians

---

83   Today, many internet archives around the world display interesting photographic records of war-time Calcutta, as captured by Kodak-carrying GIs.

84   Ibid., 270-272.

in the city: the military and the expatriate. People made adjustments for the War, but the rhythm of colonial life remained, albeit with a few changes. British expatriates shelved any plans they had for leave; the sea route back to the mother country had become quite dangerous due to the numerous German U-boats prowling the water. Many decided instead to spend their annual holidays at one of the various hill stations in other parts of India.

During the early days of the War, Mum and Dad confined themselves to establishing their life in Calcutta. Dad was extremely busy, since the War meant that Metal Box received a steady stream of military contracts. Mum and Dad had acquired the services of an *amah* who took me daily to the gardens of St. Paul's Cathedral opposite. The *amah* also helped Mum in the apartment. Judging from the numerous, surviving family photographs of this period, my parents spent their spare moments visiting with friends, swimming, making the occasional visit to a cinema, and taking me for walks to the Victoria Memorial, which was a short distance from the apartment.

The Victoria Memorial[85] is an impressive monument that was built and dedicated to Queen Victoria. Lord Curzon suggested its creation. Sir William Emerson designed the building that took as its architectural theme the style of Belfast City Hall; but he also included numerous Mughal elements in the design. The building was constructed over a period of 15 years from 1906 to 1921 on an accessible, pristine location in the *Maidan*. The Victoria Monument is made of white Markrana marble. During the Raj, when I was a little boy, it was surrounded by beautifully landscaped gardens with many winding pathways and was flanked by two large water tanks.

Japanese Bombing Raids on Calcutta, December 1942

Thursday, 24 December, Christmas Eve, dawned a clear, sunny and breezy day. Mum sat at the dining room table getting ready to prepare a list of the day's shopping. Today, she only needed to buy some vegetables and so there would be no need for her to go to the markets. If she needed bread, milk, eggs, meat or fish, these had to be bought from the New Market. But

---

85   Chaudhuri, ed., *Calcutta, the Living City. Volume 1: The Past*, 256-259.

during this era, many vegetable and fruit sellers came to the house carrying their produce in wicker baskets. The doorbell would ring and all Mum had to do was to see what they were selling and make her choice. They offered a wide range of vegetables and fruit. The seller squatted outside the front door and would weigh the purchases using hand-held scales that were balanced with round metal weights. Then, after a short pause, while he gauged her demeanour, the merchant told Mum the price. She would then show him her best, disapproving look. Round One of the bargaining ritual had started.

Mum would ask, "Why are the onions 4 annas a *tola*[86] when two days ago the price was only 2 annas?"

The merchant would respond, "But, memsahib, today I have paid too much more for them and so they are 4 annas."

Mum would counter, "But to go from 2 annas to 4 annas is double the price. I will give you only 2 annas, 8 pies. And that is my last price."

"But, memsahib, my family, my children. They are so young and I will not earn anything." Then the utter despair look on *his* part emerged as if on cue. He would cock his head, put his hand out slightly, shuffle from one squatting position to another and say, "Please memsahib, let us agree on 3 annas."

Now there was a momentary pause, a planned pause to show him that she was seriously considering his offer, glances were exchanged and, after a respectable time delay, Mum would utter the words that he wanted to hear most, "*Acha* (OK), 3 annas, but now pick me out good clean onions." Then he would bring out old newspaper pages from the *Statesman* or *Amrita Bazar Patrika* and package the vegetables up for the short trip to the kitchen pantry.

This wonderful little ritual repeated itself daily, as the merchant went from apartment to apartment on Chowringhee Road. It was a simple system of commerce that satisfied all parties: it got the deal done, while allowing all parties to indulge in the bargaining game. Bargaining was very much part of the commercial fabric of the city. On this particular

---

86   A *tola* is a traditional Indian unit of mass equal to about half an ounce.

Thursday, after purchasing her fruits and vegetables, Mum went back to finish off her coffee and plan her day.

Shortly after noon, the siren sounded. Mum and Dad had practised air raid drills before, so Mum knew what to do. She quickly went to fill up the water jars with fresh drinking water and we all went to the nearest designated air raid shelter, in St. Paul's church priory, just 300 ft. from where we lived. The priory, located in an apartment mansion, had a large entrance hall. Here the air raid warden directed people to designated areas, where we all sat down and waited. Nothing further happened; when the "all clear" siren sounded again, Mum took us back home. Dad had gone to work for his 6 a.m. to 6 p.m. shift. Metal Box operated round the clock because of the War. In the distance Mum could hear the drone of aircraft approaching and soon the sirens started to wail all over Calcutta. Instead of running for the shelter again, she closed all the window shutters, switched off the lights and lit a candle. In the distance she believed that she could hear the sound of anti-aircraft guns. Then she heard the first explosions. They seemed awfully close. At that point, she could do nothing and was worried about Dad.

Dad came home early that afternoon. He was relieved when he saw Mum. She asked him why he had come home early and he told her that there had been a Japanese air raid on the city. The managers at Metal Box did not know which parts of the city were affected. Unsure if there would be any follow-up air raids, the company decided to close the factory down and send their employees home to be with their families. The "all clear" finally went just after midnight. War had finally arrived in Calcutta and many people did not know quite how to react.

Japanese planes bombed Calcutta between 20 and 24, December, 1942,[87] but their attacks were directed mainly at the port facilities. Even

---

87 Madushree Mukerjee, *Churchill's Secret War: The British Empire and the Ravaging of India during World War II*, 94. Numerous eye-witness accounts of the bombing can be found at the following websites: http://www.bbc.co.uk/history/ ww2peopleswar/stories/50/a5756150.shtml, https://indianvagabond.com/2017/09/ 04/japanese-air-raids-on-kolkata-during-wwii/, https://www.indiatoday.in/ education-today/gk-current-affairs/story/japan-bombing-calcutta-world-war-2-1108404-2017-12-19

so, other parts of the city, including Chowringhee, were hit. It is likely that the Christmas Eve attack experienced by my mother was targeted at Europeans; fortunately, few people were hit in these raids. Due to Calcutta's pre-eminently convenient location, many wartime goods had entered India via the city's port facilities, but no one had anticipated these air strikes.

Many believed that the main target would be Howrah Bridge, but the Japanese only managed to bomb Kidderpore docks and Dalhousie Square. The damage was minimal and the bomb craters that could be seen in Dalhousie Square were very small. Despite the material damage being slight, the damage to the morale of Calcutta's citizens was immense, for they now realized how vulnerable they were to air attacks. Their fear prompted a great exodus from the city. The roads leading to Howrah and Sealdah railway stations were clogged with a river of fleeing humanity. Cars and trucks of all types were fully laden. Sometimes there were even birds in cages balancing precariously on the top of the trucks. The city's bullock carts, with goats and cows tethered to the rear, were on the move as well. *Ghora gharries* (horse-drawn carriages) packed with people and their baggage fought for space on the crowded thoroughfares. The poor horses strained under their loads. Some people had actually harnessed their donkeys into action to move the family's belongings. A general panic had overtaken the population, who were determined to reach relative safety somewhere nearby in the countryside or in other rural areas.

At the railway stations, agitated people completely blocked access to the ticket offices. They were like a football crowd that had panicked and were trying to storm the exit gates. For some people, money was no object if it meant getting a ticket on a train out of Calcutta. For the black-market ticket sellers, it must have seemed as though all their paydays had arrived: they could earn a full month's wages in one day. The final destination of the trains was irrelevant to many. People just piled into the carriages, occupying every nook and cranny. When the carriages were filled, people scrambled up to the roof of the train; when there was no more space on top, they found little footholds on the exterior of the trains from which they could hang, sometimes balancing with one foot securely jammed into a single foothold and holding on with one hand.

Mussoorie

The closeness of the Japanese march south, the fall of Singapore, and the push into Burma made people in Calcutta acutely aware that the War had arrived on their doorstep. Intense speculation on this new threat became the main topic of conversation among people in the city. The many refugees who had started to arrive in Calcutta after the fall of Singapore told stories about the Japanese treatment of foreign nationals and atrocities committed against local civilian peoples. These stories dominated the print in the newspapers and talk at dinner parties and in the clubs. Dad had good friends in Batanagar, the Surys; they regularly discussed these new developments and contemplated their next moves. Dad decided that the threat was serious enough to send Mum and me to Mussoorie, a hill station well away from the action. Mrs. Sury and her son Tommy joined Mum. We have a lot of family photographs of this stay in Mussoorie that include me, wearing my *topee*, while playing with my new friends in a sandpit. The photos indicate that I also spent time riding on the backs of mountain ponies, not a happy experience, and one that has probably contributed to my lasting aversion to horses. I was only two years old at the time and so cannot remember a single detail of the time spent in Mussoorie with Mum.

As the Allied response and active war resistance to the Japanese improved and the Japanese advance through Burma was stalled, the perceived danger of a Japanese invasion of Calcutta diminished; Dad decided to recall us from Mussoorie.

The Bengal Famine of 1943-44

During this period of shock and confusion, Bengal bore witness to one of its greatest tragedies, namely, the Bengal Famine.[88] This appalling episode began in 1943. At the time, Bengal had one of the highest population densities in India. It also had a primarily agricultural-based economy with rice being the principal staple food crop. Due to the increasing military importance of Calcutta and with the presence of so many armed forces,

---

88   The best analysis of the famine I have found is in Tom Keneally, *three famines*, 26-28, 32, 39, 75-100, 158-159, 181, 210.

the competition for and acquisition of all foodstuff supplies, especially rice, was paramount.

The fall of Burma to the Japanese caused an enormous problem for the Allies in Bengal. Burma had been one of the principal sources of the rice imported into Bengal. Prior to the outbreak of war, India imported 15-20% of its rice needs from Burma, most of it destined for Bengal. For the eight years previous to 1943, Bengal had had particularly poor rice yields, which had necessitated importing additional rice from Burma.

The panic associated with the War, political unrest, and sheer greed prompted growers, merchants, and landlords collectively to take action to protect their commercial interests. If the grower felt that the rice that he grew would not help to earn him enough money for the coming year, he simply removed surplus rice stocks from the market and hoarded it in hopes of getting a better price later. Nature played its part. In 1942, Bengal suffered both a devastating flood, resulting from a tidal wave, and a cyclone that destroyed much of its rice crop. Farmers were forced to live off the seed that should have provided the next crop of rice in 1943.

The military command that required rice for the war effort tried to impose price controls, with the result that landlords and merchants further withheld their supplies until market conditions improved. All of these actions converged into a perfect storm: rice became virtually impossible to find. All the conditions for a famine were in place. Profiteers now controlled the supply of rice and other foodstuffs to the market. A black market in the basic necessities and other essential food products emerged and the price of food escalated by 600% in six months.

To further compound the effects of the famine, the Allied forces confiscated or took over many forms of land transport as well as the thousands of boats that plied the river Hooghly, and other tributary rivers and the Sundarbans. They wished to prevent these boats from falling into the hands of the Japanese, should they invade, but this action drastically curtailed all fishing and other river farming activity without any plans to replace the supply of fish or other farm produce. Soon the effects of the famine on the populace were noticeable. Starvation spread rapidly from the city to the countryside. People left their villages, making their way to the larger, urban centres like Calcutta in the belief that food could be found there. This influx of starving people only increased the competition for food.

The Allied forces, affluent Bengalis, expatriate Europeans, and other elites in the city competed for the stockpiled foods, but at least they had the resources to do so. Inexplicably, the British, despite the critical shortage of rice, continued to ship part of the remaining rice stocks to the Middle Eastern and European war fronts. Hoarding, stockpiling, price inflation, and profiteering went unchecked; British indifference to the plight of the Bengali people contributed substantially to the emerging famine. Poor people and peasants died in their hundreds of thousands soon after the availability of rice evaporated. Many more died later. Some charitable government programs, religious institutions, and other humanitarian organisations set up food kitchens to feed the hungry but this was a pathetically small gesture compared to the full magnitude of the problem and only partly addressed the hunger issues in Calcutta. Help in the countryside outside Calcutta was virtually non-existent. The hungry scavenged the city for food, including the garbage dumps. Churchill and his British war government, despite pleas from Lord Mountbatten and General Wavell, were totally uninterested and rather contemptuous of aiding the people of Bengal during this famine. Many people collapsed in the streets. There was hardly a footpath in the city where one did not have to walk over or around the emaciated, starving bodies of people on the brink of death. The *Maidan* was converted into one, large, impromptu deathcamp for the sick and dying. The health and hygiene of the city declined, becoming unbearable, with so many people now suffering from diarrhea and dysentery. The daily death toll of people climbed into the hundreds and the authorities could not keep up with the removal of bodies. Many bodies became bloated and started to putrefy under the heat of the relentless Bengali sun. The toll on human life was horrific; it is estimated that between 2,500,000 and 3,000,000 people died of starvation in the state, most of them in Calcutta.

I remember Dad telling me many years later that, despite the tragedy and the obvious scenes of distress everywhere in the city, the evening life of Calcutta continued relentlessly. Not even a visible famine could interfere with the vulgar, expatriate, lotus-eating lifestyle. He remarked that, practically every evening, you could see the British, wealthy Indians and military officers getting out of their cars at the entrances to the Grand and Great Eastern Hotels, night clubs, Firpo's and other restaurants. The members of the Raj were dressed up to the nines, walking over and around bodies on the streets, with handkerchiefs covering their noses to escape the stench and unpleasant odours as they went on to their parties, dinner, and dance engagements. At times it seemed that the city had a full calendar of black-tie events to match those of the magic period between the wars. The upper echelon of the city showed its worst side during the Bengal famine; Dad mentioned that the everyday scenes of the famine were so terrible that you could not escape them even if you tried. He had to negotiate, on a daily basis, the sight of starving and dead persons littering the footpaths and streets when he made his way to work on his bicycle.

Mum told me that when she went to the markets it was sometimes difficult to move. Whole families and groups of families took up residence on the streets and footpaths and she had to walk around not only the living members in such groups but also over many of the dead bodies that were all around her. The fringes around the *Maidan* were crammed with people, as every available habitable space was sought by a sea of suffering humanity.

The famine lasted into late 1943 and then gradually the situation started to improve as supplies of rice and other foodstuffs became more available.

Cargnellis and Racek

Shortly after Mum and Dad moved into Chowringhee Road, they got to know Fredrik and Henriette Cargnelli, an Austrian Jewish couple who lived in an apartment on the third floor of their building. Henriette had flaming red hair and cast a strikingly grand figure. She did not socialize very much, in contrast with Fredrik, who developed a great friendship with Mum and Dad. Their apartment was handsomely appointed and had access to a large terrace from which there was a great view of St. Paul's Cathedral opposite and up and down Chowringhee Road. Henriette prided herself on her furnishings and crockery collection. But the one question that Mum and Dad would have liked an answer to was why so many of the cups, plates and saucers had the P&O Shipping Line logo on them. Dad soon ascertained that Fredrik Cargnelli was an agent who represented F. R. Racek in India. This company had been incorporated in India in 1925 in order to represent the German kerosene lantern companies F.R. Racek, Feuerhand and E & G in Berlin. Racek had some of the hurricane lanterns badged initially with the Feuerhand logo, then with F.R. Racek, and eventually as the EFAR brand.[89]

Hurricane lanterns (also known as wick, or coal oil lanterns) were portable kerosene lamps with a burner attached to the fuel tank. Their primary function was to provide light. The lamp had a cotton wick that was the light source; the lower part of the wick was dipped into the kerosene which was drawn up into the wick by capillary action. The wick was enclosed within a glass chimney that protected it from the elements and prevented the flame from being extinguished. The glass chimney slotted into a holder that allowed air to reach the wick and produce a thermally-induced draft. The glass chimney was pinched at the top, which allowed for an efficient combustion of the kerosene and hence provided light from the clean, smokeless, yellow flame. The height of the wick could be adjusted by a ratchet wheel. The light intensity could be adjusted by changing the exposed surface area of the wick exposed to the flame. During the 1940s, the main market for these hurricane lanterns was primarily in rural India, as the numerous villages across the country either had no electricity or extremely limited access to electricity. Some small, urban centres had very limited electrical distribution, so hurricane lamps were also of use in those communities.

Early in 1943, Fredrik Cargnelli mentioned to Dad that F.R. Racek was concerned with two problems caused by the War: the difficulty and high cost of importing the hurricane lanterns from Germany, and Indian government import restrictions. India at this time had very scant foreign exchange reserves; this shortcoming severely limited Cargnelli's ability to pay for overseas imports and then on-sell into the market. The immediate problem was that the final price paid by the villager had become, in many cases, quite prohibitive. So Cargnelli, cognizant of Dad's background and experience in the operation and management of machinery, raised the question as to whether it would be possible to develop and manufacture

89 They also badged the E&G lanterns with the EFAR logo (based on the F.R. Racek name).

a simpler hurricane lantern, suitable for the Indian market, that would be much more affordable to the villagers. This became the challenge that Dad was to work on.

While at Metal Box, Dad had befriended a Muslim co-worker named Shahadat Khan, who came from Dhaka, a city that was located in what was then called eastern Bengal. Shahadat was a smart and experienced machine tool operator at Metal Box and worked in the same department as Dad. They both became interested in the idea of producing a locally-manufactured, hurricane lantern. Their main challenge was how to start. They decided, while at Metal Box, to use the existing machine tools to try and produce a prototype that would be based on the EFAR brand. They soon realized that most of the elements that made up the lantern comprised parts extruded from tinplate. At that time, tinplate was a material source readily available in India. Heavy metal presses were used in the extrusion process and could produce the lantern fuel tank, the handles, the base plate, and the top chimney from a sheet of tinplate. The customised dies to produce these extrusions could readily be made on metal turning lathes. Within about 6 months, they had produced a working model that could be used in Indian conditions. In addition, their prototype was light and could serve as a workable replacement for the imported lantern.

But designing the lantern was only the beginning. They needed capital not only to buy the machinery - presses, lathes, drills, etc. - but also to pay the rent for suitable manufacturing premises. In addition, they needed to generate working capital to meet on-going income and operational expenses. The answer to where they could buy machinery came from Metal Box itself. This was wartime and the army was their prime customer. They knew there would be surplus production machinery as the War started to wind down; so, Metal Box would be seeking to dispose of some of their machinery. Dad and Shahadat were now faced with a decision about what to do next. F.R. Racek had promised to provide them with the seed capital to start the company, including the rent and start-up costs. Dad and Shahadat would provide the labour and they would work for wages.

News reports all indicated that warfare in their region was nearly over. So, Dad and Shahadat started looking for premises from which to start their venture in June and July. They settled on a garage in Royd Street, running off Free School Street and within walking distance of Park Street, an important thoroughfare in Calcutta. In the lead-up to the move, they had acquired a lathe, a metal press, a drilling machine, and welding equipment. The power distribution in the garage was upgraded and they started to acquire their hand-operated tools. On 24 August, 1943, Dad and Shahadat resigned from Metal Box and started on their business venture. Initially, they took in small jobs from the growing engineering community, work that could best be categorized as the production of specialized tools, dies, machine tools, molds and cutting tools, machine repair, fitting and turning and grinding. But at the same time, they began preparing all the dies that would be needed for the eventual production of hurricane lanterns.

Within a year at their Royd Street location, they had produced a few working models that were acceptable for Indian conditions: lanterns that were light and portable and easily protected from the elements. Fredrik Cargnelli put these prototypes to a trial in the countryside. People who lived in the villages appeared to be happy with them. Minor changes were made to the lanterns and now they thought about moving to a limited production run and, in the longer term, full mass production. They confined themselves initially to low production runs; all these early hurricane lanterns were absorbed by Fredrik Cargnelli's existing dealer network and sales started to improve noticeably.

But, some production issues needed to be resolved. The lantern's outer shell and frame was pressed from thin, galvanized tinplate sheets; this raw material was now the subject of strict import controls, as no supplier of this commodity existed in India. The prevailing reason for the limited supply was India's practically negligible foreign exchange; whatever amount became available was strictly rationed among higher priority users. But lanterns had their own value: they provided a cheap alternative for lighting in the over 90% of Indian villages that had no electricity. Because of this fact of rural life, my father was able to argue for an allocation quota and soon got a priority allocation. This was an important first step to his being able to step up production.

So, in this fashion, the F.R. Racek hurricane lantern brand was born. Much still had to be accomplished: for instance, my father needed to establish a relationship with a glass supplier to provide the globes for the lanterns and he needed to establish a Calcutta distributor and a country-wide dealership network. The original product proved to be popular and whatever they produced was sold immediately. Most of the product was handled through dealers located in Calcutta; their primary market was the Bengali village hinterland.

American GIs: Phil Seeling, Pat Gould and Frank Schuster. Martina's birth, 10 October, 1944

The latter months of 1944 saw the campaigns coming to an end in Burma as a result of numerous successful guerilla attacks against the Japanese by the Allies. Expectations of surrender heightened. The road linking India to China had now been opened to traffic; the Burma Road was cleared and regular transportation of war supplies had resumed.

During the War and because of the need for war supplies and logistical support to the Allies, there had been a steady buildup of US personnel in Calcutta. Their numbers eventually reached about 400,000 men and women. These US personnel included not only the military, but also construction personnel, naval dockyard operators, and transportation and logistics experts. There was significant construction activity in and around Calcutta, building new roads and improving old ones, and constructing airfields and pipelines to provide fuel to these air bases as well as other military installations located on the India-Burma border.

In early 1944, Dad met three American GIs through his past work at Metal Box. These GIs belonged to the logistics branch of the US Army. Pat Gould came from Breckenridge, Colorado, Frank Schuster was a potato farmer from southern Texas and Phil Seeling, I think, came from Chicago. They soon became regular visitors to our home; I believe that, initially, the appeal may have been Mum's cooking, which they all enjoyed. They drove into the courtyard below our apartment in their jeep and the car horn announced their presence. Soon we would all be sitting around the dining table over food enjoying each other's company. They always came with gifts for Mum and Dad. For Mum, they brought Chesterfield cigarettes; for Dad, it was usually some beer or Bourbon. Alcohol was very difficult to obtain in Calcutta and the black-market prices were prohibitive.

On 10 October, 1944, Martina, my sister, arrived in the world. Our new GI friends often brought presents for Mum and the new baby. They also became a good source for hard-to-get medicines and they continued to help Mum and Dad whenever needed.

Over the months, they and my parents became very good friends, and it turned out that they had a mutual interest. Both Phil Seeling and Pat Gould loved skiing; one day, they told Dad about their plans to go skiing in India. Even though Dad had been in India for over 5 years, he had not really thought about skiing. I don't think he had ever thought that India had a skiing area with all the requisite facilities and infrastructure. The American army offered its officer class the opportunity to travel quite far afield in India when they went on leave. One of the places that they were allowed to visit was Gulmarg (8,690 feet above sea level) in Kashmir, where they could ski. Pat Gould, who lived in the ski resort of Breckenridge, Colorado, would soon have ascertained this. Indeed, many GIs had visited Gulmarg. What is more, an American had already won the Ski Club of India downhill championship! So, Dad listened attentively when he heard that Pat Gould was making plans to go skiing at Gulmarg on his upcoming leave. Dad did not need much arm-twisting to commit to skiing with him.

1944/45 Ski Club of India Championships

In January 1945, Dad searched far and wide in Calcutta for suitable "winter" clothes for the snow and cold weather. He had no ski boots but was reassured that these could be obtained in Gulmarg. He travelled by train to Srinagar via Delhi, and then by rickshaw to the hotel for a short stay in the Vale of Kashmir. Dad had factored a few days in Srinagar to meet up with Bobal, his old Czech friend from Batanagar, and the man who supplied us with our Christmas trees.

Srinagar, the capital of Kashmir, is a lovely city crisscrossed by a network of canals which all gravitate to two very large lakes: Nagin and Dal. The canals leading to Dal Lake are busy with floating market produce and *shikaras,* the distinctive gondolier water taxis (similar to the Venetian gondolier) that ferry passengers back and forth across the lakes and in the canals. The Jhelum River runs right through the middle of the city. From Srinagar, there is a clear view of parts of the Pir Panjal Himalayan mountain range. Some of the surrounding agricultural lands are irrigated by runoff from the canals surrounding the city. The locals could often be seen knee deep in these irrigation ditches keeping them open and active and closing them off when water needed to be diverted somewhere else. A common sight that would have greeted Dad was that of hay and straw bales of various sizes stacked in the trees and, in some cases, hanging from branches, which kept them out of reach from hungry cows and the occasional flood. The roads of the city were replete with two-wheeled carts drawn by teams of oxen. Some carts had canvas canopies supported by a framework of bamboo. At night these carts, usually parked by the side of the road, doubled as overnight shelters for their drivers, who slept on top of their cargo, but were protected from the rain by the canopies.

One of the great attractions of Srinagar was living on a houseboat moored on the banks of Dal Lake. Dad had booked his accommodation on one of these. They were part of the early history and cultural traditions of the people. In the past, there apparently had been an imperial edict prohibiting land ownership by non-Kashmiris. Man's ingenuity knew no bounds, so the solution became a houseboat parked on a lake. Many wealthy British and Indians had, over time, acquired their own houseboats and moored them in Dal and Nagin lakes, the absolute premier location being Srinagar. At the time of the British Raj, houseboats became home to many people after they had been denied land grants in Kashmir. When the British discovered this beautiful place and started to go there on holiday, many of them wanted to live on the lake. Very soon the smaller houseboats morphed into larger and larger boats so that today they offer quite luxurious and spacious accommodation for visitors.

The hulls of these houseboats were built of cedar wood and many were over 50 years old. Walnut trees proliferated in the forests around the valley and the wooden interiors and paneling of the houseboats were made from walnut wood panels into which were carved quite intricate, traditional, Kashmiri designs. A popular motif was Chinar or vine leaves, as well as flowers such as roses and the lotus; these were carved along the border panels or even filled out a complete surface. The houseboats were usually 70 ft. long and 12-18 ft. wide. They were comfortably appointed with all the modern conveniences. Elaborately-carved wood paneling and fittings were complemented by rugs and Kashmiri carpets that covered the floors of the living areas. At the front of the houseboat were steps that lead from the living area right to the water's edge; every morning, *shikaras* laden with vegetables and fruit would pull up to these steps. The houseboats that were rented out to expatriates like my father had three bedrooms with exquisitely hand-carved walnut, Kashmiri-style furniture, a combined extended lounge room and dining room and kitchen at the rear. The curtains, carpets, linen and ornaments were produced by local cottage industries that still enjoy a good reputation worldwide today. For some quaint reason, the houseboats all tried to outdo each other with their choice of names like Shalimar, Prince of Wales, Rose of Heaven, Heaven on Earth, Your Country, Shelly Anne and White Horse. These houseboat names clearly originated with the British; however, the style of the houseboats is unique to Srinagar.

Dad spent two restful days in Srinagar; after catching up with Bobal, his thoughts now focused on Gulmarg. On their last evening in Srinagar, he met up with Phil Seeling for dinner with Ken Hadow, then president of the Ski Club of India. Ken was a knowledgeable and interesting person; he introduced them to the world of Indian art and architecture, skiing and mountaineering in Kashmir and the northern Himalayas.

In the morning, Dad and Phil left together for Gulmarg by bus. Gulmarg was located in one of the six mountain ranges in Kashmir known as the Pir Panjals. The trip from Srinagar is quite beautiful, as the road wends its way past orchards, tilled fields and rows of poplar trees. The bus dropped them off at an intersection near a short, sealed road leading to a turnabout, the end of the road before Gulmarg. Nedou's Hotel was about two miles from this sealed road and all food had to be carried in by porters and ponies to cater to the needs of the approximately 100 people who lived in the hotel and some of the outlying accommodation huts. The process of replenishing the hotel's provisions was repeated on a weekly basis during the winter months. At the end of the sealed road, people wondered if they would have to hike two miles in the snow. However, on arrival at the turnabout, a swarm of brown human bees, porters dressed in brown pants, shirts and shawls, engulfed visitors, all shouting and pointing at themselves saying, "Sahib, Sahib, take me, me very good porter. Me strong. Me very good." This was a bit confusing until someone mentioned that they were *all* in the employ of Nedou's; so, my father picked off the closest three and handed his luggage over to them.

The porters ushered Dad and Phil to the pony compound to choose their four-legged taxi, the mountain pony. These ponies looked like survivors from a Kashmiri gulag. Dad's common sense said, "Hruska, pick the strongest looking pony!" But they all appeared the same. So, he mounted one and started his journey to Nedou's. Only much later, did he find out that these were the famous Himalayan mountain ponies: incredibly strong, reliable creatures. At length, they arrived at Gulmarg; the views were spectacular. From here, Dad could see the whole Vale of Kashmir. Gulmarg was nestled in what is known as the Meadow of Flowers, a huge, shallow, saucer-shaped basin. Since it was winter, the meadow was covered with snow. In the distance, across the valley, he could see the magnificent Himalayas. Crowning this view was his first sight of Nanga Parbat, the ninth highest mountain on Earth, with a summit height of 26,600 ft. Nanga Parbat is the westernmost bulwark of the Himalayan mountain range and is located in the Diamer district of Gilgit-Baltistan in Pakistan. I am sure that this first view was the start of Dad's on-going love affair with the Himalayas.

Gulmarg could best be described as a "hardship" ski resort, as it had none of the facilities or amenities that might be expected in a modern ski resort. Nevertheless, the trusty mountain ponies took Dad and his American friend right to the front door of Nedou's Hotel in the valley. This hotel was the Headquarters of the Ski Club of India, so Dad managed to rent all his ski equipment, boots and other gear there, although there was no guarantee that he would get both skis from the same manufacturer! A veritable miscellany of people from the US and British military, diplomats, and some wealthier British and Indian nationals who had previously skied in Europe and elsewhere, gathered at Nedou's.

Dad was allocated a self-contained, free-standing, weather-beaten cabin close to the central building, which housed the reception area, dining room, lounge area and bar. Dad noticed that the cabin had two wooden frame beds, a chair, table, and stove. At the reception, arrangements were made to assign Dad a personal room bearer and another servant to look after the fire, and to keep the ski gear clean and the skis waxed. Dad decided that the stove had probably been installed in 1889, when Nedou's was built;

it really struggled to heat up the room. He looked doubtfully at the two blankets provided for the bed and wondered if he would freeze during the night. At least he had his bottle of brandy nearby, the original mountain revival medicine in which he fiercely believed.

The central lodge had better heating for its guests, which helped create a cosy, general atmosphere. Small groups gathered and introduced themselves to each other. These people were to be Dad's hotel companions for the next two weeks. Here, he made his first acquaintance with a hot toddy: rum mixed with honey and hot water. He rather enjoyed it! The ample choice of food in the dining room, a mixture of European and Balti cooking, tasted good. In Nedou's Hotel, as in hill station hotels in other parts of India, the day started with a nice touch. An elegantly turbaned room bearer arrived early to help Dad greet the new day with a pot of Darjeeling tea, snuggled under a flowered tea cosy. Breakfast was served much later in the central building.

The ski area was located in the Aparbhat mountain range on one side of the Gulmarg basin at approximately 9,800 ft. The ski terrain was a powder snow skier's dream. However, this was 1944 and there were no ski lifts from the hotel to the start of the ski runs at the top of the mountain. A single, small, tow rope operated on the upper slopes. The upper reaches of the Aparbhat mountain range could be reached either on foot or on those wonderful Himalayan mountain ponies.

The snow trail to get to the upper reaches was about 3 ft. deep and the staff at Nedou's had already carved out a path, approximately 3 ft. wide, for the ponies to carry the skiers to the top of the timberline. This hand-carved and groomed pony trail climbed another 3,300 ft. to the Kongdoori, a bowl-shaped area below the summit of the Aparbhat mountain range. The path for the ponies in some sections of the climb was so steep that, when my father sat on the pony, he could not see over the top of its head, even though the ponies were short in stature: when my father sat in the saddle, his feet practically touched the ground. The *ghora wallah* (horse guide) led his pony up the trail. Dad's personal, Nedou's Hotel-provided, ski porter followed behind leading another mountain pony that carried skis, stocks and backpack. These ski porters were quite remarkable; they wore brightly-coloured turbans and a brown woolen scarf that covered their ears and mouth. Once they had covered their singular moustaches, they were recognized by the skis they carried; otherwise they were indistinguishable one from the other. Aside from ski equipment, the ski porters carried a surprise. After they had strapped the skis, poles and backpacks onto the backs of the ponies, they kept their hands warm by carrying, in a wicker basket, a clay pot full of burning coals. They passed their hands over the coals periodically.

The remarkable thing about the mountain ponies is that they stood all of 12 hands high. They probably, at some stage, had come from the Tibetan high plateau, where they were used to carrying all types of goods over the 16,400 ft. passes. They were small when compared to a normal horse, but they were extremely strong; they resembled a slightly oversized Shetland pony. So, every morning, a snake dance caravan of skiers made their way up the mountain. This pony caravan was affectionately given the nickname "Ponycular" by the skiers. On the way up, the *ghora-wallahs* cried out, "*Horsch, Horsch*" which apparently meant, "Look out." This cry was adopted by the skiing community on the ski slopes whenever a collision seemed imminent.

Before my father departed for the slopes, his ski porter waxed the underside of the skis according to my father's reading of the snow conditions. The hotel provided a selection of ski waxes to meet all possible conditions. The ski porter would look at a guest as if he had lost his judgement when he chose a wax, but reluctantly would do the guest's bidding. A small Ski Club of India hut was located at the top of the timberline. This was the hangout for all the skiers on the mountain whether they needed to rest between runs or when they set off to go to the towline to get up to Mt. Apharwat. The *chowkidar* (caretaker) of the hut was a welcoming fellow in his orange turban, and impressive beard. He greeted skiers with a smile and a cup of steaming tea in a deep, white, chipped enamel cup. The ski community used their newly-acquired, Hindi words to get some sugar: "*Thoda chini mujhe dedho*" ("Give me some sugar") or "*Kala chai, bilkil dudh ne manta*" ("Only black tea, no milk"). As the skiers waited, some took another opportunity to re-wax their skis and check their gear.

The Ski Club of India had taken the time to mark out various trails - Red (most difficult), White (intermediate) and Blue (easiest). A small army of porters used wooden boards to stamp down the main trails, but powder ski hounds had enough other trails to explore and get enthused about. Those who knew how to ski in powder could enjoy their skis carving out a spoor trail from 8-12 inches with a plume of fresh snow that flowed past their ski boots. The whole ski area had numerous fir trees on the slopes, spread out about 30 to 45 feet apart; the more imaginative skier could use this generous tree coverage as a giant slalom course.

During the first week, Dad spent most of his time skiing the Red Run, getting used to the ski terrain on his borrowed skis. The Championship races were scheduled for the second week. The ski course was set to take place in a basin, a rather narrow section at the top but widening out lower down. Years later, he told me that, if he had tried to *schuss* the course, he could have achieved some pretty exotic speeds. So, he planned to break the speed with a few well-planned turns.

During the first week, Nedou's put on a convivial "Après Ski" gathering in the lounge area. Many framed photographs of visiting guests at various Christmas celebrations were displayed on the walls. They even had the flags and banners exhibited from affiliated ski organizations around the world. Ski activity on the mountain usually ceased by about 4:30 pm, when people skied down to Nedou's from the top of the Apharwat plateau. Skiers could ski directly to the front door of their cabins, get out of their bindings and hand them to their ski *wallah*, who would then prepare their skis for the morning by applying more wax to the underside. The guests were a diverse group: many British officers were present, wearing their civilian clothes, consisting of Harris Tweed jackets with leather elbow patches, checked shirts, corduroys or cavalry twill pants and, of course, colourful cravats (apparently, they were allowed to wear their *civies* when on leave); also present were American officers in their uniforms. Moustaches - handlebars and other varieties - were well trimmed and some were even waxed. Some of the guests had brought their wives along. There was also a smattering of smartly-attired Indians and turbaned Sikhs in attendance. The ladies looked magnificent in their pastel-coloured ensembles and the current foot fashion of the ski set, namely, an adaptation of the famous Gilgit Boots used by the British army; these were long leather boots that reached up to the knee. In one corner of the lounge stood an old piano that had seen better days but was still remarkably in tune. As my father entered the room, a Lt. Gareth Wynne-Jones was seated at the piano playing, "You are My Sunshine"; a small group of men and women had joined in and were singing heartily. A little while later, a turbaned waiter rang a gong and the guests proceeded to supper.

At the beginning of the second week, the competitors for the 1944/45 Ski Championships of India had an early start. At the hut, the racers were making their final preparations. The indomitable Ken Hadow orchestrated the proceedings from the hut and got everything ready for the forthcoming races. The dedicated skiing fraternity in India affectionately knew him as the "Mr. Ski" of India. He had the responsibility for getting the ski trails ready and setting the gates for the slalom course. He issued the competitors with their bibs and ensured that they all had one practice run. In the finals of the slalom, Dad sliced his way through the slalom gates to the finishing line; his recorded time edged out Major Bagot, the winner from the previous year. Kathie Skarrat, an American from Lake Tahoe, won the Ladies Slalom title. She was stationed in India at the time, working with the American Red Cross. The men's downhill was scheduled for the next day. It had an unusual format, as two skiers raced off in a simultaneous start. The winner from each run progressed towards the eventual final if they were successful against winners in other races. Even though there was a small field for the Championships, Dad won the downhill again from Major Bagot and surprisingly won the Ski Championship of India 1944/45. This championship win of Dad's was a complete surprise to me when he told me about it much later in life. I had no idea, growing up, that he was a championship skier. On his last day in Gulmarg, Dad skied for pure pleasure with Pat Gould and Phil Seeling; they just enjoyed skiing, the setting, the views and the Apharwat hill. All three probably wondered whether they were dreaming. Had they really just had two wonderful weeks skiing in Kashmir and had Dad just unexpectedly walked away with the Ski Club of India championship? As he left the hotel, making his way to Srinagar and the train back to Calcutta, Dad vowed he would return some day.

CHAPTER 4

End of World War II and the Experience of Independence in India

The Second World War ended in Europe on 7 May, 1945. The War in the India-Burma Campaign effectively ceased a bit later, in mid-1945. All further Japanese war resistance in the south-east Asian theatre of operations came to a halt with the dropping of the atomic bombs on Hiroshima and Nagasaki by the United States in early August 1945. Japan finally accepted the full surrender terms on 15 August, 1945, in the Pacific and in Burma on 28 August, 1945. The full formal Japanese surrender took place on 2 September, 1945, in Tokyo harbour.

93B Ripon Street – The Early Years

Originally, Dad operated out of a garage in Royd Street before building a factory on the much larger premises of 93B Ripon Street, where the business continued until it was eventually sold some three decades later. The war had ended and normal business in Calcutta had started to recover.

It soon became evident that Dad and Shahadat Khan needed to change the company's business name to reflect the fact that their business was now predominantly the manufacture of hurricane lanterns. They chose the name, "The Universal Lamp Manufacturing Company," although the brand name that they used was *Kisan* (the Hindi word for farmer). The address at Ripon Street was located in a predominantly residential area and, as the city had not zoned the area and buildings at this address as to primary function, they went ahead and converted it into a factory that could handle a manufacturing operation. A new warehouse building was started. While this facility was being erected, talks began in earnest with banks and private financiers who could provide the capital to buy all the presses and other machinery for the larger manufacturing operation. As soon as another smaller, separate building was completed and all the utilities connected, Dad and Shahadat decided to make this building the tool shop, which would be managed by Shahadat. He would be responsible for making all the dies needed for the hydraulic extrusion presses for the tinplate and the production of any other specialized equipment necessary to produce the lanterns. Then, part of the machinery that had been located at Royd Street was moved to this new facility.

Their small-scale business prospered and, in its heyday, would employ over 500 people. The *Kisan* brand of hurricane lanterns in India became synonymous with quality; soon, competitors began to emerge in Bombay and Delhi.

Decision to Remain in India

In late 1945, life in Calcutta started to return to normal. Czechs living in India now had to confront decisions reflected in the *realpolitik* of war's aftermath. For many expatriate Czechs, thoughts of returning to Czechoslovakia must have been uppermost. The new Czech Republic had only come into being in April 1945.[90] In the case of my Mum and Dad, they had heard from others and had read in the press that, in the backwash of the War, the Czech economy had been shattered; some parts of the country lay in ruins and jobs were extremely difficult to find. It was obvious that

---

90   Hugh Agnew, *The Czechs and the Lands of the Bohemian Crown*, 221-222.

considerable time and money would be needed for Czechoslovakia to rebuild its infrastructure, institutions, and economy. The decision was complicated for my parents. Dad was no longer an employee in someone else's company; he had begun his own business. The early results had proved encouraging. On the other hand, for Mum and Dad, the emotional wish to return home was strong. They longed to see their family and country, even if, with the passage of time, the realities of the political and economic situation had tempered their personal desires.

Towards the end of the Second World War, there was a concerted push by the Czech Communist Party, together with the support of Russian Communists, to seize control of Czechoslovakia. In the 1946 parliamentary elections, they managed to get just over one third of the vote;[91] it was obvious that their influence in the country was growing. After the war, the Czech Communist Party became part of a coalition government and eventually took full control of the government in a coup d'état in 1948.[92]

During these uncertain times, and with the news of the growing emergence of the Communist Party, Mum and Dad had been in close contact with their families and friends. The strong message from them was to remain in India and not to return to Czechoslovakia. In early 1946, Mum and Dad finally decided that their immediate future now lay in India. At the time, I had turned five and Martina, my sister was just fifteen months old. For us children, it meant that we would grow up in an English-speaking world rather than a Czech one. The full weight of this decision only dawned on me much later in life, when I mused about how different our lives would have been had we returned to Czechoslovakia and lived as a family in our homeland. At the very least, I would have been able to make complete sense of all the hooks and dashes on written Czech words and even speak Czech correctly! But, my life would most certainly have followed a very different path.

---

91 Agnew, 225.
92 Ibid., 229-232.

Background to the Great Calcutta Killings of August 1946

No sooner had they decided to settle into their new lives in India, than Mum and Dad had to confront another face of India: never-ending political, labour, and religious unrest. The brutal religious strife between Hindus and Muslims came to a head with the Great Calcutta Killings of August 1946. These killings need to be considered in two related contexts: first in the national and then in a Bengali context.

British direct and indirect rule over the past two centuries in India contributed much to the political and religious turmoil in the post-war era. On the political front, their rule in India, despite its many able administrators, was cautiously conservative. They really had no reason to extend the benefits of education to Indians or access to better paying or responsible jobs in the civil service. And, of course, Indians had little part to play in the commercial and industrial "big picture," except in a support role.

On the religious front, since 1923, there already had been a push for the idea of a two-nation country separated primarily along religious lines: namely, Hindu and Muslim. A clear partition of India into Muslim and non-Muslim areas dominated the political dialogue. The leading Muslim politician at the time was Mohammed Ali Jinnah. Muslim interests - a minority in India - were being advanced by the Muslim League. Ironically, in his early years, Jinnah had espoused Hindu-Muslim unity. As a young man, Jinnah had gone to London to study law and had been called to the bar. He had a Muslim background but apparently was not a fundamentalist. He was definitely a man of the world: he apparently loved his whisky and cigarettes and was a very sharp dresser.[93] But he also had a reputation for personal honesty and integrity. On his return to India, he became politically engaged and, for ten years, he took part in the Hindu-Muslim opposition to the British.

Gandhi had returned to India from South Africa in January 1915 and taken up his non-violent protests against the British over excessive land taxes and discrimination.[94] One of his many goals was the achievement of full Independence from any sort of foreign domination. This included

---

93   Alex von Tunzelman, *Indian Summer: The Secret History of the End of an Empire*, 90-92.

94   Nisid Hajari, *Midnight's Furies: The Deadly Legacy of India's Partition*, 26.

putting an end to the Indian caste system (at its simplest level, a very old form of social stratification) and the idea of "untouchability" (a form of sanctioned repression of the lower castes by the privileged higher castes); the improvement of women's rights; the reduction of poverty; and a dilution of British economic influence over Indians.[95] He was elected President of the Indian National Congress in 1921.[96]

The other important player in Indian politics at the time was Pandit Jawaharlal Nehru. Nehru was born into a Brahmin family from Kashmir on 14 November, 1889, (coincidentally, also my birthday – same day, different year!). He studied in England at Harrow School and then Cambridge University. Subsequently, he became a barrister and returned to India in August, 1912. Nehru had an early nationalist pride but decided to be more politically active against the British after witnessing a shocking event: British troops had committed an outrageous crime by firing point blank into a crowd of 10,000 unarmed Indians gathered to celebrate a Hindu Festival at Amritsar in the Punjab (this event was also known as the Jallianwala Bagh massacre). Nehru became an early follower and close associate of Gandhi. They were an odd couple. Gandhi was a spiritual man while Nehru had no time for religion. But they both shared strong views about Indian Independence. Initially, they espoused a preference for a centralized federation. Between 1920 and the 1930s, the Indian independence movement became very active and grew rapidly. They envisioned that this centralized federation should initially be a socialist, secular, democratic society based on human values and dignity, one that valued peaceful co-existence within the ambit of the complicated structure and culture of Indian society.[97] Their independence movement was highly visible in numerous passive confrontations with the British government, during which Gandhi and others were imprisoned.

In 1925, Gandhi assumed presidency of the Congress Party for a year, but he preferred to focus his energies for the three years after that on writing about national issues, rather than on taking an active role in day-to-day politics. At the end of that period, Gandhi retired from the political

---

95   Ramchandra Guha, ed., *Makers of Modern India*, 148, 157, 165-169.
96   Durga Das, *From Curzon to Nehru & After,* 96 -97.
97   Ibid., 134-135.

scene, which was fraught with community issues and legislative controversies. His goal was to take a more active role in the serious task of nation-building from the grass roots upwards. Nehru was then elected President of the Congress party in 1929.[98] In 1930, Gandhi began the Salt Satyagraha (civil disobedience), his first major, non-violent protest action. The Salt Satyagraha was aimed directly at the British monopoly of salt production and distribution. He led a protest march to the coastal town of Dandi, collected salt and thus technically broke the law by "producing" salt.[99] Shortly thereafter, a series of Round Table conferences occurred to define and explore the future Constitution of an independent India with a final conference - albeit poorly represented with no participation by the Congress or British Labour Party - leading to the 1935 Government of India Act.[100] In 1931, Lord Willingdon began his tenure as Viceroy of India.[101] His British India Office mandate was in part to work with those willing to cooperate with the British. Gandhi, Nehru, and the Indian National Congress did not fit into that category. Therefore, Willingdon imprisoned Gandhi, Nehru and a further 80,000 Indian activists. Gandhi was eventually released in 1933. The civil disobedience movement was called off in 1934.

Under the 1935 Government of India Act (passed by the British Parliament to outline principles for the governance of India prior to the attainment of Indian Independence), one of the provisions was the introduction of direct elections. Despite opposition by the Indian National Congress and the Muslim League, the Act stipulated that elections had to occur. These elections took place in late 1936-37. The Act also stipulated that there was to be one-third Muslim representation in the Central Legislature.

The Indian National Congress party came to power with a decisive majority gained in most of the states. Even in the Punjab, the Muslim party had failed to get a majority. These 1937 elections became the catalyst for some of the later tensions between Hindus and Muslims. Jinnah proposed to Nehru a coalition government in some of the states where the Muslim vote was sufficiently close to that of the Indian National Congress. Congress

98   Ibid.
99   Joseph Lelyveld, *Great Soul: Mahatma Gandhi and his Struggle with India*, 203-204.
100   Ibid., 206, 214-220, 226-227.
101   von Tunzelmann, *Indian Summer: The Secret History of the End of Empire*, 86-87.

had no need to offer anything to Jinnah. Nehru refused and the differences and aims of both parties hardened and led to heightened tensions and foreshadowed later conflict.[102] The alarm bells had rung for the Muslim League, so they aligned themselves with Jinnah's current objective for a partition within India.[103] Shortly after the elections, the Punjabi Unionist Party, along with the Muslim premiers of Bengal and Assam, local religious leaders, the *pirs* (Sufi spiritual leaders), the *maulvis* (Sunni religious scholars) and the *mullahs* decided to back Jinnah and his drive for partition, even though Muslims across the country were not a very homogeneous group. The seed had been planted for the eventual drive for partition and the future establishment of Pakistan.[104] The open question now became whether the Muslim League wanted a separate state or a confederation.

In the intervening years of world war, the Muslim League position gradually hardened on the goal for an independent Pakistan. No party had properly assessed the rights and responsibilities of secular and democratic leadership and thus the Indian National Congress had been crude in the execution of its right to rule. This only further hardened the Muslim identity and their push for partition. The real tragedy of the situation was that, in India, where different cultures, belief systems, traditions and identity cut across all religious communities, it had been difficult to define, for instance, a Muslim by his religious beliefs exclusively. In general, the Bengali-speaking Muslims in eastern India had very little in common with the Punjabi Muslims and even less with the Pashto-speaking Muslims living in the north-west frontier region, or most Sunni Muslims in Lahore. Similarly, the Hindu Brahmin from Bombay or New Delhi had little in common with the language, dress and food of a Brahmin from Madras. Superimposed on all these cultural traditions and religious differences, lay a British mindset that tried to define and place communities into silos based on religion. Naturally, this colonialist approach exaggerated existing tensions across the religious divides.

---

102   Ibid., 181-182, 191-192.
103   Moorhouse, *India Britannica*, 241-242.
104   In Jinnah's March 1940 address to the Muslim League in Lahore, he argued very forcibly for a "separate Muslim homeland." The full speech is cited in Ramchandra Guha, ed., *Makers of Modern India*, 215-218.

After Lord Linlithgow had committed India and its two and a half million troops to fight on the Allied side in the Second World War, the Congress Party offered their wartime support in return for self-government when the war ended.[105] However, the British found ways not to commit to this self-government request by stalling at every opportunity. The Congress Party and Muslim League leaders must have been dismayed, for it appeared, after the War, that Independence was even further away; but domestic and international events provided them with a bargaining chip. The United Nations was putting serious pressure on Britain to devolve after the War. In addition, as the War wound down, and with India in domestic turmoil, an impoverished and exhausted Britain was now in the mood to hasten its imperial disengagement with India.

On the other hand, relations between Hindus and Muslims worsened and became truly toxic. The Congress Party viewed the idea of Pakistan as unrealistic and refused to share power with Jinnah and the Muslim League. Elections were looming and Congress remained confident of a resounding victory. Even though the Congress leaders were still in jail,[106] Muslims became increasingly afraid of Hindu dominance. Jinnah used this time to press Muslim interests with the British.

January 1946 National and State Elections

After the national and state elections held in 1946, the Congress Party emerged as substantial victors in the Hindu majority areas (923 seats) and the Muslims in the Muslim majority areas (425 seats). Thus, any expectations that the Muslims had of a meaningful coalition government evaporated. The Congress Party had also secured an overwhelming majority of 70% of the seats while the Muslims generally won most of the rest, including Bengal. Other minor parties, such as the Communist Party of India, the parties that represented the lower castes, and the Trade Unions had also won some representation in government. The Congress Party, however, made most of the running for the push towards Independence. This became particularly evident in Bengal, with its significant Muslim

105   Hajari, 35-36.
106   Ibid., 42-43.

population. But Bengal had a problem. An unfair land system operated there, whereby the wealthy Hindu landowning class controlled the land. The people who worked the land were predominantly Muslim, various downtrodden castes, and tribal people. These workers had to contend with mounting and unsustainable debt and, in some cases, mortgage burdens. Their situation had progressively worsened since the 1937 elections and, after the 1946 elections, with no coalition government, the resentment of these workers towards their Hindu land owners had become a powder keg waiting to explode.[107]

The British still looked for a meaningful solution in trying to resolve the political impasse between the Hindus and Muslims. They had tabled a plan in 1946 to establish a Union or Indian Federation based on three large state groupings.[108] An individual state could secede from a state grouping by popular vote but only after Indian Independence had been declared. However, they could not secede from the Indian Union. The concept of the Union was thus not compromised. But even though Congress had a majority in the Constituent Assembly, Congress Members of Parliament had no appetite for the British Plan; they rejected it, while Jinnah supported it.[109]

The 1946 elections result meant even greater resistance from the Central Government to all Muslim efforts to get an independent Pakistan. Nationally, the country was splintering along community and religious grounds, and this manifested at the local level. The growth of Hindu nationalistic organisations that espoused the primacy of Hindus caused a lot of this fracturing and unrest. They had close affiliations with both the National and the Bengal Congress Parties, and they had been responsible for transforming a religious agenda into a political agenda.[110]

---

107 Narendra Sarila, *The Shadow of the Great Game: The Untold Story of India's Partition*, 210 ff.
108 Hajari, 47-48.
109 von Tunzelman, 142.
110 Bengal was a particularly fertile ground for insurrectionist political protests. Political parties of different persuasions aligned themselves against Britain and agitated via strikes, protest marches and anti-British slogan shouting. In Bengal, the Indian National Army and Subash Chandra Bose were in the forefront. The political volatility was also manifest in other parts of India. See Sukanta Chaudhuri, ed., *Calcutta, the Living City. Vol II*, 23-33.

In Bengal, Muslims represented the minority of the population in urban areas, with most of the Muslims living in largely agricultural East Bengal (present day Bangladesh); this posed something of a dilemma for them. In Calcutta, Hindus represented about 65-70% of the population. At the state level, the Muslim League held power in Bengal. Their opponents were the Congress Party and an ultra-nationalist party, the Hindu Mahasabha,[111] whose main supporters were drawn from the rich Marwari trading community. The "Marwaris" were immigrants from Rajasthan to Bengal. Bengalis had given them this name. They were the entrepreneurs, generally very wealthy, and operated at all levels of business. They had become the dominant economic force, together with European capital, in the Bengal and Calcutta economy.[112] A controversial Chief Minister, Hussain Suhrawardy, much revered by the Urdu speaking Muslims in Calcutta, but detested by the Hindus, led the Bengal state government.

Hindus and Muslims gravitated to those parts of the city where their communities were dominant. Muslims tended to live in Northern Calcutta and Hindus, as well as the Europeans, tended to Central and Southern Calcutta. Even though they held state political power, the Muslims in Calcutta consisted mainly of the poor: factory workers, rickshaw pullers, servants, tailors, cobblers, and artisans, with very few middle-class merchants or business people.

Frustrated in achieving his national political goals, Jinnah, as the main representative promoting Muslim aspirations, called for peaceful demonstrations all over India. Mr. Jinnah announced on 29 July, 1946, that "Direct Action Day" would be observed throughout India on 16 August. All Muslims throughout India were directed to observe the day as a holiday while also calling for a *hartal* (strike) in the Muslim-governed states. The aim was to affect civic and commercial life as well as transportation.[113] In

111 The Mahasabha was formed in 1906 or 1907 and is a party, or movement, that reflects right wing Hindu nationalist policies based on a belief that India is a Hindu nation. See Hajari, 59-60.
112 This is an extremely abbreviated reference to the Marwaris, their origins, and their economic importance. A more comprehensive account of the Marwaris is to be found in Sukanta Chaudhuri, ed., *Calcutta, the Living City. Vol II*, 109-116.
113 Hajari, 12-14.

Bengal, the crucial Constituent Assembly comprised the Muslim League, with its 36 members, and Congress with 32; two members were independents. The Assembly agreed to observe the *hartal*.

The aims of this particular *hartal* were intended to demonstrate how strongly the Muslim League felt about Pakistan. The League had a formidable ally in the many Muslim-owned newspapers in the country. *The Dawn* newspaper, published in Delhi and founded by Jinnah, published a lead article on 16 April, 1946, which stated:

Today is Direct Action Day

Today Muslims of India dedicate their lives
and all they possess to the cause of freedom
Today, let every Muslim swear in the name of Allah to resist aggression
Direct Action is now their only course
Because they offered peace but peace was spurned
They honoured their word but they were betrayed
They claimed liberty but were offered Thralldom
Now Might alone can secure their Right.[114]

The Hindu-owned press also presented their opposing, provocative, and inflammatory articles and distorted reports. Many politicians and labour leaders continued escalating their irresponsible rhetoric against each other in public. For the first half of August, speeches by both Congress and Muslim League public officials at large meetings in Calcutta had been inflammatory and violent in their character, all directed against the opposite community. Most Calcutta old-timers and Europeans knew from previous experience that Direct Action in India could mean violent action in the city. On 1 August, 1946, the Muslim majority in the Bengal Assembly fueled feelings further by declaring that Direct Action Day would be a holiday.[115] The Chief Minister Hussain Suhrawady ordered a public holiday and called for a rally to be organised at the Ochterlony

114 Yasmin Khan, *The Great Partition: The Making of India and Pakistan*, 64.
115 Sukanta Chaudhuri, ed., *Calcutta, the Living City. Vol II*, 25.

monument in Calcutta, where he would address the assembled crowd. This monument, situated in the *Maidan*, stands opposite the Grand Hotel.[116] In Calcutta, these decisions, including the calling of strikes, had historically been the monopoly of the Hindus, not the Muslims. Even the Sikh community sided with the Hindus. The British feared the worst and brought in more troops but restricted their movements.

This collision of issues and hatreds helped to unleash in Calcutta a period of uncontrolled violence that claimed many lives in a very short period of time. The details are clouded in controversy and each side has its own version about the course of events that led to the massacre. The British view was that both sides were to blame. The Congress view was that the Muslim League and, in particular, the Chief Minister of Bengal, Suhrawady carried the blame. The Muslim League viewed the situation as one that had been exploited by the Congress Party in a predominantly Hindu Calcutta to seek revenge on Muslims and teach them a lesson; in short, it was taken as an opportunity to kill as many Muslims as possible.

Events of 16-19 August, 1946

Friday 16 August, dawned lazily and quietly over Calcutta. The monsoon rain threatened. The weather was already warm and quite humid. The city stirred slowly. The rickshaws plied the streets already either pulling their established clients to the markets and downtown offices or moving slowly up the sides of roads seeking new customers. Because a *hartal* had been called, no trams were visible, but the buses were operating.[117] The pavements were not very busy, as the Hindus had already started to erect barricades in the northern part of Calcutta in order to hinder Muslims from getting to the Ochterlony monument for the rally. Muslims would have to find alternative routes, so marching processions proceeded via Howrah Bridge.

At this early hour, the police were completely oblivious as to what was to come, even though there had been reports that some Hindu shops in

---

116 Hajari, 14.

117 Since the trams and buses tended to be operated by the city, they would be less likely to join the *hartal*. However, trams are easier to damage and this might be why they were not running that day.

the northern part of the city had been torched because they had remained open during the proclaimed *hartal*. Other reports filtered in that some people had been forcibly pulled off buses. The police prepared for the post-meeting time at the Ochterlony monument when all the speeches would end and the crowds would start to disperse. As the time for the meeting drew near, the crowd started to gather in large numbers. The number of incidents began to increase by the hour. Reports of violence and hooliganism had already reached the assembled crowd. The police fired some warning shots into the air and used tear gas.

The crowd at the meeting scheduled for four o'clock had swelled by this time to over 30,000. Mr. Suhrawady's speech proved to be quite incendiary, fueling tensions even more. The actual meeting became increasingly disorderly, and the milling crowds agitated. Some people were intoxicated solely from alcohol and others from the more explosive combination of alcohol and nationalistic fervour. They started to shout their slogans with loud chants of, "We'll fight, we'll seize." Some people had posters with a provocative portrait of Jinnah dressed in white battledress, riding a white horse and charging into the infidels. As a token gesture to the police, Mr. Suhrawady ended his speech with an appeal to the crowd to disperse peacefully and return home directly at the end of the meeting.

Some people yelled that riots had already broken out and that Muslims in some parts of the city had been killed. The Chief Minister tried to assuage the crowd with a statement that the military and police had the matter in hand. But rumours and stories rippled back and forth through the people gathered at the Monument. As everyone dispersed back into the streets, many Muslims in the crowd started an orgy of looting. No shop owner escaped the violence. The situation had now become extremely explosive.

The Chief Minister had not counted on the presence of a large number of *goondas* (violent troublemakers) who, as soon as the meeting ended, went directly to the many nearby shopping areas and started to loot, smash windows, and burn Hindu houses and shops. By now, the number of violent incidents had spread Calcutta-wide; the local police and the British troops were losing control. A general curfew was called for the city at 6 pm.

Initially, there was looting; then, the rioters started to burn the buildings by piling all available inflammatory material up against the walls of the structures. Fire was the weapon of choice as it forced people out of their houses into the streets where they could be attacked and killed. The prime motivation of the mob was revenge. Now, the massacres started: Hindus against Muslims, Muslims against Hindu. At the end of the evening of 16 August, reports from hospitals indicated that there were about 200 dead and perhaps 1000 injured. The viciousness towards each other was pitiless.

Late in the evening, the situation appeared calm as in the eye of a storm. But, early the next day, on 17 August, dead bodies started to appear in the streets. Now the "Killings" resumed in earnest. In some streets, the authorities loaded the bodies onto barrows to be taken away. The curfew had been extended but no one heeded this order. The onset of dusk and then nightfall only released another unbridled orgy of violence. What had started as a trickle now became an absolute torrent of killings. The aim of the participants followed the script: namely, kill, rape, maim, loot, and burn. The criminal element on both sides, whether Hindu or Muslim, seemed to be in charge of parts of the city. The police and British troops were powerless for, as soon as they restored some sort of calm to one street, the killing continued unabated in the adjacent alleys, hovels, and slums. No one could escape this terror as the streets began to fill with idle men seeking their prey. The night of the 17th and the early morning of the 18th were the worst for savage butchery. Fires burned everywhere in the city. Police and troops now resorted to the use of live ammunition, with orders to fire into the crowds to disperse them; but this only had the effect of transferring the killing spree to some other street or alley.

The 18th saw no abatement of the killing, looting, burning, and rape. Despite the military presence and the introduction of light-armoured vehicles and tanks, rioters had now commandeered taxis and even buses in order to move more rapidly in their murderous onslaught outside the reach of the authorities. As the police and troops got tired, reinforcements came in from encampments and other police districts north of Calcutta. Corpses littered the streets everywhere; the people charged with removing the bodies could not keep up with their pitiful task. No one had been spared, not even women and children. The mutilations and savagery exacted on the bodies reflected the hate and passion of the two communities. Some of the worst killings occurred around Calcutta's many markets, where shopkeepers stayed with their families to protect their market stalls. In Shobabazaar Market, it seemed that every available area was covered in corpses. Rickshaw stands had not been spared, as most of the pullers were Muslim. Late in the evening of the 18th, the authorities started to get control of the situation. Now began the major task of clearing away the corpses lying in the street and establishing safe areas for the survivors. This slight reduction in violence allowed medical teams to help the wounded.

The fires and killing had spread to central Calcutta, including Chowringhee Road, where Mum and Dad lived. Park Street was not spared; like the poorer areas of the city, it had also been the scene of fires, looting and other acts of wanton destruction. Mum and Dad dared not leave their home; they lived on what they had managed to stock up in the week prior to the riot. From the relative safety of their apartment, they could hear the noise of sirens and the low roar and rumble of the armoured vehicles moving through the streets.

The rampage against people and property continued unabated until 19 August. The city had by then come to a total stop. On 19 August, a trickle of shopkeepers started to open their doors. Public transport slowly started to operate again on all the routes. It appeared that the lunacy had finally come to an end. By 21 August, Calcutta had become quiet again. The killing, which had reached a crescendo on 17 and 18 August, was now finished.[118]

The Aftermath of the Great Calcutta Killings

"The Killings" were a horrific event that presented Calcutta in a most disturbing light: a city that was quite capable of cannibalising itself through religious hatred. What everyone had witnessed was a moving terror that seeped into every neighbourhood. The heart had been ripped out of the

---

118 This description of the Great Calcutta Killings is recounted from numerous sources. Included amongst these are the eye-witness testimony of my father and a personal family friend, Mr. Suren Chatterjee. In addition, a valuable recounting of the events is to be found in Hajari, 12-21. The most detailed commentary on the events can be found in the following: Dinesh Sinha and Ashok Das Gupta, *1946: The Great Calcutta Killings and Noakhali Genocide: A Historical Study*. The full report can be accessed online and read in its entirety.

small business sector: shops had been vandalized, looted, and burnt. Even the ramshackle dwellings of the poor had been destroyed and set on fire. The roads were now a repository for furniture, broken glass, bricks, and pieces of broken concrete. Anything that could easily be ripped out or carried off had disappeared. Burnt-out shells of rickshaws, bullock carts, and cars littered every street.[119] Some parts of the city still had smoldering fires; we could smell and feel the smoke. But this was the material aftermath. What no one could escape, however, was the human toll. Everywhere we went we saw dead bodies: dismembered, mutilated, beaten, and burnt. As the days passed after the killings had ceased, the heat caused the remaining, exposed, uncollected corpses to become bloated and a stench diffused over parts of the city. In some parts of Calcutta, the vultures circled the skies ready to scavenge human remains. City authorities started with the final clean-up; corpses were gathered up and stacked one on top of the other on street corners until carts and trucks could pick them up for disposal. These pitiful *tableaux mortes* bore witness to the ferocity, viciousness, and barbarity of this murderous rampage. At the end of the killings, on 19 August, the authorities estimated that between 6000 and 10,000 people had been slaughtered. No one will ever know the true human toll. However, the real message now implanted in all our minds was how easy it is for any community to embrace the concept of hateful retribution.

This catastrophic riot of 1946 was followed closely in time by partition in 1947, when Calcutta lost part of its productive and agricultural hinterland, not to mention part of its linguistic tradition. Levels of trade in pre-partition Bengal were much stronger than after partition. Calcutta also took another serious blow, as refugees who chose to leave East Pakistan flooded into Bengal. With this new influx of people, homelessness, slum growth, and concomitant hygiene and health issues followed. The city could no longer cope. I believe that much of the genesis of Calcutta's present-day problems, at many levels, stem from Partition.

---

119 There are many photos of this time available online. I have used some of them to augment my memory.

Effect on My Parents

The Europeans who lived in the city and who had followed the political events knew that they were living in the middle of a tinder-box. The word had been passed around to the British and European communities to be prepared for communal violence between the Hindus and Muslims. Before "The Killings," Mr. Cargnelli had warned Dad about possible violent unrest. Dad therefore closed the factory down two days before the strike and advised all his workers, especially the Muslims, to go home and remain indoors. He also added that it would be prudent if they made some preparations - gathering food and water - in case they had to remain indoors for any length of time. Many had heeded his advice and had stocked up on provisions for a few days in case they could not get to the markets. Prior to the eruption of violence, Mum and Dad had already witnessed the protest processions in the city, many of them along Chowringhee right in front of our apartment block. They had heard the slogans that people proclaimed loudly in these marches. As with all protest marches, the slogans were generally very repetitive. Some echoed a plainly patriotic tone like "*Jai Hind Jindabad*" (Long live India) or, if they were on strike, the slogan was, "Metal Box. *Ban Kharo! Ban Kharo*" (Metal Box. Shut it down! Shut it down!). These fairly peaceful processions seriously affected the traffic flow on the roads and streets. We knew enough to stay clear of them. But this time, the mood was much different.

Dad told me that, when the violence erupted, he and Mum knew that something was happening, but could not gauge the extent of the troubles. They visited the Cargnellis, and we all gathered on their small terrace. From here, we could see down onto Chowringhee and towards the *Maidan*. Black smoke filled the sky. On the first night of the riots, my parents clearly saw the night sky glowing towards the direction of Howrah Station; this reddish light was the result of the numerous fires that had been started in that part of the city. They heard the noise of police and military vehicle sirens speeding to areas of concern. The news bulletins provided by All India Radio never quite portrayed a realistic picture of the emerging events.

At the time of the Calcutta Killings, Martina was barely two years old and I was six. After the city had regained some sort of calm, Dad decided that it would be prudent if he ventured out of the house to the New Market to get some fresh food, milk and some tinned goods. He took me along and we went in a taxi. I still remember the stench of decaying bodies and also the sight of bloated, dismembered and headless corpses. As we drove past the *Maidan*, we saw large packs of vultures fighting to get at the remaining corpses lying on the grass. At the Market, a few shops were open: the *unda wallah*, the poultry section, the *sabzi wallahs* (vegetable sellers) and Baborally's, where we bought our tinned foods. Dad stocked up here on coffee and a few other necessities. Many shops in the New Market were totally shuttered. Shopkeepers were naturally quite apprehensive about the relative quiet that seemed now to have settled over the city. I am surprised that, even today, over seventy years later, I still occasionally relive these horrible times. But it is only now, as an adult, after having read and written about the events of 1946, that I can actually understand the historical context and the communal and religious patterns that sparked this appalling episode.

Mum and Dad only spoke about these events sporadically. I believe that this experience had seared itself into their minds and radically revised their understanding of the country that they now called home. This was not Czechoslovakia, nor the Calcutta they had come to in 1937; this was something new, or maybe it was something that had always been there, but that they had never seen. "The Calcutta Killings" definitely re-shaped their thinking about Indian culture and I know that they made quite an impact on my father.

Dad realized that "The Killings" were not an isolated incident but were more symptomatic of a much larger fundamental distrust between Hindus and Muslims. He fully expected more religious strife in the city and understood that, with his predominantly Muslim work force, he was laying himself open to potentially serious trouble in the future. There was too much at stake and so he resolved that his hiring practices had to change; after "The Calcutta Killings," he made a point of engaging many more Hindus than Muslims.

The Universal Lamp Manufacturing Company at This Time

By the late 1940s, Dad's business was well established, even though the factory was still very basic. It consisted of a single, two-storey, residential dwelling situated centrally to the rear of a compound enclosed by four boundary walls with one access to the street. This building had been converted into the packaging, checking, and dispatch area. Dad built a small painting shed at the rear of the premises, well separated from all the other facilities, where finished lanterns, minus the glass chimney, could be spray-painted. Most of the workers on this production and painting side of the business were Hindus.

To the right of the main entrance was a small structure that had accommodated the servants of the previous owner. In the early years, this was converted into a tool-making shop. Initially, its size posed no problem, but later Dad expanded the structure to house the lathes, turning machines, drills, grinders, welding machines and hand tools that produced the dies to press the lantern shapes out of tinplate sheets. This tool-making shop ensured the maintenance of all the moving parts machinery. This part of the factory was remarkable in the early days by the make-up of its workforce. I remember Dad telling me that, while working at Metal Box, he had formed an opinion that Muslims were very gifted at operating all kinds of machinery, including lathes, turning machines, drills and other associated equipment. Therefore, his partner, Shahadat Khan, had hired Muslim machinists and tool makers. Opposite the tool shop, the skeleton of a main factory building intended to house the production facilities, including the hydraulic presses, neared completion. By the late 1940s, the original presses from Royd Street had been moved and some were already operational. In order to secure his power supply, Dad then added a larger generator to augment the electricity requirements of the factory, since the power supply from the Calcutta Corporation was unreliable.

The factory grew organically. There was no grand plan. After Dad had purchased the land and established the factory, the Municipal Council designated the zoning as "residential" (previously it had had no designation). This, in effect, completely eliminated any future expansion options. Over time, every available space was developed. Although he was effectively constrained in being able to acquire more property in that area by the zoning stipulation, there were no by-laws prohibiting the unpleasant side effects of manufacturing, such as noise or chemical pollution. As a result, there were no mufflers to deaden the noise from the heavy presses. And the painting shed operated without an air filter that might have captured the pollution from the painting process. This was long before environmental considerations were in the public eye. 93B Ripon Street was a typical production facility started after the end of the War, where the emphasis was on getting operational quickly, making a profit, and providing jobs.

The Universal Lamp Manufacturing Company initially employed about 100 people full-time. In order to service the needs of these workers, entrepreneurs started to sell *paan* nearby, set up tea stalls, or sell *bidis* (Indian style cigarettes) and western style cigarettes. There was an astrologer and palm reader located next to someone who had set up a barber shop. Other people worked as *mochis* (shoe and sandal repairers) or sold petrol at the nearby gas station. There was even a roadside entrepreneur who patched and repaired tires. In this way, the factory supported many more than its 100 employees.

In Calcutta, space is rarely wasted. In any street, such small shops would be clustered next to each other, often near a factory or office building with a large workforce. Frequently, these shops spilled out onto the pavement so that pedestrians would have to make their way onto the actual road in order to avoid stepping on someone's sales patch. The diversity of small-scale sellers was fascinating to observe. There might be a vendor with a small jute mat, selling fruit. Next to him, someone selling religious calendars and small clay statues of a Hindu god. Ripon Street was busy and full of cars and rickshaws, as well as the odd cow meandering from one side of the road to the other, usually in slow motion, checking out the debris for food. Pedestrians had to be careful as the tail would flail to the right and stiffen as the cow left its signature calling card; this steaming cow pat would later be retrieved, when partially dry, as fuel for someone's earthen-ware stove. The bullock carts in the street were laden with all types of goods. They would push through the many pedestrians trying to negotiate their way along the road. This was the Ripon Street that Dad had to negotiate every day, first with his bike, and then later with the car that he purchased in 1946. He was now mobile and, with his new Citroen and personal driver, often visited his dealers, who were predominantly located in the Burrabazar area of Calcutta. Each day, with his cycle bell or car horn in full song, the gates of the factory opened and he would disappear into the sanctuary of the Universal Lamp Manufacturing Company.

Dad's business did well because the pace of electrification in Indian villages was pitifully slow. After the War, the demand for hurricane lanterns really started to accelerate. Apart from the imported EFAR brand of lanterns, there was one other manufacturing competitor located in Bombay on the west coast of India. By about 1950, Dad's factory employed over 200 people and the production capacity had increased significantly, as more machines were added to the factory floor.

Expanding Their Social Circle in Calcutta

After the War, Mum and Dad remained in contact with friends in Batanagar, but also started to expand their social net, making new friends from amongst the expatriate community living in Calcutta. Late in 1945, they met and became friends with the brothers Sasha and Zygmunt Kahan, who had come from Poland and therefore shared a geographic affinity with Mum and Dad. I remember another gentleman called Soyka but have very little information about him except that he also came from Poland. They were all regular visitors to our house and most of my memories of them were associated with the dinner table, where they had come for Mum's cooking. In early 1946, through our neighbours, the Cargnellis, Mum and Dad met an Austrian doctor from Vienna, Dr. Ronald, who became our family doctor. They also met another Austrian Jew, a Dr. Tauber, who became the family dentist.

Our immediate neighbours on the second floor at Chowringhee were Halina and Stanislaw Bujakowski. The Bujakowskis had an interesting background. They were an adventurous couple, having travelled from Poland to Shanghai from 1934 to 1936. They were an early version of the modern-day backpacker. Stanislaw served in the Polish Air Force during the War while stationed in Britain; after the War, the Bujakowskis ended up in Calcutta. I believe that he worked in the aviation industry. They had a son, Jeremy, one year younger than me, whom I got to know at North Point. We lost contact early on, but Jeremy later gained my notice by competing as India's first, I believe, and sole winter athlete in the Innsbruck winter Olympics in 1964 and again in Grenoble 1968 in the alpine skiing competitions. Mum had a very close friend, an Anglo-Indian lady named Dorothy Watson, who lived alone at No. 54 Chowringhee Road. Dorothy was a great companion for Mum, visiting our household regularly. She was a senior secretary at Imperial Tobacco, but unfortunately had been rejected by her family for reasons unknown and now lived alone. Dorothy and Mum spent a lot of time together, especially as Dad usually went to the factory at 6 o'clock in the morning, preferring to work when the weather was not too hot.

Mum and Dad drew most of their friends from the non-British expatriate community. This was natural, I suppose. I am certain that, as recent newcomers to Calcutta, with limited English and restricted access to the traditional British clubs, there were very few opportunities to meet British expatriates. They may have felt more comfortable with people who had a similar background and history to theirs. In any case, from a business point of view, Dad had no need to interact with the remaining British expatriates who worked in the many British head offices, like Imperial Chemical Industries, British Tobacco or the P&O Shipping Line. But my parents still had many people to choose from amongst the other expatriates.

Dad's first car, the Citroen he had purchased in 1946, had been originally owned by Sasha Kahan, who was underwhelmed with it and wanted to get rid of it. Sasha had wanted to race it at Alipore. A short car-racing track, basically up and down an unused runway, had been established there for Indian and expatriate motor sport enthusiasts. The Citroen lacked the power that he needed for racing. This car, a Model Traction Avant 11CV, was a front wheel drive with a gear change lever located on the dashboard to the left of the right-hand driver's position. It went on to achieve legendary status during our stay in India. During its lifetime, from 1946 to the mid 1970s, it managed to do about 466,000 miles. As the years passed by, it started to rust, parts failed, and it got more and more difficult to get replacements. Dad used to produce some of these parts at the factory. I remember that, towards the end of its life, it had parts from many other makes, including the front headlight of a Morris Minor.

Early Calcutta Club Life

In 1946, as people started to re-establish their lives, it was as though colonial life had never died in the dark days of the War or been seriously affected by the communal upheavals of that year. British cultural influences showed no signs of waning even though the writing was on the wall about the Indian drive towards Independence. Club life had existed before and during the War. The British were absolute masters at creating little entertainment oases in their imperial cities, cloning versions of similar clubs back home. These clubs enabled expatriates to cocoon themselves away from the harsher realities of life in Calcutta. Here, dressed in their blazers and white linens, in evening gowns, or dinner jackets and white bow ties, the British tried to shut out the real world of India, a world of heat and dust, chaos, masses of people everywhere, crazy and undisciplined traffic, and numbing traffic jams. All these clubs presented a wonderful, main entrance door, guarded by a tall, elegantly uniformed, turbaned Sikh who held it open and greeted patrons as they entered. Like the wardrobe entrance in C.S. Lewis' book, *The Lion, the Witch and the Wardrobe*, which led the children into a magical kingdom, the doors to Calcutta's clubs led to sporting facilities, swimming pools, close-clipped grass lawns, deck chairs, lounge rooms, reading and smoking rooms, restaurants, bars, and dance floors. Calcutta provided clubs that matched all social classes, wallet sizes, egos, intellectual curiosity, culinary tastes, and sporting needs.

Sports lovers could choose from the Cricket Club, the Football Club, the Rackets Club, a Rugby Club, and a Rowing and Cycling club. Calcutta even had a noted tennis club, the South Club, where members could find themselves playing tennis with some of India's former and current Davis Cup heroes. Some of the more opulent clubs, like the Tollygunge Club and the Royal Calcutta Golf Club (incidentally, the second oldest golf club in the world) could boast exceptional golf courses.

The premier club, the Tollygunge Club, was situated on a 100-acre prime property. It was founded in 1895 by a Scottish banker, William Dixon Cruickshank. The Club gave members access to the most modern and luxurious facilities, and its services were excellent. It offered its members golf, tennis, squash, indoor and outdoor swimming, horse riding and amateur equestrian sports. Dad mentioned that, in the early years, there had been a local joke that you could ride a horse to your next golf shot. Members probably considered this a bit more progressive and sportier than being carried to your next shot on a divan or palanquin; mechanized golf carts were still unknown. For the less sporty, the Tollygunge had a bridge room, a billiards room, a club shop, and a reading room to match any in England. However, this club, with all its amenities, would not admit Indians or non-British Europeans as members.

The Saturday Club was one of the oldest in Calcutta with a rich English cultural influence; it offered access to a wide range of facilities. Here non-British Europeans and wealthy Indians *could* become members. It was also the club that was geographically the closest to us in Chowringhee. It offered not only a fine kitchen serving a wide variety of cuisines but also an English Pub. The Saturday Club was housed in a grand old building; it was popular and drew many pot-bellied senior executives onto the tennis courts, into the swimming pool, or the Club's amply stocked indoor and outdoor bars. The Club also had many clay tennis courts, the same tennis courts where, in later years, Dad would try and create a "Davis Cup" player out of me by contracting a current Indian Davis Cup player, named Akhtar Ali, to coach me. Naturally this fast track experiment failed dismally.

The Calcutta Club, founded in 1907, was a social club whose first president and patron was H. H., the Maharajah of Cooch Behar. This club had no perceived racial discrimination but a noticeable economic barrier existed which excluded the genteel poor, and this included many British civil servants who did not meet the club's income requirements. During Mum and Dad's time, the Calcutta Club remained a popular meeting and watering hole for the wealthy in the city. Clubs such as the Tollygunge Club, the Saturday Club and the Calcutta Club usually provided open membership to the many British and other mercantile firms in the city.

The Dalhousie Institute and the Rangers Club, on the other hand, were enlivened by the carefree, happy-go-lucky spirit of Calcutta's large Anglo-Indian population, who provided the manpower that kept many of the engine rooms of India's British institutions - the railways, the trading houses, the jute mills, the banking and insurance industries - operational and running.

Each of these clubs kept up its own traditions and charms. Many of the bars in these clubs resembled English pubs. Phalanxes of *malis* (gardeners), working in unison, squatting on the grass, gave the lawns a "short back and sides," and kept the gardens immaculately weeded. Comfortable deck chairs were spread out on the garden lawns. Many preferred the cool patios where the ladies would play bridge or mahjong from late morning to late afternoon under the ever-present *panka* (the ceiling fan). This was an ideal situation to learn about, or create and disseminate, the most recent gossip. For some, discussions about the coming holidays were laid out in great detail, if only to enter into the pecking order of status and wealth. The word "England," was replaced by "home." The men populated the bars or lounges and, as the orders for G and Ts (Gin and Tonic) or "*chota* pegs" (small shots of Scotch) took their grip on soft minds, the balmy evenings, replete with smoke and the fumes of alcohol, often ended up with lusty singing of popular tunes from "home."

The bartenders in many of these clubs acquired distinctive nicknames. And all clubs offered superb catering facilities and an interesting choice of food. Many even had their signature dishes and drinks, whether it was the wonderful steaks at the Royal Calcutta Golf Club, served by bearers in starched white jackets and trousers, the fish and chips at the Swimming Club, or the Chinese food at the Saturday Club. And every club had its own version of *Nimbu Pani* or *Nimbu Soda* (fresh lime water or soda), probably the favourite drink in Calcutta to help those who felt the heat.

The one club that Mum and Dad were really keen to join was the Calcutta Swimming Club. Because of the searing heat and humidity of the summer months, they sought relief through swimming. The Club had superb facilities. It possessed a large 100 ft. indoor pool and, outside, an even larger pool that measured about 75 by 200 ft., one of the largest in India. At first, even though some long-standing, respectable club members had sponsored Mum and Dad, there had been some reluctance to accept their membership application, because they were not British. At the front door of the Swimming Club, there was a very prominent sign on a wooden stand that stated in beautiful gold letters: "No Indians allowed." Much later, in a well-publicized event in 1967, I believe, a member of the Bengal State legislature, together with a few supporters invaded the Club and went to the outside pool and dove in; this act of defiance signaled that this racist era was finally at an end. For my parents, not being British was enough to delay their membership. However, there had been a few precedents about membership established during the war years; so, after a long processing time, Mum and Dad were finally accepted. The Swimming Club became a major part of the life of our family. The outdoor pool had a 15 ft. grass fringe and the Club provided simple recliners; we went in the morning armed with a book or magazines and spent the day by the pool. Mum loved swimming, the breaststroke being her favourite stroke, and this is how she would pile on the laps, effortlessly progressing through the water. The food at the Swimming Club was very good, so the family would often meet there in the late afternoon for dinner. On Sundays, my parents used to meet with all their friends at the Club and catch up on the news of the week.

Decision to Send Miki to Boarding School and Departure for North Point

Until 1946, I attended kindergarten in Calcutta. But, with my sixth birthday in the offing, Mum and Dad had to make their next decision, namely, where does little Miki continue with his schooling. In Czechoslovakia, this would have been an easy decision. I would probably have been sent to the local school on a daily basis and returned to the family home every afternoon. But this was India. Calcutta had two reputable day-boarder schools: St. Xavier's in Park Street and La Martinière in Rawdon Street. Mum and Dad had to decide whether they wanted a religious-based education for me near home, or far away in Darjeeling. Those were the choices. St. Xavier's College, a Catholic school, had been founded by Belgian Jesuits, who still ran it. It enjoyed a very good reputation, especially in the sciences. By way of contrast, La Martinière, also a reputable school, focused on the humanities and drew most of its students from the middle to higher class Hindus. The majority of their teachers were taken from the Anglo-Indian community, most of whom were either Catholic or Protestant. The Anglo-Indians had a reputation for being excellent teachers and the school had a Christian character about it, but no particular religious affiliation. Teaching an appreciation of the rich, Indian cultural heritage was virtually non-existent at any school. This was, after all, a British colony, so the curriculum at any "acceptable" school naturally had a European bias. Either of these schools would have been a good choice.

I think my parents' ultimate decision to send me to boarding school in Darjeeling was made because this was what the other Czech parents were doing. As simple as that. Mum and Dad had continued to make periodic visits to Batanagar to keep in contact with friends still living and working there. On some of these visits, they discussed the schooling issue. The prevailing wisdom at the time seemed to be that a boarding school was the best option. This was what the British expatriates did, mostly sending their sons to boarding school in England. But Mum and Dad did not have any English connections nor did they have the financial means to pay for an English boarding school at that time. So, boarding school in India was the answer. But which school? Two Catholic boarding schools were considered: one in Naini Tal, situated in northern India, and the other at North Point in Darjeeling, which had the advantage of being relatively close to Calcutta. Not coincidentally, Darjeeling was where most of the Batanagar Czechs sent their sons and daughters: the boys to North Point, the girls to Loreto Convent. My parents learned that the Belgian Jesuits ran North Point school as well as St. Xavier's and had a reputation for being great educators and disciplinarians. That made their decision easier. Since Dad's business had increasingly prospered, they could afford it.

This is basically how the decision regarding the appropriate school for my education was made. My parents obviously wanted to give their child the best possible education and, if that meant a boarding school 400 miles away from Calcutta, so be it. In the 1940s in India, this was quite an acceptable thing to do. No great thought was ever given to the emotional needs of the children. No one asked the important question, "Is it right to send our six-year-old child to boarding school for nine months out of every year?"

Christmas eve 1946 was a subdued affair. We had a small, imitation tree that year. Mum had prepared a modest Christmas dinner. A few gifts lay under the tree. My own thoughts were subsumed by the fast-approaching shift to boarding school in Darjeeling. Looking back on this turning point, all I can recollect is being told that I would be going to boarding school. At the age of six, how does a boy comprehend what such a separation from his home would mean?

After Christmas, I spent a lot of time with Mum assembling my school "wardrobe." Appointments were made and kept with my tailor, where Mum and I would examine the "suitings": yes, this is what material for coats and trousers were called. The tailor conveyed the relevant measurements for my torso to his assistant, fittings were arranged and taken, and soon the long grey and blue flannel pants, the short grey pants and blue blazers materialized and sat on the counter in a pile ready for payment. My blazer even had a North Point badge stitched onto the left breast pocket. We then went to the shirt shops and inspected the "shirtings"; after all, blue and white shirts were part of a boarder's dress ensemble and had to be made by hand. This was definitely not the age of T-shirts and golf shirts. The rest of the "wardrobe" was carefully assembled and placed in a suitcase with underwear, socks, black Bata shoes, Dunlop plimsoles, etc. There was no room for reading material or other diversionary objects. Basic, simple and practical. So, all the enrolment arrangements were made, all the clothing and uniforms procured, and name tags ordered and attached to every conceivable item of clothing; the school year would start in March 1947.

Then the dreaded day arrived; Mum and Dad drove me to Sealdah Station to an assembly point for all the young North Pointers. Any attempt at personal intimacy with Mum and Dad would seem formulaic or forced. There were no heart-to-heart parent-to-son talks, no advice offered, no positive messages given, no indication of when I would see them next. What was Darjeeling? Where was Darjeeling? What did it look like? I had no idea that it was a hill station situated amongst the greatest and highest mountains in the world. Today, this early moment of departure has left quite a few scars. In retrospect, at least to me, it was probably the first nail in my emotional attachment to Mum and Dad. I also feel that this early experience forced me to become very independent and less and less willing over time to take my emotional, or any other, problems to others. I remember crying as I looked at my parents gradually fading out of sight on the railway platform. How different it is for children today, with closer attachments and involvement with parents being the norm.

And, so, began seven years of boarding school in Darjeeling, and the start of ever-lengthening distances between me and my family that lasted until the end of my university years. In hindsight, there were some serious consequences to their decision that I had to confront in later life but, at the time, we had absolutely no perception about any future outcomes. It is an absolute wonder to me that most of the Czech boys and girls of my generation emerged from these boarding schools as decent, normal people armed with a good, all-round education and no lasting, visible hang-ups. But I still can't wrap my head around how anyone can justify the separation of child and parent during the child's most formative years.

Push Towards Indian Independence

After the "Great Calcutta Killings," further sporadic riots between Hindus and Muslims fanned out beyond Calcutta. The violence in Calcutta spread to Noahkali,[120] the neighbouring state of Bihar, the United State (now known as Uttar Pradesh), the Punjab, and also to the North-West Frontier.

Viceroy Lord Mountbatten was sent to India in March 1947 to oversee an orderly and peaceful withdrawal of British troops and associated colonial administrators from India. He wanted at the same time to give some flesh to the postcolonial boundaries of India that would accommodate the aspirations of both Hindus and Muslims. In many ways, Mountbatten was right out of his depth, as he failed to understand either the nuances of Indian politics or the collective aspirations of either the Hindus or the Muslims. All he wanted was a peaceful withdrawal; but this objective collided with the ardent Hindu and Muslim ambitions for Independence. The British had rejected outright the vote taken in the Constituent Assembly against their grouping plan proposal. It now became increasingly clear that the partition of the sub-continent loomed. Mountbatten tried to find a way forward by working with all the principal personalities, including Gandhi, Nehru, and Jinnah. He still had many brushfires to extinguish: for instance, the fiercely tribal Pashtuns of the North-West Frontier state did not trust Jinnah and wanted their own state. Further, in the northeast of India, the Naga tribes wanted their own state: Nagastan.

After appearing to have settled all these differences, Mountbatten set 15 August, 1947, as the date for the full independence of India from Britain, with a full transfer of power. However, there were no borders. In typically

120   Sinha and Das Gupta are informative on these events.

naïve fashion, the British sent Sir Cyril Radcliffe, a London barrister, to establish the borders on both the western and eastern flanks of the sub-continent. Cyril Radcliffe, who had never been to Asia, arrived in India 36 days before the date of the partition to draw the lines to split one of world's largest and most ethnically diverse countries.[121]

Radcliffe's simple logic included looking at a map and deciding rather arbitrarily on the boundaries. He knew nothing of nor sought to under-stand village or broader community structure in the various regions. The randomness of this line drawing on a map left literally millions of people on the wrong side of the ethnic and religious divide. In Punjab, his misinformed map-making was catastrophic, as his arbitrary decisions reduced Muslims, Hindus, and Sikhs to a minority, depending on where the lines were drawn. He finished the map on 9 August, but neither Nehru, Gandhi, nor Jinnah were informed. This underhanded behaviour was a masterstroke from the British perspective, for how could Britain be held responsible for any consequences when they would be leaving the colony within a week.

This combination of naïveté and incompetence was made even worse in the way that Radcliffe and Mountbatten divided Bengal primarily on religious grounds. It seemed that, in drawing up the boundary lines, the objective was to get the maximum number of Hindus on one side of the line and Muslims on the other and discount any agricultural, economic or trading considerations that affected these two groups. Therefore, in drawing one line on a map, Mountbatten established East Pakistan, sepa-rated from West Pakistan by the width of the Indian sub-continent and, in the process, condemned the Muslim majority in West Bengal to years of rural poverty and backwardness.

....

121 There was never any hope that he could take into account the cultural issues across this vast continent. The Punjab, in particular, posed many problems that were not adequately addressed in his deliberations. There was no time to consider the demographics thrown up from census reports, nor the geographical lay of the land, the rivers, the mountain ranges, the uneven spread of the agricultural hinterland, the transportation infrastructure (roads, river traffic, rural transportation links, etc.). It would have taken years to make fair and equitable judgements of where the boundaries should be set.

To understand Mountbatten's actions, it is useful to understand something of the conflicted and confusing colonial history of Bengal. In 1765, eight years after Robert Clive's victory, the nominal Mughal emperor of northern India, Shah Alam II granted to the British East India Company the office or jurisdiction of a *dīwānī,* namely the right to collect the revenues of Bengal, Bihar, and Odisha. In 1773, Warren Hastings became the first British governor-general of Bengal, which had by then been established as the pre-eminent colonial state in India, using Calcutta as its capital. The Governor-general of Bengal was the chief executive of British India and had powers of superintendence over the other British presidencies, in Madras and Bombay.

In 1854, Bengal was placed under a lieutenant governor. From that point onward, the government of British India was distinct from that of Bengal. But, even with this change, Bengal was deemed to be too large for one administration. Therefore, in 1874, Assam was transferred to a separate chief commissioner. Then, in 1905, Bengal was partitioned into two states, each under its own lieutenant governor: one governing western Bengal, Bihar, and Orissa; the other eastern Bengal and Assam. In 1911, because of continued opposition to partition, Bengal was reunited under one governor, Bihar and Orissa under a lieutenant governor, and Assam once more under a chief commissioner. At the same time, Delhi became the capital of India in place of Calcutta.

In 1935, the Government of India Act was passed, which subsequently resulted in the establishment of Bengal as an autonomous state in 1937. This remained the situation until the Indian subcontinent was partitioned into the two dominions of Pakistan and India after the British withdrawal in 1947. The eastern sector of Bengal, largely Muslim, became East Pakistan (later Bangladesh); the western sector was first called West Bengal and then Bengal after Bangladesh was established.

However we attribute the causes of these hasty decisions, history affirms that the consequences of Radcliffe's borders were tragic. Indeed, they would later have catastrophic results for millions of people, stunned to suddenly find themselves a religious minority - that is, on the wrong side of the political border. On 15 August, 1947, India and Pakistan formally achieved their sovereignty. On this Independence Day, Mum and Dad stepped out onto Chowringhee Road and witnessed jubilant people shouting, "*Jai Hind, Zindabad*" (Long live India!). Nehru delivered his famous speech titled, "India's Tryst with Destiny."[122] This Declaration of Independence led to panic in many regions, as recently created "minorities" sought to reach those regions where they could become part of their own perceived majority. And this fact alone led to a massive transfer of population propelled by religious tension and fear. This ethnic divide fueled a murderous rage that engulfed all those poor people on trains, buses or even those who travelled on foot. Numerous armed bands attacked migrating people, irrespective of their chosen means of transport and soon India witnessed yet another orgy of killing, raping, looting, and burning. It made the "Great Calcutta Killings" pale into insignificance. The British army was powerless to help, as its own Muslim soldiers fled to Pakistan and the Hindu soldiers to India. Soon these disenfranchised military men joined their compatriots in their own killing spree. The signature image of this savagery was the trains travelling through the countryside with all their passenger carriages full of butchered corpses.[123]

It is estimated that in excess of half a million people were slaughtered in the event that is known as "Partition." But India had achieved her independence from Britain and a separate Muslim state named Pakistan had been created with two parts - West and East Pakistan - separated by the Indian sub-continent. The changes in India's political and economic situation altered the lives of many people immediately and inexorably. Soon after Partition, there was a steady stream of British expatriates returning to the "mother country," and Muslim Bengalis making their way to East and West Pakistan. Anglo-Indians, together with non-Indian minorities like the Armenians, Jews and Europeans who had been caught up in

---

122 Jawaharlal Nehru delivered this famous speech to the Constituent Assembly of India in New Delhi on the midnight approaching August 15, 1947. The full speech can be heard on YouTube at: https://www.youtube.com/watch?v=0nbXrv0dFYY

123 Numerous books have been written about Partition, some from a Pakistani perspective, some from an Indian perspective and yet others from a British perspective. I have found the following works useful in my own reading: Narendra Singh Sarila, *The Shadow of the Great Game: The Untold Story of India's Partition*; Nisid Hajari, *Midnight's Furies: The Deadly Legacy of India's Partition*; Durga Das, *India: From Curzon to Nehru & After*; Ramachandra Guha, ed. *Makers of Modern India*.

Calcutta because of the War, sought out more welcoming countries than Britain, leaving for Canada, Australia, New Zealand, and even Europe. Many of these people were abandoning a city that had been their home for generations.

Nehru became the first Prime Minister of an Independent India and introduced a mix of socialist planning and free enterprise measures to repair and rebuild the country's ravaged economy. He also took the external affairs portfolio and served as the Foreign Minister throughout his tenure as Prime Minister. With the completion of its constitution in 1950, India emerged as an independent, secular and democratic republic. Nehru became deeply involved in the development and implementation of the country's five-year plans that, over the course of the 1950s and 1960s, saw India become one of the most industrialized nations in the world.

Nehru also had deep concerns that so many Indian people could not read or write; he wanted to implement a mass education program to release Indian society from the limitations that ignorance and religious traditions had imposed. He knew that industrialisation was needed to feed the growing population and that continued illiteracy denied people the skills required to participate in the development of India.

My Family's Decision to Remain in India

Calcutta, October 1947

Dear Bedek and Boženka, Babi, and everybody in Otrokovice and Loučka:

As always, we send our love to you from Calcutta. We are all well. Miki has now started boarding school at North Point, a Catholic, Jesuit-run school about 400 miles from Calcutta, in a small hill town called Darjeeling, located in the Himalayas. He started there in March of this year; his first few months were difficult for him, but I hope that he will feel better for the rest of the year. He will be coming back to Calcutta for the Christmas holidays beginning at the end of November to the start of March when he again returns to school.

As you all know Mirek has moved to larger factory premises and now employs about 250 people. His business has become very successful and it keeps him busy. He is trying very hard to secure import licences from the Central government for the raw materials, namely tinplate, which is required to produce the hurricane lanterns. As a result, he has to travel to Delhi quite a lot to get these licences for the factory. But everything here moves so slowly and they tell you that it will be taken care of but never tell you when. And whenever you have to deal with any sort of government department, either the national one or the state one, you have to deal with mountains of paper and forms. As his English is still not good, he sometimes has difficulty answering some of the questions on these forms.

Well, a lot has happened here in Calcutta. We have lived through some of the worst religious riots between the Hindus and Muslims. We never expected that there would be such hatred towards each other and here, especially in Calcutta, there is a tendency for their disagreements to be settled through bloodshed. But what has shocked Mirek and me has been the savagery of their attacks. During the War, we knew that we were relatively safe in Calcutta even though we had an attack from Japanese aircraft. Fortunately for us, they dropped most of their bombs in the harbour area. Calcutta became an important city during the War and there were many American, British and Indian troops here. We got to meet some nice American boys and they used to bring us good coffee, chocolates and, for me, Chesterfield cigarettes.

However, since Indian Independence in August, we have noticed an increase in the processions and protest marches in the streets and we have never felt totally comfortable, as these events can sometimes get completely out of hand. Most of the marches take place on the street right in front of our house. We can hear them shouting all their slogans. Usually, there is a person walking at the side of the procession who screams out some question or demand and then the response comes back from literally hundreds of marchers. They carry posters and placards: most are crudely made but they are great rallying points for the marchers. I usually stay indoors with Mirek and tell the servants to venture out only when the procession has passed.

Mirek and I have frequently discussed the possibility of returning to Czechoslovakia. We have been following all the political developments in Europe. When we go to see our friends in Batanagar, we learn that Czechoslovakia has had a National Front government since August 1945, made up of three socialist parties, something we are not too excited about. Even though there is a minor Catholic People's Party from Moravia and the Democratic Party, we decided to wait and see what would play out in Prague. The general view here in Batanagar is that there still seems to be too much Soviet influence in Czechoslovakia. Clearly President Beneš is trying to minimize the Soviet influence, and we believe that he still hopes that they will allow the country to develop independently. However, it appears that the Communists are winning more and more support and also gaining seats in government. Now that Gottwald is the new prime minister, and many communists have key positions in government, we realize that the political situation there is very unstable.

Mirek and I have discussed where our future should lie and we have decided that we will remain in India. Now that India is independent of Britain, we need to get ourselves new papers and, as a result, we are planning to become Indian citizens. Further, Mirek has only recently started this new business, which has become successful. The other problem that we have to confront is that Miki has so far grown up in an English-speaking world and Czech is a completely strange language for him. We do not think that it would be right for him to leave his current school and start again in another country with a language that would be difficult for him to learn quickly. With our new Indian citizenship and passports, we hope that we can travel to Czechoslovakia to see you all soon without the fear of any political consequences. After all, we did not leave Czechoslovakia running away from this current political regime.

So, it is going to be very difficult for us as a family knowing that we may be separated for long periods of time, but rest assured that we have plans to visit and help as much as possible. I hope that you will understand our decision but it is in the best interests of our family here.

Please pass on the news to the family and remember that you are always in our thoughts.

Love Marta, Mirek, Miki and Martina

First Visit to Czechoslovakia

With Dad's business running smoothly, Mum and Dad had saved some money for the first time since they came to India, and it became only natural that their thoughts turned to helping their extended family. They had left Czechoslovakia nearly nine years before, they had survived a war and even now, with the anticipated political instability in Czechoslovakia, Dad decided that Mum should visit her family and at the same time try to help them with whatever means they had at their disposal.

After Mum and Dad had acquired their Indian citizenship, they immediately applied for their Indian passports so that they could travel. The passports took some time to arrive, due the delays in ascertaining the right forms to fill in. Mum applied for an entry visa for Czechoslovakia, which they duly obtained from Delhi. But one of the great irritants of having an Indian passport was that you needed to have a visa to travel to practically every country in the world; and, in those days, you also needed to forecast both the date of entry and exit, as well as how many times you needed to cross the border. Nevertheless, their Indian citizenship and the acquisition of passports were the first overt signs of a new beginning in a new country and a sense of belonging to a place they could call home. Finally, a departure date was set for mid-February 1948, with a return at the end of March or early April. Mum greatly looked forward to going back to see her family and friends after such a long time.

However, what Mum did not realize when she left for Czechoslovakia was that the country had sunk into political turmoil. At war's end, the two liberating armies in Czechoslovakia, the Americans and the Soviets, withdrew their forces in October and November 1945. Elections were held in the country on 26 May, with the Communist parties of Bohemia, Moravia and Slovakia managing to get about 40% of the vote. They now controlled the key cabinet posts in the government.[124] However, despite coming together to draft a new Constitution and implement a 2-year economic recovery plan, there were continuous disagreements about the implementation and direction that the Communists wanted to take. In addition, the foreign policy appeared to be anchored not to the interests of their western allies, but to those of the Soviet Union, which then had Stalin at the helm. With the prompting of the Soviet Union, the Czech government rejected the Marshall Plan,[125] a huge, American-funded, recovery package aimed at rebuilding Europe. The battle lines had now been set with the West confronting the East, something that would come to be called "The Cold War." External pressure from outside was now being placed on the Czech Communists to get rid of the other parties by whatever means. The Communists co-opted the assistance of the communist-influenced trade unions and introduced legislation to target the middle class and the wealthy and generally started to stir the political pot. A lot of unrest ensued, and incidents were manufactured and used by the police against the non-communist parties. All the pre-conditions for a communist-inspired putsch were in place. The Communists forced President Beneš into forming a new government with mainly communist ministers. The

124   Hugh Agnew, 225-227.
125   Ibid., 227-228.

country experienced all sorts of labour strikes, mass demonstrations and political unrest, which came to a head on 25 February, 1948, when Prime Minister Gottwald forced President Beneš to resign.[126] The path was now clear to establish a Communist state.

Mum arrived in the country in mid-February and remained in Otrokovice, staying with her family. Uncles Noris, Rudolf and Karel had been quite apprehensive about the developments in the country and advised Mum that she should consider cutting her visit short and returning to India. Uncle Noris feared what might happen if the Communists put a clamp on the borders. Mum wanted to stay, but Uncle Noris contacted Dad in Calcutta and advised him of the situation and told him that he should convince Mum to leave. Dad then sent an urgent telegram to Mum advising her to leave immediately and she reluctantly agreed. Uncles Noris and Karel accompanied her to Ruzyně Airport in Prague. The first hurdle was to get a booking on a flight out of the country. She managed to do this with great difficulty. However, she had a much more testing time convincing the border police that she be allowed to leave at all, as she was an Indian citizen who had been born in Czechoslovakia. The border police were not impressed. To their shallow way of thinking, she was still a native Czech and should not be allowed to depart. There were a lot of arguments going back and forth. Mum then demanded that she be put in contact with the Indian Embassy in Prague which, in the end, had the desired effect; they eventually relented and let her fly out. After I talked with my cousin Karel in April, 2010, he made it quite clear that both Uncles Noris and Karel at the time feared that Mum would not have been allowed to leave; my cousin thought that she had been very lucky. And thus ended the first dramatic trip back to Czechoslovakia.

Defenestration

On her return to Calcutta, Mum heard the news that Jan Masaryk, the son of Tomáš Garrigue Masaryk, the founder and first President of Czechoslovakia, had been found dead below his apartment window, apparently a suicide. However, this actually appeared to be another

126 Ibid., 231-232.

defenestration episode; most people believed that it was a political assassination.[127] I mention the word defenestration because, in the Czech historical context, it has quite a history. The word comes from the Latin: *de fenestra*, literally meaning "out of the window," so "defenestration" means either somebody or something being thrown out of the window. What has all this to do with Jan Masaryk's death? Defenestration is a peculiarly Czech phenomenon. Most of the acts of defenestration in Czech history have taken place in the city of Prague but have had much broader consequences in Czech history.

The first act of defenestration took place on 30 July, 1419, when the poor monk Jan Želivský and his Hussite supporters stormed New Prague's town hall to negotiate with 14 municipal bureaucrats. The bureaucrats were unwilling to deal with the grievances of the Hussites. So, Želivský mustered them all, including the mayor, to the top of the Town Hall tower, where they were thrown over the parapets to land on erect lances below.[128] As a result, King Vaclav was forced to negotiate with the Hussites and control of Prague passed to the non-Catholics. Politicians warmed to this new sport and another defenestration took place in September 1618, this time at the Old Town Hall tower. On this occasion, members of the Czech nobility had a difference of opinion with the Czech king, the Archduke Ferdinand of Austria; however, this time the victims were the king's governors, Václav Bořita and Vilém Slavata. These men were also given flight lessons straight out of the window, but they survived, apparently landing in a bog.[129] This result encouraged the Protestants to remove the Catholic king and install a Protestant king, all of which angered the imperial court in Vienna. The Austrians promptly sent a large army to teach these Czechs a lesson, which they did at the Battle of White Mountain. After this battle, the Czech nation was forcibly reduced to nothing more than a region in the Habsburg Empire for 300 years, until the formation of the First Republic after WWI.

Jan Masaryk's 1947 defenestration essentially signaled the end of hopes for democracy in Czechoslovakia for another four decades. Two weeks prior

127 Ibid., 233.
128 Ibid., 44.
129 Ibid., 66.

to Masaryk's death, the Communists took control of government. The people suspected foul play in Masaryk's death, and they became apprehensive and uncertain about the future of the Republic. In the late 1940s, they voted with their feet, and departed the country in their thousands to different parts of the world. As a postscript, many years later, an investigation into the circumstances surrounding Masaryk's death concluded that he had indeed been thrown out of the window, something that was demonstrated by a professor of bio-mechanics; the laws of physics proved beyond any doubt that the distance separating his body from the palace walls could not have come from a simple leap but more likely from an energetic shove, probably by two men. But who? Here suspicion falls on Moscow and its secret police, the NKVD (the original well-spring of the KGB).

But one conclusion is inescapable: namely, that this event signaled the start of a 41-year communist tyranny that effectively sealed any hope that my parents may have had of returning to live in Czechoslovakia.

The Czech communists were now linked by a virtual Iron Curtain to East Germany, Poland, Hungary, Albania, Bulgaria, Romania, and the Soviet Union, thus forming the alliance that came to be known as the Warsaw Pact. Europe was now divided into two camps: the one symbolizing the ideals and aspirations of the communist world; the other symbolizing those of the democratic West.

Aerial View Batanagar (Batanagar News reprint 1939)

*Daddy and Miki Outside
Batanagar Home*

Dad in Civil Defense Service

Mum and Miki in Mussorie

The GI Friends - Pat Gould, Phil Seeling, Frank Schuster

Gulmarg Ski-ing.—On the left of the picture, is Hruska, Ski Champion of India for 1944-45. With him is Major Hadow, Kashmir representative of the Ski Club of India.

Dad 1944 Indian Ski Champion

Kashmir Gulmarg, the Apharwat Range, the Site of Ski Championships

Dad in Downhill Race. 1944 India Ski Champion

Mummy, Daddy, Miki at the Victoria Memorial, Calcutta

The Remarkable Dandia

CHAPTER 5

The People of Calcutta

For about a century before Independence, Calcutta was predominantly inhabited by Bengalis and the British. The British East India Company had established its commercial headquarters in a city that offered many advantages that supported trade. Calcutta was located on a river with port facilities and easy access to the Bay of Bengal. It was the focal point for bringing the produce of the rich northern agricultural hinterland to markets. The city provided an abundance of cheap labour, thus enabling its enterprises to prosper enormously and this, in turn, helped to foster a wealthy trading elite. By the early twentieth century, Calcutta had become the economic powerhouse in India and it was, in many ways, a microcosm of Indian society. What follows is a very personal description of the social face of Calcutta through the lens of my family's experience.

Bengali Culture, A Rough Sketch

My family's encounters with Bengalis were mainly with the urban middle class of Calcutta. By the time we arrived in the late 1930s, Indian contact with the British was the longest and most sustained of any place in the colony. It was a complex and somewhat convoluted relationship. For instance, Clive's original victory over the Suraj-ud-Daulah at the Battle of Plassey was partly financed by Bengali merchants from Calcutta and the subsequent victory celebrations were hosted by Bengalis.

The urban middle class of Calcutta proved to be quite amenable to adopting those aspects of European culture that interested them. The Bengali middle class, in particular, found a certain intellectual appeal in discussing western history and politics, philosophy, science, religion, and literature just as much as they did those same aspects of their own culture. By setting aside cultural barriers, educated Bengalis were thus able to absorb those aspects of European culture that suited their individual cultural identity.

Bengalis, in my opinion, are the intellectuals of India. Many Bengalis were comfortable with the British education system, since it appealed to their intellectual proclivities. What is absolutely undeniable is the Bengali leaning to the arts and the spoken and written word. It was completely normal at the time that my parents moved to India to find Bengalis who could speak and write fluent Bengali, Sanskrit, Hindi, and English. Moreover, many Bengalis that we knew were as comfortable reading the English classics like Shakespeare, Dickens, and Wordsworth as they were with their own Hindu and Bengali literary figures. In Mum and Dad's time, the city hosted numerous Indian classical music concerts, live theatre, and art exhibits, all of which were well attended. Today, one of the largest trade book fairs in the world is held each year in Calcutta, where there are still entire streets, like College Street, lined with bookshops.

The educated Bengali not only had a love affair with the spoken and written word, he had an opinion on most subjects, including politics. Some of the best coffee houses in India are to be found in Calcutta and this is where, in my father's time, Bengali intellectuals would gather. The dialogue and exchange of ideas was king. This clever coffee shop banter is called *adda*. It is a form of intellectual jousting on the larger political and social issues, as well as neighbourhood issues. Subjects could range from global politics, to food, to Indian cinema, to the merits of traditional (Indian) versus alternative (western) medicine. During these sessions, copious quantities of tea or coffee vanished as soon as they hit the table.

Ignited passions at an *adda* could explode and lead to table thumping and the serial smoking of cigarettes. Indeed, the atmosphere of Calcutta's coffeehouses was redolent with the smell of cheap cigarette smoke. But, all in all, I think the *addas* were a catalyst for a great deal of spontaneous creative thinking.

When Dad and I went to visit the India Coffee House on Chittaranjan Avenue (quite close to the end of Chowringhee Rd), we would generally find it full and would be lucky to find a spare table. In Calcutta's heat and humidity, the standard order was for an iced coffee in a large glass. We would find tables nearby, each with four or five Bengalis in animated discussion. In coffee houses, there appeared to be an unwritten code of behaviour. There was never a raised voice; the strength of an argument was an indicator of the speaker's feeling. Sometimes, when the discussion got animated, a person might allow himself a mild table thump with the two middle fingers and proclaim, "*Shabash*" (Well done). The discussion was sometimes interrupted by the sound of a slurp from a coffee cup. But this was normal, for here a slurp was acceptable behaviour.

West Bengal Police Commissioner
Surendra (Suren) Nath Chatterjee

After India gained its independence, the West Bengal State Police reorganised to fit the new realities of an independent nation. In Calcutta, Surendra Nath Chatterjee, or "Suren" as we later knew him, had been appointed, I believe, to the post of Commissioner of Police in Calcutta. I am not sure when or where Mum and Dad first met him, but I think that he may have already been retired from his position in the Police.

Over the years, Mr. Chatterjee became a close family friend. I know that "Suren" was how Mum and Dad addressed him but, of course, my sister and I knew him as Mr. Chatterjee. He was relatively short in stature, with a round face, a little bit portly and his hair was thinning. However, he was for us a larger than life person. He had a love affair with his pipe, which he caressed often and quite tenderly. He told us that it calmed him, but my perception was that he played with it and cleaned it far more than he actually smoked it. Suren was a very intelligent and articulate man who had a powerful command of English and who had read widely in both western and Bengali literature. He became our resident historian on Bengal and India, our philosopher teacher, our window onto Bengali and Indian classical music and cultural mores; it was always fascinating to listen to him. I still remember how he prefaced some perspicacious thoughts with, "You know, you need to read this into that comment," or "You know, it is only a minor thing, not important, but...." We understood that Suren was going to enlighten us when he prefaced a sentence with, "You know...."

I remember that Suren invited Mum, Dad, and me to a family wedding reception, which we attended, as well as other related celebrations. Prior to the wedding, we went to a musical soirée where the concert program included instrumental classical music and also some *Rabindra Sangeet*. The performance carried on into the late evening and provided us with a totally new experience, although we did not actually understand what we had heard. When we next saw Suren at our home, we mentioned this to him; so, he initially gave us the short form explanation of what we had experienced. But then he started with his signature "You know...," and proceeded to give us a potted history of Indian classical music. He linked some of its development from the Muslim Mughal emperors and the songs and dances of courtesan culture - in particular, the *Tawaif* (female singers and dancers and their accompanying strings and tabla drums) - to the development of musical instruments like the *sitar*, *tabla* and *sarangi* and older musical forms like the *ragas* and *talas*. He told us that the evolution of this music could be traced back over a thousand years or more. He touched on the art of improvisation and notation forms in Indian classical music. He described how Hindu musicians took this repertoire and other musical forms and brought to the West a changed and transformed Indian classical music in the modern era with musicians like Ravi Shankar.

To say that Mum and I understood everything that he told us would be dishonest, but Suren could take any subject and make it interesting. He was particularly strong on history; it was Suren who told us about the effect of the Second World War on Bengal, about the Bengal Famine and its causes, about the reasons for Partition, and about the various Indian and Bengali resistance movements - both inside and outside India - against the British. Through him we learnt about many aspects of Bengali culture. He was never dull. If he disagreed with a point of view or a comment, he would never show his disagreement openly; there would be a wry smile and he would add, in that ever-charming Bengali way, that there might be another way of looking at an issue. His natural charm and bonhomie enveloped us all; he was always calm, he was the master at reducing tension, and he was always the perfect gentleman. We loved our "Mr. Chatterjee." He visited us often but I never knew whether he really came for the beer, the scotch whiskey, the Czech cooking, or his favourite accompaniment for tea, namely Arrowroot biscuits. That remained his secret. As for food, his tastes were incredibly western: soup, roasts and Irish stew.

At one point, yet another strike had occurred at my father's factory and the whole office administration, six persons including Dad, were subjected to a *gherao* (a strike tactic used in Bengal) where, in this case, the striking workers locked the management and other office staff in their office until their demands were met. This particular lock-in lasted two hours during which time it was impossible for my mother to communicate with Dad. Well, when Mr. Chatterjee found out what was happening, he tapped into his network in the police, and managed to get a police presence to the factory and free all the office staff.

Much later in the 1970s, Dad engaged him in the company as our legal consultant and advocate for labour issues. Mr. Chatterjee brought with him skills in the Bengali way of expression that proved useful in Dad's correspondence with State and local government departments and other Bengali Institutions.

The Marwaris

The Marwaris originated in Rajasthan and were people of property and significant wealth. They moved into many other parts of India, but especially into Bengal, which had become the centre for British traders; accordingly, the Marwaris developed strong ties to the British East India Company until it all came apart in 1763 and their influence waned. Bengali Hindus then began to gain the ascendancy, but Marwaris started to move back into Bengal from about 1850 onwards, when Calcutta again emerged as an important economic centre. It was primarily the linking of Calcutta with the rest of India via the railway that drew the Marwaris. The railroad provided access to moderate and large sums of capital which made it advantageous to re-engage with the city. Calcutta was essentially "Open for Business." The Marwaris virtually took over all of the *Burrabazar* (Large Bazaar) area of Calcutta and made this the centre for their financial, mercantile, and trading interests. Their culture and entrepreneurial dynamism were quite unique and became a force in Calcutta. In time, they took control of most of Calcutta's economy.

As the struggle for Independence was taking place, the Marwaris, mainly under the influence of their most successful industrialist G.D. Birla, threatened to fight the British on the economic front. Birla, who was in favour of a non-violent solution, aligned himself with Gandhi and, as a result, when Independence came, was in the dress circle to increase the influence and business interests of the Marwaris. Because the interests of the Marwaris were paramount to the Bengali economy, Dad could not ignore them. In fact, it was the many Marwaris operating from Burrabazar who provided the dealership network that was essential for the distribution of Dad's hurricane lanterns throughout Calcutta and then the wider country.

Importantly, it was Dad's dealings with the Marwaris that created a business ethic that stayed with him for all his life in India. However, this same business ethic that had worked so well in Calcutta failed him completely later on in Australia, where it met with the western practice of written agreements and contracts. In Calcutta, your business reputation was created and grew with your ethical behaviour; you sealed a verbal agreement with a handshake. Your word was considered to be a contract. Your trustworthiness grew with your adherence to this simple principle. Dad lived his entire business life in Calcutta true to this ethos. He developed and won the trust of many Marwaris, who became an essential part of the success of his business. I remember vividly when he had cash flow problems, yet still had to meet payroll deadlines, there being no automated deposits into bank accounts in those days, he had to put together quite large sums of cash money. So, he would go to Burrabazar to see his own dealer, Mr. Jhunjhunwalla and, sure enough, the money would be prepared and the deal sealed with a handshake. In response to this favour, Dad would "throw in" an additional case or two of hurricane lanterns. I remember the efforts that Dad made to ensure that the money was repaid as soon as possible after his cash flow problem had eased. As a boy of fourteen or fifteen,

I did not quite understand what was going on, but Mr. Jhunjhunwalla always made sure that I got my Coke and *rasogollas* (a divine, extremely sugary, Indian sweetmeat) while I waited in his store for Dad to finalise his business dealings.[130]

The Parsis

Another group of people who had a very small presence in Calcutta, but a large impact, were the Parsis. They were followers of the Zoroastrian religion from Persia, but they certainly had an influence on Calcutta life through their entrepreneurship, their industry, and their influence on the arts. Many of the prominent Parsis were known for their philanthropy and also for their early effect on the development of the Indian film industry. The Parsi community in Calcutta were very westernized and progressive. According to my understanding, the Parsis were instrumental in bringing the English-language newspaper to Calcutta as far back as 1780. Mum and Dad got to know some Parsi people; they enjoyed a close friendship with the Batra and the Irani families. The Iranis were more business associates of Dad. The Batras, however, were very much part of Mum and Dad's social circle and, in the immediate post-independence years, they went to many events and dinner parties together. What I remember most was the wonderful, striking, classical elegance of Mrs. Batra and her all-welcoming charm.

Calcutta's Beggars

It is hard to decide whether begging was a desperate attempt to live or whether beggars were part of a large business scam. Probably a bit of both. Some beggars were truly destitute and many were poor people who gravitated towards Calcutta as a last recourse in the hope of finding work. But there is considerable anecdotal evidence that many actually had savings accounts at banks.

Calcutta had (and still has) its fair share of beggars, from the genuine to the professional, from the healthy to the sick and lame, from the outcast to

---

130 An excellent detailed summary of the history of the Marwaris in Calcutta is described in Sukanta Chaudhuri, ed., *Calcutta, the Living City. Vol II: The Present and the Future,* 109-116.

the deserted, and from the young to the old. We were always aware of their presence in the streets and were guaranteed a confrontation with beggars no matter where we went, marked out as we were by our skin colour. They were everywhere, near the temples and bathing ghats where Hindus congregated, and especially near the shopping areas like New Market or other venues like the cinemas and restaurants. After a while, even the locals became hardened and ignored them totally. Professional beggars, mainly those with grotesque deformities, tended to stalk their "marks." Foreigners were the mobile lighthouse beacon that represented wealth. What to do? Being confronted with this situation every day meant that we had to make some harsh decisions. Most of the time we ignored them and walked straight ahead, not because we were uncaring or indifferent to their plight, but because, if we stopped to give a beggar some money, no matter how small an amount, in an instant, hundreds of eyes within 100 feet would have noticed and descended *en masse*. Then the foreigner was in real trouble and it took some genuine nastiness to get away from the hordes closing in. The best option was to beat a hasty retreat to the nearest shop or to the car and, once in, stare blankly at the rearview mirror.

Any time that we got out of the car and started to walk away, there would invariably be a little tug on trousers or dress. As we wheeled around, at first, we would see no one but, as soon as we looked down, we would notice the little person who was the "tugger." Most of the time, it was a young child in tattered pants and singlet but sometimes it would be an adult beggar, usually lame or without legs, who pushed himself forward using his hands while perched on some sort of contrived "skateboard" with wheels. We would try to walk faster. But often we were prevented by the milling crowds. Frequently, these poor souls would contort their faces into an expression of pleading desperation with one hand making pointing gestures to their mouth and the other hand pointing to their stomachs, singing, or it appeared to be a form of singing, "Please sahib, no mother, no father, no brother, no sister, no auntie, no uncle, no friend, no help, no food, very "*bukha*" (hungry). Please sahib, some *baksheesh* (spare money)." Sometimes they just looked at us blankly and talked to us with their eyes.

In the car, we were not safe and, even with the window wound up, there could be three or four faces pushed against it looking at us directly and pleading so agonizingly for some *baksheesh*. Sometimes a destitute mother would thrust her emaciated baby against the car window pointing to the child and asking either for *baksheesh* or powdered milk. It was a harsh experience, but a fact of life in Calcutta. We became, in a way, numbed to their presence and learnt to adapt, as it was impossible to exercise any individual charity with the sheer numbers that were involved. We soon learnt to exercise a selective form of charity which, through its selectivity, could be construed as cruel. The general practice in any spontaneous act of generosity was to give the beggar a coin without looking directly at him or acknowledging any awareness of his presence. Mum had one rule with beggars: she always gave coin to destitute single women, with a baby or young child, since they probably were the most vulnerable within this group, likely widowed or abandoned by the husband. In India at that time, losing a husband meant that you lost your only means of support. This also became my rule for giving money to beggars. Another group that we helped were old and frail women, for they were totally without any support and really needed help.

Calcutta had an army of professional beggars and their continued existence on the Calcutta streets is testimony that it was a rewarding profession for some. This is not easy to write about, but every person who has lived in or travelled to India has been confronted by beggars and must develop his or her own response to this reality.

Calcutta's Rag and "Other Items" Pickers

Another element of the Calcutta population that we encountered on a daily basis were the rag pickers: the scavengers whose work in many ways could be considered a social service, since they kept Calcutta's garbage within manageable proportions. The garbage heaps and dumps were regularly scoured for items of "interest" or genuine economic value. Paper was a valuable commodity and any item of paper that was not glued tight to an advertising hoarding or a pole was a candidate for recycling. Amongst this collecting fraternity, there were rag pickers with particular skills. Some specialized in bottle collecting, some in shattered glass, some in aluminum cans, others in paper or discarded clothes and shoes, and others in wood, coal dust and even cow dung. The cow dung liberally expelled into the streets was seen both as a gift from the cow and a source of income. There existed a whole industry in the *bustee* (slum) areas of South Calcutta of cow dung collectors, usually women, who sought out these piles of brown, steaming splodge. The tools of their trade were their bare hands. They shaped the dung into a form of fat *chapatti* (patties) half an inch thick, mixed some sawdust into it, and slapped the patties onto the side of any available vertical surface or retaining wall to dry. They marked these cow patties as their own with intricate geometric patterns and, when the patties dried out, sold them as a form of fuel. When fully dried, these patties fetched a price of about Rs 4-5 per gunny sack. The cow patty trade was conducted by the lowest castes. All in all, Calcutta's army of rag pickers sketched out a meagre living from all this scavenging work. I admired their enterprise. As an aside, I also have to admit that tea brewed over a cow patty-fuelled fire by a street vendor was quite flavoursome.

City of Manual Labour

Even though Calcutta supported a large and thriving professional and business class, I always think of it as a city of manual labour. Deep in Calcutta's poorer districts, there were millions of people engaged in a daily struggle to survive. Most of them had no regular job, but they daily offered the one commodity that came cheap in Calcutta, namely the energy from their pitifully undernourished bodies. Calcutta was the ultimate body shop. These desperately poor people competed with animals to provide a service. In Calcutta during my parents' time, cattle or bullocks drew carts with goods; but, in the very same street could be found two people yoked to similar carts. In fact, some of the animals were freer than the poor. Cows routinely wandered the streets of Calcutta unmolested. Calcutta employed all forms of human pulling power in its streets. People pulled the barges along the canals. They pulled rickshaws. They rolled large petrol drums - full or empty - along the street. They carried all sorts of heavy gunny sacks suspended from bands stretched across their heads. Who can guess about the weight they carried this way? But, somehow, they managed. And when they delivered their load, they might be seen looking down sadly at their payment, then holding out their hands as if to say "Is that all?" This is an image that can be found all over India, even today, multiplied countless times. This massive, manual labour work force contributed to the Indian economy in a significant way. It was very difficult to witness this aspect of Indian life, but it was an essential component to the social and economic fabric of India during those times.

The Dhobi

In their early years on Chowringhee Road, my parents hired a *dhobi* (washerman) to do the laundry; he was, in fact, one of the most important people in our domestic life. At that time, there were no washing machines, no special washing soaps or soap powders; doing the washing meant spending a lot of time over a bath tub scrubbing and scrubbing and rinsing and then trying to find a place to hang up the washing to dry. So, in stepped the *dhobi*. He came once a week to pick up the washing from Mum. She made a list of the items to be washed, and he would go to his favourite washing place, be it a pond or large tank or even the river and then the traditional washing method took over. What this meant is that he literally thrashed the "dirt" out of the garment or item by first rinsing in water, twisting it and then slamming it down on a flat rock or stone. One of the great sights along the riverbank was to see a row of *dhobis* doing this in unison. The item to be washed was raised above the head like a scimitar, given a twirl and in a coordinated release brought crashing down on the stone. This procedure was repeated many times and, *voilà,* the dirt had been "beaten" or "thrashed" out. There was, however, one item of clothing that you never gave the *dhobi*, namely, your shirts or blouses, as they would be returned with all the buttons smashed into small pieces. Once the washing was done, the *dhobi* dried the wet clothes at his favourite spot, over a garden wall or on a flat roof or even a clothes line. And when all this clothing had dried, the specialist ironers moved in and, armed with their coal-fired flat irons, finished the job. The following week, all memsahib had to do was to check off the items against her list and give him the next batch of washing. Over time, the dhobis learnt how to do the shirts and blouses without smashing the buttons, so some small progress was made.

Darzis

In the early 1950s and later, when people met at any type of social gathering, the gender dynamics proved to be quite interesting. At most parties given by the British expatriates, the men and women tended to split up. The men reminisced about their old schools, their university, their sport and, once these subjects had been exhausted, their conversation gravitated to problems with their staff at work. By contrast, the Americans liked to have their wives around them while they cradled their scotch and bourbon. The American men showed an interest in local and international affairs and the women were very interested in telling all and sundry about the latest handicraft shop that they had discovered. At the British parties, the wives would invariably compare notes about their tailors, the insufferable heat, the amount of time before they could take home leave and, of course, problems with their servants.

There was a subtext associated with one's *darzi* (dressmaker). There were hardly any shops where a person could find fashionable women's clothes that could be bought off the rack. But a cheap and easy option existed. It was possible to buy high quality material and there was an abundance of women's fashion magazines, like *Vogue* and the German fashion magazine, *Burda*. Many of these were outdated, but they included dress patterns; a fertile imagination, together with a dress pattern, could lead to your own creation. Thus, a good *darzi,* with excellent sewing ability and charging a reasonable price for dresses and other garments, contributed to the expatriate's social standing. Having a good *darzi* that you could recommend to your friends was seen as a big plus in this society.

It took Mum a long time to find and educate her *darzi,* who lived in Middleton Row and operated a hand-powered Singer sewing machine. There always seemed to be a ritual to working with the *darzi*. It usually started with Mum buying some material for a dress. The pattern came out of magazines, in particular, *Burda*, which had many dress patterns for all occasions. The *darzi* could not make sense of the intricacies of the dotted lines going everywhere but at least he got an image of the dress that memsahib wanted. He squatted before Mum, tape measure wrapped around his neck and a white chalk in one hand. While Mum sat in the chair, they communicated in sign language. The quality of the finished product depended greatly on the effectiveness of this communication. The tape measure would appear and numbers would disappear into the *darzi*'s notebook. More often than not, he would bemoan the fact that there was not enough material and he needed twice as much. But Mum had learnt early on that *darzis* were basically interested in the surplus material in case they made a mistake and had to start again. The *darzi* hoped that he could translate Mum's vision into the finished product and, more often than not, he got it right. Thus, a sense of fashion survived in the city.

Anglo-Indians

One of the most tangible results of British colonialism was the presence in Calcutta of many Anglo-Indians. The origins of this mixed-race class could be traced back to the arrival of the British East India Company, its militia and administrators. As with all other colonial and imperial ventures, the Europeans who arrived to establish trade and keep the peace were men, alone, and without their families. In a short time, liaisons developed between these men and Indian women. If an Indian woman became pregnant, she was often cast adrift, ostracised by her own family; many would take to prostitution or some other menial work to survive. The instances of children born to a white mother and an Indian male were so rare as never to be an issue. But what became of the progeny of bi-racial unions? If the European male had the means and the inclination, he set up housekeeping and educated his half-caste children. In a few instances, the civil servant or soldier in question would marry the woman who had given birth to his child, but this was rare. Why? Essentially a mixed marriage meant his career in the administration or military had run its course; and a return to the "mother country" with an Indian wife was totally out of the question. Whether as part of a legal marriage or a housekeeping arrangement, the children of these liaisons soon became numerous enough to represent a sizeable portion of the population.

Although marginalized in many ways, Anglo-Indians could be considered to have a few advantages. In some cases, having a white father meant that the child was raised in an English household, dressed in a western fashion, was familiar with English customs, learnt English, and was probably familiar with Christianity. Unlike the Hindus who married people who came from the same caste or background, Anglo-Indians could either marry up with whites or down with non-whites. Anglo-Indians were attractive people and had a reputation for being intelligent. Since they were often well-educated, they became a principal choice for lower level administrative jobs, although their mixed race definitely kept them from advancing above subordinate positions. This must have frustrated many intelligent Anglo-Indians. Indeed, they suffered an inverse form of racism, whereby the British preferred them over Indians to provide the knowledge and experienced operational and maintenance skills to prop up British infrastructure, especially in the areas of colonial administration, defence, telegraphs, the post office and railways; yet, the British imposed a glass-ceiling for the promotion of Anglo-Indians based on race. As time went by, many Anglo-Indians found positions in the police force, customs and medical services and, most especially, the running of the railways, either in their administration or operations. Ironically, Anglo-Indians also encountered a promotional ceiling in the armed forces where they were often by-passed, in this instance, by Indians for promotion.

I could never quite understand why, despite all these barriers to normal commercial or administrative life, the Anglo-Indians remained loyal to their British masters in many facets of life, in particular in their use of the English language, adoption of some of their customs, and adherence to Christianity.

As a whole, the Anglo-Indians were a much-maligned community. They were ostracized and not much liked by the Indians and they did not fit into the British view of the "right sort" of people to represent the colonialists and their administration. During the pre-independence period, some Anglo-Indians did prosper, not only economically but also in social power and status. It is said of the Anglo-Indians that, without their contribution, Britain would have had difficulty in progressing from the simple marketplace to the economic heartland, from local producer of merchandise to supplier of the Empire, and from a trading company to a colonial government.

Despite their exclusion from high office in all the British-controlled ventures and the civil service, Anglo-Indians were determined to acquire the best education possible for their children. Precluded by the prevailing racism of the times from educating their children in England, they sought education locally, becoming educators themselves. In fact, they found their niche in Indian society as teachers. As soon as missionaries started to establish their schools in Calcutta, like La Martinière and St. Xavier's, whether Protestant or Catholic, Anglo-Indians came to dominate the teaching staff. This was certainly the case at Protestant schools like La Martinière; while at Catholic schools like St. Xavier's, they supplemented the teaching contingent, working with priests and Catholic lay-men. After Independence, their job opportunities dried up. Teaching positions that would have previously been in their purview went instead to Bengalis and other Indians. They were caught in limbo: they had access neither to a "British fatherland," nor an "Indian motherland." Historically, their contribution to India was immense. For my family, it was in education that the Anglo-Indians made a truly great contribution to our life in Bengal and Calcutta. They were the teachers in North Point, Darjeeling, where I attended, and at the girls' Loreto convents in both Calcutta and Darjeeling, where my sister went to school.

Latter-day Arrivals to Calcutta

From the 1920s right through to the 1950s, Calcutta grew rapidly, accompanied by a diversification of its ethnicities. The many pre- and post-independence political and religious upheavals and natural disasters (predominantly, the flooding of the mighty rivers to the north: the Brahmaputra and the Ganges) brought in thousands of Indian refugees. In addition, the city attracted many economic and political migrants from Europe and elsewhere; these were people who had fled unrest and wanted to place as much geography as possible between themselves and conflicts at home. Mum and Dad were part of this latter-day group. Other Europeans arrived to establish banking and industrial concerns for their parent companies. Still others were entrepreneurs seeking economic opportunities, or escaping persecution, as was the case with the Armenians. The social face of the city reflected this cosmopolitan mix of people in its restaurants, cafes, clubs, churches, sporting associations and interest groups, as well as in their associated cultural and social mores. Mum and Dad enjoyed this mélange of people, where they found many of their friends.

Missionaries

Oddly enough, even though my parents were not religious people, some of their close acquaintances in Calcutta were missionaries. Indeed, our family life was intricately woven with three of them. There is a long history in India of European missionaries working as teachers and publishers. The Jesuits had had a limited if persistent toe-hold in India since the time of St. Francis Xavier, who had come to India in the mid 16th century. But, the British East India Company essentially prohibited missionaries from setting foot in Bengal until the early 19th century, when Baptists in England forced the question in Parliament. Having won their case, the Baptists, under William Carey and William Ward (a trained printer),[131] quickly established a press at Serampore north of Calcutta and set to work translating Christian texts into Indian languages. So respected was Carey's knowledge of Indian cultures and languages that he became an instructor at Fort William College, the premier Orientalist college in India. As in other British colonies, the administration had neither the interest in nor the capacity to operate schools, so most missionaries were suborned from the outset to the field of education.

After the beach-head established by the Baptists, the Church of England arrived in Bengal, establishing numerous mission colleges in Calcutta for boys and girls. Their work extended to the outlying villages. It was from this religious community that my parents became friendly with Major Ken Hadow (of skiing fame in Gulmarg), who worked tirelessly among the poor. It was the Anglicans who established the famous St. Paul's School in Darjeeling, the Protestant counterpart to the Catholic school at North Point. The Catholic Church also opened numerous schools in the city for all classes of people; in addition, they operated orphanages and charitable organisations.

Father Barré

The first truly wonderful friend of the family in Calcutta was Father Barré, a Belgian Jesuit who held a position of some authority at St. Xavier's College. He was the person whom my parents approached when they made their

---

131   Geoffrey Moorhouse, *India Britannica*, 86.

initial enquiries about a suitable school for their son. Over the ensuing months and years, he became an admired and valued part of our family. My fondest memories of him were at the dining room table where he animatedly demolished my mother's Czech cooking; he often remarked that it was a welcome break from curry and rice. He was a wonderful raconteur and storyteller, his stories deriving from his personal experiences as a Jesuit in India. He especially excelled in recounting vignettes of his life in Bengal.

Father Barré was the son of a Belgian farmer. He had an imposing, strongly built figure and an immaculately trimmed white beard. He had come to India when he was twenty, believing he would only stay for three years to work in and assist the Belgian mission in Calcutta. Forty years later he was still there and had learnt to speak Bengali. From an initial passive, assistant role in the Mission, his work gradually took him into education at St. Xavier's and his pastoral duties involved him with the poor and the outcasts of Bengali society. In all the time that we knew him, he drew his strength from those he cared for.

There is one memory of Fr. Barré that has remained with me over all these years. It was a Sunday and he had dropped in to join us for dinner. I am not sure whether there were others at our table but he proceeded to tell us about his experience on that day. Father Barré regularly visited the jail in Alipore, which housed petty criminals. He hoped to help and provide comfort to those of the inmates who were receptive to his overtures, and then meet later with their families who lived in other parts of Calcutta, in order to pass information on to them about their jailed loved one.

This Sunday, he got up early, but noted that much of the city had already been astir for many hours. The early morning was cool and pleasant. For Calcutta's many poor, the daily struggle for survival, the eking out of a living, was never dependent on an alarm clock. He had finished saying Mass for his congregation in St. Thomas Church, near Park Street. The congregation rose and started to empty the church, milling about, and eddying past him. He offered a word here, a comforting look there, and a friendly handshake everywhere. This Sunday appeared to be routine, which meant that he would now embark on his usual visit to the Presidential Correctional Home for petty crime (commonly referred to as the Old Alipore jail). This was part of his work: a visit to members of his other constituency.

He prepared for the trip across town on his Vespa, packing a few food parcels, some personal letters for the inmates and his trusted *chata* (umbrella). The night before, there had been the normal intense, seasonal downpour and the streets were flooded. Father Barré appreciated his scooter even more at times like this. He loved his Vespa, which enabled him to negotiate the chaotic city traffic of Calcutta and the equally run-down roads with none of the frustrations that beset truck and car drivers and rickshaw pullers. Father Barré drove his scooter carefully, unsure where the pot holes lay under the water. The trusted scooter carrying his imposing figure struggled along as the roads narrowed and the skyline of the city fell abruptly from sixty-foot high brick dwellings, to modest structures of ten feet and then to simple wooden huts. Eventually he was riding by dwellings built of mud, cardboard and sheet metal that housed the poorest people.

The streets around the jail were flooded. The nearest strip of exposed land was on the footpath near the main entrance. Father Barré brought his scooter to a stop. Basu was the outside guard on duty.

"Salaam, Basu. Is it OK to park here?" asked Father Barré, as he stroked his white beard.

Shaking his head from left to right, Basu replied, "Salaam Father, no problem father-ji with parking. You please leaving your *chota gari* (small vehicle) there. I will look to it."

Father Barré entered the jail, after having satisfied the usual check-in formalities with the guards, and greeting the Jail Superintendent, Shri Mr. Chakhraborty. He then began his rounds. The jail was depressing as only Indian jails can be. The hygienic and sanitation conditions assaulted his senses. Most of the walls were covered with pear-shaped streaks of bright, red, betel juice, spat out onto the walls by hundreds of *paan* chewers over the years.

He acknowledged some of the inmates without breaking step, stopped to talk with some, and with others he passed on letters or messages from family and friends. He also took their messages and letters in return. In this way, Sunday after Sunday, he brought comfort to the wretched inmates, most of whom were famished, diseased, or stooped with pain and despair. He had become their lifeline to the outside world and their families.

He completed his visit; the amount of time spent at the jail was never an issue. As he reached the entrance gate, another tropical rain shower erupted and he decided to wait under cover until the squall passed. The sheet-like downpour felt like flecks of crystal on his cheek. As he waited, he noticed another person waiting near him. Fr. Barré spoke to the man and ascertained that he had just been released from jail. Poor soul, he had been incarcerated for six months for stealing. He was very concerned about his family and how they had survived this period alone without his support.

His name was Baswant, gaunt, with furtive eyes and a wiry face. Father Barré guessed his age at anywhere between 30 and 40 years old, but it was hard to tell. He lived in a crowded *bustee* (slum) near Howrah.

"Is your family still there?" Father Barré asked.

Baswant shrugged. "Who is knowing, father-ji?"

Father Barré sensed the man's disquiet. He asked him, "Would you like a lift to your home on my scooter, Baswant?"

Baswant replied softly, "I am of many thanks to you. But I have no money and my *ghar* (house) is near Howrah Station. Is that too far?"

Going to Howrah would be a major detour for Father Barré. But he realised Baswant wanted to get home quickly to his wife and children. He said, "You will have to hold on tightly, Baswant. It's going to be a bumpy ride and it will take time."

The rain subsided and, as they emerged into the humid, steaming atmosphere; the priest noticed that a traffic policeman was busy writing a parking infringement notice for his Vespa in his little brown book.

Father Barré looked at the traffic officer directly and asked, "Salaam, Officer-ji. I am just about to leave. Is it possible not to issue a parking fine?"

"Sorry, Sahib. Law is law. This vehicle is breaking law of non-parking areas. It is not allowable under Traffic Code 3-B, sub-section 5A, as amended in 1948. The fine for this offence is Rs. 20." It was essential that he could make reference to this obscure sub-clause in the Calcutta statutes relating to traffic violations. This extra bit of offered information was important, as it indicated to others that this traffic policeman had some education and training.

He added, "I must do my dutiful duty. I am very sorry."

"Off course, Officer-ji. You must do your duty. I do not want to cause you any problems with your superiors."

Father Barré took the parking notice politely, folded it and stuffed it into his briefcase. He got onto his Vespa. Baswant took his place on the Vespa's apology of a rear passenger seat. Before setting off, Father Barré again listened respectfully as the traffic policeman lectured him on the do's and don'ts of parking in and around the jail entrance. Fr. Barré politely assured him that he would take note of his warnings for the future. Taking leave of the policeman, he engaged the gear, slipped the clutch, and off they went in subdued silence. Baswant was more intent on hanging on than in trying to talk. Riding on a Vespa was a new experience for him. As they neared Howrah, Baswant guided Father Barré nearer to his home in the *bustee* (slum). As he disembarked, Baswant asked Father Barré to come in and meet his wife and children. At the dwelling, Father Barré noticed the strain in the reunion between Baswant and his family. He seemed to be an unexpected surprise. Gradually his children emerged and once the children had recognised Baswant, they hovered excitedly around him. Baswant was happy as he clasped his children. His wife offered Father Barré some tea in a clay cup, which he politely accepted.

As the priest prepared to go, Baswant stopped him and said, "Father you have been very kind to me and I am wishing to give this small gift to you."

He proceeded to present Father Barré with a small brown notebook. The priest was quite perplexed at this gesture, but accepted it gratefully. He was quite curious about the gift. What could this very poor man be offering? His surprise turned to absolute delight when he saw that he had the traffic policeman's parking and traffic infringement book. He even saw the very last entry: his own parking infringement notice. A broad smile came to Father Barré's face and he looked at Baswant, paused, and embraced him. In this city, a gift of kindness from a pick pocket manifests itself in many ways.

Father Ante Gabric

Another remarkable friend of our family was Fr. Gabric. I am not sure how we met him; I believe that it may have been through Father Barré, but I remember him from quite an early age. He visited us at least once a week, usually staying for lunch, and we were always happy to see him.

Father Gabric was born in Metković, Croatia, on 28 February 1915, one of nine children; eventually, he found his vocation in the Jesuit priesthood. He came to India after the War to do missionary work. Like many of the missionaries who came to Calcutta, he planned to spend about 5 years there doing pastoral work, but ended up staying for the rest of his life. Initially he worked in the city. He was quite a remarkable man and a very talented linguist. Early on, he taught himself to speak and write Bengali; our friend, Mr. Chatterjee, a native Bengali speaker, often commented that Fr. Gabric was totally fluent in the Bengali language. He also later became a fluent speaker and writer of Hindi. I vividly remember one Sunday mass when he gave the sermon in his impeccable accent-free Bengali to his congregation. This ability to converse in Bengali helped him enormously in his pastoral work. The details of his early years in Calcutta are not known to me but, when he became a regular visitor to our home, he had already established a small shelter for orphaned and abandoned children in the parish of Mariapally, some 50 miles away in the district of Baruipur in the Sundarbans,[132] south of Calcutta.

Baruipur district was located in the extreme south of Bengal where the River Ganges ends and the river breaks out into a large delta with its myriad tributaries and islands and where the waters from the three great rivers - the Ganges, the Brahmaputra and the Meghna - finally empty into the Bay of Bengal. The Sundarbans are home to the largest mangrove forests on earth; they cover about 3,800 square miles with 60% in present-day Bangladesh. The area is home to the Royal Bengal Tiger and a wide range of other animals including crocodiles, venomous snakes, spotted deer, and birds. Because of the annual flooding of the delta, a large layer of silt is regularly deposited on the land. The resulting soil supports agriculture and is an important hinterland for Calcutta. It is also a region of high rainfall and humidity. This coastal area often suffers from floods caused by the many cyclones that originate in the Bay of Bengal as well as tidal surges,

132 Some believe that the name "Sundarbans" is derived from the Bengali *shomudro-bon*, which literally means "sea forest," but it is most likely associated with the *Sundari* trees.

due to its low-lying topography. These cyclones carry a lot of sea moisture and, over the years, some of the land has become quite saline, which lowers crop yields. The people who live in this area are very poor and their crops, livestock, and fishing afford them only a meagre livelihood. This was most probably the reason that Fr. Gabric chose to work there; he was drawn to the poorest and most needy people.

Over time, Father Gabric continued with his construction program at Mariapally. At first, he built a small school, then a refuge for the abandoned and homeless. Later, he built a medical dispensary that provided first aid to the surrounding people. When he had completed these early projects, he built additional schools to take care of the different age groups and then came the construction of the church. After the church was consecrated, he built a larger dormitory style refuge that was urgently needed to look after the orphans who had started to come into his care. In that very poor district, there lived a lot of families for whom female babies were an unwelcome economic burden. The parents could not afford the dowry and, if they could not marry the girl and send her to the groom's household as soon as possible, she was just another mouth to feed. So, for many families, it was easier to abandon their new-born baby girls. This was accomplished by leaving the baby on the steps leading up to the front door of the church. Father Gabric took on the responsibility of feeding, clothing, and taking care of each one.

When I last saw Father Gabric at Mariapally in the late sixties, he had about 420 orphan girls in his care. But this abandonment scenario had evolved into a wonderful story of hope. He gave the children some basic education, teaching them to read and write. As the girls reached maturity and came of marriageable age, he then sought out suitable husbands for them in the surrounding district. He made sure that his girls married husbands who also had some basic education and promising work prospects. The girls were not illiterate and therefore employable. This allowed them to escape the practice of being used predominantly as additional help in the home. By this time, he had attracted quite a lot of helpers, including many of the girls who had decided to devote their own lives to helping the poor.

Some of Father Gabric's girls went on to become teachers at Mariapally and others went on to become members of Mother Teresa's Sisters of

Charity in Calcutta. Essentially, Fr. Gabric's schools were providing a service to the poor that ought to have been supplied by the West Bengal government. Consequently, there were not enough of these schools to serve all the poor children, but their very existence meant hope for many. Fr. Gabric was fighting an engrained set of traditions based on superstition and prejudice. The children came from illiterate homes. It therefore took quite some time for education to be not only understood but appreciated by the families. I remember that, one day when we visited him, he introduced us to a young boy who had learnt to sign his name. This simple accomplishment became a reason not only for great celebration among his school friends but also a source of immense pride for the boy, as he demonstrated to us his newfound skill. The happiness etched in the boy's face was noticeable and we all delighted in his triumph. No longer would he have to use a thumbprint as a sign of acknowledgement or recognition; now he could sign his name.

Father Gabric also took in and looked after people who had become refugees as a result of warfare (in Bengali, *Muktijuddho*). When Bangladesh separated from West Pakistan, many lost their homes and property and took refuge in Bengal. At other times, when the crops failed or had been destroyed by a cyclone or by floods, Father Gabric took it on himself to find the necessary food in the city to feed those affected. He lived a simple life and his example helped others to have a greater sense of community and humanity towards each other.

We all noted that there was a wonderfully positive chemistry between Father Gabric and Dad. They had a sincere admiration and respect for each other. Dad would move mountains to do anything for him. But the most immediate tangible help that Dad could provide him was access to the skills and facilities available at his factory. So, over the years, a steady stream of carpenters, plumbers, builders, painters, electricians, other specialists and materials wended their way to Mariapally to help Fr. Gabric build and maintain his sanctuary.

As Fr. Gabric's pastoral work grew in Mariapally, so did his challenges. Over time, he received financial support from people and organizations around the world. I saw the large correspondence that he had with these patrons, acknowledging their kind words of support; their donations, usually came in the form of cheques, postal money orders, and sometimes cash. His challenge was how to convert the foreign donations into useable Indian currency. For this particular problem, he had some sort of financial understanding with Dad, whereby Dad would exchange into rupees Father Gabric's foreign currency donations. Dad gave him the prevailing Reserve Bank of India exchange rate plus an additional ten per cent. Dad was happy with this arrangement, and both parties were satisfied. Father Gabric got more rupees for his foreign currency than if he had exchanged the cheques and cash at the local banks and Dad got foreign currency that he could use outside India. During the 60s, 70s and 80s, it was very difficult to obtain foreign currency. With his rupees in hand, Fr. Gabric descended on Calcutta once a week, meeting all his contacts in the markets to buy food (predominantly rice), pharmaceuticals and whatever else was needed at Mariapally. And let us not forget that he made this excursion to Calcutta week in and week out over a fifty-year working life. It had to be done, as so many people were dependent on him. Whenever he came to Calcutta, he would always drop in to our house for some lunch and Dad always made available to him the Citroen and the driver so that he could do his business more effectively.

Fr. Gabric became known as the priest who extended his pastoral care to all the peoples living in the Sundarbans. He fed the hungry, he provided clothing to those who needed it; he even helped to acquire land for those who needed that. He provided shelter for the homeless and he taught and cared for the abandoned children. And, as I mentioned above, he even became a marriage broker, arranging marriages for his wards to suitably screened candidates. He told us that, through the sheer example of his life, he had been successful in changing the ways of some of the *dacoits* (robbers or armed bandits) who lived and operated in this area. One day, he was ambushed by a band of *dacoits* who wanted to rob him but found there was nothing to rob; instead he offered them food and drink and spoke to them about his way of life. They were so surprised by this that some members of the band asked for his pardon, changed their ways and eventually became strong members of his congregation. No wonder that Mother Teresa often referred to him "… as a holy man for God and humanity." The people of the

Sundarbans also referred to him as the "… holy man of the Sundarbans," so great was their respect for him.

Fr. Gabric had a dry sense of humour. I remember on one occasion when Dad, a friend from Sydney, and I visited him at Mariapally. We stood by a large water reservoir where a lot of boys and girls were swimming and splashing about. It looked like any scene where children have fun in the water. I noticed that the water appeared luminous green, with some sort of algae growing on the surface. Concerned, I asked him if he was worried that the children might contract some virulent infection from the "apparent" green filth on the surface of the water. He looked at me, laughed, and replied that he had no such fears, since there were probably more vitamins - yes, he said vitamins - in this water than we had in our local water supply in Calcutta.

In July 1976, his parish bishop decided that Fr. Gabric needed a holiday and so he came to visit members of the Croatian community in Sydney. While there, he also visited us and many of his other friends from Calcutta. He even brought us two carpets that had been made at Mariapally. I believe they are still being used by my sister. During his time in Sydney, he baptized my sister's daughter Gaby and other babies from the Czech community. This was the last time that we saw him, but if ever there was a person whom we esteemed it was Fr. Gabric. He remains to this day the man whom I most admired as a child, and he is a constant source of inspiration to me as I live my life.

Father Gabric died on 20 October, 1998, exactly 50 years to the day after he first set foot on Indian soil; he is buried at Mariapally near the grotto adjacent to the church compound. It is a fitting memorial, and later some water and soil from his native Croatia were added to his grave at the request of his parishioners as a sign of their deep affection for him. In his life of completely selfless devotion to his community, he lived like a Bengali, devoted to his Sundarban community and to my family as well. We are so grateful that we were privileged to know a good man, to share bread with him, to laugh and cry with him and in some small way to be inspired by him. Today there is a move, both by the Calcutta Catholic archdiocese and the Croatian Jesuits, led by Cardinal Josip Bozanic, to initiate proceedings in the Vatican to have Fr. Gabric beatified and possibly later declared a saint. I hope they succeed.

Mother Teresa

Mother Teresa founded her new order, "The Missionaries of Charity," in Calcutta in 1950. Her mission's intent was to provide physical and pastoral care for the destitute and dying of Calcutta, people whom society had jettisoned and who had been left on the streets to fend for themselves or die. Mother Teresa was born in Skopje, Macedonia and joined the Sisters of Loreto at eighteen. This order had missions in India, where she was sent, formally took her vows as a nun, and initially taught school. But soon the crushing poverty and the poor people's suffering and despair affected her to the degree that she devoted her life to working for this community. Mother Teresa's mission was located near the Kalighat Temple. She worked in many parts of the city, offering the dying a final resting place and some dignity, helping the destitute, or those with broken spirits, and the hungry, sick and suffering. In the early years, she struggled with her ministry but then volunteers and funds began to materialize. In the course of doing his work with the poor, Father Gabric got to know Mother Teresa. Then Mother Teresa contacted my father, after Fr. Gabric whispered in her ear that he knew someone who could help with her non-pastoral problems. Soon, Dad was extending the same services to Mother Teresa's mission work as he had to Fr. Gabric. Dad supplied whatever work she needed from within the resources of the factory. If she needed an electrician, word about her need came from Fr. Gabric to Dad and soon an electrician was despatched to her premises. The story was the same whether she needed a plumber, carpenter, or bricklayer.

The Armenians

The Armenians have been a presence in India since antiquity. It is believed that there were Armenians in Alexander the Great's army and that they also established trading settlements on the Malabar coast and in Kerala. Certainly, from the eleventh century onward, Armenians were part of the overland caravan trading routes through Persia, Bactria, Tibet, and beyond. We also know they were invited to settle in Agra, India, by the

NO WAY BACK HOME

great Mughal king, Akbar, in the 16th century.[133] They were, in general, economic settlers. They built a church in Chinsurah in Bengal in 1685. It is the
second oldest Christian church in Bengal. They were already well settled in
Bengal before Job Charnock arrived.

There is quite an interesting bit of information about the Armenian presence in the area where modern Calcutta now stands. In the graveyard of
the Armenian Church in Armenian Street, Burrabazar, there is an intriguing
inscription which reads, "Rezabeebeh, wife of the late charitable Sookias"
and the chiselled date in the gravestone reads "21 July, 1630." If this date
is correct then it would predate Job Charnock by about 60 years. An error
perhaps, but who knows; in any event, the Armenians proffer this information as further proof that they were in Calcutta well before the British
arrived.[134] It is thought that they became the money lenders to the British East
India Company. Their earliest ties with Calcutta were certainly economic.
Their strength was their status and reputation as merchants and traders, but
they lost their pre-eminent position with the advent and rise of the British
Raj. In the 1950s, 60s, and 70s, the Armenians had a thriving community in
Calcutta that functioned at many levels. They had a reputation for being very
smart businessmen in real estate, as jewelers and goldsmiths, and in profes-
sions such as engineering and law. They also contributed financially to the
development of the city and were appreciated as philanthropists. An early
wealthy Armenian, Johannes Carapiet Galstaun was involved in building
development and real estate and, even today, in Park Street, one of the largest
residential buildings in the city - named Galstaun Mansions - can still be
seen. Another Armenian, Arathoon Stephens, built two of the major hotels,
the Grand and Everest Hotels, which today are owned by the Oberoi group.
Mum and Dad had a few Armenian friends including their dear friend Coco
Mackertich, to whom I shall refer later.[135]

133 See "Julfa v. Armenians in India," *Encyclopaedia Iranica* www.iranicaonline.org/
     articles/julfa-v-armenians-in-india
134 Geoffrey Moorhouse, *Calcutta*, 36.
135 An excellent detailed summary of the Armenian presence in Calcutta is presented
     in Sukanta Chaudhuri, ed., *Calcutta, the Living City. Vol I: The Past*, 54-55.

Other Communities

During the war years there were several nationalities present in Calcutta. Mum and Dad had a few friends who came from Poland. Many of them remained in Calcutta well after the War and left in the mid-1950s for other destinations, like Thailand and Hong Kong; some even returned to Europe. Among the Poles, Mum and Dad socialised with the Kahan brothers quite regularly. There were also people from Austria including Dr. Ronald and Dr. Tauber, mentioned previously as our family doctor and dentist respectively. Dr. Ronald was an interesting person. At some stage, and I do not know all the details, he became the personal doctor to the King of Nepal. At this time Nepal was, to all intents and purposes, "closed" to the west; Dr. Ronald would disappear for days and we would find out later that he had gone to Kathmandu to attend to the medical needs of the King and the royal family. This early link to Nepal became quite useful to Dad. If anyone wanted to go trekking or mountain climbing in Nepal, they had to get permission from the Nepalese government. This was a difficult process and many were refused permission. But Dad managed to get the permission he needed, through the intervention of Dr. Ronald with the King, in order to embark on his 1952 expedition to Sikkim and Nepal.

One of the more interesting characters in Calcutta was Boris Lissanevitch. He had a chequered past. Early in his career he had been a ballet dancer in Diaghilev's Ballet Russe. His dancing career took him to South America and all over Europe. Eventually he found work in India after a tour of Ceylon, Malaya, Indochina, Shanghai, and finally Calcutta. It was in Calcutta that Boris found his niche. During his travels he had picked up a few skills, including knowing how to cook well. While in Calcutta, he became a good friend of the Maharajah of Cooch Behar, who had a house in Theatre Road not far from where we lived. They used to go tiger shooting together. But, sometime during this friendship, they came up with the idea of a nightclub/restaurant in Theatre Road and, in 1936, their dream was realised. They called it the "300 Club." I am not sure whether Boris was a manager there or a part owner; nevertheless, the 300 Club became the watering and partying hole for many of the wartime pilots, Calcutta's socialites, Maharajas, fringe society dwellers, hanger-ons, and the wealthy. The club's main caché was its exclusivity, which depended on social standing, money, and perhaps even notoriety. The 300 Club had a reputation for parties where guests were invited to greet the dawn with a hearty breakfast. Needless to say, the 300 Club had a fine restaurant. Mum and Dad got to go to the Club as guests of Coco Mackertich, an Armenian friend who was one of its members. The attraction for them was the fine food and the 300 Club's signature dish, which was "Chicken Kiev," something Boris had introduced into Calcutta's culinary repertoire. I am not sure how long the club lasted but it had closed by the late 1940s.

Boris' real fame is that he can rightly be said to be the father of tourism in Nepal. Dad and I stayed at his hotel in Kathmandu, the Royal Hotel, where, if memory serves me, he had a pet horse or donkey that had free reign in the building; one encountered this pet everywhere. Dad knew Boris quite well from Calcutta and the 300 Club. I remember that we once visited his house at Ichangu, a few miles to the north of the Swayambhunath Temple. At that time, Boris' house was in a rural setting, where he kept a few white pigs from Yorkshire. I still recollect Boris trying to corral these pigs into a pen. He had the pigs face the wrong way and hit the lead pig with a stick. The reaction of the pigs was "one step forward and three steps back. In this manner Boris met his objective and soon the pigs were in their enclosure. Dad and I were beside ourselves with laughter. Boris was a gregarious man and a wonderful host and I remember well his private lounge room that was a treasure trove of Tibetan and Nepali antiquities. I was especially taken with a magnificent Tibetan saddle done in silver, which was displayed prominently in this lounge. Boris' life story has been admirably captured in Michel Peissel's book, *Tiger for Breakfast*.

After Independence many companies, especially banks, established branches in Calcutta. In the late 1950s, a Netherlands bank operated in the city. Dad did his business banking there, and he and Mum became very friendly with one its executives. His name was Gerrit (Gerry) van der Griendt and this friendship continued well after the van der Griendts left India. Gerry later worked at the Dresdner Bank in Hamburg; whenever we visited Hamburg, we always went to see him. In fact, Gerry got me my first job in Germany after I graduated from Sydney University as an engineer.

Another community that was well represented in Calcutta was the Chinese. The Chinese had been regular visitors to India, but the first settlers can be traced to about the 1770s. They were skilled workmen and crafts people. As their numbers grew, they diversified into businesses of various kinds. The community in Mum and Dad's time numbered about 5,000 people and our contact was mainly through their fine restaurants, their shoe shops in the New Market, and their skill as carpenters. Dad employed Chinese craftsmen to build specialized furniture for the factory. Mum and Dad quite often took us to the famous Nanking Restaurant that I believe was located in Blackburn Lane or close by. These were memorable outings indeed and were a treat for us all. However, this domestic tranquillity was destroyed when an on-going Indo-Chinese border dispute escalated into full-scale confrontation in October 1962: China invaded India. This lamentable situation put the political fate of the Chinese in India into serious jeopardy. In the aftermath of a cease fire in November, the Indian Government rounded up over 2,000 Chinese, most of them from Bengal, and interred them in camps in Rajasthan. When the bulk of these Chinese were released in about 1965, many left India and either returned to China or emigrated to Canada, Australia, Europe, Hong Kong, and other Asian countries.

Calcutta Stock Exchange

At this point, I feel that I should introduce the reader to the Calcutta Stock Exchange, since one of the family's closest friends was a member. This was the world of Coco Mackertich. I have never forgotten the day he took Dad and me on a guided visit through the Exchange and its environs and gave us a fascinating insight into the running - inside and outside - of this esteemed establishment. The Calcutta Lyons Range Stock Exchange was located in the vicinity of the hotel district near the Writer's Building complex, which was the administrative home of the State Government of West Bengal. The Stock Exchange was housed in a delightful Victorian building with an impressive entrance that led directly into an extremely crowded trading floor above which was a second-floor balcony. Outside the building, scribes, banging away on their typewriters, packed the alleyway where the Exchange was housed. They shared the lane with fortune-tellers, food hawkers and the ever-present beggars. The external walls of the Exchange at ground level were covered by the splotchy "red paint" of spat-out *"paan."*[136]

Inside the Exchange, the brokers were resplendent in their black coats and button-down white shirts. Most of them were Marwaris, Jains, Parsis, and wealthy Bengalis. The brokers normally spent their eight-hour day sitting in drab offices with small windows, with the *Calcutta Statesman* opened to the financial pages from which they tried to glean the next "sure bet" investment. All the while, they continually worked the phones. Documentation was not a strong point of the Exchange. If regulatory agencies required proof of a buy or sell transaction, the record would inevitably have been "lost or mislaid." If absolutely required by an official agency, the brokers would turn to the expert forgers located outside the building. These entrepreneurs would then create the requisite documentation. Forgers were thus part of the Exchange family.

But what set this Stock Exchange apart from its other counterparts around India were the external brokers. There used to be a mountain of rabbit warrens, resembling empty 3 by 3 ft. tea chests that were stacked neatly one on top of the other directly across from the beautifully porticoed entrance to the building. In each square of this veritable honeycomb, open to the street, sat the outside brokers, phones cupped to their ears. Each warren was connected to the interior of the Stock Exchange building by what appeared to be dedicated phone lines. The interesting thing about these external brokers was that they traded on the Stock Exchange on behalf of the lower classes, including minor civil servants, cooks, small shopkeepers, etc. I remember Coco telling me that the average trade was about Rs. 50 and that they dealt in quite small share parcels. How the companies dealt with these investors on their share register was anyone's guess. But capitalism had obviously reached out to the lowest echelons of society.

Constantine (Coco) Mackertich

Another dear friend of the family was the very wealthy and eccentric Armenian, Constantine (Coco) Mackertich and his wife, Alice. Alice

---

136 *Paan* is not swallowed; when its users have done chewing it, they just spit it out onto a convenient wall or the nearest available surface: hence the numerous *paan* bedaubed surfaces in Calcutta and elsewhere in India.

was an elegant lady always immaculately coiffed and dressed; she had an uncanny resemblance to the actress Merle Oberon. We all knew her husband as Coco. He was born on 4 January, 1895, to Martin and Adile Mackertich. Coco's parents were quite wealthy; their fortune had been founded in the finance industry, especially in share broking. At an early age, Coco had been duly introduced into this world and the family bought a seat for him on the Calcutta Stock Exchange. He became even wealthier. He owned houses and apartments, which he rented, as well as the horses that my mother and sister used to ride. Unfortunately, he was in a loveless marriage and he and his wife had come to some arrangement, living in separate parts of their house. But despite this, he was a wonderful man and an adopted member of our family. We could not imagine an informal lunch or a dinner party at our home without Coco.

He was one of a kind. He was not tall. His head had a slick of white hair pasted on top; a beautiful stiletto moustache adorned his upper lip. He dressed like an aristocrat from "turn of the century" England, a grandee with an ebony walking cane that sported a sleek silver embossed deer head handle. Coco was an absolute picture in his immaculately creased, grey, pinstriped trousers, coloured waistcoat, heavily starched shirt and collar, his black cravat, fob chain, and morning coat. His tie was always secured by a beautiful pearl pin. To round off his attire, he wore elegant lace-up boots and white spats. Coco seemed at times to have stepped straight out of a Toulouse Lautrec painting of the Moulin Rouge night club in Paris. Casual wear for Coco meant knickerbockers, a style of men's clothing featuring a baggy trouser that went down to the knees. With his "knickers" he wore his matching, light, Shetland patterned sweater over a cotton shirt, a yellow silk cravat and Argyle socks. For this clothing combination, instead of spats he wore his two-toned shoes, usually black and white. He loved this style of clothing and cut a truly distinctive figure in Calcutta society. Coco's signature statement and most memorable accoutrement was a silver flower holder for the daily red rose or carnation that he wore on his left lapel. But this holder was unlike many others. It could actually hold water and did not leak. I do not think that anybody in Calcutta dressed quite like this at the time.

Coco lived in a large, two-storeyed house on Lower Circular Road. His wife Alice lived in the upper part of the house and Coco occupied the main floor. The house grounds were large enough to keep stables for 4 race-horses, and pens for two goats and a cow. Coco loved horse riding; every morning his horses would be walked to the Calcutta Race Course where he, my mother and, sometimes my sister, would exercise them around the Calcutta Turf Club racetrack.

A visit to Coco's house was an interesting experience that presented us with many surprises. After Coco had married Alice, his parents sent him to undertake the "grand tour" of Europe and North America and, as was the wont of those who could afford to undertake such a journey, he returned with Venetian glass, grandfather clocks, large porcelain vases and bowls, and diverse antique bric-a-brac. The furniture in the house was a treasure trove of highly polished European and British antiques from the late 19th and early 20th centuries. The large drawing room had weathered sofas with dilapidated cushions that had seen better days and some occasional tables for coffee and tea. Wonderful Persian rugs covered the floors even though many had started to show their age and had become moth-eaten and threadbare, with frayed corners or missing edges from years of exposure to Calcutta's climate. The oil paintings captured scenes of Rome, Venice, Paris, the French Riviera, London and New York. During his world tour, Coco had been introduced to and partied with many Hollywood stars in their select American and European playgrounds. On one feature wall he displayed signed photographs from many famous film stars of his generation: Douglas Fairbanks, Myrna Loy, William Powell, Merle Oberon, Stan Laurel and Oliver Hardy, Charlie Chaplin, and others. Here and there, portraits of various dignitaries and possibly even members of his family and important Armenian Church figures hung on the walls or filled the silver photo frames resting on occasional tables. Many travel mementoes and objects made from Georgian silver filled the display cabinets. The ceilings supported some of the finest Venetian crystal glass chandeliers from the famous Murano factory near Venice. One cabinet held other glass objects like *aventurine* - glass with threads of gold - and *millefiore* (multicoloured glass).

Coco had some musical talent. He played the piano very well and, when playing, he used to sway back and forth like Liberace, sometimes with a furtive look over his shoulder, as he accompanied the music with a song. He had a favourite tune and, whenever the opportunity presented itself, he started with "Rose of Picardy." The only thing missing from this picture was the Liberace candelabra. He also had an old "pianola" piano that accepted music rolls. Unfortunately, with the passage of time, many of these rolls had torn and could no longer be played. However, whenever I found a "good one," I loved to sit pedaling away, making the piano-roll spin and watching the piano keys get magically depressed to play in tune, synchronised with the notes.

The curtains in Coco's house were made of some heavy material, probably brocade. In the dining room near these curtains, a long piece of corded sash dropped from the ceiling and, when Coco tugged on it, servants magically appeared. I often wondered if these curtains ever got washed. They gave me the impression that they would disintegrate into a small pile of fragments if exposed to the slightest gust of wind. His house was like a museum and, as the years passed, all these treasures tarnished and gathered dust. I think that all this faded glory reflected Coco's loss of interest in the house and its upkeep. The years and the Calcutta climate exacted their toll and everything showed its age. Even the paint was flaking off the walls.

Coco possessed a unique collection of cars. He could choose from a 1924, royal blue, Singer 10, four-seater Tourer, where two passengers could occupy an upholstered dickey seat in the rear, or a vintage, silver, 1928, Rolls Royce Phantom 1, also with a dickey seat in the back. He had another spare Rolls and I suspect that Alice used that car. On the other hand, it might have provided spare parts for the one currently being used. I imagine that Coco used the Singer for his social outings and, when he needed to go for his business appointments or a visit to the bank or Stock Exchange, then the Rolls became the vehicle of choice. When he used the Rolls, Coco always had two "footmen" with him, one being the spare driver and the other an actual footman who jumped out and opened his door. Style, sheer style. One of my fondest memories of this magnificent car was Coco driving and the two attendants, regaled in full white uniform, sitting in the dickey seat sweating profusely in the midday sun and fierce humidity. We often went out with Coco in his Rolls Royce for a spin around the racecourse or on the Red Road near Fort William. These roads had no built up areas surrounding them and so we could ratchet up the speed quite a bit.

Among my many fond memories of Coco is visiting him for high tea with Mum and Dad one day when we were accompanied by a friend. As we entered his house, he asked us to be very careful where we stepped and advised us how to manoeuvre ourselves around his *objets d'art*. At the main entrance stood a preserved, stiff, elephant foot intended for umbrellas and walking canes. There were some moth-eaten tiger and leopard skins scattered in between the Persian rugs around the floors. He had a billiard room but the cloth was torn and threadbare and the cues so warped that they could have outfitted Robin Hood's merry men with bows! The odd cobweb had found a permanent home high up in inaccessible places near the ceiling, where fans groaned noticeably as they did their figures of eight, since the fastenings attaching them to the ceiling had come loose.

Coco called for tea to be served. We sat at a tastefully decorated table. All the crusts had been trimmed off the cucumber sandwiches. There soon appeared another silver platter with dainty cakes supplied by Flury's, a local Swiss owned and operated patisserie in Calcutta. Tea was served to us in exquisite English porcelain, the teapot covered with the requisite tea-cosy. Coco liked his tea black, but Dad and I happened to prefer it taken with milk. I had the temerity to ask for milk. Guess where the milk came from! The servants brought the cow to the nearest French door close to our table where she was milked before our eyes. Straight from the cow to the table. Fresh as fresh can be; so, Dad and I had our milk, albeit a tad warm. Coco loved Calcutta and, with his persona and lifestyle, he was definitely in the right place at the right time. In the Calcutta of the 50s and early 60s, all this dressing up and his other indulgences were still acceptable and appropriate.

We adopted Coco and he us. Since he had no children, he treated my sister and me as his own. The circumstances of our family's coming to India meant that my sister and I had no uncles and aunts to enjoy in Calcutta. Sure, we had our genetic aunts and uncles in Czechoslovakia but geography precluded them from being part of our daily lives. So, dear old Coco became our "de facto" uncle. We affectionately called him "Uncle Coco" and he became part of our growing up. When he came for a visit to 53 Chowringhee, he always brought a small gift for us, mostly a packet of sweets or chocolates. When Mum and Dad went for a walk in the *Maidan* or in the gardens of Victoria Memorial, he would join us. When we went to visit him at his home in Lower

Circular Road, we invariably made a detour to the stables with Uncle Coco; he always had a plate of cut apples and carrots on hand so that we could feed his beloved horses. He knew that we loved to ride in the dickey seat of his Rolls Royce and so he often took us for a spin, much to our delight. When Mum and Dad came to Darjeeling to visit me at boarding school during the Pooja Holidays in October, Coco also came for a visit. He had his holiday house there, but it too required extensive repairs and suffered from neglect and lack of use. So, he stayed at a hotel. In Darjeeling, when our family conducted our 1950s version of boulevarding from Chowrasta[137] to Keventers, a dairy products outlet, we made our obligatory "pit stop" for a milkshake and cake and Coco joined us.

Darjeeling at this time of the year was full of characters that could have been plucked straight out of a P.G. Wodehouse novel. People gathered at the Planter's Club, and later the Gymkhana Club. Men dusted off their old school cricket and rugby blazers and paraded in a moving, zebra-decorated panorama. In this atmosphere, no one cared that Coco still cut such an antiquated, yet dapper figure. His moustache was always waxed and twisted to perfection, the tips being equidistant from each nostril. For his holiday in the hills, his idea of appropriate dress was the Shetland tweed, with vest and tie. The ever-present flower holder in his lapel sported a freshly hand-picked red rose or carnation. Coco never failed to disappoint. Even in Darjeeling, he joined us for our canter and, despite the fact that he was astride a Himalayan mountain pony, he rode bolt upright in the saddle, allowing the pony tender to lead him at a slow canter as we went for our ride around Birch Hill. All in all, Coco loved our family and we loved him. We were the family that he never had and we delighted in him and his eccentric ways. I miss him and am grateful for all the wonderful memories.

When he died on 5 February, 1975, the Armenian Church became the principal beneficiary of his substantial wealth. Today, he lies buried at the Armenian Church in Tangra, Calcutta.

137 This area was also called Chowrasta Mall. Chowrasta is literally the meeting point of four roads: ("*chow*") means "four" and "*rasta*" means "roads."). It is at the centre of Darjeeling, located next to Observatory Hill. Chowrasta commands great views of the mountains, valleys and several tea gardens.

CHAPTER 6

Family and Business Life after Indian Independence

We live in a wonderful world that is full of beauty, charm and adventure. There is no end to the adventures that we can have if only we seek them with our eyes open.[138]

Jawaharlal Nehru, first Indian Prime Minister

Darjeeling *Durga Puja*

In October 1948, when I was seven, Mum and Dad came to Darjeeling to visit me for the *Durga Puja* holidays. At this time of year, for a ten-day period, in various parts of India, this annual Hindu festival celebrated the Hindu goddess Durga, but also other deities such as Shiva, Ganesha, Lakshmi and Saraswati. At North Point, the school declared a ten-day

---

138 As quoted in Jason A. Merchey, *Building a Life of Value: Timeless Wisdom to Inspire and Empower Us*, 74.

holiday. If a boy's parents visited Darjeeling over this holiday, he was allowed to leave school and stay with them at their hotel. This was the only opportunity that parents got to meet their sons during the school year. Whenever Mum and Dad visited Darjeeling, I could look forward to ten days with them at the Windamere, or at the Mt. Everest Hotel. We passed the time by taking excursions to Ghoom or Kalimpong, or in visiting Tiger Hill to see the sunrise over the Himalayas. Or we simply strolled through Darjeeling, one of the most popular of the hill stations during the British Raj. At Chowrasta Square, there were mountain ponies which we often hired for long rides. Writing weekly form letters home never quite had the same caché as direct personal contact. After nearly eight continuous months at the boarding school, I really enjoyed the opportunity of speaking with Mum and Dad in person, at least as much as a young child could.

When we went for our walk around Birch Hill, there was a section, as we rounded the hill in the vicinity of North Point School, where we saw in front of us the full expanding view of the Himalayas, including the stunning view of the third highest mountain in the world, Mt. Kangchenjunga. I could see that Dad was captivated by this magnificent vista. He had recently joined the Himalayan Mountaineering Club in Calcutta and had met quite a few of the members who had already made small treks into Sikkim and Nepal. Nepal was still virtually "off-limits" to those of the trekking fraternity, since they needed to have a permit to go there and these were not easy to come by. But Sikkim was possible and, combined with the fact that my father's factory was now well established and profitable, he could afford to take time off to go trekking. So, 1948 witnessed the beginning of my father's experiences in the Himalayas.

At the Himalayan Club, Dad had recently met Trevor Braham and they had become quite good friends. Trevor was a son of the British Raj who had gone to school at Darjeeling and begun his own thirty-year love affair with the Himalayas there. Trevor mentioned that he was in the process of preparing for a trek to Sikkim in November 1949. He then talked about the possibility of Dad joining him but no firm commitment had yet been made. I believe that the 1948 visit to see me in Darjeeling convinced Dad that he should at least try it once and see for himself what trekking in these mountains entailed. Would he enjoy the experience or not? I think he decided to go with Braham because it was an ideal opportunity to learn about trekking from an experienced mountaineer.

Windamere Hotel

The Windamere Hotel was and is a charming little hotel situated behind Chowrasta, under historic Observatory Hill. Chowrasta, the large open square at the top end of Darjeeling was the well-spring from which the town of Darjeeling grew. The shopping mall and all the restaurants and other diversions that Darjeeling had to offer were centrally located near Chowrasta. Swirling clouds and mists often caressed the hillsides and, when these lifted, the majestic sight of the Himalayas, 25 miles distant, was revealed. The Windamere Hotel was centrally located to the life and diversions of Darjeeling. The Hotel enjoyed a reputation as one of India's classic colonial hotels; it had opened as a boarding house in the nineteenth century and was converted into a hotel in 1939. By that time, Darjeeling had become the tea-growing centre of India and the Windamere Hotel, the "hotel of choice" for all the English and Scottish visitors who sojourned in the town to escape the heat of the plains. A legendary hotel manager during this era was an Englishwoman named Mrs. Brewster, who ran the place like an English country house. Early every morning there would be a knock at each bedroom door by a Nepali servant bringing a tea biscuit and a fresh pot of tea hidden under a giant tea cosy, to help start the day. The rooms were decorated in a style reminiscent of the 1930s; each guest room had a fireplace and every bed had its own signature hot water bottle. The clock ruled in this establishment. The ringing of a bell by a Tibetan doorman announced the various meal times. Photographs and mementos of bygone eras hung on the walls everywhere and engulfed the seating areas. As I inspected these gems, my mind would wander and I would imagine the many stories behind them.

Darjeeling

Darjeeling is the queen of all the Himalayan hill stations. I like to think of it as a gift of the British Raj to India. The original name of Darjeeling was Dorje-ling; it used to belong to the kingdom of Sikkim.[139] Over time, it became a very popular place for colonial families and started to attract better facilities, hotels and other infrastructure. It also afforded the visitor a chance to see a wide variety of peoples from the Himalayan regions. These included Tibetans, Nepalese, Sikkimese, Bhutanese and the Lepchas. Mainly because of its location, its spectacular scenery, easy-going way of life, pleasant climate and clean air, Darjeeling also started to acquire a permanent European population, which included Christian missionaries from every corner of the earth. These missionaries - the Belgians, the British, the Irish and North Americans - built and ran the great boarding schools that were and are still found in Darjeeling. The Jesuits ran North Point School (in Darjeeling from 1892), which I attended as a boarder; it was intended mainly for Catholic boys, but it also included a smattering of Protestants, Buddhists, Muslims and Hindus. The non-Catholic boys were excluded from the never-ending round of religious obligations that had "Catholic" boys like me on our knees in prayer for three hours every day. The nuns ran the Loreto Convent School for girls (established 1842); like St. Joseph's, it accepted children from non-Catholic denominations. Darjeeling also had Protestant schools like Mt. Hermon, St. Paul's (established 1864), Goethals (established 1906), Dow Hill (established 1898) and others. Many of these schools enjoyed the reputation of being among the best scholarly institutions in the country.

Darjeeling had some rather eccentric characters. Rumour had it that a Jewish rabbi lived there who doubled as a jockey at the weekend mountain pony races at the race track at Lebong, located about six miles from North Point. Another interesting character who spent a winter in Darjeeling was

139 In the Tibetan language, "dorje" means thunderbolt and "ling" means a place or land, giving us "the land of the thunderbolt." Prior to 1816, this land belonged to Nepal which had acquired it after defeating Sikkim. A border dispute between Nepal and the British led to a war. The British, led by General Ochterlony, defeated Nepal; subsequently, through an 1816 Treaty, the Nepalese handed over 2,500 sq. miles of territory to the Rajah of Sikkim. The British (through the auspices of the East India Company), saw opportunities in what is now called the Darjeeling area and therefore arranged a transfer in 1835 of the area to their authority from the Rajah of Sikkim. They then made plans to develop a town, which is known today as Darjeeling.

Maurice Wilson (1898-1934), an ex-British soldier, mystic, aviator, and putative mountaineer. His claim to fame was that he wanted to climb Mt. Everest to prove that, through his strong faith and fasting at the roof of the world, he could eliminate all evil on earth. The inspiration to climb Mt. Everest came after a transformative healing event related to his war experiences and from reading accounts of the 1924 British expedition. Initially he failed to get permission to enter Tibet. But Wilson was not dissuaded from his quest and spent a winter in Darjeeling fasting and meditating and planning another attempt, albeit an illicit one. He engaged three sherpas and, in March 1934, his group slipped out of Darjeeling disguised as Buddhist monks. They eluded the authorities and managed to get to the famous Rongbuk monastery on the Tibetan side, where they augmented their supplies from equipment left by previous expeditions. Unfortunately, Wilson died in his attempt, but reports indicate that he managed to reach 22,600 ft. before he succumbed to the mountain.[140]

Darjeeling was a fashionable destination of choice for those desiring to escape the searing heat of Calcutta. Even the West Bengal government moved its parliament on a seasonal basis to an imposing Government House built in a pristine location near Birch Hill. And, of course, Darjeeling was the centre of the Indian tea industry where, arguably, some of the finest black tea in the world is still grown. English and Scottish tea planters owned, managed, and operated the tea gardens that draped the hillsides around Darjeeling and its valleys. With all these diverse groups of people in Darjeeling, the town developed its own life style. Darjeeling had a Gymkhana Club where members could indulge in all sorts of sports, including tennis, swimming, and roller-skating. In its early years, the Gymkhana Club was the venue for the celebrated "ghost" dance where all the guests regaled themselves in white, flowing, fantastic costumes. For non-sporting people, there was ample opportunity for gossip while sipping endless cups of tea, munching on cucumber sandwiches and participating in the "thés dansants." Among the amenities at Darjeeling was a reasonably

---

140 Audrey Salkeld provides the full story of Maurice Wilson in the chapter, "The Mad Yorkshireman," in Peter Gilman, ed., *Everest: The Best Writing and Pictures from Seventy Years of Human Endeavour*, 47-48.

large hospital to cater for the growing expatriate community. I know about this first-hand, as I had my appendix removed in the Planters Hospital.

But Darjeeling had another claim to fame aside from tea gardens, boarding schools and a retreat from the plains. High altitude climbing and trekking expeditions used Darjeeling as their starting point for expeditions into Sikkim and Nepal. Kangchenjunga dominated the skyline in Darjeeling with its massive outline. Its majestic form, in many ways, resembled a giant bookend for the eastern end of the Himalayan chain. The mountaineering expeditions that assembled in Darjeeling got their trekking permits there, if these were required. They recruited their *sherpas* and porters and obtained all their provisions there. It is no wonder that Darjeeling became a magnet for mountaineers and trekkers.

The dominant geographical feature in Darjeeling is known as Observatory Hill, which served as a powerful religious symbol for Hindus and Buddhists alike, drawing both groups to the Temple of Mahakal (originally built in 1782, now dedicated to the Hindu God Shiva) in a spirit of harmonious coexistence. A monastery existed on Observatory Hill in my time. Numerous other Buddhist monasteries and Hindu temples littered the hillsides in and around Darjeeling. Ghoom, located along the railway line about 18.5 miles before Darjeeling was the location of the famous "toy train" loop. Then, as now, the Darjeeling Himalayan Railway owned and operated the narrow gauge, or "toy train." The train gradually gained height as it climbed from the plains below Darjeeling by undergoing a series of zigzags and loops such as the one located in Ghoom. As the train chuffed its way up the mountain towards Darjeeling, passengers could see agricultural terraces that looked as if they had been sculpted by someone carving wedges from a side of roast beef. In many cases, the terraces reached from the bottom to the top of these hillsides. The well-known Sampten or Yiga Choeling Monastery with fifteen stunning images of the Maitreya Buddha (the coming Buddha) was also located in Ghoom. In the monastery, many ancient palm leaf and paper manuscripts were displayed in the Tibetan script.

One of my favourite activities in Darjeeling was to go to Tiger Hill to see the sun rise over the Himalayan mountain range. My abiding image of this glorious experience is of seeing the first rays of the sun hit the tops of the mountain peaks which, a moment before, had been bathed in a ghostly white. It was as if a candle were being lit. As the sun continued to rise, the colour of the mountains changed from pale white to blush pink to a deep red to a full bright white as the sun breasted the horizon completely. Even Everest was visible 99 miles away in the distance. The privilege of witnessing this event, reminds me of the poem, "Sunrise on the Hills," by Henry Wadsworth Longfellow:

> *I stood upon the hills, when heaven's wide arch*
> *Was glorious with the sun's returning march,*
> *And woods were brightened, and soft gales*
> *Went forth to kiss the sun-clad vales.*
> *The clouds were far beneath me....*[141]

1949/50 Expedition to Sikkim

During the period from November 1949 to early 1954, Dad made three expeditions into the Sikkim and Nepal region. For the 1949/50 expedition, he joined Trevor Braham as part of his trekking team. In 1952 he went to Sikkim with his own team, as was the case two years later in 1954, when he went to the Kangchenjunga region in Nepal. Since many mountaineering experiences are similar, I will only include here those occurrences that were specific to my father's treks. I should add that, although writing this account many years after these events took place, I am personally familiar with the natural landscapes and travel conditions that he confronted. In addition to my own experience in the Himalayan region, I also have available Dad's memorable photographic and film record of these trips. I have used all of this background information in creating the narrative that follows.[142]

After Mum and Dad returned to Calcutta from visiting me during *Durga Puja* in October 1948, Dad got in touch with Trevor Braham at the Himalayan Mountaineering Club. He indicated that he wanted to take

---

141 Henry Wadsworth Longfellow, "Sunrise on the Hills," 10.
142 The photographs and films, with my own commentary, have been restored, digitised, and lodged with Athabasca University. They are available at this university website: http://digiport.athabascau.ca/hruska/

up Trevor's offer to join him in the Sikkim trek, which was scheduled for November in the coming year. I wonder now whether Dad gave *any* consideration to the fact that I would be home for the holidays during this period and that he would be away in the mountains. Probably not, since the forthcoming trek was taking on a life of its own. After a year of preparations, including trying to get fit by playing tennis and going for long walks in the *Maidan*, Dad felt prepared for this challenge. The big adventure started early one morning in late October 1949.

I can imagine that, after he left our flat at 53 Chowringhee Road, Dad negotiated the usual marathon obstacle course through the streets of Calcutta as he made his way to the Sealdah Railway Station. The road struggled through endless randomly scattered houses and half-finished brick structures where one or two floors had been completed but whose yet-to-be-constructed roof still displayed an aerial farm of steel rods protruding from the building and reaching for the sky. Had the owners run out of money to complete these buildings, or did they dream of adding another floor some day? At every busy street crossing, a traffic policeman with a whistle in his mouth stood on a half sawn-off petrol drum in the middle of the crossing, attempting to manage traffic with his hand signals. Every so often, one of these traffic policemen descended from his petrol drum, either in despair, or to take a pee break by the side of the road, and smoke a *bidi* to calm himself down from all the chaos around him. More delay. On a good day, the trip to Sealdah Railway Station took 35 minutes to negotiate. Today it took 45 minutes. Finally, Dad arrived.

He made his way to the large information display to find out which platform the Siliguri Express would leave from at 8:42 p.m. Siliguri, about 370 miles from Calcutta, was the final destination for the train; it was situated in the foothills about 5,250 ft. above sea level. Dad engaged a railway porter to carry his luggage, which also included a pair of skis and poles, because he had plans to try some skiing on a Himalayan glacier.

The ticket examiner at the platform entrance gate looked at the skis and asked pensively, "Sir, what are these long planks of wood and these short bamboo sticks?"

"They are skis. I am going on a trekking expedition to Sikkim and I want to ski on some of the Himalayan glaciers."

"But sir. I am not understanding. What are you meaning with "ski"? I do not know this word. It is not normal luggage for train. It is some form of equipment, am I not correct?"

Dad looked at him and noticed his genuine confusion and replied, "These planks of wood, as you call them, are what we call skis. They are attached onto your mountain boots with a buckle and you can then slide on snow down the mountain doing turns and all sorts of other things. The shorter sticks, are called ski poles. You hold onto them with your hands in order to steer or guide yourself down the mountain."

"So, this is not normal hand luggage, I take it."

"No," replied Dad. "This will have to be placed with my other luggage in the storage or sleeping compartment of the train."

Other railway staff approached to examine these "planks" and, being satisfied, shook their heads back and forth and agreed, "*Acha* (Okay), it can be done." With this issue resolved, my father passed through the ticket gate onto the platform.

The Siliguri Express left Sealdah Station every night at about nine and took ten or eleven hours to get to Siliguri, arriving about 7 or 8 a.m. The arrival area outside the immediate station perimeter at Siliguri was situated in the countryside and was surrounded by a green carpet of grass and a few, small, scattered bushes. Here and there, water buffalo swished their tails over their backs, scattering the flies that irritated them. The coolness in the air was noticeable. Dad looked eagerly at the impressive foothills, hoping to see some mountains, but they were still hidden. After Dad had retrieved his luggage and skis, he found a taxi, negotiated a price and departed for Gangtok, about 70 miles away. The first part of the road trip took him through the lower reaches of the Terai forest where, sometimes, the traveler was lucky to catch a glimpse of tigers, leopards or wild elephants. I still remember that, one year, on the way to school in Darjeeling, I saw a leopard crossing the road.

The Gangtok road meandered through the foothills, with the Teesta river on its right for quite some time. Soon the taxi reached the winding road that clung closely to the side of the hill. The countryside changed dramatically. On one side of the road, there was an uninterrupted view falling away into the valley through which the Teesta ran. On some stretches of road, the taxi slowed because small groups of people squatting by the road-side were breaking up rocks into small stones with small hammers; this was the road repair crew, a common sight to this day. Three hours after crossing a bridge over the Teesta river, the taxi finally reached Rangpo, the India-Sikkim check-point, where border formalities were completed. After a short break, they reached Gangtok, some 24 miles away.

In Gangtok, Dad met up with Trevor Braham. In 1949, Sikkim was still an independent Himalayan kingdom run by the Namgyal royal family. Two other independent Himalayan kingdoms bordered Sikkim. Bhutan lay to the east and Nepal to the west. Tibet lay to the north. Sikkim had quite an interesting history. From the 9th to the end of the 18th century, it was a dependency of Tibet, and it was from Tibet that Buddhism had been introduced into the country. In the 17th century, Sikkim became a monarchy. Over the years, it endured many turbulent times with Bhutan and Nepal. After more political affrays with its neighbours, Sikkim became a British Protectorate in 1890. After India's Independence in 1947, the Bhutanese people rejected a move to join India formally, but Nehru even-tually established a special protectorate status for Sikkim and its people. In effect, Sikkim became an autonomous state except in the areas of foreign affairs, defence and communication.

The mist had already moved in from the valley as they arrived in Gangtok towards dusk. The noise of the day had abated, only interrupted by the sound of music that occasionally blurted out on a loudspeaker somewhere. Gangtok had a few "hotels" to choose from; so, when Dad and Trevor first saw their hotel room, it was a bit of a shock. The furniture was basic. The bed had no sheets and some of its cross section wooden planks were missing. Deciding that the floor would likely offer more comfort, Dad unrolled his sleeping bag. The evening had become quite cold. Fortunately, the hotel room had a log-fueled fireplace. In the morning, the fire had long since died out and the cold air inside the room felt bitingly crisp. Nevertheless, the view outside heralded a clear day. In the distance, the mountains presented a beautiful sharp outline against the sky.

At this early hour, life stirred on the main road. The shopkeepers were already busy. They had removed the shutters from their windows and drawn back the curtains or protective cloth from their displays. The vegetable sellers had already mapped out their turf with their underlay cloth or cardboard and laid out their produce. Soon the pavement took on the appearance of a Persian carpet with the confused colours and shapes of all the vegetables and fruit spread out everywhere; the vendors held out their chosen items for customers to try and hopefully buy. The housewives of Gangtok moved between these pavement displays, checking the freshness of the vegetables prior to any purchase.

The houses of Gangtok sprawled down along the line of the hill slope. The houses were built so close on one another that it seemed that a person emerging from one house was but a stepping-stone from the roof of another house. It was clearly a Buddhist community. Scattered throughout the town were a myriad of prayer flags attached to large bamboo poles. When the wind blew, they resembled a forest of underwater sea weed. As the prayer flags fluttered to and fro, they sent their earnest tranquil messages to the heavens and hopefully brought calm to their supplicants. The mist usually clouded the town in the mornings but this soon cleared, opening up more glorious views of the mountains.

In Gangtok, Trevor Braham and Dad made their preparations to go on trek. They met up with the famous *Sherpa*, Ang Tharkay, who had assembled a team of four other *sherpas*. Ang Tharkay was one of the most experienced and capable *sherpas* of his time. He had gained a reputation as an exceptional *sirdar* (leader), a manager of the *sherpas* who accompanied expeditions. Ang Tharkay had climbed with Eric Shipton, H. W. Tilman, Maurice Herzog, Gaston Rebuffat, Lionel Lachenal, and others, all of whom were pioneering giants of Himalayan mountaineering in the early twentieth century. He had been on Kangchenjunga in 1931. He had also climbed on Everest in 1933, 1935, and 1938. He had been on Nanda Devi in 1934, and K2 in Pakistan in 1937. Ang Tharkay, both as a climber and as a person, had earned himself high praise from all who knew him. Later, he became famous when, on Annapurna, a 26,250 ft. peak, he carried a very badly frost-bitten, French climber, Gaston Rebuffat, on his shoulders from a high-altitude camp to base camp. With Ang Tharkay's help, Dad and Trevor spent the next few days in Gangtok buying non-perishable items of food like rice and flour. They also made arrangements to hire some mountain pack ponies to carry all their gear.[143]

The path was not always clear, so Trevor and Dad often had to clamber over large rocks or the odd tree that had fallen over. But the trek had been strangely beautiful, as they were accompanied by the sounds of birds in the branches above. On occasion, the sunlight broke through the tree canopy illuminating the colourful plumage of those birds. As the trekkers started to gain some altitude, the forest began to thin and, when they entered a clearing, they saw a mountain range in the distance, forming what appeared to be the serrated edge of a saw.

Dad and Trevor now followed the path along the Teesta River. For much of the route, no identifiable trails were evident, so they had to move along sections of the river on make-shift bamboo bridges that were attached to the cliffsides abutting the river. Ang Tharkay carried Dad's skis, so moving along these bridges was quite a challenge for him. When crossing rivers, they sometimes found better-constructed bridges with improvised bamboo handrails. Other times, the team crossed the watercourses like circus tight-rope walkers on two logs strapped together. The early going at altitudes between 2,000 and 7,200 ft. proved difficult, which slowed their progress. Often, they encountered a wet trail, redolent of decaying trees, bushes and leaves, skirting small waterfalls and streams. At night, they stayed in the guest houses at Dikchu, Singhik and Chungtang. One of the wonderful features of staying at these resthouses was that they were looked after by *chowkidars* (caretakers) who were very friendly and hospitable; these caretakers took so much pride in their resthouses that they cultivated beautiful little flower beds to decorate the sides of the building. Any positive comment on their gardens brought a proud smile.

Near the guest houses were small groups of inhabited huts. Here, Dad saw his first yaks and learnt quickly to keep a respectful distance from these unpredictable animals. At the back of some huts, Dad found a few yaks tethered to a makeshift rail. It turned out that this would be the source of his fresh milk. He noticed some men squatting by the yaks yanking at

143 This team can be seen in my father's 1949/50 film, which can be found on his mountaineering website: http://digiport.athabascau.ca/hruska/

something that was hidden in a forest of hair and out of which emerged a jet of milk liberally sprinkled with torn, thickly-matted, yak hair. Dad tried yak milk but I still remember him saying that you could only drink it after you had extracted all the yak hair from the liquid. The locals used yak milk to make yak butter and a cheese called *chhurpi*. A spoonful of yak butter was regularly added to a cup of tea as a taste enhancer. All I can say from my own experience is that, if you enjoy drinking tea with a slimy, oily surface on top, then yak tea is for you. Tibetans and Nepalese consume yak butter tea in large quantities. But yak butter also has other uses, whether in festivities, as fuel in lamps, or when carved into religious sculptures.

As Dad surveyed the village, he noticed women standing in the entrances of their homes as they looked curiously at the new arrivals in their community. Shy children wrapped their arms around the legs of their mothers against a noisy backdrop of barking, mangy dogs running aimlessly around. Dad was offered a cup of *marwa* (a local brew made from fermented millet seeds). He said that it tasted a bit like cider that had passed through an unwashed sock. But it had the kick of a mule and it definitely lifted his tired spirits and relieved his aching muscles.

As Dad and Trevor pressed on, the well-worn and well-known trekking trails all but disappeared. The terrain was rough, especially near river beds. Soon the expedition reached a place where the Lachung and Lachen rivers merged to form Sikkim's main river, the Teesta. This junction was known in the local dialect as the "Meadow of Marriage," because of its scenic beauty. From this spot, the expedition members could see the Kangchenjunga massif in the distance. Dad always mentioned that the great pleasures of trekking were the omnipresent views of the wonderful mountains, as well as the hills and forests he was walking through and those that beckoned from a distance. At a place called Chungthang, they veered to the east so that they could follow the Lachung River, which was fed by the melt from the Khangkyong glacier located directly to the north. Dad was planning to try skiing on this glacier. They camped at the *chowkidar's* hut at Lachung.

Shortly after they left Lachung, they turned further east and followed the Sebo river that bisected the Sebo Valley. They were now about 9 miles from the Khangkyong glacier. They camped at Dombang, where they encountered some locals who grew and harvested medicinal plants. In this region, rhododendrons and juniper grew in great profusion. Dad often mentioned that one of the other great joys of trekking in the Himalayas was walking on a hillside under a forest canopy of rhododendrons. It seemed like he was walking under a suspended, scarlet carpet.

Soon they reached the glacier, made their camp there, and rested before they started to explore. Trevor Braham was very interested in this unknown area and wanted to examine possibilities for further routes both to the north and west. Various small groupings of mountain peaks surrounded their campsite. Over the course of the next three or four days, the trekkers made little forays into and up over this glacier and ice-fall region. Some sections of the route proved to be steep and difficult and required some measure of climbing skill. They climbed at an altitude of about 15,000 ft. This was a new challenge for Dad, as it was his first, real, high altitude, climbing experience. Unfortunately, he was starting to exhibit the early signs of altitude sickness. He was becoming increasingly lethargic and found it difficult to hold down food and water. Despite this setback, Dad persevered. The sight of many majestic mountain peaks like Pauhunri (23,000 ft.) and other unnamed peaks ranging in height from 21,600 to 23,000 ft. were a relieving balm to any feelings of discomfort.

They struck camp in this region and investigated the surrounding area to ascertain the best route to proceed further. A few visible mountain passes loomed on the horizon. However, any serious approach for a crossing required a survey, which would tell them if that approach were at all possible. There had been virtually no expeditions of note into this area and images shown on the available maps did not necessarily match the terrain they saw before them. Many of the maps showed a "cloud" in the area with a comment such as "Believed to be eight peaks in the area."

Their movement over this glaciated region was made even more difficult by the changeable daily snow conditions. On some days, they trekked over soft snow. On other days, they encountered hard snow. They struck their next camp at an altitude of about 16,400 ft., which gave them another staggering view of the amphitheatre surrounding the glacier and Jongsong Peak, Tent Peak, Nepal Peak, Kangchenjunga, and Kabru to the west. Close by, they saw the striking profile of Chombu. I remember Dad telling us how they spent time surveying and enjoying this beautiful mountain, coming to the conclusion that it probably could not be climbed with the equipment available at the time. This part of Sikkim had been visited by very few westerners, so they felt extremely privileged to see both the known and uncharted peaks. I truly believe that Dad's ongoing love affair with this part of the world was cemented during these days.

As they descended to the lower reaches of the glacier and with less danger presented by crevasses, Dad decided to put on his skis and try his skill on its surface. Trevor Braham, in his book, *Himalayan Odyssey*, writes, "As he glided smoothly, noiselessly down the long slopes the *sherpas'* reaction had been first one of amusement then of envy" (56). It must have been quite a sight as he descended, with his skis making turns in the pristine snow against the backdrop of the impressive mountains to the west. After Dad completed his skiing experiment, they moved on and reached the bottom of the glacier where dangerous crevasses began to appear. The party roped themselves up to cross the difficult terrain. At the end of this day, they struck camp in a region with small lakes and some scrub, prior to making for the hamlet of Mome Sandong the next day. However, it was here that Dad's health took a turn for the worse. He found it hard to cope with altitude sickness; his condition worsened and he became seriously dehydrated. Nevertheless, he decided to continue to their next objective, namely, the mountains of Chomiomo (22,400 ft.) and Kangchenjau (22,600 ft.). I mention these two mountains here, as they were to become the main climbing objectives for his later expedition to Sikkim.

They followed the Jakthang Valley to get to Mome Sandong, and tried to overnight in two Himalayan Club huts but these had fallen into disrepair and were unusable. Further down the Lachung Valley, they kept close to the Lachung River and passed through the little settlement at Yumathang. This place is etched in my memory. Every time we saw the movie of this trek, Dad always mentioned that this "....was one of the most beautiful valleys he had ever seen...." with the rhododendron-draped hillsides and the mountains providing a backdrop behind. There is no doubt that, with this initial experience, his appetite for trekking had been well and truly whetted. I am sure that he had already started making plans for his next expedition. It was here at Yumathang that Dad finally decided to abandon the trek due to his worsening altitude illness and, with the assistance of a *sherpa,* made it back to Gangtok, Darjeeling, and eventually Calcutta.

1950: Second Visit to Czechoslovakia

After the shortened visit to Czechoslovakia in 1948, Mum keenly wanted to go back to see her family. In 1946, while she was in India, her father had died of tuberculosis. She felt badly that she had not been able to see him again while he was still alive. So, she was determined this time to take clothes and other articles to give to both sides of the family to help them through very difficult times. In January 1950, when I was nine years old, Mum and I left for Czechoslovakia; we travelled first to Vienna, and then caught the train to Otrokovice where my Uncle Noris and Aunt Boženka met us. We stayed at Loučka for the first two weeks. I remember this visit well because, in Loučka, I spent a lot of my time on the upper level of the barn where the rabbits resided. Once I fell asleep holding one of the rabbits that Babi bred for the dining table; sadly, I suffocated it as I apparently hugged the poor thing to death. Today, whenever I visit my remaining relatives in Loučka, they still remind me of this unfortunate event. But, even more than the death of the little rabbit, I remember the wrath of Babi and her capacity for some pretty colourful language that would have surprised even Dad.

Mum really enjoyed this visit, as she got reacquainted with her mother, brothers, and sisters. And I got to meet the rest of Mum's scattered Czech family for the first time. After Loučka, we went for a week's skiing to Vrbno pod Pradědem, located nearby; this was where I was first introduced to skiing and, for that matter, actual snow. The family photos of this visit attest to my earliest exploits on skis, but Mum commented that I seemed to be a fish out of water. After Vrbno, we stayed with Uncle Noris in Otrokovice. Whenever we went to Czechoslovakia, the centre of activity revolved around Uncle Noris. He was my mother's oldest brother, the second born and the self-designated "Patriarch" of the family. He had a very small apartment and I remember that the sleeping arrangements were challenging. I camped on a mattress on the floor in the lounge. Mum got the couch. The room was so small that it resembled a "mattress" camp at night.

This visit was, in many ways, a trial run to see how easy it would be to travel to the country in the future. My mother also wanted to gauge how the family had managed during all the turbulence of the war years and the political upheavals leading to the communist takeover. In addition, she was interested to ascertain what sort of life they had under the Communists. During this visit, she realized that her family and Dad's would need a lot of help in the coming years. Since some of the family were Communist Party members and some were not, Uncle Noris made it very clear that we had to be careful about being too open in expressing our personal views of life under the communist system. This was because we did not know if we would be reported to the authorities. Any such disclosure would have made life difficult for many. At nine years of age, I was too young to understand any of this, but Mum fell in line with this caution and agreed that the only place where open discussion was possible was within the four walls of Uncle Noris' apartment. We departed in mid-February to return to Calcutta, since I had to get ready to go back to boarding school in Darjeeling.

Communal Violence and Departure of Shahadat Khan

After Dad's return from Sikkim, he had to face another emerging problem in the early growth of the factory. The post-independence period in India witnessed many refugee migrations between India and East and West Pakistan. After the Partition of 1947, over 250,000 people sought refuge in Bengal alone from East Pakistan. This torrent of people continued to increase, with a further 600,000 (1948) and 182,000 (1949) people moving to Bengal.[144] The reasons for these migrations were many, but both the Hindus and Muslims felt that they had become strangers in their country pre-partition; in the post-partition period, many felt increasingly disenfranchised. In those areas of the country where they were the minority, each group had encountered not only shrinking public sympathy, but harassment, persecution, and religious intolerance by the prevailing majority.

---

144 Sukanta Chaudhuri, ed., *Calcutta, the Living City. Vol II: The Present and the Future*, 72-73.

Many refugees had pre-partition ties with both Calcutta and Dacca in East Pakistan. In December 1949, there was an outbreak of violence in Khulna,[145] the third largest city in East Pakistan, which rapidly spread countrywide and set off a new migration of refugees between Bengal and East Pakistan. This had then sparked yet another round of reprisal violence against Muslims in Calcutta. Since Independence, there had remained a terrible climate of fear for Muslims in the city. Even though all of these events were of peripheral interest to Dad at the time, he hired many Muslims in his young company, and this unrest and violence caused them to fear for the safety of their families and themselves. Many of these workmen were experienced toolmakers, including Dad's partner, Shahadat Khan, who decided to leave Calcutta in mid-1950 and join the exodus to Dacca and East Pakistan, where they felt that they would be safer. The loss of Shahadat Khan was a major blow for Dad; it effectively brought to an end the long friendship based on mutual respect that had started at Metal Box. The problem was exacerbated when Shahadat encouraged many young, experienced, Muslim tool-makers to go with him to Dacca.

As if the artificial magnification of religious and cultural differences was not enough to unsettle the city, the sheer number of refugees made things even worse. There was a veritable flood of people from East Pakistan into Calcutta; this caused huge problems for the city, including overcrowding, a further proliferation of slum areas, a breakdown of the already outdated and inefficient sanitary infrastructure, lack of food and clean water, and the corresponding problems associated with disease and crime.[146] These were difficult times for Mum and Dad. Dad had to recruit Hindu workers and train them; otherwise, the factory would have had to close. I believe that it was during this period that Dad decided to take on more Hindus than Muslims because of his previous experiences with social and religious strife. Somehow, the factory continued to operate and produce lanterns and Dad kept his dealer network happy. It is mere conjecture on my part, but the survival of the factory must have created its own tensions in my parents' daily lives. Even so, I am sure that Mum played her part to provide

145 Ibid., 73.
146 Ibid., 142-143.

the necessary moral support for Dad during this period. It could not have been lost on them that they were living in a political tinderbox with all the religious and political differences at play.

The Great Tibet-Assam Earthquake of 15 August, 1950, at 2:09 p.m.

On Tuesday, 15 August, we were at school in Darjeeling sitting down at our desks in the main study area when, at 2:09 p.m., all the seats and desks started to shake violently from an invisible force. None of us knew what was happening but the Jesuits ordered us outside immediately into the large, open quadrangle.

What we had just experienced was one of the largest earthquakes ever to hit the region. The epicentre of the earthquake was at a town called Tajobum in Arunchal Pradesh, a state in the north-eastern part of India, east of Darjeeling. The strength of the earthquake measured 8.7 on the Richter scale, very powerful. At the time, it was the sixth largest earthquake of the century. The quake affected the border regions with China, caused over 1,000 fatalities and was felt throughout north-east India, Sikkim, Bhutan, East Pakistan, Burma, and as far away as Calcutta.

I mention this earthquake at this juncture, since it played a role in Dad's subsequent trek to Sikkim planned for November in 1952.

Mum's First Mental Breakdown

It is not possible for me at this distance in time to ascertain whether Mum's first mental breakdown in April 1951 was the result of an acute emotional, physical, or psychological collapse. But the anecdotal evidence suggests that Mum became unable to function in a social context, likely suffering from acute depression. How and when the symptoms of a mental breakdown (weakness, uncontrollable crying, confusion, feelings of worthlessness, disorientation, loss of self-esteem, sleep problems, guilt feelings, despair and tiredness) manifested themselves, I don't know. I was ten years old and away at school much of the year. All I do know is that the situation became so serious that our family doctor, Dr. Ronald, felt that her condition was best treated away from Calcutta, since the circumstances of living in the city during the aftermath of war and of having to stay in India separated by half a world from her family were obviously weighing her down. In addition, her personal life must have been difficult, with one of her children away most of the year in boarding school and only the comfort of a six-year-old at home. Finally, with my father at the factory most of the time, she may also have felt it even more difficult to cope on her own. What is more, I discovered in recent years that there was a significant history of depression and suicide amongst her siblings. In any event, whatever the causes, in those days and in that place, no professional support existed in Calcutta for her.

Dr. Ronald had a good friend who lived in Switzerland and, after they discussed Mum's situation, he recommended to Dad that she go to Geneva to be under the care of Dr. Edwige Fatzer. Dad arranged for Mum to travel to Geneva immediately. After assessing her, Dr. Fatzer felt that the best treatment would be in a sanatorium that a good friend and colleague managed and where they had been using a radical method of therapy: electro-shock to the brain.

Prior to Mum's breakdown, Dad's business was always on his mind and he had become completely pre-occupied with its growth. With this success, I believe that there came a sense of entitlement and, possibly, a need for some self-indulgence or a feeling of "I have earned this!" He had, after all, gone on a trek to Sikkim in 1949/50 at the very time that the whole family should have been together from November to January. With this feeling of entitlement came neglect of his family. Whether he ever perceived the consequences of his actions, I cannot tell. Mum, however, had a real feeling of disengagement from Dad, since she had accepted the responsibility of caring for the children and the running of the household alone. This was a situation that was not enough to sustain her emotional and personal needs, and led, I believe, to a feeling of abandonment.

As Dad's business success fueled his sense of importance, he felt that he got his recognition - business success, money, adventure - from the surrounding society of Calcutta and not from his family. There had always been a tendency for Dad to make the family decisions without discussion or consultation. We were a very Dad-centric family. After all, why should a self-made man who had taken risks and succeeded on a business level take advice from anybody, whether about business or about personal matters?

I remember the effect it had on the rest of us quite well. When I returned for the Christmas holidays from Darjeeling, he would be off trekking and therefore absent for the first six weeks of my long school holiday - that is, for most of it. I have often wondered if he ever realised how this affected us, especially Mum, who had to look after a very young Martina and a boy who, since the age of six, had hardly ever seen his father, aside from a short time over the Christmas and New Year breaks. He probably did not anticipate or sense the increasing degree of alienation between himself, Mum, and the children.

In many ways, he was a man of this colonial generation, feeling that having a family and taking care of them amounted to ensuring that their living and material needs were taken care of. I do not believe that he thought further than that. His son and daughter were getting the best education that he could afford. He believed that Mum's needs were being met by his providing financial security for her and the children. Her personal needs were being met by the small coterie of friends that they had. And, after all, her life was a mirror of the lives of the British expatriate wives. In this context, he could concentrate on his business and look after its success. I think my father considered himself a good father to us and a good husband to Mum. But their personal relationship was beginning to unravel. Dad was only too willing to accept the model of English colonial family life. But his family roots, as well as Mum's, had been much, much simpler and she could not accommodate or indeed believe in this colonial model of living and caring. This alien form of family life, when she contrasted it with what she had had in Czechoslovakia, still seemed very strange to her and it caused all sorts of tensions that became destructive for what should have been a happy Czech family. The growing unhappiness that my mother felt started to build up and eventually the gates of her personal dam broke and she suffered her breakdown.

Dr. Forel and the Psychiatric Facilities at Prangins

Based on the recommendations of Dr. Fatzer, Mum became a patient of Dr. Oscar Forel, who was a very distinguished psychiatrist in Switzerland. Dr. Forel was the son of a renowned brain surgeon, Dr. Auguste Forel, and had spent most of his life as a practising psychiatrist. He had also founded the psychiatric clinic at Les Rives de Prangins. The clinic, located in a huge park area of 37 acres, is situated in a pristine location facing Lake Geneva and has spectacular views of the Alps. After her arrival in Geneva, Mum went directly to the clinic to undergo her psychiatric rehabilitation. There is some indication that Mum may have been subjected to electro-shock treatment but the details are conflicting and very sketchy. Dr. Forel mentioned to me when we visited him at his home at St. Prex on Lake Geneva, that they had to use electro-stimulation but the context may have had more to do with a revival of her heart than a specific therapy application. No one can now say for sure which therapy was practised; but, after about two months in Switzerland, the clinic released Mum and allowed her to return to Calcutta in June.

1951: Family Skiing Holiday in Austria

After Mum returned to Calcutta in mid-1951 and, while she was still recovering from her treatment in Switzerland, Dad decided that the family should all have a skiing holiday later that year. We would go to St. Anton in the Arlberg region of Austria. With his background as a champion skier, he wanted Martina and me to learn to ski. We left just after Christmas and flew to Zurich, where we caught the Arlberg Express heading for St. Anton. I was eleven years old and can still remember the excitement as we got into our compartment, pulled down the window and watched the imposing alpine countryside rolling through Switzerland and Austria. At Bludenz in Austria, we got our first view of the snow-covered Arlberg mountains. Langen was the next stop. Soon we entered the 6.5-mile-long Arlberg tunnel; the next stop was St. Anton station, immediately after the exit from the tunnel. Travelling through the tunnel seemed to take an eternity but, once we emerged and saw the mountains, our spirits lifted. St. Anton was to be our home for the next seven weeks.

Directly adjacent to the station stood the only large hotel in the village, the *Hotel Post*, which dominated the landscape. After registering, we got our rooms, threw open the windows and looked out onto our own winter wonderland. St. Anton had a sprinkling of alpine style houses and a few smaller pensions scattered throughout the village. On one side of the railway track, the full extent of the impressive ski terrain opened up, together with the only cable car and two or three smaller T-bar ski lifts. On the other side of the hotel, a narrow strip of land bordered a small mountain stream and led directly to the steep sides of a heavily forested mountain. My parents had their own room and Martina and I shared another. We all wondered what to expect from St. Anton. We knew that, in the morning, we would get outfitted for skiing and enroll in the famous (at that time) Arlberg ski school, which taught the Arlberg ski technique.

In 1951, St. Anton was a relatively small ski resort and not as well-known as the famous Swiss ski resorts, like Davos and St. Moritz. With the advent and development of alpine ski teaching techniques, St. Anton became, in many ways, a winter secret waiting to be discovered. Nothing at this time indicated that it would later acquire the outstanding reputation it now has as a winter sports centre. When we were there, Hannes Schneider already lived in the United States, having moved there in 1939. He had become one of the foremost figures involved in the development of Arlberg alpine ski techniques not only in Austria, but in North America as well.

Skiing in St. Anton started with peasants and farmers using all sorts of boards and planks of wood and poles to slide down the mountains. By 1900, proper skis, albeit crude and simple, but serving their function of sliding, were already in use. In the Tyrol region of Austria, where St. Anton is located, ski clubs were being formed. Skiing as a sport really took off with the advent of the railroad. Hannes Schneider had originally been a mountain guide and ski instructor associated with the *Gasthof* (Guest House) *Post* and developed the first systematic method of ski instruction, including the teaching of various manoeuvres such as the snow plough and parallel turns.

Thus, at the wonderfully impressionable ages of six and eleven, Martina and I enrolled in the famous Arlberg Ski School and started to learn how to ski. The skiing mystique enveloped us at this early age, starting with our snow ploughs, "bend ze knees," "schussing," and "stem Christies." Moving between the ski lifts, the Galzig cable car station and Nasserein ski lift became second nature to us. All I remember of this peaceful time was the wonderful harmony and closeness that finally existed in our little family circle. St. Anton, this wonderful ski village, had woven its magic on us. At times, we felt that we had become part of the local community. Everybody had a *"Grüß Gott"* welcome in the morning and the shopkeepers who knew us waved as we walked through the village.

Dad had his own surprise. He found out that the director of the Arlberg Ski School was none other than Rudi Matt, the legendary Austrian skier in the pre-war days and against whom Dad had raced at Innsbruck in the 1936 Alpine World Ski Championships.

The *Hotel Post* was a family-run, friendly hotel and we all loved staying there. I believe that Walter Schuler owned the hotel. We all became quite friendly with him and often, after a day's skiing, Martina and I took his cocker spaniels for a walk through the nearby forest on the other side of the river. We also got to know some of our ski instructors quite well. Three of them became friends. The names of Rudi Draxl, Otto Schneider and Johann Fahrner come to mind. Martina and I made rapid progress with our skiing and gradually moved up through the classes. Towards the end of our stay, I even got promoted into the men's class; I am not sure what Dad made of this development. Mum skied with a private ski instructor now and then; and often, after a break from formal lessons, the family would ski together.

1952 Expedition to Sikkim

In November 1952, Dad made his second expedition into Sikkim. His first experience had been enjoyable despite his having to depart early due to altitude sickness. He had been fortunate to have made his first trek with such an experienced mountaineer as Trevor Braham. Dad now had a much better appreciation of how he needed to prepare for one of these treks. He had a whole year to get ready. This time, he had set himself the goal of climbing a minor peak, namely Mt. Kangchenjau, in northern Sikkim.

He left in mid-November, but this time he left his skis behind. He flew to Bagdogra in a Dakota DC-3 for what seemed an eternity, across the endless, yellowish-brown, rice fields that dotted the landscape of Bengal. The DC-3 seemed to fly from one scattered cloud bank to the next. Then the plane began to lose altitude and, from his window, he could see the first outline of the forested foothills.

He then made his way to Darjeeling by taxi. He bought a few provisions for the trek in Darjeeling and then went by bus to Gangtok along the same route taken in 1949. In Gangkok, he assembled a small group of six *sherpas* to accompany him; but, this time, his trekking team included two *sherpanis* (women *sherpas*), who were expected to carry the same loads and do the same work as their male counterparts. Taking *sherpanis* on a trek turned out to be a masterstroke, as they more than held their own against the men, and they brought some unique additional skills to the trekking team. In the first place, they were better cooks than the other *sherpas*; but they could also repair clothing, including climbing boots; they could negotiate better with the travelling Tibetan herders when they needed to supplement their provisions; and they always had a cheerful disposition: never complained and just went about their work.

In the early stages of the trek, Dad retraced the route from 1949, making his way to Lachung and camping again at the *chowkidar's* (watchman's) hut. From Lachung, they did not go to the east but instead went straight north along the Lachung *Chu* in one of the "most beautiful valleys" (Dad's own words) to Yumathang and then on to Mome Samdong. On 15 August, just 3 months earlier, the area had been hit by the great Tibet-Assam earthquake that had devastated the region. The icefall on the lower portion of Chombu mountain 20,875 ft. had fed the Sebu *Cho*. During the earthquake, a large portion of this icefall collapsed, sending great chunks of mountain and ice into the Sebo Cho causing the lake to burst and empty its contents. The released waters from the lake formed a tidal wave that had swept everything in its path and caused severe damage down the whole valley. This wall of water had been responsible for destroying half of Lachung village and had swept away many suspension bridges that crossed the Lachung Chu. The route from Lachung to Mome Sandong was therefore now quite difficult and Dad had to find his way over boulders and moraine debris. River crossings that had been previously quite challenging had to be treated with extreme caution as they were now very hazardous. They camped near Mome Sandong at a site close to a few scattered small lakes but near scrub and juniper wood, which they burnt not only for cooking, but also to provide warmth. The Himalayan Club had built small mountain huts in various locations, but the hut at Mome Sandong lay in ruins, and was totally unusable. The surrounding area did not leave much available room for cultivation. There were a few potato fields nearby, together with a small number of unherded yaks and goats.

This time they reached the Sebu La Pass 17,560 ft., where they got a close-up view of Mt. Kanchenjau 22,700 ft. and all its challenges on the later, planned ascent. Crossing this pass proved to be hazardous due to the state of the ice underfoot and they all had to use crampons. Dad noted that many of the approaches on the mountains appeared to resemble "blue" ice and he had serious doubts that crampons would even make any impression on it; so, he prudently decided to give up his attempt to climb Mt. Kanchenjau, feeling that it would be far too dangerous. He was disappointed but he was a realist. From Sebu La Pass, looking north, Dad told me that the scene was unlike anything he had ever seen. The light here was very bright and the enveloping cold air felt like a sharp knife on the cheek; not a sound could be heard anywhere. From this spot, he had a clear unhindered view towards the Tibetan plateau. As they rested near their tents, enjoying a cup of tea laced with Dad's favourite mountain medicine, brandy, he again looked in absolute awe across the valley of Mt. Kangchenjunga 28,170 ft. to the southwest.

The next morning, they trekked into new territory, occasionally meeting Tibetan herders. On one occasion, these herders were very happy to sell Dad half a side of sheep to replenish his provisions. That evening they all feasted well on the spit-roasted sheep. They then explored the many areas in the vicinity of Kangchenjunga and its glacier.

From here they returned to Darjeeling where the members of the expedition disbanded. Then Dad made his way back to Bagdogra. The engines of the Dakota DC-3 clicked over once, twice, three times before they spluttered into life in a white cloud of engine smoke. The flight lasted two and a half hours. Shortly before landing at Dum Dum Airport in Calcutta, Dad noticed streaks of rain running across the window. A torrential downpour had hit the city. The plane landed and bumped into the numerous pools of water on the uneven runway. The passengers alighted and ran from the rear steps to the entrance gate of the airport. They were drenched. He picked up his ruck sack and looked out over the heads of the bustling crowd, seeking Phul Mohammed, his driver. They made contact and soon he was leaving the perimeter of the airport, on a rain-drenched road, home to Chowringhee Road.

Jammu/Kashmir Visit

In January 1952, Dad was planning a business trip to visit his friend, Bobal, who lived in Pathankhot, near Gulmarg, Kashmir. Dad originally planned to meet with Bobal, conclude their business, and then fly with me on to Srinagar and Gulmarg, where we would spend a week doing a bit of sightseeing. In particular, he wanted very much to visit Gulmarg with me.

Unfortunately, after we left Bobal, the weather worsened and it started to rain heavily and incessantly, causing severe flooding in Srinagar. The airports at Jammu and Srinagar were closed indefinitely. We spent a week in Jammu cooped up in an awful hotel waiting for the weather to break. We could not even fly out to Delhi due to the rain and low cloud cover that made flying with a DC-3 very hazardous.

Cooped up inside the hotel as we were, we did not appreciate the historical significance of Jammu as much as we might have. We did not know, for example, that Jammu had featured in the ancient Indian saga, *The Mahabharata*. About 12 miles from Jammu at a place called Akhnoor, there were excavations that suggested a link with the great Harappan civilization. At Akhnoor, remains from the Maurya, Kushanshah, and Gupta periods have been found. Jammu also featured in the stories of Timur or Tamerlane - a 14th century conqueror from Mongolia - and his campaigns in Central Asia. All around us were places of great historical interest and we were blissfully ignorant of them while we waited for the weather to improve.

So, what promised to be an interesting visit to Kashmir ended up in disaster; eventually we managed to get out and fly back to Calcutta. Dad was extremely disappointed, as he had wanted so much to get to Gulmarg and show me the scene of his skiing triumph in the Ski Championship of India. But I was not as disappointed as he since, for once, I had actually managed to spend time with him.

Last Year at North Point

Dad and Mum became good friends with Gerrit van der Griendt and his wife Inge over time and, in the course of their friendship, Gerrit suggested to Dad that he take out an educational insurance policy, just in case Mum and Dad decided that my future education needs could not be totally satisfied through North Point. I later discovered that they took out this policy with the thought that I might want to go on to university in Europe. The concern was that any degree obtained in India would not have been accepted at face value outside the country. Furthermore, they wanted to make sure that my command of English was as good as possible. This led my parents to explore boarding school options outside India. But where?

Father Stanford, a Canadian, was the rector of North Point in 1953/54 and Dad asked him if he had any suggestions about boarding school options abroad. Father Stanford mentioned that he was familiar with a Catholic boarding school in Lancashire, England, called Stonyhurst, and it just happened that the present rector, Father Vavasour, was a personal friend of his. Father Stanford approached Father Vavasour to ascertain whether it would be possible to take me and, after Dad had satisfied himself that the insurance policy would pay for the annual fees for the next five years, he made a formal application to Stonyhurst on my behalf. The school's only stipulation at the time was that I needed to wait for one year; during this time, they wanted me to do the common entrance examination. If successful, I would then have a place.

Stonyhurst advised the addresses of colleges in Europe that catered for this bridging year and suggested that I spend the time at Aiglon College in Villars-sur-Ollon situated in the beautiful French-speaking part of Switzerland near Lake Geneva. Villars also just happened to be a ski resort. I enrolled at Aiglon in anticipation of sitting the entrance examination at year's end. Fortunately, after a year in this Swiss college, I duly passed these examinations, met all the requirements of the college, and was then offered a place at Stonyhurst starting mid 1954. So, this fortuitous insurance policy paid off handsomely for Dad. As for me, I had the dubious fortune of going, yet again, to another boarding school. The long summer holidays at Stonyhurst were from July to mid-September and Dad said I could come back to Calcutta for these holidays. But it didn't always turn out that way.

1954 Last Expedition to Kangchenjunga

In October 1954, Dad made his third expedition to the Himalayas but his first into Nepal. This part of Nepal is sparsely inhabited. His expedition started again in the cloying heat of Sealdah Station, surrounded by hundreds of people in their old, faded dhotis, sweating profusely, while waiting for the announcement of the departure of the Calcutta-Siliguri Express.

He stayed a few days in Darjeeling, using the time to assemble his trekking team and buy all the supplies that he needed. After they had completed their arrangements, he and his team left Darjeeling, making their way into the Kangchenjunga region via Sandakphu through the bamboo glades and the rhododendron forests.

Here he trekked through numerous valleys and passed through small villages where a few Bhutia families farmed and tended their yaks, sheep and goats, and grew potatoes. Always there was the ever-friendly *chowkidar's* house where they camped and restocked their supplies. They went into numerous glaciers, the massive mountain peaks acknowledging their presence. They got as close as possible to Kangchenjunga and Jannu. They even managed to trek north to the Tibetan border via Lhonak. From Lhonak, they turned north into the Lhonak glacier, made a small detour into the Tsisinla glacier, and trekked to the base of Janak Chuli 23,260 ft. (previously called Outlier Peak), where they established a campsite at a small lake. From here, they had spectacular close-up views of Drohmo Peak 22,470 ft. and the Kangchenjunga massif to the south-east. After this detour, they returned to the Lhonak Glacier and continued north to the Tibetan border, where they saw Nupchu 19,800 ft. to the south-west and Lashar Peak 22,730 ft. to the north.

They returned down the Lhonak Glacier to Kambachen and made their way to the Jannu Glacier where they had extraordinarily spectacular, close-up views of Jannu 25,300 ft. and Mt. Sharpu 23,200 ft. After some time spent on the Jannu glacier, they returned to Ghunsa, and Darjeeling via the Yamatari Glacier, Phalut, and Sandakphu. Then it was time to return home to Calcutta.

1955: Family Skiing Holiday in Austria

I believe that the failed visit to Gulmarg in 1952 may have been the catalyst for another skiing holiday *en famille* in St. Anton. Our previous holiday there had left all of us with many warm feelings about the place and so we went again and stayed in the *Hotel Post*. I am not sure what the St. Anton locals thought, but I heard some murmurs amongst the staff about this "Czech Maharajah" from India who brings his family for six weeks to Europe to ski. No one in Europe, apart from the really well to do would even consider a six-week skiing holiday. Mr. Walter Schuler, who owned the *Hotel Post*, again gave us excellent rooms. I remember once going to pay the hotel's weekly bill with travellers' cheques for only 70 English pounds per week for a family of four, accommodation and full board. When I think back on this time, I shake my head in disbelief, but skiing holidays were not so popular then in Europe as they are now. Also, Europe was still recovering from the aftermath of the War and many people had not yet re-established themselves financially after its ravages.

There were a few changes evident in St. Anton. More pensions and small hotels had been built to boost the village's accommodations. A new, large, triple chair lift had been built to carry skiers up to Gampen; this lift had opened up a whole new and challenging ski terrain. But St. Anton was still a long, sprawling village with traditional Tyrolean style houses hugging a narrow main road.

Again, we were outfitted with new ski gear and enrolled in the ski schools. I moved into the top class for children; Rudi Draxl, our ski instructor, mentioned that, if my skiing improved, I would get promoted into the senior class, possibly being able to ski with Dad. It had been fun re-acquainting ourselves with St. Anton. The faces of our old ski instructors remained the same, the only change being that Otto Fahrner had gone to America to marry a ski heiress and start a ski school in some resort on the east coast.

We quickly progressed through the classes and, after starting in the junior class, I found myself in the adult class with Dad. The two of us got to experience new and more challenging ski terrain. I still vividly remember one magical day after we had had an overnight dump of snow; our ski school went to an area for some deep powder snow skiing near the Galzig cable car station, where each of us got to create our own tracks through the snow. Everyone has these wonderful skiing days when the skis move effortlessly through the deep powder, with the tips rising up to the surface as you prepare to make your jump turn and then the ski tips are buried again as you fall into the deep powder once more. Well, this day the powder came up to our chests and it felt simply exhilarating as we carved turn after turn in the virgin snow. And so the days turned into weeks and our skiing improved all the time as we moved up through the classes.

Mum and Dad decided that we would spend the last two weeks skiing at Lech, a much smaller ski resort that is part of the Arlberg region. Lech had a wonderful old church, the Church of St. Nicholas, which had been built in the Gothic style and dated from about 1390. In 1954, Lech was linked by road to Zurs, St. Christoph, and St. Anton. Today these resorts are all interlinked with ski lifts; but, in 1955, we could ski from one resort to the other by climbing up to the relevant peak and skiing down to the next village. These places were relatively unspoilt and the mountain backdrop and skiing, whether at Zurs or Lech, was simply phenomenal. Dad had arranged that two ski instructors - Rudi Draxl and Johann Fahrner - come from St. Anton to ski with us. In fact, they became our "private" ski instructors. As a young boy, I thought that all this was unbelievable; our skiing abilities improved by leaps and bounds. Anyway, these final two weeks were a fitting end to our skiing holiday.

But all of this did not happen by chance. I now know that the first seeds of some of Dad's thinking for his life after he stopped work had begun to germinate prior to and during this holiday in St. Anton in Austria. At the time, nobody, not even Mum, had any inkling about what he thought he would do after he finished his working life in India. We all believed that India was going to be our home forever. But mountains and skiing were in his blood and, for the first time, he was speculating that, if the family left India, a move to a ski resort in Austria - for instance, St. Anton - might be ideal. Later on, Dad would often describe this as his vision of the ideal life post-India. He dreamed of owning and operating a ski chalet catering to about 20-25 guests in the mountains. Mum would work in the kitchen as the cook. Martina would perform all the chambermaid duties, Miki would be the handy-man cum gopher, doing this and that including shovelling snow and Dad's role would be… well, Dad saw himself as working behind the reception, greeting visitors with a happy smile. In the evenings, his role would change and he would be the self-appointed mingler with guests, the storyteller and raconteur-in-chief regaling everybody with his stories of Czechoslovakia, India and his exploits as a climber in the Himalayas. This "division of tasks" thinking on Dad's part was to repeat itself much later in Australia with the same level of success.

Only much later, did I realise that the presence of Rudi Draxl and Johann Fahrner in Lech had not been a random event, but had been planned. Dad had already started to talk to them about the possibility of buying land; oddly enough, Rudi and Johann, who were related, just happened to have a block of land available for sale. Dad didn't see it coming.

Helping the Family in Czechoslovakia

The success of Dad's business in India allowed him and Mum to support both their families in Czechoslovakia for many years. Beginning with clothing and moving on to medicine and other material goods, enough of their parcels managed to get through to make a difference to the Hruskas and the Krobaths, even with pilfering from Czech customs officials. If someone in our "Indian" family went to Czechoslovakia, that person would take an extra suitcase of clothes and other items and deliver them to the "Czech" families with Uncle Noris' assistance. Later, when I got to know the extent of my Mum and Dad's support and generosity, and how much my father had helped the family during the tough years under Communist rule, I held him in very high esteem for his largesse. Even today, when I speak with the surviving members of my mother's family, they all speak about how the tangible support that they got from India helped them cope with the daily drudge that had become Czech life.

The Money Run, Summer Holidays and the Arrival of Charlie

In Stonyhurst, the summer holidays went from July to the end of August and most years I went home to Calcutta for this holiday. For Mum, and especially Dad, my visits to India were important. During this time in India, because the government still had a foreign exchange problem, many people had to find "creative" ways of obtaining foreign currency. As I have mentioned above, in Calcutta there were many religious organisations that were dependent on donations from abroad, mainly in the form of cheques, money orders, or even cash through the mail. However, when they went to exchange these negotiable financial instruments for cash at the local banks, they got a pathetic rate of exchange and the donations' possible impact on the missions and their work was considerably diminished. So, my father offered a solution. He was prepared to buy these financial instruments at the nominal Indian rupee exchange rate plus a small margin, which effectively meant that the missions could get a "bit more bang for their buck." He had this arrangement with Father Gabric and, much later, with Mother Teresa. In return, Dad received the cash and many cheques signed over to his name and this is where these summer holidays became important for, on the return leg, Dad needed me to stop for a day or two in Zurich, Switzerland. In effect, I became the "bag man" for the family business.

I loved these interludes in Zurich. I would take a stroll down the famous *Bahnhofstrasse* (Railway Street) to *Paradeplatz* (Parade Place). Practically every German-speaking city has a *Bahnhofstrasse*, but there is only one real *Bahnhofstrasse*. Running from the Zurich Railway Station down to the lake, this grand street was the epitome of elegance with its Rössli tram, which ran down the middle of it. Extremely elegant shops filled both sides of the street, shops that had an air of exclusivity with a price tag to match. If a person liked Swiss watches, then *Bahnhofstrasse* had the whole of the Swiss watchmaking industry's output on display to seduce any discerning buyer. The choice ranged from such relatively modestly priced watches as Rolex, Omega and Movado, to the more upmarket models from Girard Perregaux, Audemars Piguet, and IWC Schaffhausen. But the shopper did not need to be a millionaire to enjoy *Bahnhofstrasse*. Here and there were scattered many small food stalls, selling Pretzels and simple bread rolls with (pork, veal or beef sausage with mustard). *Bahnhofstrasse* was home to many well-known and fine department stores like Jelmoli, Migros and Globus where anyone could buy a reasonably priced meal. So, a 15- or 16-year-old in short pants and blazer could strut like a "rupee millionaire" in *Bahnhofstrasse* fortified with a currywurst, bread roll and sauerkraut as he wended his way to *Paradeplatz* to do his banking.

Paradeplatz is one of the best-known squares in Zurich. Here can be found the headquarters of two or three of the biggest Swiss banks, including the Union de Banque Suisse (UBS) and the Credit Swiss Group. Our "family" bank was the UBS. Each year, on my way from India back to England, I would make my way there and, at the reception, would ask if I could see my father's contact without having a prior appointment. This gentleman apparently managed Dad's affairs at the bank. I would sit and wait in an elegant reception room with a huge chandelier in the middle, but nobody asked me if I would like a drink. Someone had obviously visually gauged my importance and even a Coca Cola had not been worth the gesture. After about 10 minutes, a gentleman would meet me and escort me to the fourth floor where I would go to his office. He made me feel very welcome. After all, today's small, unimportant client might be tomorrow's big client or money launderer.

I took out the little bundle that Dad had given me and handed it over to him, according to Dad's instructions. The man counted out the various bank cheques and currencies, sorting them into various piles, converting all this "negotiable paper" into Swiss francs, and crediting the corresponding amount to Dad's account, showing me a copy of the original receipt. I kept the duplicate, as the original would stay with the bank. No record of these transactions ever went to India officially. After this important and serious bank transaction, I departed, having done my work as a courier. I then made my way to one of the most famous chocolate shops in all Switzerland, Confiserie Sprüngli for a hot chocolate and cake, the "payoff" for being a bag man! On my return to England from the Christmas holidays in India, I would make the journey again to Zurich, have another meeting with my Swiss bank contact, and another hot chocolate.

When I returned to Calcutta from England for the summer Holidays in 1955, Mum and Dad met me at Dum Dum airport and I noticed that Mum was very pregnant indeed. My initial reaction was one of indignation, based on the fact that no one had bothered to mention it in any letter to me at school. I felt very much left out and it took me some time to get over this shock. Once things had settled down, I became absolutely thrilled at the prospect of a new arrival; but, at the time, I did not take in that there would be a 15-year age difference between the new arrival into our family and me. The new baby was expected in September. I had already returned back to school when the news arrived that I had a brother named Charles Christian, or "Charlie" for short. A legendary story started to circulate that the new baby had somehow managed to get his little fingers around the nurse's thermometer and wave it back and forth like a fly fisherman. And, thus, the legend of "*El Pescador*" (the Fisherman) was born. These fishing skills manifested themselves much later, but we all feel he was born with them. Unfortunately, the age difference and the fact that we were living our lives in different parts of the world meant that any meeting with my brother Charlie in any year would be fleeting. I wasn't to develop a solid relationship with him until we were both adults. The arrival of Charlie changed the family dynamics; now, most of the attention was focused on him, quite natural since I boarded at school in England and Martina, eleven years older than our brother, attended school in Calcutta. For me, it was one more wedge that distanced me from my parents and the family as a whole.

Keeping in Touch with the Czech Language, Czech Traditions, and Culture:

Speaking Czech

Even though Mum and Dad had been effectively cut off from Czechoslovakia because of the Communist regime, they still managed to keep part of their Czech heritage alive in Calcutta. The first and most obvious link was that they still spoke Czech at home. In the first few years, and as they slowly started to make strides with English, Czech remained their prime means of communication. In Batanagar, within the Czech expatriate community, Czech still ruled the day. As a result, both my sister and I were the beneficiaries of this practice. We heard the language and we imitated Czech phonetically and, what is more, we could speak it quite proficiently; but we had no clue whatsoever how to spell or write it. That came much, much later for me. But it is a testament to this early exposure to the Czech spoken in the house that our pronunciation was quite correct. Later on, after many years, when we were finally unleashed on the family in Czechoslovakia, we were able to carry on meaningful conversations with our relatives. Naturally our vocabulary failed us sometimes, but that was understandable since we did not have daily exposure to the language in English-speaking India.

Czech Language

If anyone is contemplating learning Czech, then he or she may be seriously driven to consider joining the Benedictine monastic life, taking a vow of silence or, better still, just jumping out of a window. Consider the tongue-twister below:

> *Měla babka v kapse brabce, brabec babce v kapse píp. Zmáčkla babka brabce v kapse, brabec babce v kapse chcíp.* (Grandma had a sparrow in her pocket and the sparrow made a sound. Grandma pressed the sparrow and it died).

You can recognise the vowels and, saying it out aloud may not be a challenge, but it is a brave student of the language who tries to get his mind and tongue around these words. On the other hand, for Czech speakers, the sound is so pure, so rich and so exact; my sister and I felt privileged to have membership in the exclusive club where the pronunciation of these wonderful words fell easily.

And now we come to another challenge. Consider the following little sentence. But where are the vowels?

> *Strč prst skrz krk.* (Stick your finger through your throat).

How do I start? It is the only language that I know of (aside from ancient Hebrew) that allows the speaker to speak out the sentence even though there is not a single vowel in it. No problem for us Czech speakers as we can effortlessly say these simple words without slitting our throats.

Below is the tongue-twister that Dad used to tell me over and over again so that I could get the feel of the language and, today, after nearly eighty years it still flows languidly, effortlessly from my lips. Aaaah! How wonderful!

Tři sta třiatřicet stříbrných křepelek přeletělo přes tři sta třiatřicet stříbrných střech. (Three hundred and thirty-three silver quails flew over three hundred and thirty-three silver roofs).

Today Czech is spoken by an overwhelming majority of Czechs in the Czech Republic. Some other languages can also be heard like Slovakian and the gypsy language, Romany. Czech, Slovak and Polish belong to the strand of languages known as the western Slavic languages. Russian and Ukrainian belong to the Eastern Slavic languages. But Czech stands out for the complexity of its structure and the torturing of its vowel sounds!

Czech Swearing

There were some definite drawbacks to learning Czech the way we did. My parents came from simple peasant stock and the polite way of expressing a sentiment or simple request was not one of their strong points, especially in the case of Dad. An attentive ear like mine would listen to his words and, as any dutiful son would do, if Dad used the words, I believed that they had to be correct. Thus, I continued to use these expressions until I was about 40, innocently thinking them to be not only grammatically correct but also polite until someone one day kindly corrected me. I was attending a gathering of Czechs in Sydney and our hostess had prepared a splendid table with food and drinks when Mother Nature beckoned. I went up to my host and calmly asked "*Musím jít srát! Kde je záchod?*" (literally "I need to have a crap! Where is your bathroom?") in my best articulate Czech. Well, a look of stunned silence came over my hostess and she calmly took me aside and explained that there actually existed a polite way to make such a request, namely "*Kde máte záchod?*" (Where is your bathroom?). That's it, short and sweet. Well, from that moment on, I became much more careful with my use of the language!

Dad had a formidable array of curses. Most languages have, as a minimum, at least three categories of cursing: religious curses, curses that involve your relatives and/or parentage, and curses that refer to parts of the human body. Dad loved the religious variety. So, from an early age, we heard expressions such as *krucifix* (crucifix) or *Ježíš, Maria, Josefe* (Jesus, Mary, and Joseph) or *Herrgott sakramente* (God Sacrament) when he became frustrated at something or someone. So, it was natural to invoke the church or heavens; but these were really mild curses.

If Dad was annoyed when someone at the factory had misunderstood an instruction or stuffed up somewhere, then we heard quite a litany of curses, like *zatraceně or krucinál* (damn) or *sakra* (blast it, or hell) or *magor* (retard). I never heard him use some of the cruder Czech equivalents of the famous English f... swear word. But the real star of Czech swearwords is the use of *do prdele* which in English literally means "up yours!" Compare this with the English form of "go to hell." Another very common Czech expression that Dad used was *polib mi prdel* (kiss my rear/ass). But the real gems were associated with comments about persons that he had no time for or who were, in his opinion, stupid and who only seemed to occupy space. For this we got from him such gems as *hňup* (half-wit), *blázen* (fool), *hajzl* (bog), *trouba* (nitwit) or *debil* (moron). And, thus, as good listeners, my sister and I heard all these new words, learned these expressions, and used them often. And I must admit that I loved the sound of some of them such as *hňup* or *trouba*!

Traditional Czech food

Traditional Czech food in Mum and Dad's time was not exactly what one would call slimming, or even healthy, but it was thoroughly satisfying. Their diet was based on meat, copious quantities of starch and on what could be grown locally. And because so much of traditional Czech food is based on pork products, it is perfectly matched by the true star of Czech gastronomy - the wonderfully flavourful Czech beer. It is quite ironic that a country with such a solid intellectual history, and that has given the world great classical music, literature, architecture, folk music, visual arts, and an especially creative experimental theatre has such an uninspiring cuisine. A glance at any Czech menu suggests that this is a country of carnivores. Czechs love their meat, whether it is the cheap and fatty range of salamis and smoked or cured meat, or the more wholesome roast pork, chicken, or beef. I think that if there were ever to be a meat-eating Olympics, the Czechs would win the gold medal for meat consumption. And they wouldn't even qualify to enter the vegetable eating competition. As far as the token concession to vegetables goes, potatoes, cabbage, tomatoes and cucumber salad do get a nudge, though once the Communists were removed from the scene, a wider range of vegetables started to make an appearance on diners' plates. One would be forgiven for thinking that this fare was meant to provide energy to dig up roads or fill potholes! But some habits die hard and the love affair with meat swimming in sauces, accompanied by shovelfuls of cabbage, has survived the Communist era and is still all too common in the Czech Republic.

Besides animal protein, Czechs have a hard time excluding carbohydrate stodge from any meal, especially in the form of knedlíky (dumplings). The Germans and the Austrians have their own versions of this moderately hardened plasticine but the Czechs will proudly tell you that they can cook theirs with all sorts of additions like bacon, bread pieces, etc., and in over 30 different ways. Need I add that this culinary delight gets digested very slowly. But the Czechs treat their *knedlíky* with great reverence. And helping them digest this fare again is the justly famous, Czech beer. I sometimes wonder if the eating is secondary to the enjoyment of the beer, arguably one of the finest in the world.

Being landlocked, Czechs don't get to enjoy a variety of fish and so any exposure to fish rests predominantly with trout, pikeperch (also known as zander), pike, and carp from the rivers. Carp is one of the traditional foods that appears on the Christmas table. But there is one area of the kitchen where the Czechs excel and that is in the area of baking. Czechs love their cakes, pastry and cookies. When I was a child, virtually every Czech household had a wonderful array of baking to offer their family and friends.

So, this was the food world that my parents grew up with in the province of Moravia; their culinary ideas and experiences were shaped within this framework. And this was what I enjoyed as a child in my parents' home in Calcutta. Of course, as soon as I went to boarding school in Darjeeling and then in Lancashire, my own culinary horizons changed. It may have been this drastic shift from the comfort food of my childhood to the questionable joys of boarding school fare that has given me a lifelong preference for sausage, cabbage and dumplings!

Czech Food in Calcutta

Dad was never a very great friend of Indian food, in particular curries and heavily spiced dishes. The closest he got to enjoying Indian food was *tandoori* chicken, which is marinated in yoghurt and a variety of spices. It is not very hot on the tongue and its uniqueness is that it is cooked inside a large *tandoor* (a bell-shaped clay oven) at very high temperatures. It is also usually served dry with an accompaniment of onions, lime, etc. As an aside, whenever Dad and I visited Delhi, he always made a point of visiting Moti Mahal's restaurant in Old Delhi, which had the reputation of preparing the best *tandoori* chicken in India at the time. These were memorable experiences for me.

Access to good beef was always a problem in Calcutta. Since the cow is a sacred animal in India, they were generally slaughtered only when they could hardly stand up; then the Muslim butchers got access to them and prepared the remaining flesh for sale. In consequence, the available beef was old and stringy. But at least you could make a stew out of it. And so, when a suitable portion of beef became available at the meat sellers in the market, we would have a Calcuttan version of *Szegedinsky Guláš* ("goulash," from "Szeged" in Hungarian). While it may not have been possible to replicate in Calcutta the wonderful array of spices that went into this goulash, Mum used an equally interesting array of Indian spices. Perhaps I should call this dish *Calcuttinsky Guláš*. And naturally, when there was goulash, there could also be a goulash soup! I should add that we were all good friends of garlic, just like Mum and Dad were used to at home in Czechoslovakia.

Pork, on the other hand, was obtained from Hindu butchers, so we often had pork dishes on our table. Getting fresh cabbage at the market sometimes posed a problem but, when it was available, our Indian cook Dandia would make *zelí* (pickled cabbage), which Mum had introduced him to. However, in contrast to Czechoslovakia, India offered us a wonderful array of vegetables and fruit at the markets. So, I can say that my parents' culinary experience expanded significantly through living in India. Rice became a staple in our house. After all, traditional Czech cooking had to be modified in Calcutta to match the climate and the availability of local ingredients and spices.

Fortunately, in Calcutta, young chickens were available, as well as geese and ducks and these birds appeared on our table regularly. The smaller chickens that I remember from Calcutta had a unique taste and were much more flavourful than their modern western counterparts. They were probably a different variety from the much larger, "Arnold Schwarzwenegger," chickens of supermarkets today. In the 50s and 60s, chickens were purchased live at the market, and then killed and plucked at home. We could not buy deep frozen chickens or fresh chicken pieces, as is the case in the west today.

I am reminded of one memorable incident when I was a child at home that had a big effect on Mum. We had a small kitchen, hardly enough room to swing a cat. It was a typical urban Indian-style kitchen. It had an apology for a gas stove standing next to a preparation table that was next to a separate water sink. Under the sink was a large drain with a two-brick height retaining wall surrounding the drain. It also had a tap, so this was the area for cleaning food, hence the retaining wall so that water could not flow back into the rest of the kitchen. This area also served other purposes, like the execution of chickens and consignment of their mortal remains to the cooking pot. So, on one occasion and only one, Mum decided that she would be the executioner and got hold of the poor chicken, in the prescribed way, or so she thought; she grabbed the sharpest knife and went to slit the throat. But she did not cut deep enough.

Until then, the chicken had been quite passive but it certainly awoke with a start as the sharp knife slid across its neck. It let out a loud squawk, its wings started to flail madly, its legs oscillated up and down and the blood started to squirt out of its neck. Mum's grip on the poor bird had not been secure, and so, she let go. Well, pandemonium broke out in the kitchen as the poor bird flew haphazardly round and round like a released gas balloon. As it leapt and flew about the kitchen, it bumped into walls and cupboards, spraying blood from its throat everywhere. Mum panicked, not knowing what to do and ran to the kitchen door, yelling for Dandia, who emerged and soon pinned the bird down on the floor. Dandia took off its head in one well-timed chop and peace reigned again in the kitchen. Then the prolonged clean-up commenced before the chicken could be served. Mum remained very subdued and quiet that evening and I do not know whether she enjoyed her chicken dinner. This experience was the first and last time that she took on the role of chicken executioner; she left all subsequent dealings with chickens, geese and ducks to Dandia. But chicken still remained on the Hruska household menu!

Mum and Dad had a Czech friend, Křižká, who missed home cooking. He started to make his own sausages and smoked meat. Occasionally, we were able to buy some of his produce, which made the carnivores in our home content. He particularly loved what he called, and I hope that this is correct, *Utopenci*, sausages that had been pickled in vinegar, oil, onion, red pepper, and different spices. He loved to eat this with bread and a rather good Indian beer called Kingfisher.

My fondest memories of my mother's Czech cooking happened when she made wonderful Czech *palačinky* (crepes) filled with jam or fruit and coated in whipped-cream, almonds, cinnamon or sugar and sometimes accompanied by ice-cream. And then there were the incredible *ovocné knedlíky* (fruit dumplings), and the memories of family dinners with nothing but these dumplings on a large plate with melted butter, quark cheese and icing sugar! The only sounds at the table were those of chewing in silence. Sheer culinary pleasure cannot, indeed must not, be interrupted by conversation! Mum also made the most excellent *koláče* (cakes) filled with different fruits, jams or made with almonds and other nuts. She baked large batches of these cakes and they became part of the family Christmas baking ritual. They were always offered to friends when they came to our house, a custom that had prevailed in Czechoslovakia when she was a girl.

Growing up in a Czech family, we children were constantly reminded by Mum and Dad not to waste food; so, we were encouraged to finish everything on our plate. Many a time, I would hear Mum add, "Think of all the starving millions in India. You must finish your food!" And we did. At this age, we had no idea what all this traditional Czech food was doing to our arteries.

Czech Christmas in Calcutta

Czechoslovakia has many wonderful national and regional traditions associated with Christmas. There are two main Christmas celebrations: one on 5 December and the big one on 24 December. The festivities on

5 December commemorate St Nicholas and are associated primarily with children. In Czechoslovakia, this is known as *Mikuláš* (festival of St. Nicholas), a festivity formally observed together with the Advent season of the four Sundays leading up to Christmas. In Europe, Christmas and St. Nicholas are synonymous, especially in Germany, Holland, Austria, and Switzerland. Each household indicates to external passers-by that there are children in the house and, on 5 December, *Mikuláš*, dressed as a bishop and carrying a bishop's staff and mitre, knocks on the front door. He is accompanied by a *čert* (a horned devil) who usually has a long red tongue or rattling chains and an *anděl* (a winged angel). I believe the symbolism portrayed to us here is that *Mikuláš* is meant to reward children with small gifts; the devil comes to punish naughty children; the angel, in turn, protects the children from the devil. If a child has been naughty, at least he has until 24 December to reform and be good! In the Czech tradition, *Mikuláš* usually brings gifts such as fruit, chocolates, or even nuts. The punishment for bad behaviour was never exacted in our household, but I am sure that the presence of the devil meant something appropriate would be done.

I am absolutely sure that this tradition was perfect for Czechoslovakia, with cold weather and snow on the ground; but, though Mum and Dad told me about *Mikuláš*, they decided that we would forego this northern hemisphere tradition in India and just concentrate on 24 December. Even so, I have always believed that Dad would have made a great *Mikuláš* and Dandia a believable devil (although his character was probably better suited to the angel). When I was little, in my imagination, Coco Mackertich would have made an even better St. Nicholas, dressed in his traditional morning wear, carnation in his lapel, moustache waxed and wearing spats. The devil would certainly have taken notice of Coco.

In Calcutta, just as in Czechoslovakia, the arrival of the Christmas season meant the start of intense baking activity. Mum reached back into her memories of Christmas in Třebíč with Babička for the time-honoured recipes of baking, collectively known as *vánoční cukroví* (Christmas baking). These included some of our favourites like *máslové pečivo* (buttered bread), *důlkové koláčky* (jam-filled thumbprint cookies), and *vanilkové rohlíčky* (vanilla almond crescents rolled in confectioners' sugar). For days, the smells that came from the kitchen wafted through the house, but all this baking came to an end in a crescendo with the baking of the *vánočka* (braided Christmas bread). Mum would bake enough *vánočka* to feed the French Foreign Legion, including all our friends and enough to fill the plates put on the dinner table at Christmas. The excess cookies were packed into all sorts of storage boxes for later use.

In the lead-up to Christmas, Mum and Dad did their Christmas shopping and, when we were young, we never knew when this shopping happened, nor had any indication of where all these gifts were hidden away in the apartment. We knew that something was afoot but we feigned ignorance. Nevertheless, for my sister and me, the days leading to Christmas Eve caused a lot of excitement.

There were no real traditional trees available for sale in Calcutta's markets. Many people made do with a replica, but Dad wanted a real tree and the nearest place that we could get it was either from Darjeeling, where we knew nobody, or from Kashmir. Dad's friend Bobal in Pathankhot knew the defined tree specification - height 5 feet, perfectly conically shaped, and a point at the top of the tree so that we could attach a Star of Bethlehem. An order would go out in late November to Bobal. Dad allowed a month for the tree to arrive, which was usually about a week before Christmas Eve. Even though the conifer was from Kashmir, it resembled the trees we had seen in magazines like *Colliers* or the *Saturday Evening Post*. In other words, it not only looked like a Christmas tree, it *was* a real Christmas tree.

In Calcutta, Mum and Dad adopted the British custom of exchanging Christmas cards with family and friends, even though this had not been something they did in Moravia. But they did decorate the tree according to Moravian custom. Mum brought out her Czech Christmas tree decorations and we used to help her decorate the tree. Mum used to put a few glass ornaments on the tree, but she also placed some of her gingerbread baking, a few red apples, and small mandarins on the tree. The top of the tree had its Star of Bethlehem, but candles were a problem. In the early years, she had tried real candles but these were a worry: we could never get proper candleholders, so we dispensed with the real candles and used an electrical strand of candle-looking lights instead.

December 24, Christmas Day, meant "frenzy," but only for the one day. In the morning, there was the endless answering of the doorbell as many of

Dad's dealers and business associates came to offer their "Christmas gift." Even though they did not celebrate Christmas, their "gift" usually comprised a basket filled with goodies. There was always a healthy representation of fruit, confectionery and chocolates from Flury's or Trinca's and other gifts. And, usually buried under all these offerings, there was a bottle of Johnny Walker whisky, which was a most welcome supplement to the household: whisky was not only difficult to get, but also quite expensive.

As the countdown towards *Štědrý večer* (Christmas Eve) continued, the feverish activity associated with preparations started around noon and quickly escalated. At our home, we had a large dining room table around which we managed to seat 10-12 people. Both the Dandias did all the cleaning in our little apartment for Christmas. Mum gravitated to the kitchen and checked that everything that needed to be there for the dinner was present and accounted for. Mum summoned Paidya, one of Dad's tool makers from the factory; he did the table decorations and all the fancy napkin folding. Mum brought out a few select items from her Bohemian crystal collection. I remember that the baking was always served on these beautiful crystal plates. Having nuts, especially walnuts, had become an important part of the evening and they also found a home in a beautiful crystal bowl. And the wonderful part of all this is that some of this crystal is still being used in my own household and that of my sister; each time I see one of these pieces, it reminds me of our Christmas in Calcutta.

Late in the afternoon, Mum and Dad would have a cup of coffee on the verandah near the tree and we would get to sample some of Mum's baking. I remember that the almond crescents were rationed as these could fly off the plate in a flash. But we all enjoyed this quiet moment together before Christmas dinner and before the rest of the festivities erupted. I remember, aged about five or six, another little custom that we had before Calcutta became so polluted. Mum insisted that not a single candle could be lit on the dinner table until the first star came out. So, we all crammed in front of our small balcony and looked out for the first star and, when found, then and only then could we sit down for dinner. But this custom lasted for only two or three years, at which point, with Calcutta's pollution haze, we could have been standing at the balcony all night waiting to see a star and we would have gone hungry!

At around 7 o'clock in the evening, the first guests started to arrive. Most came from my parents' circle of friends in Calcutta. Practically every year we had Coco Mackertich, Suren Chatterjee, Josef Kintr, Fathers Gabric and Barré and, while they lived in Calcutta, Zygmunt Kahan and Sasha. Sometimes the Cargnellis from upstairs came down. Sometimes the Batras. One year, we entertained many of the principals of the Czech circus that had been touring India: Herbert and Rudolf Tichy, and Eva Ochenašova - who later on, I am told, became a film star at home in Czechoslovakia. And I will never forget the famous, or shall I say, the infamous Daša Krásná. She smoked like a chimney stack and, during the evening, some of the smouldering ash from her cigarette fell onto Mum's lace dining cloth, one of her prized possessions from home. Mum displayed amazing self-control, even though wisps of steam appeared to be coming out of her ears and nostrils. Mum made out that it was not a problem, brushing away the incident through gritted teeth, but I am sure she could have reached over, grabbed the goose on the plate, and smashed it over Daša's head.

Finally, dinner arrived. If Christmas fell on any day except Friday, we would have chicken noodle soup or, better still, chicken liver dumpling soup with noodles, followed by roast goose or duck with dumplings, roast potatoes, green beans and carrots and the obligatory buckets full of gravy. If Christmas fell on a Friday, we usually served fish, a *bhekti* with potato salad and some vegetables, out of deference to our religious priestly company. It is ironic to think that, when we lived in Calcutta, we used to think that *bhekti* was a fish quite unique to India. But, in fact, it came from exactly the same genus as barramundi that we later came to know so well in Australia. Father Gabric always started with a small prayer and blessed our meal and, once the religious part was dispensed with, we got down to the serious business of eating. We could not buy wine anywhere, so Dad provided the local Kingfisher beer. The *vánočka* graced the centre of the table. Dinner was always a happy occasion, but we children wanted to get it over quickly; we wanted to get to the tree. As a finale for dinner, Mum always served her wonderful apple strudel with coffee and tea together with her baking.

In our apartment, the dining room had two large doors. One solid wood door led to the bedroom and the other, a large glass door led into the verandah. The verandah door had curtains to hide any view of what lay beyond. The verandah could also be accessed from the bedroom. At some point in the dinner, Mum rose and made her way to the bedroom. When questioned, she gave the same reply each year: "I have to go and turn the light on to help *Ježíšek* (Baby Jesus) find his way to the tree." If we children had not found any traces of presents prior to Christmas, the illusion was preserved that indeed *Ježíšek* had brought the gifts and placed them under the tree.

Mum and Dad tried to maintain some of the family traditions that they had grown up with. I remember that they used to place a small bowl on the table, which had a bulb of garlic in it and next to it a small jar of honey. The tradition asked us to believe that the garlic was a source of strength and protection and that honey deterred evil. But, with the passing of time in India, many of these traditions disappeared from the celebration of Christmas at the Hruska household and it became more an occasion to celebrate with friends over a good meal in a spirit of bonhomie.

And then the big moment arrived. The dining table was cleared and everybody retired to the verandah with their drinks and made themselves comfortable. Somehow, magically, the base of the Christmas tree had become resplendent with gifts. Mum passed around plates of her Czech baking and we sat by the tree enjoying the lights and decorations for a short while, a very short while indeed. I remember these more as quiet occasions of reflective introspection surrounded by close and dear friends rather than a boisterous and noisy affair. We sometimes sang a well-known carol but these occasions were few and far between. Mum took on the role of giving out the gifts. As a small boy, I got a lot of Meccano sets ranging from Set 1 to 8.[147] I also got clothes. Mum had always been a knitter and so, on many occasions, our friends and I got a sweater or socks. These also accompanied pants, singlets, underpants and store-bought socks - thankfully, not knitted! Mum loved giving knitted gifts. But sometimes, the odd,

147 Meccano was the most popular construction sets for boys for several decades in the mid 20th century. It was a metal-based model construction system full of structural and mechanical components, shaped elements, wheels, axles, and nuts and bolts to connect the pieces together. Meccano was so durable that it could be passed from one child to another.

balsa wood, model airplane or book were there and these were always welcome. We always had a gift for each of our guests and they responded in kind: Coco got us the best chocolates from either Firpo's, or Flury's.

Midnight Mass in Batanagar and Singing

We had another important Christmas tradition. Even after my father left the company, we always celebrated Midnight Mass at Batanagar. My parents' faith was informed more by their values and the way they lived than by any overt religiosity. When all the Christmas Eve celebrations had concluded at home and all our guests had left, we piled into the Citroen to celebrate midnight mass. After a 45-minute drive, we gathered in the small church located at the northern end of the Batanagar Czech community compound. The church was small and totally adequate for a typical congregation at Sunday mass. But, on this special night, the church filled to overflowing. Women and children sat in the seats and pews at the front, inside the church. The rear doors of the church were thrown open and the men and latecomers spilled out onto the small pathway and grass verge leading to the church entrance.

The mass was said in English but, as a concession to the Czech community, some of the carols were sung in Czech. I will always remember the wonderful voices that rang through the church. Many of these Czechs, most of whom came from Moravia, which had a rich musical tradition of song, had wonderful voices. When you looked around at the many faces, they were singing their hearts out. Emotions ran high and many of them had tears in their eyes as they thought of home, which was currently unreachable, and families and friends whom they had left behind. I always felt the warmth of the occasion, created by the wonderful singing; the finale that was truly uplifting at the end of the service came when this group of people started singing the Czech national anthem *"Kde domov můj?"* (*Where is My Home?*). The music was written about 170 years ago by the composer František Škroup as background music for a comedy. Hearing and understanding the beautiful words of this anthem, led us to appreciate the collision between nostalgia for home, the memory of loved ones left behind and the sheer pride of being Czech in a strange land.

Here is the first stanza of the anthem:

Kde domov můj, kde domov můj?	Where is my home, where is my home?
Voda hučí po lučinách,	Water roars across the meadows,
bory šumí po skalinách,	Pinewoods rustle among crags,
v sadě skví se jara květ,	The garden is glorious with spring blossom,
zemský ráj to na pohled!	Paradise on earth it is to see.
A to je ta krásná země,	And this is that beautiful land,
země česká domov můj,	The Czech land, my home,
země česká domov můj!	The Czech land, my home.

We visited with other close friends living in Calcutta like the Křižkás, the Schwardalas, the Gartleys and the Batras on 25 December and Mum brought along all her baking for them to savour.

Mid 1950s: Emerging Political and Labour Problems

From the early 50s to the late 60s, Calcutta underwent dramatic change at a political and social level. In the early 1950s, the Congress Party governed with a majority in the West Bengal Legislature. However, gradually, a shift started in Calcutta politics towards the Communist Party. There are many views about why this occurred but there appears to be a consensus that there were two principal reasons.

Probably the most important was the change in Calcutta's demographics; the increasing problems and pressures associated with millions of refugees had greatly contributed to the decline of the city. Over the years, from the aftermath of the Great Famine to the trauma of Partition, the city experienced enormous growth from the influx of those refugees, which only exacerbated its already strained infrastructure and dwindling resources. In a short time, many mini-slum communities had developed in various parts of the city. The few industries that were located in the city's poorer areas attracted even more slum dwellers, as they sought work close to where they lived. The *bustees* (slums) took root, competing with planned development for space and access to public utilities. Most, if not all of these *bustee* areas, had either limited or no access to clean water or proper sanitation. The West Bengal government rarely made adequate appropriations in their state budgets to keep up with these slums. Some parts of the public utilities still belonged to private interests: for instance, electricity generation companies. Private entrepreneurs were not disposed to making capital investments[148] in the slum areas when there existed little prospect of ever recovering their investment, let alone user fees. What made matters even worse were the continual turf battles between government agencies over who should do what, when and where. In government circles, this resulted in a total inability to deal with infrastructure and a paralysis of action. I'm not aware of any government initiated, systematic analysis of the problems during this era, so the West Bengali government cannot be accused of being affected by "paralysis through analysis."

Coinciding with this massive influx of refugees into West Bengal, people drifted from the rural countryside to Calcutta whenever they were flooded or dried out, or when the market for agricultural produce collapsed. These farmers and agricultural workers gravitated to the city hoping to find work, which was always something in extremely short supply. And, predictably, these displaced peoples supported political parties that offered them the "sky," a rosy way of life that could only be delivered if the party won a majority in the West Bengal legislature. In West Bengal, the parties that appealed the most to these homeless and dispossessed people were on the radical left, namely the Communists, because they were not in power.

A second mitigating factor in finding any solution to the political and social issues that plagued West Bengal in the 50s and 60s was the Bengali intelligentsia who, by and large, controlled the political and administrative domain to the almost total exclusion of the business communities, which were dominated by the Marwaris, Chinese, Punjabis, Armenians and other Europeans. The Bengalis seemed to have a basic distrust of these commercial groups. They also had a longstanding infatuation with a left-wing political agenda and ideology that had been influenced in part by their

---

148 In Calcutta, the West Bengal Government had a policy of importing their provision for power from state agencies. These same agencies often failed to meet their commitments. There is an informative overview of Calcutta's power supply in Sukanta Chaudhuri, ed., *Calcutta, the Living City. Vol II: The Present and the Future*, 128-132.

favoured son, Netaji Subhas Chandra Bose, as well as Soviet, and even Chinese Maoist, communist models. That being said, the Bengalis knew that they could not afford to antagonize the business community through raising taxes. If they had done so, there would have been a flight of capital out of the city to other parts of India, jobs would have been lost, and the city would have gone further into decline.

The coming together of these two forces created another perfect storm in Calcutta. On the one hand, there was a totally ineffectual government and complete inability of the Calcutta Municipal Corporation to deal with the city's infrastructure problems: they could not raise enough extra money through taxes to even begin to address the pressures associated with an ever-increasing *bustee* population. On the other hand, they were ham-strung by their antipathy towards commerce.

The quality of life in the city was noticeably affected. The gap between rich and poor widened. With so many disaffected people in the city, life became one round of endless protests. Calcutta evolved into a city of strikes and slogans. The art of the political and anti-commerce street poster emerged. Buildings, walls, and any free, street-front windows were an invitation to post messages against business. There was no differentiation between big or small business. Calcutta's labour warfare was enmeshed in the art and language of strike polemics. With increasing frequency, Calcutta experienced erratic failure of its utilities. Poverty was evident at every turn. Once restricted to outlying areas, slum dwellings now spilled over into the streets. And, everywhere, disaffection took root in those people who had only recently arrived.

First Stirrings in the Family about Leaving India

Against this backdrop, Mum and Dad, (I believe that it was more Dad), started to give serious consideration to leaving India. In the mid-50s, he had already started to transfer money out of the country, but these precautionary measures had not been enough to make a clean break with Calcutta. Numerous issues still needed to be addressed, like where they would live, how much capital would be necessary, what to do with the business, and whether they could sell it in its current location in Ripon St. which, since the establishment of the factory, had been re-zoned as a residential area. Would Dad have to re-establish the factory in another part of the city, preferably in an industrial area? Another serious issue that Dad had to confront was whether he could repatriate the proceeds of any sale of the factory legally and what, if any, would be the conditions of such a transfer? Many of the problems at this stage seemed insurmountable but the seeds of an eventual move away from Calcutta were planted and my parents began to make their plans.

In late August or early September 1956, Dad made a trip to Europe during which he visited Czechoslovakia to see his mother in Buchlovice. After leaving that country, he went to St. Anton and spent some time there. Then he went on to Zurich to attend to some banking matters. In October, he came to England to visit me at Stonyhurst. I remember being pulled out of class mid-afternoon; we met in a general reception area near the main entrance. After greeting each other and exchanging all our news on family and friends, we sat down.

Dad pulled up a chair next to me, opened a briefcase and pulled out a large photograph of St. Anton and pushed it across to me. I took the picture and looked at it. The area shown on the picture was familiar, but then I noticed what appeared to be a marked-up circle around a bit of pasture in the middle of the photograph.

"What is this circled area?" I asked.

"That's our land in St. Anton. I bought it from Johann Fahrner and some of his farming neighbours. He had some excess pasture land and wanted to sell it. The price was acceptable and so I went to the public notary's office and finalized the sale."

I looked at him incredulously and again at the picture and back to him and enquired, "What do you want to do with the land?"

He said, "I want to build a chalet there for the family after we leave India for good!" I was stunned and did not know what to say. As a 16-year-old with hardly any capacity yet for serious critical thought, all I could think of was living in Austria, a lot of skiing and having to learn German! A short silence followed and then Dad added, "Of course, I still have to negotiate with Johann for access rights to the property, but I am sure that will not be a problem!"

"You mean, that you bought a block of land with no access rights! Is that possible at all? And what happens if they do not sell you the access rights? Does this mean then that you will not be able to build?" He looked at me with an expression of surprise and I got the impression that this logical next step to his plan had yet to be addressed!

I now started to see the very temporary, exciting dream waft away out through the window. Dad, however, was very optimistic about the whole affair throughout our whole discussion. I regret not asking him about what he paid for this bit of cow pasture because there is a postscript to this tale. Of course, it turned out that the landowners who had land bordering on this property decided that they would not provide him access. Later I found out that he had to sell it back to Johann and his farmer friends at a significant loss! But for non-humans, access had always been available and the Austrian dairy cows wandered in an out of this wonderful property, bells around their necks ringing and glocken spieling with great abandon. Yet, Dad could not even get a grass royalty for this privilege. So much for the great Austrian land fiasco!

The Search for a Home Continues

After he left me at Stonyhurst, Dad made his way to Canada. He had also made some oblique reference about checking out Canada as a possible destination for the family after India in case his dreams for St. Anton did not materialize. He had some friends from his Bata and Calcutta days, the Surys, who now lived in Ottawa and also another acquaintance living in Vancouver. But this was the start of winter. After completing his mission through Canada, he came away with the startling conclusion that Canada was much too cold for his liking; he therefore deemed that it was not a suitable place for us to live. Which is odd, when I think of his love of skiing!

I have since wondered what the conclusion might have been if he had travelled there in summer and spent some time in the mountains or at a lake. If we had gone to Canada, we would all probably have learnt to skate, to love ice hockey instead of rugby (we had not yet discovered golf), to go camping and rub shoulders with bears instead of sharks and snakes and spiders, and become adept at adding "eh?" to the end of all our sentences! And the skiing would have been great! But this was Dad.

Totally single-minded in his decision-making. Mum obviously never had any contribution to these important decisions. So, we later learnt that Australia was the new destination of choice. End of story, no ifs or buts! I suspect that another important reason he chose to settle in Australia was that many Czechs in Batanagar and Calcutta had already started making plans to leave India and settle there. So, in keeping with the herd instinct, Australia and the city of Sydney became the chosen land!

In September/October 1957, Mum visited Australia for the first time. She brought along Martina and Charlie. I believe that they also went to New Zealand, probably for a holiday but, on their return to Sydney, they rented an apartment at Kirribilli. Here they met up with their old friends from Calcutta, Bob and Ina Gartly, now living in Sydney and, through them, got a reference to a friend of theirs, Dick Forbes, who happened to be the bank manager at the Commonwealth Bank, Milson's Point Branch. Mum opened up an account at this branch and Dad started to transfer money into it. I believe that the eventual aim was to use the transferred funds to buy land in Sydney and build a house.

Dick Forbes lived at the lower end of Edinburgh Road in Castlecrag, one of the more interesting suburbs in Sydney, on the North Shore. Castlecrag is a peninsula jutting into the harbour about five miles from the city and has quite an interesting history. Originally, it was a suburb planned by Walter Burley Griffin, who previously had had a chequered relationship with the Australian government in relation to the creation and development of Canberra. Even today, his legacy is evident in Castlecrag, as many examples of his houses still stand in the suburb. In 1958/59, Castlecrag was relatively undeveloped. From about two-thirds of the way down Edinburgh Road (the only main street in the suburb), apart from the houses built on either side of Edinburgh Road, the rest was dirt track or just "bush." Nevertheless, there already existed plans to open up some new roads to connect to the lower end of Castlecrag.

In late 1958 or early 1959, on a visit to Australia and after visiting the Forbes, Dad noticed that there was a small street opening up called Linden Way and about six or seven blocks of land there were being prepared for sale. Dad's initial reaction had been to buy four or five of these blocks, as they all had absolutely stunning views of Middle Harbour, the Spit Bridge and further beyond to the Tasman Sea. At the time, Dad thought that this would be a much better investment than placing his money in a long-term investment at the Commonwealth Bank. The average price of each block at the time was approximately 1,800 Australian pounds. When Dick Forbes heard about this plan, he advised Dad that this would be an extremely risky thing to do and that he should only buy one block of land to build the family home. At the time, we did not know much about Australian banking or the real estate investment scene in Sydney and what we did not realize was that Australian bank managers needed to have some larger customers on their books with money invested in the bank's financial products. This would be viewed favourably by Dick's bosses. We also did not appreciate that Australian bankers of the 1950s and 1960s did not have the same financial expertise as their Swiss counterparts. Dick Forbes won the argument, and Dad bought a large quarter acre block of land on Linden Way. As it happened, the land probably had the best views over Middle Harbour and beyond. Forbes also suggested an architect, John Brogan. Soon Dad started preliminary discussions with Brogan to come up with some proposals for a house.

Australia

In July 1959, I finished my education at Stonyhurst and, before I left Europe to return to India, decided to go to Czechoslovakia and also St. Anton. I suppose that my interest in St. Anton had been more related to this fantastic block of land - Dad's folly - and what could have seduced him to think that this could ever be a home for us. The land was indeed beautiful and afforded the owner a sweeping view over St. Anton but the only residents that currently enjoyed the view were Austrian Simmental and Pinzgauer cows, probably owned by Johan Fahrner. In late August, I returned to Calcutta, still not knowing where my future lay. I had an opportunity to go to the London School of Economics, but this option at the time did not quite appeal to me, as it would have meant even more time spent away from home. This question was uppermost on my mind. I had been at boarding school since the age of six and had seen my parents for less than three months each year. To my simple way of thinking, I needed to reconnect with them, as I really did not know them - nor had I had the benefit of a parent's involvement with children. In many ways, they were strangers to me. Sure, they had provided me with a good education and met all my material needs, but I felt absolutely no connection to them at all on a personal or emotional level. Many years later, I came to realize that this was the high price that I had to pay for the blind belief that boarding school competed favourably with hands-on parenting.

I sought direction from them on the simple question, "What next?" When I had finally settled back into life in Calcutta, it soon became apparent that a decision had now finally been made about where we would live. Mum and Dad had committed to moving to Sydney, Australia. They had already bought land there and then I found out that an architect had been working already on a house design. I remember sitting down with Dad to look at artist impressions of the new house. The sketches portrayed an impressive looking building, but it was hard to visualize against the contours of the land.

Slowly the intent behind the impressive plans started to emerge. This was to be a home for the extended family. Dad's vision was that Martina, Charlie and I would live there. We would all have our own rooms and bathrooms. There would be large indoor and outdoor living areas and the house would have a pool. The scale of the house was truly enormous. Then Dad added that he hoped that when we all got married we would continue to live in the house and establish some sort of communal family life. A veritable harmonious Hruska ashram! At the time, I could not think beyond all of his dreams, but obviously Mum and Dad envisaged our future to be in Australia. My thoughts therefore shifted from possible study in London to university in Sydney. After I broached this issue to my parents, Dad talked to me only about my financial and livelihood support, not about my interests or motivations. So, I concentrated all my efforts on getting into Sydney University and finding a place to live. In December 1959 or January 1960, I moved to Australia, thus becoming the first person in our family to actually live in Sydney. After arriving, I stayed for a short time with the Begbies, friends of Mum and Dad from Calcutta, who were living in Manly. As a newcomer to Australia, I could not think of a better place to live than Manly, a beachside suburb, close to the harbour and the ferries that were the transport of choice to city centre. I remember those

Sunday nights when Mrs. Begbie would cook us her wonderful curries. Her cooking fame spread and soon Ivan Valenta, Johnny Křižká and I joined their family regularly at Sunday dinner. During this time, and with the help of Mum and Dad, I finally made arrangements to live at the University itself, in St. John's College.

At this point, I had not given much thought to my future studies. The University put on what they called Orientation Week, where people like me could visit various faculties and talk to students and teachers about what they did and the prospects for work. As I had some notions of becoming a doctor, I visited a second-year anatomy class. While there, a student put me off by dissecting a cadaver and at the same time enjoying his sandwiches, which he placed in a brown paper bag cradled in the cavity of the corpse's stomach. Uncertain and confused, I asked Dad what he thought I should do and I have never forgotten his response: "Miki, in Czechoslovakia, the first son should follow in the footsteps of the father. But, as I did not go to university, perhaps you should study Engineering as this most closely resembles what I did in Czechoslovakia and India." We did not have the benefit of career counselling at the time. So, after nearly twenty years of living apart from the family, these words of parental wisdom rang in my ears. And, not being a very reflective person as a result of having enjoyed a lotus-eating lifestyle to date, I accepted his advice and enrolled in Electrical Engineering. Some thirty or forty years later, as I look back at the way my life has rolled out, I sometimes wonder whether the London School of Economics would have been the better option. Maybe, but *c'est la vie*!

And, so, the first member of our family had made the permanent move to Australia – alone!

Factory Entrance, 93B Ripon Street

Shahadat Khan

Fredrik and Henriette Cargnelli

Main Factory Building

Another part of Main Factory Building

Family Apartment 53 Chowringhee Rd

Mum, brother Charley, Mr. Chatterjee

Coco, family friend Dorothy, Mr. Chatterjee

Father Gabric

Mt. Kangchenjunga from Darjeeling

North Point, Darjeeling

Mummy, Miki, Coco in Darjeeling

Dad's First Silver Sports Car

Dad Silver Sports Car

Dad's Second Sports Car

Mullick Bazaar

Dad's 1952 Sikkim Expedition

Dad encamped Jannu Glacier 1952 Sikkim Expedition

Dad with view of Jongsong Peak

Dad crossing Jongsong La pass. Langpo Peak in background

Dad's trekking team moving down valley to Mt. Kangchenjunga

Mum and Dad in the Maidan, Calcutta

Mum and Dad at a social event

Mum and Dad in Darjeeling

Mum skiing in St. Anton, Austria

*Mum and Dad skiing
at Lech, Austria*

Christmas in Calcutta

Dad in Darjeeling

Calcutta Swimming Club outside pool

Mum at Swimming Club

St Paul's Cathedral

Mum convalescing at Prangins, Switzerland

CHAPTER 7

Calcutta, the City

During the colonial era, the British derived their wealth in Calcutta, but spent most of it elsewhere. They bought lavish mansions in the English countryside, while they lived in more modest two-storey dwellings in Calcutta. These Indian homes were built in a variety of architectural styles, giving little consideration to the principles of town planning. Thus, we see grand homes with Ionic or Doric columns, and imitation European gardens and fountains luxuriating behind walls that divided wealth from squalor. Some wealthy Indians, exposed to the British imperial lifestyle, followed these architectural quirks. Witness the Malik family's remarkable, Italian Renaissance-style, Marble Palace, full of decaying European masterpieces.

As for public buildings, any European visitor to Calcutta will recognize the wonderful examples of Georgian and Victorian architecture that abound, notably the majestic Victoria Memorial, Rashtrapati Bhavan (Government House), and Fort William. These buildings, almost universally the victims of decay and neglect today, still remind the appreciative eye of their original beauty and evoke a not very distant colonial time.

Today, Calcutta is visually a city of both the modern and the old, whether evidenced in its business towers or its heritage buildings. It has grand open spaces like the *Maidan* and Park Street, as well as the lively intellectual life that can be found on College Street, with its bookshops and coffee houses. Calcutta is, after all, the home of Rabindranath Tagore, the first non-European to win the Nobel Prize for Literature (1913).

Calcutta demands your interest and attention. The city celebrates its traditions through its love of language, its intellectual and cultural offerings, its political and business life, all of which contribute to a certain style of living. It has a tradition of embracing theatre and music that is, in my opinion, unsurpassed in India. And this is a city with a love for literature and the local arts. For some years now, Calcutta has been home to the world's largest non-trade book fair, which is located on the *Maidan*. The Book Fair was started in 1974, when "some young publishers of Kolkata, sat chatting at the College Street Coffee House about how to start a rendezvous of book lovers."[149] College Street and the *Maidan* are still at the heart of cultural life in Calcutta. But my connection with the Book Fair is very personal. In 2006, I obtained my prized copies of Jim Corbett's books, *The Man Eaters of Kumaon* and *The Man-Eating Leopard of Rudraprayag* at the Calcutta Book Fair! For me, these were amazing finds - they were books that I had enjoyed reading as a boy.

The city talks to you at every turn. It makes you think. It makes you confront and question your values. It makes you an observer of life. Its exterior may lead to shock and rapid judgement for those paying only a fleeting visit; however, a more considered view reveals an utterly human and delightful place where people of all classes or status touch you, for they are generous and kind of spirit.

Mum and Dad cannot speak for themselves and so I hope to answer the question, "What was Calcutta like?" through my own senses by presenting a tableau of images and experiences through this chapter and the next. I am sure that Mum and Dad would nod in agreement for they would have also seen, smelt, heard, tasted, and touched the same. They lived the most

---

149 This passage about the origins of the Book Fair was taken from the Kolkata Book Fair website, Aug. 17, 2018. http://kolkatabookfair.net/kolkata-book-fair/history-2/

productive years of their adult lives there. This is my attempt to give some insight into many of the facets of Calcutta life that they would have experienced or confronted.

Calcutta's Seasons: Rain and Shine

Mark Twain once wrote,

> *I believe that in India 'cold weather' is merely a conventional phrase and has come into use through the necessity of having some way to distinguish between weather which will melt a brass door-knob and weather which will only make it mushy. It was observable that brass ones were in use while I was in Calcutta, showing that it was not yet time to change to porcelain; I was told the change to porcelain was not usually made until May. But this cold weather was too warm for us; so we started to Darjeeling, in the Himalayas - a twenty-four-hour journey.*[150]

Anyone who has lived in the Tropics will remember tropical downpours. Tropical rain gives new meaning to the phrases "bucketing down," or "raining cats and dogs." In Calcutta, the rainy season daily yields the sight of the rickshaw pullers or the heavily laden cart pullers struggling through flooded streets, or people fleeing to avoid the rain in whatever fashion possible. After a really hot, humid day, the rain is welcome, but only as a relief from the discomfort of the heat. When I think about the sun, I think of terms like hot, searing, sticky, and relentless. Heat defines the tropics, perhaps even more than the rain. In summer, the oppressive heat and dust affect everyone's energy levels and their mood. People who work as carriers struggle with their heavy loads. Policemen in full white dress uniform sweat profusely while standing on oil drums that have been cut in half and placed at street intersections; here the policemen direct traffic under the protection of a white umbrella stuck in the belt of their

---

150 From Chapter 54, The Project Gutenberg e-book of *Following the Equator*, by Mark Twain (Samuel Clemens).

uniform. As with any city, seasonal weather cycles dictate the rhythms of daily life.

Calcutta actually enjoys a *sub*-tropical climate. It is located on the Ganges delta and is very close to the Bay of Bengal, and thus very much influenced by the sea. It experiences three major seasons: monsoon, winter, and summer. The period between June and September is monsoon, which is when it rains and rains.

During monsoon, massive, brooding, dark grey clouds overhang the city and the Ganges delta. The sheer power of the monsoonal rains never ceases to fascinate. They bring a fleeting relief from the heat, yet also provide life to all the insect species, especially mosquitoes which, in turn, awaken and torment Calcuttans. The monsoon announces itself to the city with rippling wave after wave of rain; this is an early warning for all, for soon the city is inundated with torrential rain. People know that, in many parts of the city, there will be flooded streets and that the power will fail. Some of the tram services will be disrupted. Anyone caught in a monsoon downpour is totally drenched in a matter of minutes. Rickshaws are at their busiest in the rain. Historically, the rickshaw puller is one of Calcutta's iconic images: his *dhoti* and singlet drenched to the skin, pulling his fare through flooded streets barefoot, with his passengers taking refuge from the rain behind a dirty tarpaulin.

One of my abiding memories of Calcutta and, for that matter India in general, is the ferocity of this tropical rain. Sometimes the rain became so intense that I felt Calcutta's sins were being forgiven through a watery baptism. On some days, especially in August, the loose, wild rain lashed the city; the showers were short, sharp, intense and heavy. They always seemed to follow days of severe heat and thunder. The intensity of the rain forced us to notice it; it was not part of the background. It had its own distinctive rat-tat-tat noise, similar to that of a machine gun, as it hit the ground or the roofs of houses and low-level sheds; it had its own rhythm. If we happened to get caught in the rain, we noticed the individual droplets; they were hard and we felt them. At night, if we were sleeping during a tropical downpour, the rain acted as a salve that ensured a deep sleep. If the day had been really hot and humid and a tropical downpour had even-tuated, it brought relief to the city; our spirits rose as the air cooled and the surrounding atmosphere was again breathable. It settled the suspended dust in the air and made our world fresh again. I loved the rain. I loved to walk in it. I don't know why. Perhaps for me, it meant a subtle cleansing of the body. It certainly felt like a renewal of the spirit prior to the next exposure to heat and humidity.

During a normal downpour, people would avoid the awnings, especially those that were full of water and bulging, or those that had holes in them. Instead, people sought building recesses or bus shelters as they went about their business. The city's busiest thoroughfares were always full of pedestrian traffic. The men looked like army ants on the march, swarming forward under a sea of black umbrellas as they held up the end of their *dhotis* (loincloths) in their free hand. If the pavement became blocked, they would spill out onto the side of the road. The cars sent up plumes of spray with headlights going in one direction and red tail lights in the other.

Only when the rain stopped and evaporation had started, heralded by clouds of steam rising from the surface of the road, did the *dhoti*-clad figures who had sought refuge in buildings and doorways slowly emerge, gingerly walking around the many water puddles on the pavement as if playing hopscotch. Then, after the air moisture had departed and the heat haze had taken over, the roads would appear to be covered in oil patches with the light reflecting off the remaining surface water. As the air freshened, a silent invitation went out to all of the city's flying and crawling insects to emerge and seek their next unsuspecting victims to torment, bite, or sting.

The monsoons created their own problems for the poor people who lived in the *bustees* (slums) and who had no access to proper sewerage or drainage. What drains there were soon became clogged and the sewers overflowed. Many streets flooded and many low-lying areas resembled mini-lakes. These people suffered enormously, since their families lived in cramped quarters and the rainwater overflow often spilt into their dwellings. When the streets became flooded, public transport would grind to a halt. In time, many streets became so damaged that huge potholes developed. All this contributed to the annual cycle of decay, for there existed no systematic or periodic maintenance of the streets by the city's authorities.

At the time, our family never asked, "How do people live like this?" Instead, we were grateful to have dry living quarters and got on with our lives.

December to February is the winter season in Calcutta, a pleasant time of the year. The temperature usually varies between 12°C and 14°C and very rarely goes below 10°C. In the evenings, I remember it getting quite nippy by local standards, cool enough to bring out a short-sleeved pullover. Many of the locals got all trussed up for the cold, all 10°C of it, heavily wrapping their ears in layers and layers of scarves. Apparently the ears were seen as the most vulnerable part of human anatomy to the "cold." Often, in the winter mornings, a layer of mist, not smog, hung over the city and swathed the *Maidan* and other parks. Calcutta walkers took over the suburban streets during this early morning time, dressed to the nines. On these early crisp mornings, devotees of yoga did their exercises on the *Maidan*, along with those who just loved doing any sort of exercise. Mum loved these early misty mornings; they were her favourite part of the day.

Clear, pure, blue skies in Calcutta were rare. The skies were generally sheathed in a greyish haze. Naturally, this was also season dependent. Dusk came early to the city, but it was not the dusk normally associated with the setting of the sun. All over the city, thousands and thousands of *chulas* (small earthen or brick stoves) were fired up on the sidewalks, in the side streets, and in the bustees for the evening meal. In the Calcutta context, a *chula* was a small portable stove that used cow dung, charcoal or wood. The interior and exterior of the *chula* frame was plastered with a mud mixture and had a smooth finish. The *chula* had an opening at the bottom for the fuel source. The top may have had a grill top but was normally open so one could rest a pot or pan or even a skewer across it. The *chula* could also be used as a heater. Evening meals were normally prepared at dusk when families started to cook their *chapattis* (wheat pancakes), boil the *chawal* (rice), and prepare a vegetable dish, probably *dhal,* a dish based on red or brown lentils. The smoke generated from these stoves was a significant contributor to Calcutta's air pollution. As the smoke rose, the air took on the smell of whichever fuel was being used. So, our evenings were marked by a street-hugging smoke and perhaps, a cow dung-scented haze. When the sun started to set, it therefore appeared as a blurred, amber, glowing disc on the horizon.

I often wondered if Calcutta had a spring at all, since the transition from the end of winter to summer seemed so fast. As the summer approached, we felt the change in our bodies as we noticeably slowed down. From March to June, summer took over in Calcutta. In summer, on many a day, the skies appeared to be bleached. Even early in the morning, we knew that the temperature would soar. Any summer memory of Calcutta must include remorseless sun, searing heat, and prickly humidity. As the season changed from winter to summer, the sun went from a balmy glow in the sky to a fiery ball screened by a curtain of rippling hot air; then, the sun was fully ablaze, giving off a torrid heat. At home, the blinds in our verandah were lowered to keep the heat out. The temperature often reached 41°C in the month of May. I always felt that May was the worst month of the year. The humidity nudged 100% during summer; this made us feel lethargic and gasping for air at the same time. It penetrated into our skin, where it clung like the clammy hand of a watery death. The only relief from the pollution and the ever-present dust in the air came from the occasional rain squall that swept in from the Bay of Bengal. The cooling relief provided by these short-lived, random, daytime showers was fleeting because they were often followed by dusty, violent winds.

Calcutta's Building Practices

Building sites in Calcutta during my parents' time, and even today, are a form of organized chaos. One of the supreme building art forms practised in the city was to be seen on the walls of new buildings, which were like a canvas on an artist's easel. At the base of the building lay a jumble of building materials, bricks, sand, cement, and sticks of bamboo lying tumbled about. The bamboo poles were used to create the exterior scaffolding of the building under construction. Slowly the poles were erected into the vertical plane and tied to other poles placed on the horizontal plane. Now, not all bamboos run in straight lines, so the scaffolding structures followed the natural lines of the bamboo, which were never true to the vertical or the horizontal. The result was that little bends bulged and waggled out from the actual building under construction. Jute rope held this amazing structure together.

The construction workers built little board pathways on top of the horizontal poles; this enabled an army of workmen who balanced their loads, mainly bricks, on their heads, to bring building materials to the necessary elevation. Scattered all over this incredible scaffolding structure were the bricklayers, who moved between these bamboo structural elements like trapeze artists in a circus. Ever so slowly, the actual building inched upwards. It was always possible to distinguish new buildings from older established buildings by the size of the rubbish pile of damaged or partially unused construction material that had been left behind. The new owners knew that this rubbish pile would very quickly get smaller and disappear as human scavengers carted it away to become part of another building venture somewhere else in the city. So, we have that unique phenomenon of building debris "wandering" around the city. As the debris diminished, the walls of the new building would serve as the support for shanty structures erected by the poor. In this way, most buildings in Calcutta looked 50 years old by the time they opened.

Our Neighbourhood

St. Paul's Cathedral

Directly opposite our home in Chowringhee Road stood the Anglican Church known as St. Paul's Cathedral, which was situated in quite beautiful grounds. The building of St. Paul's started in 1839 and was finally completed in 1847.[151] Over the years, it had been repaired and partly reconstructed as a result of an earthquake in 1934. My sister and I spent many hours in the church garden, initially being perambulated there by our *amahs*. Later, as a young boy, I played there near the two water tanks and amongst the garden's exotic trees, many of which were climbable, enjoying all the adventure and exploration games that my imagination allowed.

The cathedral structure drew its inspiration from the Neo-Gothic or Gothic Revival architecture style much admired by British colonial architects. Its worship hall was cavernous and lined with stained glass windows on either side of the pews. The decoration on the interior was quite

---

151   Ibid., 168.

300

exquisite. Inside the cathedral, there were a few tombs, many with lovely sculptures of people who had lost their lives in the Great Indian Mutiny of 1857 and others who had succumbed to cholera and typhoid and even some who had lost their lives in a cyclone in the Bay of Bengal. But I think that the finest epitaph in St. Paul's is outlined below, not only because it captures in many ways the essence of British colonial India through the aegis of the British East India Company but also the premature fate that awaited many of Britain's finest youth pursuing adventure and wealth on the Indian sub-continent. I believe that it is important to understand the historical context in the case of my parents. Even though the events occurred in the past, the great city that they now lived in had its genesis in the previous events of British occupation. They were the inheritors of the cultural impact of this history and Mum and Dad had to build their lives in a Calcutta where they were reminded daily of India's history, its institutions, its dominant language, and the society around them. I was obviously too young to notice this epitaph, but when I travelled to Calcutta in the early 1990s, I revisited our home and, in particular, St. Paul's Cathedral, where I saw this epitaph and took note of it. The full text is outlined below:

NOT NEAR THIS STONE,
NOR IN ANY CONSECRATED GROUND,
BUT ON THE EXTREME FRONTIERS OF THE BRITISH
INDIAN EMPIRE,
LIE THE REMAINS OF
PATRICK ALEXANDER VANS AGNEW,
OF THE BENGAL CIVIL SERVICE
AND
WILLIAM ANDERSON,
LIEUT 1st BOMBAY FUSILIER REGT,
ASSISTANTS TO THE RESIDENT AT LAHORE:
WHO, BEING DEPUTED BY THE GOVERNMENT TO RELIEVE
AT HIS OWN REQUEST,
DEWAN MOOLRAJ, VICEROY OF MOULTAN,
OF THE FORTRESS AND AUTHORITY WHICH HE HELD,
WERE ATTACKED AND WOUNDED BY THE GARRISON,

ON THE 19th APRIL 1848,
AND BEING TREACHEROUSLY DESERTED BY THE SIKH ESCORT,
WERE ON THE FOLLOWING DAY
IN FLAGRANT BREACH OF NATIONAL FAITH AND HOSPITALITY,
BARBAROUSLY MURDERED
IN THE EDGAH UNDER THE WALLS OF MOULTAN.
THUS FELL THESE TWO YOUNG PUBLIC SERVANTS,
AT THE AGE OF 25 AND 28 YEARS,
FULL OF HIGH HOPES, RARE TALENTS, AND PROMISE OF
FUTURE USEFULNESS,
EVEN IN THEIR DEATHS DOING THEIR COUNTRY HONOR:
WOUNDED AND FORSAKEN THEY COULD OFFER
NO RESISTANCE,
BUT HAND IN HAND CALMLY AWAITED THE ONSET OF
THEIR ASSAILANTS;
NOBLY THEY REFUSED TO YIELD,
FORTELLING THE DAY WHEN THOUSANDS OF ENGLISHMEN
SHOULD COME TO AVENGE THEIR DEATH.
AND DESTROY MOOLRAJ, HIS ARMY AND FORTRESS;
HISTORY RECORDS SHOW THE PREDICTION WAS FULFILLED,
THEY WERE BURIED WITH MILITARY HONORS
ON THE SUMMIT OF THE CAPTURED CITADEL,
ON THE 26th JANUARY 1849,
THE ANNEXATION OF THE PUNJAB TO THE BRITISH EMPIRE
WAS THE RESULT OF THE WAR,
OF WHICH THEIR ASSASSINATION WAS THE COMMENCEMENT.

THE ASSISTANTS TO THE RESIDENT AT LAHORE
HAVE ERECTED THIS MONUMENT
TO THE MEMORY OF THEIR FRIEND

Park Street

About four blocks from our home on Chowringhee Road heading toward New Market, a right turn took the resident to Park Street, the closest thoroughfare that Calcutta had to a boulevard. The street began at the western end of the *Maidan* and ran all the way down to the commercial district of Park Circus. When Mum and Dad lived in Calcutta, there was a statue of Sir James Outram at the intersection. Later, Outram's statue was removed and replaced by a statue of Mahatma Gandhi, surrounded by a ring of small flower gardens. Park Street offered Calcuttans the best fine dining experience, coffee shops, restaurants, ice cream parlours, bookshops, magazine vendors, and other small stores. Notable eating-house names in my parents' time included Flury's, Trinca's, Blue Fox, Park Restaurant, Kwality, Olympia, and Moulin Rouge. Park Street was our place to meet up with friends in its many coffee shops and restaurants. These places added a pleasant international character to the city when compared with the other large cities in India. Most of these places offered music provided by small bands and Saturdays meant jam sessions, with the musical flavour of the month provided by well-known crooners like Pam Crain, Braz Gonsalves and Louis Banks. Isaiah's Bar, a seedier establishment, just down the road on Free School Street, catered to a clientele who were prone to brawls and drunken behaviour. One of the roads running off Park Street was Middleton Row; Loreto House dominated much of the street. My sister, Martina, went to school there.

Park Street represented the cosmopolitan heart of the city. At the Park Street and Middleton Row intersection was a Swiss patisserie and confectionery coffee shop, called Flury's. It was the best-known coffee shop in Calcutta; people loved to meet there to enjoy, not only the coffee, but some of the best cakes, biscuits and savouries in town. Mr. Flury had a daughter named Josette, who was my first serious infatuation. I believe the shop was originally co-owned by two Swiss families. At some point, they had a serious difference of opinion and fell out. As a result, Trinca's, another coffee shop, was set up about 100 yards away from Flury's. This was much closer to Chowringhee Road. Trinca's became a favourite venue for the business community. Dad used to go there and indulge himself with their signature, multi-layered, club sandwich. Trinca's sometimes offered a tea dance at 4 o'clock. However, as popular as Trinca's became, if we wanted to plan a tea or birthday party, we ordered our cakes and biscuits from Flury's.

Magnolia's was always the coffee and milk bar of choice for the younger crowd who came to listen to a lonely jukebox that spewed out songs by

Pat Boone, The Kingston Trio, and Harry Belafonte. Inside, apart from the energy expended on the dance floor, young males loved to preen themselves, especially their hair. The smell of Brylcreem anointed the nostrils everywhere. If the comb broke as a result of an over-zealous combing action, the boys could soon replace it from the street vendors outside who specialized in exotic, greasy hair products and combs to meet any hair or wave requirements. I remember there was also a hobby shop called Hobbyco where I used to go with Mum to buy miniature, balsa wood plane kits and meccano sets. Also on Park Street was an apology of a department store called Hall and Anderson's where, just prior to my returning to school in Darjeeling, Mum and I made our obligatory visit to purchase cheaper shirts and underwear.

When Dad and Mum decided that we needed an outing, we usually went to the Park Restaurant where they served great Chinese food. This later changed hands and reappeared as a restaurant called Blue Fox that offered Indian food and music. Blue Fox changed Dad's opinion about Indian food and became his favourite restaurant. Park Street even had a Moulin Rouge, with mini windmill and sails, though I cannot recall if the sails actually turned. Another popular restaurant was the Sky Room, known for its love affair with the colour blue and a ceiling that resembled the night sky, with a host of twinkling lights. This venue offered a sort of cabaret in the evenings. These places all had exceptionally fine cuisine and the family would often come to them for a "*burra khana,*" literally a "big feast."

Towards the lower end of Park Street is the famous necropolis known as the South Park Street Cemetery.[152] This cemetery pre-dates the Park Street of my youth and is therefore totally out of place on this busy commercial thoroughfare. When I think of the history that the Cemetery represents, I always feel that it deserves a better location than to be situated in an unremarkable part of Park Street surrounded by an uninteresting busy neighbourhood. It has a quiet serene atmosphere about it and, while it is a cemetery, provides a fascinating mirror of the history of the Raj in India. The

---

152   A description of this cemetery can be found at the following link https://www.saha-pedia.org/city-of-the-dead-south-park-street-cemetery

epitaphs etched on the headstones read like a panegyric of self-perceived sacrifice on the altar of the British Empire. A walk through this cemetery reveals the eccentricity of many tombs, from simple headstones to obelisks and even miniature pyramids and urns. South Park Street Cemetery is not a well-tended or manicured garden. Many monuments have fallen victim to the frequent monsoons that plague Calcutta; rain and high humidity have promoted the overgrowth of moss and other clinging plants. Opened in 1767, South Park Street Cemetery is a testament to the many people who succumbed to tropical disease while engaged in the struggle for king or queen and country. Many of these decaying and weathered tombs are heavily inscribed with the life histories of the dead.

South Park Street Cemetery is the final resting place for some of Calcutta's important citizens. Probably the most important tomb is that of William Jones. It is shaped as a miniature pyramid. On 15 January, 1784, William Jones co-founded the Asiatic Society, which was devoted to furthering Asian studies and research. On his arrival in Calcutta, he became totally entranced with Indian culture. Jones was an English philologist, a linguist who spoke numerous oriental languages; he was a jurist and a scholar with an interest in Eastern history, language, and culture.[153] He contributed greatly to the furthering of knowledge on Bengali law, literature, music, and other sciences.

In another part of the cemetery is the tomb of Major-General Charles Stuart (c. 1758 - 31 March, 1828), yet another British East India Company officer to immerse himself totally in Hindu culture; his passion earned him the nickname "Hindoo" Stuart.[154] His tomb is quite spectacular, as it takes the form of a Hindu temple. His love affair with Hindu culture and life extended to wearing native clothes and in taking a daily ritual bath in the Hooghly. He even encouraged English women to wear the sari. Another interesting person buried here is Henry Louis Vivian Derozio (18 April, 1809 - 26 December, 1831). Derozio was a person of mixed Portuguese and Indian birth. When he turned 17, he was appointed to teach history and English literature. Derozio himself had been a poet of some note at

153 Sukanta Chaudhuri, ed., *Calcutta, the Living City. Vol I: The Past,* 196.
154 Soumitra Das, *A Jaywalkers Guide to Calcutta,* 67.

the Hindu College. He also became a fierce patriot for Bengal; his zeal and influence on his students were enormous. He was a catalyst in the promotion of Bengali intellectual life.[155]

Most of the cemetery's inhabitants are women and children, sometimes many members of a single family, who met their death from tropical diseases, skirmishes, and war, but also from childbirth and melancholia. But there are oddities as well. The headstone of one Lucy Aylmer recounts that she died from eating too many pineapples. In another part of the cemetery lie the remains of Mrs. Frances Johnson who, at 13, married the first of her four husbands, a dapper gent with the colourful name of Parry Purple Templer. Her epitaph stands as a stark witness to the numerous ravages of cholera, childbirth, shipwreck and melancholia among the young. Many tombstone epitaphs begin with the lines: "If ever tears deservedly were shed...," a truly sad testament to the human tragedy that accompanied the colonizer in Calcutta.

Many other famous figures from Britain's' colonial period are buried here. However, from my perspective, the most telling epitaph is to be found on Grave 363 that just has the following inscription:

A VIRTUOUS MOTHER

DIED 1825

This epitaph echoes the highest praise that could have been bestowed on a woman from Victorian England; it is in essence the epitaph to the Unknown Woman commemorating the Victorian home.

Mum's Horse Riding in Winter

Our family friend Coco Mackertich owned a number of horses; these were animals that had finished their career on the racetrack, but had now found a new home at Coco's expansive property on Lower Circular Road. These horses needed to be exercised daily and so Coco asked Mum if she would join him on his early morning outing at the Calcutta Race Club exercise

155 Sukanta Chaudhuri, ed., *Calcutta, the Living City. Vol II: The Present and the Future,* 68-69, 207.

track. Mum obliged and this is how she got to go horse riding each day. Very soon, she became used to one particular bay horse, a largish animal, but as timid as a mouse; Mum loved riding him. I used to accompany Mum and sit on the guardrail watching her and the other riders put all of Coco's horses through their paces. During this hour of the morning, Calcutta was unusually subdued. The early morning air had enough nip in it that, when the horses snorted and sneezed, their expelled breath condensed quickly. After Mum had completed her morning ride and, as I had been nominated the custodian of carrots and sugar cubes, we got to feed the horses and stroke their soft muzzles.

Calcutta Swimming Club

With the hot summers in Calcutta during the months from March to June, when the temperature was generally north of 35°C and with 100% humidity, the Calcutta Swimming Club afforded many people both great pleasure and relief. The Swimming Club is located on the Strand Road, one of the more pleasant roads in Calcutta; it runs alongside the River Hooghly. The Club and its outside swimming pool were situated adjacent to and under the gaze of the Calcutta Law Courts.

The Calcutta Swimming Bath actually got its sanction to be built from the Lieutenant Governor of Bengal on 24 May, 1887. It had originally been intended as a private amenity for a wealthy group of Calcutta merchants. The present-day Calcutta Swimming Club evolved from this planned intent. Initially, it had an inside swimming pool co-located with clothing change cubicles. The much larger outside pool was built in the 1930s. House modesty rules at the time dictated that men had to wear full body costumes and women had to be completely covered from neck to knees. At first, the catering service for club members consisted of Bovril and biscuits. During the Second World War, servicemen used the Club's facilities extensively.

After the War, the Club's membership grew and further improvements were made. In the 1940s, the Swimming Club initially restricted its membership to the British. But after Independence from Britain in 1947, this membership group declined steadily, as expatriates completed their contracts with their British companies and returned to Europe. With dwindling membership, the Club decided to open its doors to the white, non-British, expatriate community. As a result, my parents and a lot of their friends became members in 1948. There was no change in the eligibility criteria for membership until the early 1970s, when the resident Europeans and other expatriates started to retire, dispose of their business interests, and emigrate to Australia, Canada, or Britain. I could never understand why Indians were precluded from becoming members. Racism is an obvious reason. But it may also have been that their community regarded swimming in public a very gauche activity. Consequently, they may not have availed themselves of the opportunity to become members after Independence. Even in later years, when membership was thrown open, the Club became more a meeting place for tea or coffee and a gossip, than a chance to cool off with a swim.

The Club had its amusing moments. After the 1967 and 1969 elections in West Bengal, it had still not torn down all barriers to membership. So, Ram Chatterjee, the newly elected United Left Front member of the West Bengal Communist and Socialist Party Alliance decided to make some sort of "public statement." He took a busload of Santhal tribesmen and made his way to the outside pool where they proceeded to strip half naked, jump in the pool at the shallow end, and prance around like excited water babies. Note that this frolicking did not occur at the deep end of the pool; otherwise the local newspapers might have had to report not only a "public statement," but also a "mass drowning tragedy."

A visit to the Swimming Club was our family's relief during the hot humid days of summer. The large outdoor pool had all sorts of tethered islands at various places. We children learnt to swim there. On Sundays, this became our family outing. Mum and Dad met up with their friends and other Czech families and caught up on all the news. Our day at the Club gravitated between long stays in the water and the unwelcome exit from the water to have a little lunch. This was no great sacrifice, since we thoroughly enjoyed the Club's famous club sandwiches. My long-lasting memory of the Swimming Club is of very pleasant and happy family occasions.[156]

---

156 The Club's history can be found on its website at: http://www.calcuttaswimming-club.com/index.php/pages/club_history

Calcutta's *Maidan*

"The *Maidan*"[157] is Calcutta's truly magnificent "green lung" for its citizens. It is the city's major, large parkland area and it provides the necessary spiritual uplift and breathing space for people who want to get away from the intensity, noise, smells, and visible struggles for life that take place in other central areas of the city. In my parents' time, it covered about 990 acres very near the river Hooghly. Many roads intersected the *Maidan,* from the Course Road that skirted Calcutta Race Course, to the Strand Road that ran alongside the River Hooghly, and the Red Road that bisected it from north to south. Over its entire perimeter, the *Maidan* is surrounded by some of Calcutta's most magnificent buildings and monuments. The impressive Calcutta Race Course and the majestic Victoria Memorial monument flank the *Maidan* to the south. At its northern end, the *Maidan* is bounded by the Ochterlony Monument, and the imposing Raj Bhavan, or the Governor's Mansion, as it was known in the days of the Raj. To the south are the Victoria Memorial, St. Paul's Cathedral, and Fort William to the west. In recent times the cricket ground, Eden Gardens, has been added to the northwest corner.

To this day, the *Maidan* is home to all sorts of leisure activities. Scattered cricket players have impromptu games there during the winter months. The cricketers pay no attention to the state of the ground so long as they can pace off the 22 yards for the pitch to have a game. Here baggy short pants are the "cricket flannel" of choice. Stumps can be three real cricket stumps, or a pile of bricks. The ball can be a proper cricket ball, or a tennis ball. But they play the game as if every match is a Test Match, with the outcome of an actual series resting on the result. The kids adopt the names of the cricketing heroes of the day. When I was a boy, their *Maidan* matches may have witnessed an "Umrigar" bowling to a "Manjrekar" or "Pankaj Roy."

157 *Maidan* is an Urdu word meaning an open space for people.

The *Maidan* was also home to people playing badminton, volleyball, and *gilli danda*;[158] to people riding horses; families having a picnic on the grass; and children flying kites and playing marbles. Then, as now, late in the afternoon, groups of students came out and sat on the grass to relax and enjoy a discussion on whatever was topical. And then there were the street musicians, snake charmers, dancing monkeys, black Himalayan bears, acrobats, jugglers and tumblers, who came out to entertain the passers-by.

Near the Victoria Memorial, opposite one of the gates, the muscle and body building aficionados flexed their biceps, triceps and whatever other "ceps" they had. Fitness fanatics were drawn to the *Maidan*, especially those interested in yoga. The walkers, clad in their *dhotis*, vests and pull-overs, came in the early morning. The walkers encompassed all age groups, with most wearing Dunlop Volley tennis shoes - the Adidas and Nike equivalents of the day. After the walkers came the joggers but they were attired in more appropriate gear. Here and there, soccer was played, either informally or in organized clubs, and often with only one goalpost. On the periphery of the *Maidan* were found some of the oldest and most famous soccer clubs of Calcutta, which even today enjoy a great rivalry, namely Mohun Bagan Club (founded in 1889) and Mohammedan Sporting.

When the weather was not particularly stifling and the temperature hovered around 25°C., Mum and Dad would go for a walk to the Victoria Memorial end of the *Maidan* where there were beautiful gardens and water tanks; here they could relax and play with us. On many occasions, I remember walking with Mum to the markets but, instead of walking down Chowringhee Road and keeping company with the traffic, we would cut across to the *Maidan* and walk there for the remaining four or five blocks

---

158 *Gilli Danda* is a very popular game that is played throughout India. It is simple and requires only the most basic equipment. All you need is a short stick that is 6 inches long and tapered at both ends (the *Gilli*) and a stick about 2-3 feet long (the *Danda*). There is no limit to the number of players, but you need at least two (one to hit the *Gilli* and one to catch it). The hitter, using the *Danda*, hits one of the tapered ends of the *Gilli* hard enough to lift it off the ground and go as far as possible. The catcher(s) tries to catch it before it hits the ground. If it falls, the batter scores points and, if it is caught, he is replaced by a new batter. The winner is the person or team with the most points. Having played this game, I can affirm that it is fun, but requires considerable skill.

to Lindsay Street and the New Market. I loved walking by myself in the *Maidan* for other reasons, namely the street vendors who sold *Jhall Muri*, a favourite snack of mine. It was basically spiced, puffed wheat served in little paper cones. Here and there were other food vendors who offered mouth-watering choices of Bengali sweets like *jelabis* and *rasagoolas*, while others sold *Teli Bhaja* and *Alu Dum*. The fixed food stalls paid for their concessions, but the mobile ones were geared to moving rapidly if the inspectors appeared. These vendors were everywhere. Most had a bamboo cane hourglass stand in one hand. They stood, carrying their stock in the other hand; on their heads they balanced a small cooking oven, some-times already burning fuel and insulated from the top of their heads by an improvised, coiled, cloth heat insulator.

The scope of the food vendors on the *Maidan* was incredible. They sold everything from home brewed tea, to *paan*, to sweet meats. The most common food vendors sold roasted peanuts, or *bhel puri* (puffed rice mixed with various spices and vegetables). Sometimes, for those perform-ing their exercises in the *Maidan* and, if they were lucky, there would be a food vendor selling some *Teli Bhaja* (deep-fried vegetables in batter), or roasted corn or maize. For those with a sweet tooth, there were ice-creams, *kulfis*, and even candy-floss. As a boy, I really felt like I had struck pay-dirt if I found a vendor selling *phuchkas* (also known as *golgappas* or *pani puris*) and variants of this treat such as *dahi phuchkas* (where the tamarind water was substituted by thick curds). How would I describe this taste sen-sation? They were hollow balls of fried flour which had been mixed with Tamarind juice, grams, mashed potatoes and red chilli and usually served in a cone made of some leaf and held together with slivers of wood that resembled toothpicks. Use of fingers accompanied by much finger licking was *de rigueur*. I needed to have a good *roomal* (handkerchief) ready for my watering eyes. Calcutta's street-food was usually prepared or served with chillies and tamarind. Street food is surely one of the great joys of India and, in Calcutta, we had some of the best as well a great deal of choice. When my parents were in Calcutta, there were even people selling a glass of water from goatskins. Mum and Dad abstained from the street food, as they were far too knowledgeable and sensible about food hygiene; but, for a young boy on his own, *Jhall Muri* was food nirvana.

Many families and friends visited the *Maidan* on weekends and holidays. If a person needed a haircut, the *Maidan* was the place to find a barber. The adults amused themselves like adults everywhere in the world by arguing and gossiping about local politics or other happenings in the city. Evening walks tended to be very relaxed and included regular stops at their favourite food stall.

At the Ochterlony monument, situated at the northern end of the *Maidan*, there was very often a meeting or political rally in progress. These rallies could be large and quite intense. Leading politicians or local, charismatic bigwigs, delivered fiery speeches that rose to a crescendo. This performance would fire up their followers, who would then march off to some place where they could shout their slogans to a crowd of sympathizers, who would respond with rehearsed phrases.

At the Victoria Memorial, families, or even a romantically inclined couple, might hire a distinctive *ghora ghari* (horse carriage), a relic of the British Raj. The horse carriages had been introduced to Calcutta in the late 1880s. Most of the horses were seriously malnourished, old, and often badly treated. Sometimes people hired these horse-drawn *ghora gharis* to go to the New Market for shopping. Others would just enjoy a ride around the perimeter roads of the *Maidan* and various city landmarks, like the Birla Planetarium. Sometimes a large, corpulent family would shoe-horn themselves into the *ghora ghari*. As they all collectively settled into their seats, the suspension springs would squeal in response. The driver would fold in the loose end of any protruding *sari* from Memsahib or *dhoti* from Sahib into the carriage before shutting the door. After taking his position on the driver's seat, he would reach for his whip and crack it close to the ears of the gaunt horses. No forward motion was forthcoming. The poor animals showed their displeasure at the sudden extra weight by swishing their tails back and forth before raising them erect and ejecting a torrent of horse dung. Still no forward progress. If the horses could have spoken, they would have bayed, "Are you seriously asking me to pull that mob in the seats? You have not fed me. I have no strength! No way!" The whip flailed over their ears. They could hear the crack, but still no movement! Soon after this non-event, the impatient and frustrated passengers would get out of the carriage and move to the nearest food vendor to appease their frustrations and seek out their next transportation option. Ah, there was a rickshaw ahead. Now, the rickshaw man might be willing....

Calcutta Zoo

Mum and Dad occasionally took me to the Calcutta *Chiriya Khana* (Calcutta Zoo). When we left our house in Chowringhee, we turned into Lower Circular Road (now called A.J.C. Bose Road) and drove past a treed section of the *Maidan* and the imposing setting of the Calcutta racecourse. We turned left at the Zeerut Bridge. The next stop was the Zoo. As we drove over this elevated bridge, and when we reached its apex and looked to our right, there was an open area with a lot of cows wandering around or resting in what seemed a state of animal bliss. We could never quite figure why this little oasis for cows existed here and so we asked our friend Mr. Chatterjee for an explanation. His response surprised us. In his own inimical style, he mused, while gently cradling his beloved pipe, "You know, I believe that this is an old age home for cows, a little sanctuary where old, tired, frail or sick cows are sent to pasture awaiting their mortal end and possibly reincarnation." Well, how considerate indeed, but understandable knowing the reverence in which cows are held!

The Zoo is India's oldest and dates back to the 1870s; even when I was a boy, it showed its age. Although it had some unique attractions, the conditions in which many of the animals were kept - cages and the areas surrounded by a moat - could only be described as pitiful. The animals lived in cramped quarters and many displayed their boredom. Keepers apparently had been attacked by some of the animals but nothing was ever done to alleviate the conditions that caused these attacks. As a child, I was oblivious to these problems. I remember seeing a very old Aldabra tortoise, apparently captured from an island in an atoll in the Seychelles. This particular tortoise had the reputation of being one of the largest tortoises in the world. Another unique animal that I remember was the Indian, one-horned rhinoceros. However, the real gems in this zoo were the two white tigers that had been acquired specifically for the Alipore Zoo. They were truly majestic animals, unfortunately housed in a cage and not a free-run enclosure.

The zoo had a large lake with an island in the middle that was home to hundreds of birds. A fence surrounded the lake. Families or groups of school children enjoying an outing would gravitate to the bird life on the lake. Many of these adults and even the children would walk along the fence line around the lake in a single file, like one long conga line. They formed a human chain with the little finger of one person intertwined with the little finger of the person ahead and behind. Smaller children gripped a *sari* or *dhoti* of the next person in line. When the lead person stopped, they all stopped and the linked column concertinaed together. When the lead person looked at a bird or animal, they all looked in wide-eyed wonder at the same bird or animal in a synchronous action. Whenever I saw these human chains, I was reminded of groups of elephants, large and small, walking single file with the trunk of one elephant grabbing the tail of the elephant in front and striding forward.

Loreto House

My sister, Martina, attended Loreto House, a strict, girls' convent school run by nuns who all sported the usual "Mother" names, like Mother Immaculata, Mother Xaviera, Mother Scholastica, or Mother Angelina. Loreto House is situated just off the very fashionable Park Street. Every school day, the convent girls were driven to school either in the family's chauffeur-driven Hindustan (an Indian designed vehicle of the day) or by taxi, accompanied by a chaperone to ensure the little darlings arrived safely. Loreto House, like the school that I attended in Darjeeling, accepted Indian and European children. For the European girls, attending Loreto simply meant that they would have a good education. However, the "convent-educated" Indian girls had a distinct advantage in the marriage market. They could look forward to an arranged marriage with a wealthy Bengali Brahman or professional. At the end of their seven or eight years at Loreto, they would be the proud holders of a certificate outlining their scholarly and cultural achievements and which implied an unwritten subtext: "I am a convent educated girl and I am ready to be married."

Social Diversions

Mum and Dad had limited opportunities for any social diversion in the early years. In Batanagar, most of the entertainment was provided through the social club. They couldn't speak English at that time and so moved in their own circle of friends. In Calcutta, however, they were introduced by their friends to a limited aspect of club life. These were the Swimming and Saturday Clubs, where they met their friends and enjoyed the club and sporting facilities. As their English improved, their social circle expanded, as did access to other social opportunities. This at least gave their life a newer flavour and something totally different to that which existed in Czechoslovakia. They now went out to the movies, dined at the numerous restaurants (some of which offered live entertainment) and entertained at home.

In Mum and Dad's time, Calcutta had least eight cinemas that I can remember that featured English-speaking films. Not all, however, were venues that my mother would attend. The top two were undoubtedly the Elite and the Metro cinemas. These were owned and operated by MGM. The Metro, originally built in 1935, started as a variety theatre known as the Palace of Varieties and became a cinema in 1938 after it had been re-modelled in an Art Deco style. The Metro liked to feature newly-released Hollywood movies. It opened with a splash in 1950 with the film *Red River* starring John Wayne. Architecturally, the Metro was quite interesting. The exterior had a slender tower and molded art deco bands running right through the façade. The interior continued with the art deco theme with hidden lights on the sides and ceiling. The auditorium had two levels: the stalls and the upper circle. Very low-income patrons were accommodated in the first few rows of the stalls for the princely sum of thirty paise. This area, in many ways, resembled a bear pit. Upstairs, the seats ranged from three to four rupees, depending on the type of film and the currency of the release. Mum and Dad liked to go to the Metro. I remember seeing *Quo Vadis* there with them, a Roman toga and sandals epic featuring Deborah Kerr and Robert Taylor (one of Mum's favourite actors). There was always the feeling of an outing when entering the main hall of the cinema and walking past the full blown-up posters of the current matinee idols and buxom screen sirens. They all seemed to be looking down at us in approval.

In 1954, the Elite was the first cinema in Calcutta to feature Cinemascope and I remember going with Mum and Dad to see *Beyond the 12 Mile Reef*, a Romeo and Juliet-type melodrama with a youthful Gilbert Roland, a curly-haired, dashing Robert Wagner playing the Greek sponge fisherman's son, and a buxom Terri Moore, who spent a lot of the film in a wet shirt. Other notable films that we saw at the Elite were the Palestinian drama *The Robe*, with Victor Mature, a swarthy, chunky actor, who was another of Mum's favourites; and the hilarious comedy, *How To Marry A Millionaire,* with Marilyn Monroe, Betty Grable and Lauren Bacall. Mum adored Lauren Bacall.

There were two other cinemas, the Lighthouse and New Empire, which my parents frequented, since they were clean, had plush seating and the air-conditioning worked. If you enjoyed films produced in England, then they were most likely to be released in one of these cinemas. And then there were the second-tier cinemas that showed all the B-grade westerns, serial films and other cheaply-produced mystery films. These cinemas included the Globe Cinema, opposite the New Market in Lindsay Street, and the Minerva. Calcutta also had its derelict, fleapit cinemas such as the Tiger and the Regal, with poor seating and no air conditioning, but with whirring fans. The latter was bug-infested and had cane seats with holes. You had to be really desperate for entertainment to patronize these filthy venues. The Regal had a nice tradition of starting all its feature films with a rendering of Tiger Rag.

Mostly our cinema experiences were fine, but there were days when everything went wrong. I remember the showing of the film *Ben Hur* in 1959. I am not sure at which movie theatre, probably the Elite. The problem was that not all the reels of the film had arrived. As the film progressed and we came to the scenes of the dramatic chariot race, we saw the chariots line up and Stephen Boyd cast threatening glances at Charlton Heston. The race started and the chariots rushed forward in a chaotic line to the first corner with the odd chariot flipping over in dramatic fashion. Then, with no apparent conclusion of the chariot race, the next film sequence showed a domestic scene with Charlton Heston confronting his lady love, Haya Harakeet, and "finding the faith," somewhat dramatically while being on hand to give water to Jesus on his way to being crucified. What happened to the race? Who won? What happened to Stephen Boyd? The film finished, the curtain came down and the movie theatre resounded with boos and shouts, but to no avail. The cinema emptied and, as this had been the 5:00 pm show, we emerged into bright sunlight, shrugged our shoulders and went to a coffee shop. It was later in the week when we found out that one or two of the reels had got lost in the mail. But this was all in the life of a Calcutta moviegoer.

To my boyish mind, it was the westerns that provided the best movie experiences. Generally, a western was playing somewhere in the second tier of Calcutta cinemas every week. In these cinemas, I experienced the ultimate in audience participation. Sometimes during the movie, if there was a scene where the "bad" cowboys chased the "good" cowboys and it appeared that they might be headed for a trap in some gulch or narrow canyon, audience members would start to shout warnings to the good cowboys, alerting them to the location where the bad cowboys planned their ambush. These audience participation instances were absolutely hilarious to experience but the involvement was all too serious. The audience was genuinely concerned for the "good" cowboys. I also loved going to the Minerva Cinema for, directly opposite, was Nizam's restaurant where, after the movie, I could get the absolutely best *kathi kabab* rolls in Calcutta, dare I also say India, bar none. The ingredients for this "delicacy" are as follows: take a *paratha* roll, put a coating of egg on it, fill it on top with sliced onions, chilli paste and a stuffing choice ranging from curried chicken (my favourite), strips of grilled meat or, for the vegetarians, *paneer* cheese. Then after heating it, you wrapped this taste sensation in a paper roll to hold, peeled back the paper and the first bite transported you to *kabab* heaven! Nizam's represented not only some of the best up-market street food but also in restaurant fare. There were no class distinctions at Nizam's: the rich, the middle class, the passer-by in a rickshaw all stopped here for a *kathi kabab* or *paratha* roll treat between their engagements.

On Chowringhee, there was a Calcutta institution that sadly no longer survives. Firpo's, in Dad's day, was a first-class restaurant, tea-room and confectioners; it also had an upstairs bar and a large dance floor. Firpo's was started by Angelo Firpo and, after the War, it became an epicure's treat, the Calcutta mecca for fine dining. After a splendid meal, diners left with some of the best confectionery from its little shop near the entrance. The location was pure dress circle and its balcony overlooked the *Maidan*. During the War, it was an officer's meeting and dining venue and watering hole. After the War, it put on Calcutta's best dinner-dances. When you went to Firpo's in the evening, you were required to be attired in *khana kapra* (dinner jackets and black bow tie for men and full-length evening dresses for women). I have a few pleasant memories of Firpo's as, every now and then, Mum, Dad, and I, along with the Cargnellis, went on Sundays for their *Burra Khana* (Big Feast) lunch.

Coffee Houses

Coffee houses have always been the great tradition of Calcutta, more so than anywhere else in India. In many ways, they were somewhat reminiscent of the great coffee houses of Vienna where mostly men came to meet, chat, gossip, discuss, and solve the pressing issues of the day, or just read a newspaper, or watch the world go by. (Women tended to congregate at places like Flury's, where they could also eat cake!) Dad's favorite coffee house was located at the top of Chowringhee Road just where Chittaranjan Avenue branched off. Most of the patrons were Bengalis. They had this wonderful art of being able to drape themselves into a chair with one leg crossed over the other at the horizontal. The *dhoti* would just allow a hint of ankle to be seen. A true aficionado would even manage to balance his sandal by his big toe. Often I witnessed the "vibration" sonata where the coffee patron would begin to shake the crossed leg. Sometimes the leg that was firmly planted on the ground would tap; and, all this shaking, vibrating and tapping would be in time. Added to animated arm and hand movements, vibrating limbs gave a heightened articulation to his opinion or story. The coffee house was the natural domain of the artist, the wordsmith, the intellectual and even people from the cinematic world. In short, the coffee house was an important part of Bengali life. I frequently went with Dad, sometimes to escape the heat of the day under an armada of ceiling fans, but mainly for the pleasure of a cold coffee with a hint of cream. How we enjoyed this treat as, all around, we experienced the noise of excited and animated philosophical musings by Bengalis of all ages sitting around a table covered in empty glasses.

How to Buy a Book at the Oxford Book Store

When we wanted to buy books, the Oxford Book Store in Park Street was the only store that mattered. I remember with great fondness this jewel of Calcutta. Every time that I went to browse or buy books, it seemed as if time stood still.

Entering the Oxford Book Store was like entering a labyrinth with deep canyons stacked with books running from floor to ceiling. Many of these books had "lived" on these shelves for decades. This was a book lover's paradise. To be able to browse at the top of the bookshelves, I learned to come attired in well-used, old clothes, for dust reigned supreme here. Some mountaineering skills, preferably those of a rock climber also helped, as the ladders that provided access to the upper level book shelves appeared to have been recovered from a previous expedition to some Himalayan glacier: on occasion, I had to jump from one ladder to an adjoining ladder. But in all cases, I needed to use these ladders to climb up the 10 feet necessary to reach the upper shelves because that was where most of the treasures could be found.

The books in the Oxford Book Store covered every subject in the known universe. The staff were always very courteous and helpful. I found that I definitely needed to tap into their intimate knowledge of the shelf's contents for, if I sought books on Abyssinian umbrellas of the 19th century, they were the keepers of this knowledge and could direct me to the appropriate shelf unerringly. Sometimes they even paved the way by doing some preliminary dusting on a shelf. Nevertheless, whenever I had climbed up the ladder and found my book, I had to be prepared for the ensuing dust storm. But it was worthwhile, for here was pure gold.

At the entrance, a man mountain with a proud bearing, sporting a turban, an even more impressive handle-bar moustache, and holding a Lee Enfield rifle of World War II vintage always greeted me very courteously. Inside, a pleasant, young, attractive lady dressed in a beautiful sari, appeared to float towards me with her hands held together, head slightly bowed, welcoming me with a *Namaste*.

"Salaam, Sahib. Welcome to Oxford Book Store."

Once past her, I was greeted for a second time by a venerable old gentleman who asked, "Sahib, may I be of kindly assistance to your goodself.

Are you looking for anything special or is Sahib just wishing to look for purposes of browsing? Please be feeling free to continue and to calling me for assistance, i.e. help, in case your goodself so desires."

"Thank you," I would reply and indicate that I wanted to browse.

If I found an interesting tome, even if it was not directly related to what I was looking for, I would liberate it for evaluation later. Persistence eventually paid off. I generally made my selections after an hour or two of browsing. Choosing a book was difficult and I had to consider carefully what I was going to leave behind.

"Sahib has made a choice. Can I help?" a store attendant would ask.

I would hand him the books and move to the teller, a bespectacled Bengali lady sitting behind an elevated glass enclosure. At first, she would prepare an invoice with at least 4 or 5 carbon copy papers placed symmetrically between its pages. The teller would then proceed to enter the title, author, ISBN number, and price of every selected book onto the first page of the invoice. She would list the price of each book on a separate piece of paper and do a manual calculation. If the sum total of this calculation was somehow not to be trusted, out came the calculator and there ensued another verification process; and, human nature being what it is, if this also proved unconvincing, the sum was re-verified on the calculator at least two or three more times. The clerk would then initial the totaled sum on the invoice. Finally, all the carbon papers would be extracted and I would receive one copy of the invoice while she dispatched the other carbon copies to other parts of the bookstore. I would move to the cashier to pay. Another lady clerk would take my copy and proceed to re-verify the sum with her calculator and counter initial her name against the sum.

Then she would ask, "Will Sahib be wanting to make payment by cash money or bank cheque?"

"Cash, please!"

I would hand over the paper notes to cover the invoice. The cashier would hold each note to the light to ascertain whether the notes were real or fake.

I would finally pay and she would countersign my invoice copy with "PAID" and then sign it.

"Where next?"

"Please, Sahib to go to the wrapping section."

I would move to the wrapping section. Here again the books were checked against the paid invoice and, when satisfied that I had paid, the clerk would wrap the books. Then the wrapping clerk would pierce his copy of the invoice onto a spike, stamp my invoice copy with "VERIFIED," and countersign again. I would then approach the exit. The books had by now been wrapped and someone else had taken the wrapped books to another table where I finally received them. Was this the end of the transaction? Had I finally finished all these checks and counterchecks? After satisfying this clerk, I would move to the door; but no, the security guard had his own invoice copy and would again verify that it had been paid and wrapped and I would get another stamp on my invoice. Finally, I would emerge into the street with my books and my multi-stamped invoice.

Why do I go into such detail about this process? Because this is one of the reasons that I love this country. Although the multi-layered drama of buying a book provided a small mirror into some of the effects of the Raj bureaucracy, it was also the very human face of business: several people were gainfully employed and it embraced a gentler way of doing things. Contrast it with the cold interface with a computer, bar code readers and printers spitting out bits of paper and I will take this quirky, human way of selling books any day.

Calcutta Post Office in Free School Street

As charming as the bureaucracy of buying a book might have been, the same cannot be said about buying a stamp at the Post Office. Let me recount an experience of simply trying to mail some postcards; the event occurred quite recently, but it might equally have happened when my parents lived in Calcutta. This bureaucratic inanity occurred at a larger post office on Free School St. There was a huge counter behind which sat, with legs crossed, an assortment of Banerjis, Chatterjees and Mukherjees every 9 or 10 feet on high chairs. I dutifully presented myself to buy some stamps at the Stamp Counter, where Shri Arun Mukherjee directed me to go to Shri Prakash Banerji at the Assessment Counter. In my mind, the virtual clock had started ticking. Prakash took the postcards, 11 in all, 7 small and 4 large and counted them. He put each one on a scale to weigh them, despite 7 of them being identical. Not one small one and a big one, but EACH ONE. Yes. Then the 4 large cards had to be verified. Then Prakash pulled out an information sheet and advised that the cards each required a Rs. 20 stamp.

Prakash then directed me to Arun's counter where I could buy the stamps. I asked for 11 stamps of Rs 20 denomination. Arun grew alarmed as he noted that the cards were of two sizes. "Oh. No, sir! That is not possible." He counted them again and verified 7 small and 4 large as his crossed right leg stirred. "Cannot be right! I have to check." Arun then went to see his boss Shri Moolchand Bose to query if the larger post cards required more stamps. And, as I gazed at this peaceful scene with my blood pressure slowly rising, I noted also that Shri Moolchand appeared to be unsure. He picked up the phone and called his superior somewhere within the bowels of the building. Finally, an answer: yes, the larger cards required Rs 50 stamps. Wonderful, so let us get on with it and buy the stamps.

But, we had only just begun, it seemed. Arun had to count them again: 7 small and 4 large. Another count to make sure but this time he looked at the scene and noted that some cards were not about India and this appeared to pose a problem. I assured Arun that there was nothing sinister about this, as we had had no time to send them off from the previous country we had visited. Seemingly satisfied, he finally opened the stamp book and counted out the requisite stamps. "Finally getting somewhere," I thought and did a small mental calculation of the amount Rs 340, reaching for my wallet. But no. Arun wanted to do another assessment about the cost of the stamps and then had the nerve to ask me for my pen so that he could do the calculations himself on paper. Not once, but twice. We agreed on Rs 340.

As I paid for the stamps, I noted that they had no adhesive on the back, so I asked if he had stamps that had an adhesive. Arun, with one hand wrapped around his heels, then calmly informed me that I had to cross the street to a small shop and buy some glue. At this juncture, I exploded and in my best and most vitriolic Hindi, with all expletives added, told him to get up off his bum, crank his arms into some sort of action and get me some glue immediately. After some protestation, he sheepishly went over to Shrimati Amrita Ghosh behind the Registrations Counter and proceeded to produce the filthiest little bowl of glue I have ever seen. He invited me to dip my finger into it in order to wet the back of the stamps and affix them to the cards.

I went across the street to buy some glue.

Then I had to wait another 15 minutes to ensure that all cards had dried before proceeding back to Prakash to get the stamps cancelled prior to placing the cards in the post box. I noticed with disdain that there was no Customer Satisfaction counter. This little episode lasted all of 55 minutes and in part demonstrates how the Bengalis are absolute wizards at replicating and indeed embellishing colonial bureaucratic practices. All I could think of as I left the Post Office was that this might have been where the term "Dead Letter Office" came from.

Calcutta Municipal Corporation

On numerous occasions, I went to a Calcutta Municipal Corporation branch building with my father when he was applying to obtain a building development permit for the new factory planned for Gobra. I believe the building was a branch office, is located in close proximity to the New Market area in Hogg Street. The office space inside was characterized by high ceilings whose prime function seemed to be to accommodate a swarm of ceiling fans that kept the place cool. I remember that parts of the red brick building, the first or second floors, had colonnaded terraces. In Dad's time, some of these colonnades had become the open air "storage" for the business and other records of all Calcutta's burghers and it had been like that for over a decade. When the city had its regular heavy monsoonal rains, rainwater would seep into these storage areas and affect the records. In fact, many of them had turned into one, large, amorphous load of water-logged, pulped paper that then fed the vermin and insect population. It remained a mystery how these wonderful bureaucrats found details of anyone's records in this mess!

It was on these occasions with Dad that I got to observe the Bengali bureaucrat first hand. He occupied a desk that had papers and files piled high on all sides. The desk closely resembled a bunker which we approached from the rear, since the front was usually blocked. What little space remained was taken up by a large manual typewriter, newspapers such as the *Statesman*, the *Amrita Bazaar Patrika* or *Hindustan Standard*, the telephone, a prominently displayed *Thacker's Directory* (a reference book of regulations applicable to Indian companies and which also projected some air of importance on its owner), and the ever-present tea cup and saucer. A stand stood directly behind the desk, serving as a repository for his *chata* (umbrella), perhaps even his *topee* (hat), the scarf that covered his ears, if it happened to be cold, and his coat or waistcoat. Nothing much seemed to happen before 10:30 in the morning after a calming cup of tea. Keeping these cups filled was the task of a host of tea vendors walking between the desks. As 11 o'clock approached, I noticed the first stirrings of productive endeavour as the clerk shuffled to the end and removed a file to work on. He would flick through a page or two, glance at the clock and sigh: only 40 minutes to lunch. He would scribble something on the file to the effect that the application form to do XYZ needed to be checked for a valid payment, since he could discern no PAID stamp on it. He would raise his hand, looking straight ahead, and flick his fingers; magically, a peon would appear from somewhere behind him. Without looking at him, the bureaucrat would request that he take the file to Section D.2 where payment was to be verified and then return the file back to him. A further two days of work were lost on this file. The clock hands now showed 12 o'clock. The hour for lunchtime had arrived. He would look around to see if his servant had arrived with his tiffin stack. At the important hour of noon, the normal lunch hour in Calcutta, the city was a buzz of domestic servants, with their tiffin stacks in hand, going to the offices where their masters worked. And, while lunch was being consumed, the servant had to ensure that fresh water was at hand. He then waited in the corridors until it was time to pick up the empty tiffin canisters, stack them, and go home.

After resuming work, the bureaucrat was either occupied on the phone or he ignored us totally, as he shuffled his papers from one pile to the next, poured his tea into his saucer and then drained the saucer with an exorbitantly loud slurp. He truly believed that this was the best way to cope with the heat and humidity. He always looked busy. It is extraordinary, but, through this seemingly impenetrable morass of paper and process, the "Babu culture" had the capacity to make things happen, just not necessarily in anyone else's desired time frame. Despite the glacial speed of this approval process, Dad eventually got approval for his new plant at Gobra.

In the 1960s, I remember a small scandal at the Corporation Building. Apparently over 50% of these clerks would turn up after 10 am, hang up their *chata*, hat or scarf, and read the paper, and drink tea. After this short on-site visible presence, they usually returned home and reappeared magically at 6:00 pm to clock off, collect their hat, scarf or *chata*, wipe the sweat off their brows and head off home for the night. And they also sometimes managed to claim overtime. Their theory was apparently that no one could be sure of their presence when they appeared to have been buried behind mountains of files and paper. This Municipal Corporation branch was quite a place and I have often wondered if it ever changed over time and, more importantly, whether the clerks had ever entered the computer age, let alone learned to cope with it. I do recall that, somewhere in another part of Calcutta, was a 5-foot high replica of a telephone on the street pavement. An inscription read, "Dedicated to the memory of the telephone that never worked."

Occasionally, there would be a dispute somewhere in the building that led to strike action. Then pens were "downed," the scarves wrapped around the neck, the black waistcoats donned, the briefcases slammed shut, and the *chata*s picked up as the bureaucrats went out on a "solidarity" or "sympathy" strike. And so, in this city, the cycle of the petrification of labour took hold. Such continual strike activity not only demonstrated the absolute power of the labour unions in Calcutta, but also a government that appeared to be utterly impotent to do anything about it.

River Hooghly

Calcutta's river, the Hooghly, is one of the tributaries of the mighty Ganges and eventually flows into the Bay of Bengal through the delta region and the Sundarbans. It flows through Calcutta like a brown ribbon splitting the city into two parts. The river is subject to flooding during the monsoon and also when the snow melts in the Himalayas. When the river is in flood, it is sometimes not possible to see the far bank at some parts of its course. But, these floods in no way deter people from living and working on the river, celebrating their religious festivals on the river, and bathing in the river.

For Calcutta, the Hooghly's commercial importance cannot be doubted. The river's existence was the foundation for the port from which jute, the agricultural produce of the hinterland, and other manufactured items were exported. This is where the famous tea from Darjeeling and Assam made its way to the auction rooms and the great tea houses in Europe and other parts of the world. As the area around Calcutta is flat, there was never any real prospect of establishing natural water storage dams. So, the Hooghly was the most important source of water for the city and this water was treated daily. The Hooghly is also prone to a build-up of silt and this influenced not only navigation but also the size of ships that could reach Calcutta to pick up cargo.

The advent of the railway and the establishment of a railhead at Howrah led the British to build a pontoon bridge that was eventually replaced by the Howrah Bridge completed in 1942 and opened to the public in 1943 (typically, it took a war to speed construction up). Since the early days of Calcutta, it was increasingly evident that the city needed such a bridge. The railway link to the rest of the country had been in place from about 1850 onwards from Howrah, but people had to be transported across the river by ferries. The precursor to the eventual fixed bridge was a flexible wooden pontoon bridge that could separate in order to allow other river traffic to pass. Eventually a cantilever bridge design was proposed and built with a span of about 1,500 feet. Today, Howrah Bridge is one of the busiest bridges in the world; in fact, people can usually walk across it faster than they can drive.[159] It serves a transportation community encompassing humans carrying loads, rickshaws, hand-pulled carts, camels, bullock carts, *ghora gharis*, cars, taxis, single- and double-decker buses, trucks, and even trams. What city in the world can boast such a mélange of transportation options!

Yes, the river is brown; it is very muddy. It was and is a symbol of life for the people and, at the same time, a transporter of death. When we stood

159 Ibid., 148. Other interesting facts and information about this bridge can be found at: http://www.factsninfo.com/2013/03/interesting-facts-and-info-about-howrah-bridge.html

at the river's edge at one of the many *ghats* that led to the water's edge and looked out on the river, we noticed all sorts of detritus flowing by. Here were cut logs or a fallen tree, there some dislodged water hyacinths and, yes, the occasional carcass of an animal or even the chalky, white body of a dead human being. And when a corpse or a carcass flowed by, the ever-present crows were perched on them, picking away at the remains.

The river Hooghly has many bathing *ghats* where Hindu devotees perform many of their ceremonial rituals. The *ghats* also served another purpose, namely, a convenient place right at the water's edge where people could do their washing. At many *ghats* were clothes lines hung with saris and other items of clothing drying in the sun. It was also at the *ghats* that people emptied urns containing the ashes of a loved one into the sacred river. The scattering of the ashes was a symbol of returning home; we often saw members of the funeral party splash and stir the river with their hands in a display of joy and happiness.

Any visit to the river underlined its importance for commerce. Upstream was the imposing shape of the Howrah Bridge and the random assembly of ugly commercial and civic buildings that bordered the river. Many of these were vast warehouses built to accommodate the jute industry. On the river, small freighters would be carrying cargo to Diamond Harbour, some 37 miles away where it would be off-loaded onto a much larger cargo ship that could not make its way into the Calcutta port area because of the heavy silting in the river. Viewed from the Strand Road, the river was about half a mile wide. The main craft plying the river were dhows and the occasional steam damper moving toward the sea. The dhows crisscrossed the river, with their lateen sails erect and fully blown out with whatever wind was available. At the helm of each one, the *dhoti* clad helmsman squatted on the deck with his feet splayed out, holding the tiller in one hand and a *bidi* in the other. If the dhow were not carrying any cargo, its prow rode high in the river; when laden, the dhow sometimes appeared to be taking on water. If the current were unfavourable, forward progress was painfully slow. But, on the river, time appeared to be irrelevant and the flow of the river traffic in many ways mirrored the ambling pace of the city.

Past the Howrah Bridge going upstream, there was a noticeable change in the character of the river. Residential buildings, some of which evoked the colonial past, had beautiful gardens reaching down to the muddy banks of the river. Further on were the remnants of a disused railway line that used to lead to a loading wharf. Scattered on either side of the river, standing out on the banks were white, Hindu temples with their own bathing *ghats*. Through this collection of houses and temples were small flashes of green where trees had taken hold and somehow survived in a bed of overgrown vegetation. Large clusters of high-water signs were ever present along the river.

When I lived in Calcutta, Dad and I had the opportunity to visit one of the city's elegant riverside homes. My Gujarati friend, Vimal, had arranged for us to visit a distant relative who lived there. On entering the property, it felt as though we had left the harsh reality of Calcuttan life behind. Passing the main entry gate, we entered a fantasy garden with water sprites and other elegant figurines spouting water out of their mouths. In the elegant, marble entrance hallway we heard a muted cacophony of bells, gongs, chimes, and clangs as the hundreds of standing clocks and timepieces that were housed in this wonderful building announced the time. It seemed this house was famous for its clocks, which had been lovingly collected over a lifetime from all over the world by their owner. They occupied every available space: the walls, the niches, and the floor. There were clocks of every size and description including the most gorgeous carriage clocks on the many mantle-pieces in this extraordinary residence. To prevent the clocks from chiming at the same time, the owner had arranged that they all went off at different times; so, every two or three minutes, we were entertained by marvelous clock music. It was an incredible experience, and another unexpected moment in the life of the city and on this river.

The Hooghly, despite its dark coffee colour, is also a river of life for the Hindu. It is one of the many daughters of the River Ganges, the most sacred river in India. This association with the River Ganges gave the Hooghly a status of reverence and even holiness. For the people of Bengal, through which the river flowed, it was a source of food and water, the basis of their livelihood, a thing to be worshipped. It was never just a slow-moving mass of water. It was part of the full life cycle, from the ceremonies of early life, to work and leisure, to all the annual festivals that commemorated the vast pantheon of Hindu gods, to the final spreading of the ashes.

Marble Palace

The Marble Palace is a merchant's home built in a neoclassical style; it resembles the impressive southern mansions depicted in the film, "Gone with the Wind." Built during the 19th century "Bengal Renaissance" that came about as the local intelligentsia responded to British rule, the Marble Palace is open today to tourists by appointment. It is an absolutely remarkable place: indisputably the weirdest, most ridiculous, eccentric, lovable and, at the same time, saddest of palaces. It is surrounded by the narrowest of alleys running off Chittaranjan Avenue. You get there through a muddle of chaotic humanity, competing with rickshaws, cows and bullock carts; suddenly, you emerge out of this jumble into the walled, overgrown grounds of a family home, whose imposing façade is surrounded by a huge unkempt garden replete with statuary (Roman, Greek, the Buddha, fawns and satyrs, etc.) and a fountain (not working) straight from Rome. There is even a small zoo in one corner of the garden, also claiming to be the first zoo in Calcutta!

Inside are six galleries, three on each floor, with objets d'art bought from visits to Europe in the 19th century. Some of these objects are valuable; the rest are worthless. Statues and busts of Queen Victoria abound, including a 12-foot high wooden statue carved from a single piece of rosewood. Some floors are made from the finest Italian marble; others from wood in intricate parquet patterns, the wood curling at the edges. The porcelain pieces range from Meissen to Dresden to Sèvres to Wedgewood; the ruby red glass vases come from Bohemia; the glass chandeliers and wall-sized mirrors from Belgium. Amongst the bric-a-brac, there are magnificent ormolu timepieces from France. And everywhere in the long galleries and stairwells, the visitor is surrounded by paintings. Their frames are tarnished and disintegrating in places and the surface paint on the images is often flaked. The canvases in these frames are covered by 150 years of grime and reflect total, utter neglect. I am told that this collection houses many fine paintings by well-known artists, including four by Rubens, a Murillo, a Reynolds and possibly a Titian!

This is still a family home; on our trip there, we met the great grandson of Raja Mahendra Mullick, who had become incredibly wealthy from rents and gemstones, and who had started this collection. He explained to us a little of the collecting philosophy of his great grandfather, who simply bought what he liked, whether it was by a great master or not. The family still carries on the individual philanthropic tradition of the Raja by feeding about 400 of Calcutta's poorest every day at noon at the front gates.

Kalighat and Nirmala Hriday

Calcutta has a patron deity named Kali, the Hindu goddess of death, who is mainly portrayed as a laughing, threatening, black figure dancing on the body of the God Shiva. She has four hands, one of which holds a severed head and another a raised sword. Kali is enshrined in the Kalighat temple. The temple is generally filled with pilgrims offering flowers and incense, normally hibiscus, and other more modest fare of rice and grains.

The temple is situated on the River Hooghly, near Keortala *Ghat*. This is the principal Kali shrine in India where the dead of Calcutta are burned and moved to their next transfiguration. It is ironic that the cremation business at Kalighat is inexorably linked with that modern-day saint of Calcutta, Mother Teresa. Very close to Kalighat is Nirmala Hriday, the home set up by Mother Teresa for the dying and destitute. The Hindu religion does not accommodate the concept of charity easily. Thus, Mother Teresa's nuns, mostly moving in pairs, rescue the sick, the dying and destitute, taking them back to their shelter. In my parents' day, there was no room at the city's hospitals for these people. At least, with the nuns, they could live or die with some semblance of dignity. As they died, they were delivered up to Kalighat to be cremated. I liked the way that this little symbiosis took place. It was hard to gauge how Hindus reacted to Mother Teresa. On the one hand, I believe they did admire her "goodness" and her charity, but whether they understood it was another question. In my observation, Hindus in general were more comfortable with the notion of working on your "inner self" (hence the importance of Yoga and Yogi in India) and so the two did not mix well, namely "inner self" and "outward good works."

CHAPTER 8

Street Life of Calcutta

People often ask me what Calcutta was like when Mum and Dad lived there. What a challenge, indeed! What do I remember about Calcutta? My memories are now a blend of the city I knew in the 1940s and early 50s as a child and youth, the city I later visited many times in the late 1950s and early 60s while in university, and later still for several decades when I went there on business. All told, my experience of Calcutta spans a period of over 60 years. Although I have not lived there for over half a century, it still feels like where I am from.

On a human level, Calcutta has always been a city of intense emotional contrasts, of gnawing poverty, of the finest virtues of human caring and feeling, of despair, but also of dreams and hopes. Its palaces stand right next door to the hovels of the poor. Calcutta often reminds me of the feelings evoked by "Suzanne," that immortal poem by Leonard Cohen, and in particular this stanza:

Now, Suzanne takes your hand and she leads you to the river
She's wearing rags and feathers from Salvation Army counters

And the sun pours down like honey on our lady of the harbor
And she shows you where to look among the garbage and the flowers
There are heroes in the seaweed, there are children in the morning
They are leaning out for love and they will lean that way forever
While Suzanne holds her mirror.[160]

As modern as Calcutta can be, it is still a city that retains some of its old colonial traditions, whether it is club life, the love of cricket and other colonial sports, the quaint trams that ply the streets, or its well-known, unique cuisine. Calcutta is known for its jam-packed, noisy, crazy streets, for the even crazier driving habits of its inhabitants, and for its rich street life, with ubiquitous food vendors, pavement dwellers, and cows. Despite the chaotic traffic, Calcutta enjoys its own pace and the slower the better. It pays to be patient here whether you are waiting for a bureaucrat to affix his signature to some document or waiting in a line for anything at all! And who knows, you may become involved in a discussion on what the government is or is not doing, or about "what is happening at the cricket." Today, there are more cars than rickshaws, but I feel that very little has changed since my parents' time.

The Streets of Calcutta

Life on the Streets

In Rabindranath Tagore's *My Reminiscences*, in the chapter entitled, "At the Himalayas," there is the following passage so appropriate in writing about Calcutta's streets:

> *This is the great advantage of the first vision: the mind is not*
> *then aware that there are many more such to come. When this*
> *comes to be known to that calculating organ it promptly tries to*
> *make a saving in its expenditure of attention. It is only when it*
> *believes something to be rare that the mind ceases to be miserly in*

---

160 "Suzanne," by Leonard Cohen. First published in 1966 as a poem in the collection, *Parasites of Heaven* (Toronto: McClelland and Stewart) and then recorded and made famous as a song in that same year by Judy Collins in her album, *In My Life*.

assigning values. So, in the streets of Calcutta I sometimes imagine myself a foreigner, and only then do I discover how much is to be seen, which is lost so long as its full value in attention is not paid. It is the hunger to really see which drives people to travel to strange places.[161]

One of the first impressions that any traveler to Calcutta gets, unlike any other city that I know, is that the pavement is home to so many of its inhabitants. These might be anyone from the genuinely homeless poor (the beggars, the destitute) to all types of permanent or transitory workers (day labourers, rickshaw pullers, paper and rag pickers, etc.). It is the final refuge of Calcutta's homeless, who have this remarkable capacity of discovering every available free space to claim as their own. They literally live their lives in the street. For this category of street dweller, owning possessions means very little. There is one item, however, that most people have and that can be carried around: namely their large calico sheet. At night, when they have chosen their place to sleep, they drape themselves in their calico sheet, fall asleep without a care about whether they block the footpath or not; people just walk around them. This calico cloth, when draped around their shoulders, also doubles as protection from the cold or rain. They erect a form of shelter where the whole family lives, cooks its food, sleeps, where they are born and where they die. The whole cycle of family life is to be found in a small area of the pavement.

There is always something happening on the pavement. During the day, women cook food, children play here, someone else is going to the toilet, or using the pavement to bathe if there is a convenient communal tap or water pump handy. The pavement is shared by all. For those seeking to eke a living, this is their refuge when the day is done. The streets assault the senses, whether it be the noise of people, or the perennial sound of car horns, the smells of cooking, or the detritus of exposed garbage. The streets are also suffused with a sense of lost hope, despair, and the utterly

---

161 From chapter 15, p. 90, The Project Gutenberg eBook of *My Reminiscences* by Rabindranath Tagore.

depressing inevitability of one day morphing into the next and the next with no change in sight.

As dawn approaches and the sun slowly spreads its warmth, the sheets shift as the street people stir and take their first glimpse of the day ahead. For some, there will be a ritual stroking of the beard and for others a combing of the hair. Others reach for a *bidi*,[162] light it and take their first draw. That first pull on the *bidi* prepares them for whatever lies ahead.

The Astrologer

"You like horoscope?" he asked, pointing to an astrological chart weighed down on the street pavement. The ash-smeared and bearded horoscope reader, sometimes bedecked with beads and unusual baubles, has set up shop for the day. He is, however, a multi-faceted horoscope reader. He can read palms and he has cards that help him to tell the future. Incense burns in the background to add to the mystique. But this horoscope reader is different. He also uses tell-all parrots and female shama birds (a small bird from the thrush family) to corroborate his own predictions, as well as provide added reassurance to his customers. A skilled parrot astrologer will affirm that these are ancient traditions and a mystic art and that he has been gifted with the knowledge to practice this form of astrology. If he uses the birds, he will charge an extra rupee; after all, he needs to provide his birds with seed. If a customer wants predictions for life's great questions, future prospects, matching of horoscopes in case of a possible future marriage, medical health astrology, business prospects, or even numerology, then he has come to the right man. Our astrologer needs to have every predictive device available to reassure his clients. He lays out all his planetary and natal charts to foretell the customer's destiny. If he is a bit more up-market, our astrologer will provide a very small stool to sit on; otherwise the expectant customer squats.

Most customers opt for a simple palm reading especially if they believe he is skilled in this art. Frequently asked questions are about the customer's love life, marriage prospects in the future, the number of children they

---

162 A poor person's cigarette, usually with some tobacco grounds wrapped and rolled up in a *tendu* leaf and fastened with a thread.

will have, potential divorce and even spousal deaths. In the Calcutta of my parents' time, there were street astrologers everywhere, ranging from the charlatans to the more serious practitioners.

The Rickshaw-Wallah

The Calcutta rickshaw, a unique form of human-powered transportation, proliferated in Calcutta at the time that my parents lived there.[163] Imagine a large two-wheeled cart, with a small, open-air, wooden cabin with seats for one or two people. To the rear of this cabin, there was a small retractable canopy, which could be drawn up when it rained, a frequent occurrence in Calcutta. During a downpour, a grimy piece of waterproof cloth attached to the canopy was lowered over the seated passengers and fastened to the frame to keep out the rain. But this effort was never very successful and a trip in the rain usually left some part of the customer wet. Protruding from the bottom of this cabin were two long shafts of wood extending about 10 feet in front of the cart and which were held together with a wooden crosspiece; this primitive transmission mechanism transferred the human energy of the rickshaw puller to momentum in the wheels. For, between these two shafts of wood, a sliver of a man, mostly skin and bones, provided the energy to turn the wheels and pull people and loads of all shapes and sizes. These rickshaw-wallahs were Calcutta's equivalent of beasts of burden, each competing against the other and against other forms of transport in a daily struggle for life. A successful day for the rickshaw-wallah answered that perennial question, "Where is the next bowl of rice coming from"?

The rickshaw-wallahs drew their clientele mainly from the lower middle class and the poor. As an adult, whenever I saw a rickshaw, I felt a sense of pity and even shame. The bare-footed rickshaw-*wallahs* resembled survivors from Bergen-Belsen concentration camp; they often pulled corpulent individuals who somehow squeezed into the narrow seat and then placed the extra weight of their shopping and other paraphernalia on the platform under their feet. These customers could have used other means of

---

163 Rickshaws still exist in Calcutta, although in vastly reduced numbers. They have been superseded by tuk-tuks, scooters, motorbikes, and buses.

travel including the plentiful yellow taxis, the trams, even the buses or the horse-drawn carriages; but, of course, these would cost more. Although the reason for using a rickshaw was generally financial, some cynical persons even went so far as to justify their use as a non-polluting form of transport. I could excuse these customers the use of buses and trams, because they were generally crammed like sardines and women passengers were often sexually harassed through lewd suggestions, catcalls and even groping, but the use of rickshaws was nothing other than exploitation by the wealthier customers.

Chinese immigrants to India and Calcutta probably introduced rickshaws to the city in the 19th century. This form of transportation immediately filled the void for cheap transport and a ready work opportunity for the many economic refugees from the neighbouring state of Bihar, a place with few opportunities for work. Some of the rickshaw-*wallahs* plied their trade for over thirty years and pulled their rickshaws for up to 12 hours a day. Despite the working conditions of the rickshaw men, they were a popular conveyance simply because they were abundant and cheap.

The rickshaw-*wallah* pulled his vehicle in all weather conditions, whether it was the blistering heat and humidity of summer or the monsoon rain. He advertised his presence on the street with a little, round, brass rickshaw bell attached to his finger by a leather thong, rather like a castanet. The tinkling sound served many functions. It invited people or carts ahead of him to make way, it was a method of attracting custom and, if he was caught in a dangerous manoeuvre, a way of indicating his panic. It was a familiar and recognisable sound on Calcutta's streets, a sound that every Calcuttan knew. The rickshaw-*wallah* coped with poor roads and uneven streets. He had to negotiate the tramlines and not get his wheels caught in the tracks, since extricating his rickshaw was difficult and oncoming trams in Calcutta did not have good brakes; nor were the trams in the habit of stopping for rickshaws caught in the tracks. The rickshaw-*wallahs* also had their enemies on the road. The state of the pavement, the many potholes, the tramlines and the tossing around created by cobblestones often caused them to zigzag all over the road. This erratic meandering by rickshaws irritated taxi drivers considerably. Their lack of patience for rickshaws may have resulted from their own problems driving 20-year-old vehicles, with apologies for brakes, bald tyres and imperfect electrical systems. It was difficult enough navigating the roads without having to steer clear of the unpredictable rickshaws. Whenever there was an altercation between taxi and rickshaw, the rickshaw-*wallahs* would always come off second best, especially since most of the taxi drivers came from the warrior Pathans and Sikhs of Northwest India. Rickshaw-*wallahs* were also at the mercy of unscrupulous policemen, who made their lives a misery if they became involved in any sort of traffic fracas; such policemen turned a blind eye in return for some money.

The fare charged for a rickshaw ride was pitiful; there was no fare meter to refer to, so a common sight in Calcutta was of customers, who had arrived at their destination, arguing animatedly with the rickshaw-*wallah* over the price of the trip. The rickshaw-*wallah* generally lost this argument. From every rupee that he earned, usually half went to his family living in another state or district, a quarter went to the owner of the rickshaw and a quarter remained for his own living expenses, including the bribes that he often had to pay to the police. This situation was immoral and outrageous, a miserable existence, a daily fight for life. But it served a purpose and offered jobs for poor, lower caste men. In many cases, the business passed from father to son.

But rickshaws also served their clients well. Apart from being popular among people with limited income, or who did not have to travel very far, they were the transportation of choice for families sending their children to schools. Many of these rickshaw-*wallahs* even received a retainer from families to carry their children to and from school. And some small businesses used the rickshaw as a way of moving goods and produce around the city.

Street Merchants

The pavement barbers had it easy. All they needed to provide was a small area where their clients could squat, making full eye contact with the barber. The barber had all his tools laid out on the ground before him: the unsterilized cut-throat razor, the combs and scissors, the home-made liquid concoctions for the face and hair and one absolutely indispensable item for any self-respecting street barber, namely his broken-off piece of mirror. At the end of the session he held and rotated the mirror around the client's face to reassure him that he had given him a close shave and haircut. The mirror also became indispensable for the customer in order to examine how well the street barber had trimmed his moustache. Once he was satisfied that the shave was *pukka* (perfect), then and only then would he part with his two annas to pay the barber.

Nearby, one might find the shoe and sandal repairer. Around him was a pot-pourri of leather off-cuts for repairing men's and women's *chappals* (sandals) and shoes. And near the cobbler, there might be a Bengali gentleman, advanced in years, sitting in front of a typewriter, his nose gingerly balancing a pair of spectacles that added to the image of "knowledge." Why a typewriter, you may ask? Well, this was a man of letters in the fullest sense of the word, a man who would transcribe the wishes of any illiterate person sitting in front of him into the most beautiful and flowery English prose. It might be for a job application, or when someone needed to plead his case before a magistrate or tribunal. Even after Independence, English was still the *lingua franca* and language of commerce and law. When used imaginatively by someone who spoke English and who owned a typewriter, it could also be a livelihood and a business opportunity.

Another category of vendor was what I will loosely call the small wall or nook vendors, who occupied a very small space with their products. During the day, natural light was adequate, but at night a candle emerged. In these nooks were the sewing machine entrepreneurs who plied their dressmaking trade. Their only asset was a Singer sewing machine, which they used to stitch together their creations while squatting on the pavement. Behind them on the wall, they either displayed some material or fashion cut-outs from magazines.

The pavements in front of the major hotels attracted the greatest flush of pavement vendors, especially outside the Grand and Great Eastern hotels. At the time, the main entrances to these hotels were situated in the middle of a covered, porticoed section of pavement. These covered pavements afforded an escape from the mid-day sun and so all the little shops and street stalls squeezed together, shoulder-to-shoulder, but they politely kept main entrances clear. Hugging the building walls were book and magazine sellers. On the side nearest the curb were the garment and jewelry sellers.

The poor student or aspiring businessman, usually armed with a virtually empty briefcase that held nothing of importance except for the daily newspaper, obtained his cotton underpants and singlets, *mojas* (socks), *kameez* (shirt), leather belt or ties from the garment vendors as he prepared for that next job interview.

Near the Lighthouse and New Empire cinemas, located across from the New Market, the pavement vendors mostly specialized in selling well-thumbed murder mysteries, love stories, science fiction and action adventure pulp fiction. Occasionally, very occasionally, a serious classical author could also be found. A thin fleck of pavement was left for the pedestrians. From these vendors I could buy second-hand paperback books, copies of Zane Grey, Agatha Christie, and Somerset Maugham, all varieties of outdated magazines, and all the Hollywood film and other women's magazines. "Girlie" magazines, which were sold at a premium, were purchased by expatriates and the wealthier Indians. They were available outside the Grand Hotel on Chowringhee Road. If a customer wanted to view <u>really</u> naughty, glossy, photographic art with more exposed flesh, he just asked for it, and out from somewhere in the stack of paperbacks a brown paper bag would appear with all types of glossy pictures and *risqué* magazines to suit every taste.

On one side of Park Street, the street vendors took over most of the pavement near the Oxford Book store and sold all types of used reading matter. After an eternity spent browsing, Dad and I would purchase our popular reading matter, which included a selection of *Readers Digest, Saturday Evening Post, Colliers, Time, Newsweek,* and *Popular Mechanics* magazines. Mind you, these were not current magazines, except for *Time* and *Newsweek*, but discards from expatriates, consulate libraries, reading rooms and hotels. Nothing was thrown into the garbage; it was all re-circulated via these vendors. On my own, I usually purchased the *Captain Marvel* and *Superman* comics and English aeronautical magazines like *Flight*. However, seeing that I was a European, the vendors would automatically assume that I wanted a "girlie" magazine and would offer these to me as well. Girlie magazines like *Playboy* and *Hustler* were considered mild and did not attract the brown paper bag treatment; but they did show the scars of wear and tear along the seams from the continuous wrapping and re-wrapping for nervous customers torn between "buy and no-buy" decisions.

The clothing vendors seemed to take over the sidewalk on either side of Lindsay Street as well as leading into the New Market car park. Here, you could buy everything from saris to *shirtings, pantings, suitings*; strange, but I never saw a vendor selling underpantings, singlettings or vestings! In some of these shops, amongst all the displayed samples, was even to be found a picture of Christ and the Virgin Mary or a Hindu God. But the most bizarre of all, and usually part of a current calendar, was a picture of Christ displaying an open heart in his left hand while his right hand made a peace sign. Bizarre indeed. In other shops, and usually located on the wall behind the cashier, were two pictures, usually facing each other, one of a saintly, humble-looking Mahatma Gandhi and, in the other, a picture of Pandit Nehru (the first Prime Minister of India) in his most youthful pose. In some pictures, Nehru was portrayed with his hand reaching out of the picture.

Also in the New Market area were the mobile vendors. Most of them balanced a pyramid of their products on their heads. The best of these were the toy vendors with their sticks and little aerodynamic fans attached to them that were in a state of perpetual motion as they spun with every whiff of breeze. And amongst all these whirling fans, secured to his body and scattered around him were plastic rattles, toy cups and other garish, stuffed animal toys. Other vendors seem to have been obliterated from view by the balloons that they carried. When they were stopped, a face emerged from out of this balloon "bush" and soon a happy child walked away with a balloon picked out from the middle of the bunch.

Shoe shine vendors proliferated everywhere and they did brisk business. They had a rhythm in their polishing that finished with a final twirl and some could even produce a soft cracking sound. How they did it, I never knew.

Some streets, like the famous College Street, had both shops and specialty pavement vendors. College Street was situated near Calcutta University and other esteemed intellectual institutions, like the famous Presidency and Sanskrit colleges. The street, and its associated side alleys, stretched from Bowbazar to Mahatma Gandhi Road, and numerous bookshops, bookstalls and little wall kiosks crowded the pavement. College Street had the reputation of being one of the world's largest second-hand book markets, with an incredible selection of books on every subject imaginable, all of which could be bought at bargain basement prices. Many of the storeowners were very knowledgeable about their book collections and knew their stock intimately; if they could not help you, they would direct you to other bookshops that could. Here, customers could find old and even rare books and, if they were prepared to engage in some healthy bargaining, could definitely pick up a treasured book that had been missing in their collection.

But College Street was not just about bookshops. On many pavements the *paan-wallahs* set up their shops. Apparently *paan* cleansed the palate and freshened one's breath; and it was reputed to have powerful digestive qualities. There were many different variations of *paan*: some sweet and others quite tart. On College Street, could be found probably the best-known *paan* shop. It was called the Kalpataru *Paan Bhander*, which specialized in *paans* that cost from a few annas right up to stratospheric price levels. This *paan* shop was a favourite of many prominent Calcuttans and testimonials from its satisfied clientele covered its walls.

In College Street, there were also many coffeehouses where customers could browse through recent book purchases with a freshly brewed cup of coffee, and perhaps take part in an *adda* with their friends.

Calcutta's Street Food

On most streets in Calcutta, there were both fixed and mobile food vendors. Calcutta's mobile street food vendors were everywhere. Some pushed a metal cart mounted above deformed, rusty wheels. Many carried a little portable brazier full of hot coals in one hand and a little portable food stand in the other. To complete this picture, the vendor sometimes balanced on his head a box containing the cooking pans, various food ingredients, and dried plantain or banana leaves on which to serve food to his customers. And what did these vendors cook and serve? They catered to every taste. The mobile "menu" varied from snacks (like *chana, masala muri* and *phuchkas*, also known as *golgappa*), to vegetarian food, to small skewers of chicken, to plain chapattis with a sauce spread for taste. *Chana* was a simple enjoyable snack made out of chickpeas, spices, finely chopped onions, chilies, fresh cardamon and doused with some lemon juice. *Masala Muri* was puffed rice, preferably roasted, with a variety of spices, chopped onions, cucumbers, coconut, ginger and chilies, and served with a dash of mustard oil. Both these snacks tasted especially good when eaten out of a newspaper-formed cone.

The fixed pavement vendors on busy pedestrian thoroughfares had "set" selling areas during the daylight hours. Some moved to quieter streets at night, but many did not. After all, they had taken "possession" of a prime selling location, so why move. For these vendors, the pavement location was a bedroom where they slept with all their wares. The fruit sellers displayed, amongst other seasonal fruit, mangoes, bananas, sometimes watermelon and, often, apples. Others specialized in vegetables such as carrots, spring onions, baby cucumbers, okra and other local varieties of vegetables that westerners could not recognize. The more affluent vendors would even display their produce in small wicker baskets. Others just lined the flat surface of the pavement, if it was dry, with newspapers or large banana leaves. Those with a larger space created a pyramid with their fruit or vegetables. Once the food vendor had chosen his spot to start selling, he would be joined in no time at all by the *chai wallah* (tea vendor).

Rabindranath Tagore wrote about tea and how appropriate it was: "Come oh come ye tea-thirsty restless ones - the kettle boils, bubbles and sings, musically."[164] Throughout the many public areas in Calcutta, the cry of the tea vendor echoed as he wandered around with his large kettle of pre-prepared masala tea, advertising, "Chai... Chai... Chai..." On his head or under his arm was a bag with all the *kulhar* (the little clay cups from which tea is drunk). There was a common ritual with drinking *chai* out of a *kulhar*. Since customers never knew if the *kulhar* was too brittle and would therefore disintegrate in the hand, they stooped noticeably forward; and, with a slightly rounded arm holding the *kulhar* away from the body, slurp up their tea. If they had some residual *paan* in their mouths, they would spit this out and sip again. After finishing the tea, customers would throw

----

164 From Tagore's *Collected Poems and Plays* accessed at https://www.poemhunter. com/quotations/famous.asp?people=Rabindranath%20Tagore&p=7

the *kulhar* on the ground and crush it. Quite noticeably, the many popular tea drinking spots around the city were well-marked with small mounds of broken clay cups.

But Calcutta also offered the upmarket tea, food, and drink vendor, who could be found near the government and commercial buildings, very conveniently located in a permanent outside wall niche or near an entrance. This site might even have had space for advertising or an ICI Chemical Industries calendar displaying Lord Shiva. Here, the customers had their tea served in a proper cup and saucer. The main customers were the *babus*[165] who had their own tea ritual. Since the tea was hot, the *babu* first poured some of the tea into the saucer, with the very confident belief that this would somehow cool the tea. He could then drink it without scalding his mouth, but he still participated in the familiar slurping sound. In Calcutta, the noise of slurped tea was part of daily life.

For other thirsty customers, there was the *bishti* (mobile water seller). He carried a large closely stitched goat-skin filled with water from which he dispensed drinks into a glass. But, like the tea drinkers, water drinkers had a style of their own. The glass cup may be *juta* (unclean or touched by other lips, unwashed after use); so, our drinker had ways of dealing with this. He might choose to pour the water from a distance directly into his mouth - similar to the way the Spanish drink wine from their pliant *Bota* leather wine pouches - or by cupping his hand below his mouth and pouring the water into the cupped hand and then drinking. The lips never touched the glass cup. This was an art and the drinker rarely got wet.

About a mile from where we lived, the fading, decrepit world of the Raj could still be found in old, imposing government offices and a few large British and European banks. These offices, though graced with high ceilings, housed row after row of ancient desks located under a bat colony of ceiling fans and inadequate lighting. Seated in these rows of simple desks were their occupants, surrounded by artificial walls created by stacks of files and files and more files. When these hundreds of white-collar workers were thirsty or hungry, they had only to step outside. They might nibble

---

165 *Babu* was originally a term of respect but, during the British Raj, the term was usually derogatory and used to refer to an Indian clerk, official or administrator.

on roasted peanuts, hot gram, sweet corn or a wide variety of cooked food. For those with a sweet tooth, the sweets man materialised with offerings of *jelabis* and *rasagoolas*. Close by, the sugar cane press man squeezed some juice from a beautifully ornate sugar cane press.

Animals of the Street

There are streets in Calcutta that seem to be taken over by dogs, many lean-looking starved dogs, some diseased and some barely able to walk. Mum used to refer to them as "pie" dogs, while others called them pariah dogs. I have since learned that a pariah dog is an actual breed of dog, with quite an ancient pedigree. All I know is that they were everywhere scavenging for food and scraps. At night in some parts of the city, jackals joined the dinner party at the various dumps.

In my parents' time, as now, all around Calcutta were garbage dumps exposed to the elements. Wherever these dumps developed, could be found the omnipresent crows who throve on their contents. Crows are sturdy birds with a high degree of intelligence. They will eat almost anything. They thrive on insects, lizards when they find them, grains, and fruit left-overs. Calcutta was, and is still, home to hawks; these birds were a regular sight, especially around the *Maidan*. Like the crows, they throve on scraps, the odd squirrel, and animal carcasses. Vultures lived on the outskirts of the city, feasting in a wing-flapping pack on animal carcasses. One sight I will never forget was a vulture sitting on an animal carcass and ripping at its flesh as it floated down the Hooghly River. Calcutta was home to many other birds including sparrows, swifts and small parrots. But, no matter the type of bird, they all shared one thing: the location of the feeding ground was somehow telegraphed to them each day and they were soon demolishing the next "delicious" garbage dump of its scraps. Among the most interesting of these birds were the mynas, which are "pesky" birds by nature; they are very territorial and can be a nuisance, even to humans. But they were masters at adapting to compete in the Calcutta environment, whether it was to the available food supply or the niches, crannies and alcoves of buildings where they built their nests.

When I think of Calcutta, I think of cows. They were everywhere and walked with such impunity through Calcutta's street that they forced humans to move around them. In India, cows enjoy a sacred status among Hindus, so we left them well alone. There have been riots caused by irreverent behaviour towards cows. Goats were another sight in the streets, though they were usually tethered, or accompanied by their owners as they led them along. When I was young, Mum and Dad would take me for a drive to either Napier Road or Clive Road and there, next to a military facility, were rhesus monkeys that would swing out of the trees. If we had halted for a look, they would climb onto the bonnet in anticipation of food. On the golf course, they were an even bigger nuisance, as they slid down from the trees to remove golf balls after a blistering drive. The golf club had special rules to deal with "lost ball due to monkey theft." Often in the streets, we would hear the rat-a-tat of a tiny conical drum that advertised to all that the *monkey wallah* (street performer who uses monkeys) was here to entertain the children with monkey dances and acrobatic back flips. If he happened to have two monkeys, then he would put on a Calcutta version of monkey live theatre, with the monkeys wearing shorts and dresses, and accompanied by music and sometimes singing. We paid a rupee to watch and the monkeys got some peanuts or a piece of fruit.

Shopping

Going Shopping for Food

In the early years, in virtually all Calcutta households, people had to buy their fresh food practically every day, since few family households had refrigerators. This meant a daily visit to the markets to shop for fresh produce, whether from a proper shop front, or a mobile vendor who pushed his cart, or even someone who had a small pile of fresh produce assembled on banana leaves in front of him on the pavement. The householder and their servant had to decide early in the morning what they needed and then go to select vendors to buy the best produce just after sunrise. Shopping early also meant that they missed the soaring temperatures later in the morning.

Shopping for food in our household developed into a predictable routine. After a party on the weekend, we needed to replenish our supplies at the market. From the earliest hours on Monday morning, Mum had already met with Dandia and the day's shopping and meals would have been discussed. Dandia provided an update on the non-perishable supplies like sugar, flour, condiments, etc. Once it had been established what the kitchen needed and also with what urgency, then Mum made the decision about the items that Dandia was responsible for purchasing and those that she would take care of.

Calcutta's New Market

One of the great shopping experiences in Calcutta is a visit to the New Market. Opened originally, I believe, on New Year's Day 1874, it was first known as New Market and later renamed the Sir Stuart Hogg Market in 1903.[166] In my parents' day, if you were into designer label shopping, then New Market certainly was not for you. I cannot recall any designer labels on sale there, except perhaps for Binny's shirts. Baborallys, one of the older legacy shops in New Market, still trades there and has been there for generations. A leisurely browse or shop in the labyrinthine interior of this market never failed to fascinate.

From Lindsay Street, the front façade of the Market was quite remarkable. It was built with a rather grandiose red brick "Gothic" style tower. In the 50s and 60s, the Market was spread out over a single level. The interior had comparatively high vaulted ceilings. Rows of wooden shop stalls ran the length on either side of a relatively narrow grid of access passages. These shops were more permanent in nature, with the shops' names advertised on the front in Bengali or English or both.

The organization of the various merchandise sections of the market had a definite plan rather like that which can be found today in any department store in the west. The florists were located in the very front entrance façade facing Lindsay Street. The shoe shops and shoemakers were located behind them. Then followed shops that sold everything from Tibetan goods (the Tibetan shop-keepers always looked resplendent in their scarlet felt boots and wearing their silver amulets as they sat on stools in front of their shops), and Nepali curios, to clothes, men's and women's

---

166   Sukanta Chaudhuri, ed., *Calcutta, the Living City. Vol II: The Present and the Future*, 118. I need to say, though, that Calcuttans paid no attention to the re-naming and continued to refer to it as the New Market.

stores, specialty food items, saris, *chappals*, Indian handicrafts, cameras, stationery, embroidery, trinkets and knickknacks, jewellry, books, and dress material. Amongst the many shops of the New Market were those that sold thousands of different styles of Indian bangles. The façades of the bangle shops seemed to have pillars of coloured glass reaching for the roof. Sometimes the shop owners and assistants passed their time enjoying a smoke on a *hookah* pipe to ease the boredom.[167]

Here in the Market were all types of people doing their shopping: young and old. The patrons - whether buying or passing through - came from every socio-economic class, from the poor to well-heeled Indians and Europeans.

I often went to New Market with Mum. She liked to personally examine and choose the fresh produce, meat and fish. The experience started the moment when we stepped out of the car at the Lindsay Street end. Hardly had our feet touched the ground before we heard the honking of taxis competing for the patronage of those who had finished their shopping, the noise of the hawkers and touts trying to get our attention and the pleading sounds of beggars. As we walked to the Market entrance, beggars without legs would propel themselves behind us on their wheeled skateboards, while women beggars, usually with a baby propped on a hip and holding another child by the hand would plead ever so for some *baksheesh* (alms). Others sometimes even grasped us by the arm to get our attention; they would point to their navel to indicate hunger as their cupped hand moved between stomach and mouth pleading for some *baksheesh*.

We would also be surrounded by a *mĕlée* of porters, all armed with their wicker baskets, wanting to carry our purchases. This very human service could be viewed as the Calcutta equivalent of the modern supermarket trolley. The advantage to these human "trolleys" was that, if we had finished shopping and wanted to browse, we sent the porter to the car and told him to wait for us there. If the basket filled up quickly, he'd return to

---

167 A *hookah* is a smoking contraption where smouldering tobacco smoke is allowed to pass through water contained in a receptacle to an outlet tube, which the smoker elaborately cups in his hand for inhalation; it was important that the inhalation tube never touched the lips as the *hookah* was passed around.

the car, where the driver would load the boot. Then our mobile "trolley" would return to find us somehow in the chaos of the Market.

My mother preferred to engage the more mature basket carriers, as she felt that they probably had families to look after. In fact, one particular porter dedicated himself to serving her, using his own personal radar to detect when she had entered the Market area. In the instant that Mum let herself out of the car, her porter would be standing near the door. If it rained, he would open up a tattered black umbrella that billowed like a mushroom over her head. The porters of the New Market worked with a great sense of pride. Many of them had learnt enough English to mention that they were registered with the New Market porter management office, and thus were considered to be honest and reliable.

Our shopping started at the bakery and then moved on to the meat and fish sections, before coming to the *unda wallah.* The egg buying process had its own charm. The *unda* man hand-picked each egg and put it in front of a naked light to ascertain that no embryo was forming inside. Once approved, he placed the egg safely in a basket shaped out of newspapers. I loved watching the ritual as the *unda* man flicked the eggs through his fingers in front of the light rather like the magician who mesmerizes a crowd with coins juggled adeptly between his fingers. Mum's visit usually ended at the flower seller, where she bought her favourite flowers: gladiolas.

To the right of the central block of shops were the stalls selling meat, fish, fruits, spices and vegetables. Here also was the live poultry. The chickens and ducks were stuffed into large wicker baskets and after the brave house-wife made her choice, the seller pulled out the live bird from within, hung it upside down with its feet tied and handed it to the porter. Our dexterous porter would then balance the wicker basket on his head while he carried the eggs and live chickens in his hands. Remarkable, quite remarkable!

Moving through this market, we were continually assailed by its sights, sounds, and smells. It took an extremely strong stomach to negotiate the stall selling meat or fish. The optics of meat presentation were very chal-lenging. The absence of refrigeration was evident and the various cuts of meat were suspended by hooks at the rear of the meat stall. A severed goat's head hung from a hook while a carcass with tail, with original hair still attached, hung from another. On the marble counter, were displayed various unrecognizable cuts of meat. Flies were everywhere. Water lay everywhere. The marble countertops and floors of each stall were continuously hosed down after preparing and packaging meat for the customer. Around the fish stalls, we waded through a sea of fish scales. Part of the service when buying fish included cleaning and scaling. This is where Mum bought *hilsa* (an oily fish that is used commonly in Bengali cuisine) and *bekhti* (the local name for barramundi or giant sea perch) and, when available in season, a wonderful bony fish call "mango fish," that Dad particularly enjoyed.

At the rear end on the fringes of New Market, were all the specialty shops that sold the imported and other smuggled tinned goods. Here also were found the delightful shops offering Bengali and other Indian specialties and sweets like *rasagoolas, jelabis, gulab jamuns*, delectable cheese and palm sugar-based sweets. My family patronized Baborallys for over thirty years and, during a visit, Baborally senior always had a chat with us while his sons did the running around in the shop to fill Mum's order. His shop stocked all the imported tinned goods and other non-perishable food stuffs from the ceiling to the floor. In one corner, Mr. Baborally sat at his desk, with all his invoices and other paper work. Mum sat in the chair closest to him and I would sit meekly in the other. Baborally knew that he would be dealing with Mum exclusively but he also spoke to me in a kind and polite manner. So, even before my rear had hit the seat, Baborally had said to his son Arjun, not a store worker, "*Arjun, chota sahib, ekto Coke me dedye*" ("Arjun, get a Coke for the little sahib"). The Coke came with a "pipe," the English word used in Calcutta to mean a drinking straw. I felt important. Then Mum would go through her list and Baborally would translate into Bengali and one of the store helpers would climb up and down the store shelves like Spiderman extracting the required item. In Calcutta, these imported cans or tins were always welcome and we never asked stupid questions about whether the expiry date had been reached. Our porter's basket gradually filled up; soon he returned to the car to unload all these items and then returned to find us, wherever we happened to be in the Market. A wonderful sense of trust existed between Mum and Baborally and, if Mum happened to be short of money to pay her bill, Baborally would say, "It's OK, memsahib, you can pay me next week." This is one of my most abiding memories. Mutual trust and a handshake were more important than a piece of paper. Later on in life, I realized that this was an old-fashioned way of getting to know people, and of developing social ties. It was a precious aspect of human relationships that I took for granted in India and that we lost when we finally left India for Australia.

On the days when I accompanied Mum to do her shopping, I always managed to drag her to another section of the Market, where they sold pets. "Pets' corner" was located in a narrow lane adjacent to the meat sellers' section. Here were all the normal household pets that we are familiar with: from the tail-wagger brigade right up to the felines, and I don't mean tender, cute, little pussy cats! If we were lucky, we sometimes saw the marbled cat, the jungle cat, the caracal and once the rare Palla's cat. Here also were numerous species of bird in small wire cages, all stacked on top of one other. Fortunately for this trade, there existed no Society for the Prevention of Cruelty to Animals; otherwise this lane would have been shut down in a trice. Eager pet owners made their choice of tail-wagger and then proceeded to give them some ridiculous exotic name like Pitti, Dattoo or Pushpu or even just plain Doggie. In another part of this corner, people could buy their own monkey or turtle or even other much larger and wilder varieties of animal. I remember seeing some pretty impressive snakes there. But I cannot forget the pitiful conditions in which all these animals had to live.

Just Another Day in the New Market

Just after the New Year, Mum was deciding whether I needed some clothes for the coming school year in Darjeeling. So, she went to the Market. As soon as the driver had parked the car and Mum had emerged, she was surrounded. These were the forward "spies" who worked for the various shops in the Market and who hoped to influence Mum to visit their shop. The competition for custom was fierce and by this "ambush" in the car park, many hoped to get their "foot in the door" early and thereby perhaps earn a small commission if Mum bought something. So, on this day like any other market day, Mum entered the chaos.

"Memsahib, memsahib, what are you looking for? My shop has everything. We are number 1 in the Market. Please, memsahib, come see my shop!"

Mum very casually said, "Today, I am looking for material for suits," and, with this remark, more than half of the forward scouting agents disappeared. The "suitings" agents all stepped forward and, as if in unison, shouted once more, "Memsahib, memsahib, please, my shop, my shop. No. 1 in market." Mum knew where she wanted to go and led the procession into the bowels of the Market. As she entered into this labyrinth of narrow alleyways, she had to watch out for porters with laden wicker baskets balanced on their heads. Often, she had to slow down as she came upon a wall of stout Bengali ladies shuffling slowly ahead in their saris and dainty sandals.

As tedious as this type of shopping could be, Mum knew that she would find what she wanted in these hole-in-the-wall shops, and the bonus was that they would be much cheaper than in the specialty "suitings" shops on the main street outside, with all their high overheads. Unlike shops in western countries, there was absolutely no way that customers could enter into one of these market shops, since the whole area from the back of the shop to the front of the alleyway resembled a giant bed or divan. On all sides of the shop, shelves that reached the ceiling carried the "suitings" materials; in the middle of the back wall, was a door that led, presumably, to a storeroom. Situated just in front of this door, the owner squatted behind what appeared to be a schoolboy's desk, which had been chopped down to half its height and which had a lid. The owner addressed Mum.

"Can I help Memsahib to make her choice?"

"Yes, I am looking for plain grey flannel material, enough to make two pairs of school pants for my son. What have you got? I want very good quality and not some *katcha* (poor or inferior) brand."

"Oh yes, madam, we have excellent flannel material. Ganesh, Shankar, flannel "suitings" *nikalo* (take down). Show to Memsahib. Madam, we have very much extensive range of flannel material and also a very good price and, for you, Madam, we have an even more, very good special price. Would Madam like a Coca Cola with pipe or some *chai* (tea) or coffee with *chini* (sugar)?" Mum would decline the kind offer and wait. Ganesh and

Shankar would get up out of their squatting position on the huge bed and move to the shelves. Soon, bolts of flannel material were being pulled off the shelves and one by one rolled out before her to inspect them.

Mum would ask, "Where are these flannel materials from?" The shopkeeper would respond, "Madam, these are the finest woven flannels that come from the famous mills of Lancashire in England." After much scrutiny, Mum would come to a decision and say, "I like this material. And how much do you charge for this material by the yard?"

He would look at Mum and in a soft voice say, "Madam, for you and only you I will give my very best price. This is the very finest material, you are very knowledgeable and you have made a very good choice; it is a fine weave, you can see how soft the material is and it comes all the way from England and is part of a special consignment which you will not find anywhere else in the Market."

"Yes, I understand all that, but what is your price?"

At first, he would read the label on the bolt, then go to his desk and pull out a pad of paper. For the next few minutes, as Mum waited, he would appear to be doing an ultra mini-maths exam as his pencil flew back and forth. After he had done all his checks, he would look up and say, "Madam, for you my very best price, is only Rs 40 per yard."

Mum would take a step back as if in shock, pause and look at him directly in the eye, but would not respond. The short silence soon conveyed the message to the owner that the quoted price was not acceptable. He would immediately come back and say, "*Acha* (OK), Madam, I will make it Rs 39 per yard and you can tell me how many yards you require!"

There was still no reaction and she would look sideways to the left and right of his shop where there were other shops selling similar materials. These sideways glances were not lost on the shop-owner, as he also knew that the owners of the adjacent stores had been following every detail of what had just transpired. One of the adjacent shop owners might even go so far as to shout an order to one of his fellow workers to pull down a bolt of the same flannel from the shelves. The man Mum was dealing with, obviously uncertain, would ask Mum, "*Acha, acha,* what does Madam want to pay?"

Mum would reply, following the 15% discount rule and say, "I will offer you Rs. 34 per yard" and wait. He would hesitate, shake his head from side to side and say to her, "But Madam, I will have no profit and I have to pay my staff and look after my large family," a standard response, as the voice took on a soft, sad tone. Slowly, he would start to order his staff to remove the rolls. Then, he would make one more effort and ask Mum, "Can mem-sahib make it Rs. 38 per yard?" Mum would say nothing and start to make the first tentative steps to the adjacent store where an identical flannel "suitings" material bolt had been pulled down off the shelves. When the owner recognized that he might lose a sale, he responded immediately, "*Acha* memsahib, you can have for Rs. 36 per yard."

Mum would order 4 yards of suiting material and also some other cloth lengths to make other items of clothing and then she would leave this section to go somewhere else in the Market. This was a game, a game of discerning who would blink first. Interactions of this kind took place many thousands of times daily in the Market and other retail outlets scattered throughout Calcutta. Living in Calcutta taught us the bargaining lessons early. It was expected and we found ourselves playing this game over really small amounts of money such that we would wonder whether we were even sane; but it was expected. So, we played along. I should add that Mum was an absolute "grand master" at these chess-like bargaining duels, demonstrating a shrewdness of judgement and a cunning that led to a successful bargaining career during her time in Calcutta.

Transportation

Calcutta's Traffic

In the mid 1970s, when I first returned to Calcutta as an adult in my thirties, and we had left the perimeter of Dum Dum Airport, I thought about what lay ahead with the drive back to the city. One of the worst road experiences always seemed to be negotiating the traffic on Chittaranjan Avenue. There would be pot-holes and a veritable canyon of four- or five-storey decrepit buildings, many with new washing flapping and drying on the windows outside. I settled reluctantly into a sort of drugged state to handle the constant stopping and starting that represented the traffic on this major thoroughfare. Many side roads entered Chittaranjan, so that the buses, lorries, bullock carts and rickshaws competed fiercely for space. The noise was appalling. The tinkling of the handheld bells of the rickshaw pullers was lost in a sea of car horns. Every car made use of its horn almost continually and, if these no longer functioned properly, then the hot-wired version would do. After all, everyone needed an outlet for their frustration! Some drivers would try to bypass the chaotic traffic by illegally entering a one-way street, only to be confronted by an oncoming car. The driver going the right way automatically would use *his* car horn. The car driver of the opposing car would stop. After being reminded that this was a one-way street, he would lean out of the window and hold out his hand, open palm facing upwards to the oncoming vehicle in a gesture requesting some patience and indicating profound regret. Then he would try to back out but, more often, he would try to allow the oncoming car enough space to pass, thereby still providing himself the opportunity to continue in the wrong direction. Chittaranjan Avenue traffic and its horn symphony: the frustration is etched forever in my memory.

Well, imagine my surprise on my return to Calcutta a decade later in the 1980s, when the air conditioned (A/C) Hindustan Ambassador hire car bypassed both the malaria-riddled swamps that surrounded Dum Dum Airport and this horror stretch of Chittaranjan Avenue. The car actually travelled in the countryside and then, all of a sudden, the road emerged near Park Circus and finally made its way into Park Street. Park Circus had become the new Chittaranjan Avenue, but mercifully it was a shorter stretch of congested mayhem compared to the former. On the other hand, the intensity had not changed. Cars came from everywhere and all wanted to compete for that little opening here or there. In many ways, the traffic resembled the movement of "dodgem" bumper cars that I had experienced at fun fairs. Some tried to drive fast, but that was next to impossible with only 60 or 90 feet to rev the engine before braking again.

This was an automotive dance where the drivers developed into an absolute art form their skill of "pushing into the gap." In some instances, the separation between cars was so close that I thought I could pass a piece of cardboard between the body panels of adjacent vehicles. Drivers could assert themselves - an older car was always helpful - and play "chicken" with the other drivers in order to maintain their position in this heaving mass of metal. But they never surrendered an inch to anybody or anything. If driving in this wall-to-wall honking mass was difficult for drivers, it was next to impossible for pedestrians. For instance, pedestrians who tried to cross streets like Chowringhee to get to the *Maidan* were embarking on "Mission Impossible." How could anyone find a gap? Even mothers and children were totally ignored when they tried to cross the road. So, pedestrians took their lives in their hands; their chance of success in attempting to cross this or any other street was minimal. I sometimes wondered if the reason that many pedestrians carried umbrellas when the sun was shining was to have the opportunity of whacking the passing cars.

If traffic was bad in the non-peak hours, it was insane at rush hour. Could it be compared with the "gaucho" madness that is so familiar in South America, but more particularly Mexico City? Could it be compared to the helter-skelter mayhem of an Italian city's rush hour, a form of brinksmanship conducted at a higher than average speed? Or was it more like the subdued, polite, traffic crawl of London? In Calcutta, the rush hour proceeded first and foremost with a total disdain of the traffic rules. Who cared if the street was officially divided into two lanes? Why not create a third or a fourth lane, even if it meant encroaching on the opposite line of traffic? It was obviously much more interesting if there were three or even four cars at the front row of a red light as everyone got ready to take off. What surprised me was that Calcutta's drivers had not just taken over the sidewalks in their perennial jockeying for position. But there were specifically Indian impediments to high speed at rush hour. There were the ever-present wandering cows to avoid, as well as piles of building rubble that had spread to the roadway. And then there was the peculiarly Indian condition of the cars. Who cared what happened to his car in this scrum when its front bumpers were attached to the front end with chicken wire, when its side panels resembled a hilly countryside, when the brakes did not work as they should, when the steering column had a play in it of God knows how many degrees, when the exhaust belched black smoke and, most importantly, when the car could only creep forward 3 feet at a time? In Calcutta's rush hour, drivers were lucky if their average progress reached the giddy speed of 10 miles per hour.

In Calcutta, drivers would hang elaborate sculptures or baubles or toy animals from their rear-view mirrors; some had a small facsimile of their favourite god in an elaborate shrine on their dashboard so that when they became stuck in traffic they could look at these holy objects and indulge in a spot of meditation or prayer! Every few minutes, cars would inch forward and then stop again for the lights at some traffic intersection. The traffic lights were a signal for all the car engines to be switched off. Switching off the engine heralded a lengthy stop. As the lights changed, engines roared to life in perfect harmony, releasing both a collective growl and a mini-mushroom cloud of thick, dirty-brown, exhaust fumes. Intersections offered the opportunity to indulge again in a colossal game of "chicken" to get across. There was a ritual to this. On approaching an intersection, the driver put his right hand out of the car indicating to an opposing car that he planned to undertake his manoeuvre and then he went for it. The hand gesture might be interpreted as a silent prayer that the opposing driver would display some courtesy. Strangely enough, it most often worked. Despite all the mayhem, there were relatively few accidents and drivers usually managed to reach their destination.

Superimposed on this mélange of cars were the Calcutta buses, usually filled to overflowing. In some buses, the shock absorbers or springs had obviously given out because, when the bus went around the corners, the rear entry platform would sometimes scrape the road due to the sheer overload of people on the bus and the number of people holding on at the back. I often wondered how the bus conductor sold tickets in this stuffed sardine tin. Sometimes, at a traffic stop or a bus stop, the conductor emerged from the front entry side exit of the bus and re-entered from the rear. Then he would start pushing and shoving through the crowds to sell bus tickets. When he eventually reached the front, the whole cycle started again. Often, there were three, four or five buses all going to Bhowanipore, running one behind the other. Could this column of buses possibly be following a timetable? People driving cars did not push their luck with a bus. If a gap was visible, it was certain that the bus driver had seen it and would gun his bus for it. His conductor - by some sort of telepathy - knew instinctively the intent of the driver and hung out over the roadway from either the front or rear bus exit to beckon other vehicles to slow down and let the bus push into the gap. With the bus, the rules of the road read, "Bus is might"!

The Calcutta trams were less chaotic. When we lived in Calcutta, Mum and I often took the tram when the car was unavailable. The tram was a pleasant ride to Lindsay Street and the New Market and, if we traveled outside peak traffic hours, invariably we got a seat. The air blew through the open windows and provided reasonable relief from the heat. But, with the passing years and lack of maintenance, the tracks deteriorated badly and the trams seemed to run along a wavy ribbon of steel, jerking along this way and that and up and down. We always avoided the trams at rush hour. The brave tram patrons embraced death as they hung out from the tram doors, one foot on a platform whilst hanging onto someone or some other support inside the tram. If the tram was too full, why not use the exterior, perhaps even the wheel arches and rims? Over the years, the rush hour grew to occupy the period from early morning to the onset of evening and still the people filled the trams.

I often walked through the large open-air tram terminus opposite the Metro Cinema. I was amazed to see not only some examples of the newer trams, but also older relics of the 1940s and 50s still in service. No tram graveyard here! They were kept in service no matter what.

Calcutta's Taxis

Calcutta was and is a city full of taxis: a swarm of yellow and black Hindustan Ambassadors that definitely own the streets. They are every-where and their numbers appear to be growing year by year. In the 50s, there were distinctly fewer taxis around such that sometimes, after going to the movies or a restaurant, we actually had to wait many minutes before a taxi appeared. The cab driver asked all the waiting passengers where they wanted to go and then chose passengers going to the furthest destination. Today, Calcutta's taxis populate the city's roads like bees in a hive. Drivers are now happy to get *any* customer. The tables have turned. I have one memorable image of this taxi world on Park Street, now a one-way street, with wall-to-wall, row-by-row taxis. Most of them were no bigger than a Morris Minor or a Fiat 124. Europeans might be excused for feeling they had to enter rear first with an imaginary shoehorn to help them slide into the back seat. Even when I was a boy, Calcutta's taxis seemed old, as though they had been reincarnated through many lives; all were pretty much dilapidated. Predominantly, Sikhs drove them; but there was the occasional Bengali driver.

Today, a friend usually sits next to the driver to keep him company. Some things have not changed. In the 1950s, when we caught a cab, there was usually a Sikh cab driver with all his friends occupying the front seat and sometimes part of the back seat. If he noticed that you needed more room, he would tell one or more of his friends to get out. Occasionally, these friends would act as signal lights for the driver, leaning out to gesture to the following cars that a left turn or a lane change was planned by the driver. At times, the friend decided that this free ride presented a good opportunity to comb his hair or beard, thereby releasing all the latest oily pomades into the air. Sometimes, a third person squeezed into the front seat with the driver and his friend. The main job of the front seat occupants appeared to be lowering the flag on the taxi-meter situated on the front left window exterior of the taxi. They were well-proportioned persons, so that if there were more than three people in your group, you found yourself another taxi with no front seat passengers.

The taxis also had some wonderful quirks. The rear passenger seats were pretty dilapidated through decades of use and neglect and I always felt I had hit the jackpot if the rear seat had no exposed spring. When customers hailed the taxi down, the driver sat behind his wheel and offered no help whatsoever to his prospective fare. The drivers also knew all the tricks known to taxi drivers the world over. The taximeter was either broken (so the driver claimed) or the meter was already running with a fare, suggesting a few miles already travelled. No amount of requests to reset the meter helped, so customers often guessed what the fare would be and could expect an argument about the fare at the end of the trip.

Many of these taxis seemed to be held together by string and straightened wire from coat-hangers: they were literally ready for the scrap yard, if such a facility had existed in Calcutta. When it rained, customers would get soaked from the leaks that were all but invisible in the cab roof, or from windows that could not be closed properly. Another common occurrence was customers picking up some sort of oil or grease stain on their clothes.

These cabs were so prone to mechanical breakdowns that customers were often forced to try and flag down alternate means of transport, sometimes in rain or even rush hour. But, there were so many of them packed so tightly on the roads that this was seldom a problem.

The electrical systems of Calcutta's taxis were an eye-opener. For instance, the driver would have a small, non-descript button on his steering wheel that had once functioned as a horn. But it had given up the ghost a long time ago. Instead, a spaghetti-like bundle of wires spilled out of the steering column. Two of these were used to start the engine by closing the circuit on the column. A spark or two ensued and suddenly there was a deep groan or belch from the engine. It did not matter that the taxi sometimes reeked of petrol. The wires did the job, so who cared! And if it worked for the ignition then why not the car light, the brake lights, or the overhead light, if it still had a bulb! And nary a thought was given to the potentially explosive presence of petrol fumes and sparks. If the electrical horn was inoperable, the driver's front seat friend would operate an older-style trumpet horn with rubber bellows, which he squeezed to produce a noise somewhere between that of a squealing pig, and the "breaking of wind." It soon became apparent that this rubber version of the old-fashioned trumpet horn situated on the side of the car sometimes also served as the de facto substitution for brakes. The continual din from these horns let each driver know where the others were situated on the crowded roads and what other drivers' intentions were. The noise was unbelievable but, magically, there were very few accidents. Once the taxi set off and joined the traffic, the driver displayed his skills. He had all the moves, the kamikaze spurts, the sudden acceleration into a tight spot, the squeezing into a place between cars. Thus, these taxis proceeded through the Calcutta traffic with a professional, if reckless, abandon. All the customer could do was close his eyes and hope for the best.

Howrah Station and Train Travel

Howrah is a suburb to the north of Calcutta that abuts Howrah Bridge. Here were some of the worst slums in Calcutta; the poorest people lived here on the streets. Many of them were displaced from the countryside; these were the victims of the annual floods that occurred on the Brahmaputra and Ganges when the snow melted in the Himalayas. They could not help themselves. How could you control a river like the Brahmaputra that, at some points, is over 25 miles wide? Some people estimated that, every year, the city acquired about 100,000 of these displaced people and that a fraction of them managed to move back later to their land. For the majority, the city and the promise of jobs was the lure and so they joined the hundreds of thousands who sought work there. Howrah witnessed thousands and thousands of daily struggles by these unfortunate people who wondered where their next bowl of rice would come from.

Quite close to the northern end of Howrah Bridge is Calcutta's main railway station, Howrah Station. The architectural style of the main façade is Grand Victorian with its exterior faced with red and white brick. Here, at Howrah Station, was an ideal opportunity to get an insight into the life and soul of Calcutta. Even in my parents' time, people from all walks of life congregated at the Station, from the daily commuters coming from outlying areas, to well-to-do and poor families travelling for personal reasons. The concourse was so jam-packed, with people filling every available nook and cranny of the railway platform, it seemed impossible that so many people could be contained in such a small area. It did not matter what time of day it was, the platforms served as temporary homes for many people, many of them enjoying a short nap. Children were all over the place. They were absolute pests, thronging around helpless travelers who, on entering the station, often had to push out one hand, shoving aside those who stood in front of them, thus creating a small passage so that they could at least move forward to their departure platforms. And at the same time, travelers had to be careful where they placed their next step for fear of treading on someone sleeping on the platform.

Much of the concourse area resembled a campground, with numerous family groups huddled around their bags and bedding rolls, and often a "*chula*," where they prepared their food. Some were engaged in animated conversation, some stared ahead blankly, some argued while the children played and amused themselves. And why? Well, many of them were poor people who had chosen to travel up-country, but did not have access to, let alone been able to read and understand, the timetables. So, they just turned up and waited for their train even if the departure was scheduled a few days later. Logic dictated that, if they had to wait for a train, they should just camp in the station and wait out the time.

The trains that entered and left the station were usually packed. Most trains were predominantly assembled with third class carriages. This naturally invited a scrum, as travellers laid claim to their position in these carriages. When the carriage doors opened, tempers often rose as everyone tried to enter the carriage at once through a door that was designed only to accommodate one person at a time.

The railway staff helped to push and shove the passengers into their compartments. As some passengers got separated from their baggage, there would be screams of despair. Square-shaped luggage and bedding-rolls were extremely useful, since they could serve as "seats" in an already crowded compartment. There was now a real frisson of anxiety. As more and more people were jammed into the carriages, some were forced to stand upright, like so many asparagus stalks. Could this be the Indian Railways version of a mobile "Black Hole"? Third class passengers laid claim to a seat, which became their home for the duration of the journey. People travelling alone would have to make sure they used the toilet beforehand so that they did not need to leave their seats for the duration of the trip. Otherwise, someone else would claim it. Those unfortunates who had to stand made sure that they hung onto something, for the trains usually started with a staccato series of jerks and tugs to gain some momentum forward. The station master would look left and right before he raised his flag; then he would take out his whistle and blow long and hard into it. A momentary shudder would concertina its way through all the carriages. The "sardine" express was underway, swaying ever so slowly and gently. Yes, forward motion could now be discerned. Welcome to third class travel in India!

People hung out of their carriage windows and ordered all types of food from the wandering hawkers, ranging from nuts, to beverages, to "*chai*," to samplings of vegetables served on small banana leaf cutouts. Small banana leaves were easy to dispose of: they were just thrown on the floor. All the railway platforms were littered with them. The idea of using garbage bins was an alien concept to most people. After all, why bother to find one when the floor was a more convenient receptacle.

CHAPTER 9

Dad's Business World and the Move to Australia

The Evolution of Dad's Factory

In many ways, Dad was lucky to have established his business in 1943, before the advent of the twin problems of political uncertainty and labour unrest that emerged with Indian Independence in August 1947. A second factor in his favour was that he began the company during the British-controlled period between December 1943 and August 1947; this meant that he did not initially have to confront the excesses of a Bengali-controlled bureaucratic system, where progress happened at a snail's pace and the love of paper would be elevated to a minor religion.

Nevertheless, "luck" is a relative term; as a boy, I never really appreciated the very difficult and unusual business climate in which he had to operate the factory. For more than two decades, he ran a business during extreme political confusion, unusually high economic uncertainty, and in the midst of a very serious religious divide between Muslims and Hindus. Just as important was the chaotic labour market, with interminable unrest, that would have driven most entrepreneurs to an early grave. That he managed to survive and keep his factory and workforce employed is a testimony to his own business acumen and to the astute people who helped him navigate the always murky and occasionally dangerous waters of Bengali labour. Through it all, he never forgot that he had both a responsibility to our family, and to the families of his workforce.

By the late 1940s, Dad established the manufacturing, assembly and packaging side of his business. But where to put the office? Eventually a space was found between the main factory and the front retaining wall of the property. The builders came in and created a useable office. I can only imagine what it must have been like to work there, with the noise from all the hydraulic presses booming directly into the area. Nevertheless, this space was Dad's office, no separate area, no front door. He shared the extremely cramped, "open plan" office with the other office staff and it never changed during all his time in Calcutta.

As I have mentioned before, in the emergent economy of post-independence India, the country's foreign exchange reserves were in extremely short supply. This shortage had serious ramifications for the country. Many industrial sectors competed ferociously for access to foreign exchange to pay for the imports necessary to keep their factories running. In the case of Dad's factory, India did not produce any tinplate, an essential raw material in producing lanterns. Once he acquired the tinplate, he used his heavy hydraulic presses to extrude the external frame of the hurricane lanterns. The tinplate had to be imported and the Indian government had to release the necessary foreign exchange to pay for these tinplate sheet imports.

Thankfully, this industrial sector was considered important. Estimates at the time were that about 80% of Indian villages had no electricity; therefore, the lanterns my father produced were deemed by the Indian government to be of national importance. So, in theory, the purchase of foreign currency with Indian rupees was never the issue. The issue revolved around getting *approval* for enough foreign exchange to buy adequate reserves of tinplate to meet a whole year's production. As it turned out, the factory would never have survived from the officially sanctioned annual tinplate quota. Dad had to resort to the black market and other manufacturers to buy any tinplate surplus to their needs to cover his shortfall. Making up the shortfall from the thriving black market for tinplate was always an expensive option, but he really had no other choice.

Although I have previously outlined how the political and social environment of Bengal affected our family's daily life, I would now like to demonstrate how the political, labour and social context affected my father in trying to operate a business in Calcutta during this era.

Mid 1950s: Migration Waves and Pressure on Calcutta

I can't emphasize enough the widespread unrest and desperation experienced by many of the ordinary people in Calcutta during the 1950s. The fear and worry were almost palpable. The city was trying to cope with waves of migration, predominantly refugees. The political migrants largely comprised refugees fleeing the unrest in East Pakistan, yet unsure of where to go. The Hindus amongst this particular group of refugees were worried and confused by the East Pakistan adoption of Urdu as its official language and the adoption of an Islamic constitution. Where did this decision leave Hindi-speaking followers of the Hindu religion? All of these policy changes disenfranchised the many Bengali Hindus who were primarily engaged in agriculture in areas that crossed the borders of Bengal and East Pakistan. In addition to these political refugees, thousands of others who were victims of agricultural and natural disasters sought sanctuary in the city. In 1953 and 1954, especially, disastrous floods occurred in Bengal. [168]

In the north of Bengal, after the annexation of Tibet by the Chinese, several thousand Tibetan refugees had escaped Chinese oppression and made their way across the Himalayas, many eventually settling in Darjeeling and scattering throughout the rest of Bengal and India. As the seat of government in Bengal, Calcutta felt the additional weight of allocating and distributing aid.

For many refugees, Calcutta offered the promise of jobs. For others, the city was a transit stop, but most of them effectively viewed Calcutta as the end of the road. All displaced peoples lived in refugee transit camps and squatter colonies that were meant to be temporary. But, with each passing

168 The whole subject of post-Partition refugees and their impact on the city is comprehensively covered in Sukanta Chaudhuri, ed., *Calcutta, The Living City. Vol II. The Present and Future*, 70-77, 85-86, 92, 97, 142 154, 156, 203 and 257.

year, more people flooded into the camps than were able to integrate into the city itself. The result was that, by 1958, over 800,000 people were still living in these urban hovels.

The pressures on the city were now enormous; it began to transform into a crowded, dirty, noisy place with thousands of people living on the streets. The overt signs of increasing poverty were everywhere. The city's planners and the utility departments had no chance of keeping up with this enormous influx of people and the concomitant need for infrastructure. The city could not keep up with any improvement plans for slums and refugee colonies. It could not fulfill its obligations to education or the care of children from displaced families. It even started to experience food shortages: the availability of useable land for agriculture was in short supply, as housing needs increasingly added to the pressure.

Emerging Political and Labour Problems

A perfect storm appeared inevitable with these converging realities. The West Bengal government had been responsible for the decisions on all the important issues confronting the city and the wider countryside. However, the need to rehabilitate displaced persons and refugees and create work opportunities for them remained unaddressed. The Indian Government, led by the Congress Party and its leader Jawaharlal Nehru, refused to make funds available to ameliorate the growing crisis. Since all displaced persons and refugee issues had basically been inadequately managed or ignored by the Bengal government, this decision by the Congress Party produced a field day for the opposition parties, in particular, the Communist Party of India (CPI). Political feelings ran high.

And how did Bengalis show their anger? Through agitation and protests. In the late 1940s and the early to mid-50s, Calcutta started to experience all sorts of protests in the form of mass political rallies, marches through the streets that disrupted city life, *hartals*[169] by the tram workers, students, bank employees, government workers, office workers in corporations, and employees of the law courts, amongst others. Because of the total

169 A *hartal* was a strike action that usually involved the shut-down of a workplace, or a public disruption through protest rallies, processions, and general civil disobedience.

disruption and potential for violent protests in the city, private companies, banks, schools, and markets would prudently close their doors whenever they felt a threat.

The Indian Government had banned Communist parties in 1948, amongst others, as a means of removing those groups that did not respect the law or abstain from violence. The ban did not last for long, however. During the 1950s and 60s, Calcutta was enmeshed in a climate of frivolous strikes. For instance, in 1948, the Communist Party of Bengal organized a "pens down" strike in the government sector where clerks ceased to work while sitting at their desks. This strike spread to some factories. In 1949, there were over 35 major strikes in Calcutta which included a *hartal*, more "Go Slow" strikes, "Pens Down/Tools Down" strikes, wild cat strikes, sympathy strikes,[170] jurisdictional strikes, hunger strikes,[171] "sick out" strikes, and unfair labour practices strikes. Calcutta experienced some truly crazy strikes like the one that occurred in February 1969, when about 3,200 trams suddenly stopped, through a carefully planned action in which unknown individuals all pulled on the emergency stop cords at a designated time on the trams. The picture that I am trying to present is that these creative forms of strike became an integral part of the Bengal industrial landscape and caused major problems for all businesses, including my father's. Numerous variations of this strike theme occurred every year; indeed, it would have been possible at that time to construct a yearly calendar organized by strikes rather than by months in the year. For instance, in 1968/69, strike incidents in West Bengal accounted for over 60% of the total man-hours lost throughout *all of India*.

In many ways, these strikes contributed to a decrease in the economic importance of Calcutta, a phenomenon that had started with the decline of shipping through the Port and went right through to a dramatic downturn in economic activity in the city, as investment dollars went elsewhere. Many companies relocated to other places in India with more stable labour relations. The cumulative effect of all this strike action, primarily influenced

---

170 The Calcutta dock workers went out on strike in solidarity with their striking Australian dock worker comrades.
171 The city employees started a hunger strike in solidarity with prisoners who carried out a hunger strike in gaol.

by the Communist Party in Bengal, had the direct effect of slowing general employment to a snail's pace in Bengal compared to the rest of India.[172]

One of the more vivid experiences of these times occurred with the almost daily, long processions that marched down Chowringhee Road. They had started somewhere beyond Lower Circular Road, probably in Kalighat, a poorer part of town. These processions comprised anywhere from a few hundred to thousands of people all marching, proudly displaying their banners. The processions had a form and structure, as well as their own rituals. The protesters usually marched in line formation, 8 to 10 persons per line; some would display their banners, which identified their industry. Many of the banners were in English. Women carrying children or babies on their hips were often prominent in the front ranks, which was meant to garner sympathy from bystanders. Alongside these concertinaed columns came the cheerleaders who shouted out loaded, pre-rehearsed questions through a loud hailer, questions that lent themselves to a two- or three-word provocative response. A frequent call was, "*Hum kya cahate haim?*" ("What do we want?"). The responding chants from the column usually ended with "*Band kharo!*" (Shut it down!). I sometimes think that the first Hindi words any foreigner learnt during this era were "*Band kharo!*"

With the growing ascendancy of the Communist Party, the political landscape in the early 1950s, in Bengal and especially Calcutta, started to change. Congress had been the dominant party all over India at virtually all levels. In Calcutta, Congress' mandate had been to provide a government conforming to Nehru's socialist ideology. Throughout the early 1950s, the Bengali Congress Party had maintained its control of patronage, pandering to lobbyists, and securing ties to business and corresponding financial contributions. Its image was as the party of the wealthy, propertied classes, and industrial interests. People generally viewed the Bengal Congress Party as an organization that was oblivious to the social and economic problems of its citizenry and the growing refugee population. The voices of disenchantment were certainly growing. All this popular agitation and confrontation in the streets began to have its first impact on parliamentary

---

172 Geoffrey Moorhouse, *Calcutta*, 293.

politics. In large part, the Communist Party controlled the streets and used these organized protests and subsequent labour unrests to further its own political aims.

Bengal Elections

The political landscape started to change from 1951 onwards, as the Communist Party made steady gains in government. The increasing despair and poverty of the refugees still presented a problem to the West Bengal government. A perfect set of pre-conditions existed for the Communist Party to make inroads into a disenchanted citizenry. During this turbulent time, the continuing industrial and political chaos led to periods of President's Rule in July 1962 (7 days), February 1968 - February 1969 (1 year 5 days), March 1970 - April 1971 (1 year 14 days) and June 1971 - March 1972 (256 days). Under the Indian Constitution, the Central Government can dismiss an unstable state government in order to maintain law and order; this certainly was the case in Bengal, with its continuous barrage of highly disruptive strikes and political unrest and disputes. And, thus, the Communist Party made steady gains electorally until their 1977 success, when they could rule Bengal in their own right. These disruptions significantly affected the running of my father's factory.

Bengal Corruption

During Congress rule in Bengal, with the huge disparity between the poor and the wealthy, corrupt behaviour became rampant, whether amongst members of the Legislature, in the governing administration, with local government councillors, or even the private business sector. Votes could be bought in the Legislature or at the local government level if the issue seemed important or, more likely, profitable enough. In my opinion, the Calcutta Corporation became the most corrupt, the incentive being that it handled all the building applications and related matters. Their illegal activities extended to providing undervalued assessments on property to minimize the taxes levied on that property in return for inducements. An investigative commission enquiring into corruption in the Calcutta Corporation found that the property under-valuations could reach as much as 50% of the actual value. Municipal taxes were based on these valuations. This corruption was integrated at both the state and municipal levels, for the Commission determined that many of the beneficiaries of this largesse were sitting members of the West Bengal Legislature. All it took to obtain a low property valuation was money or nepotism (a promise of a job to family or friends of the assessing officer). Officials of the Public Health Department were bribed to falsify findings about adulterated food. Public auctions of land by the State were not transparent; often, lower bids won the day in return for cash or other favours. In one case, a councillor was found to have been illegally evicting stallholders from one market to another. Only later, after investigation, did it emerge that the evicted stall-holders had become his tenants.[173]

The corruption extended into the judicial system where the wealthy could escape prosecution for non-payment of municipal council taxes for periods of time ranging from ten to fifteen years. The final straw came in the lead-up to the 1967 state election, when Congress Party Ministers were involved in a massive financial scandal. In this case, money that had been destined for the relief of the poor and distressed in an outer Calcutta area had been mostly purloined through corrupt Congressmen, who sat on boards and agencies that were supposed to manage the relief programs. The accounting of monies spent bore no relation to the actual work done. In addition, the nepotistic tendencies of the Congressmen ensured that these agencies were populated by their sons, daughters, in-laws and friends, and Congress Party hacks, as well as fictitious employees.[174] The scandal unfolded in 1967 and most probably led to the Communist-led coalition that included a breakaway *Bangla* (Bengal) Congress Party. The coalition won the 1969 elections by a margin of 140 to 127 seats.

Running a Business - Obtaining Raw Materials

All of this government corruption was a daily hindrance to my father's business. It was most evident in the difficult, yet essential, task of obtaining an allocation of tinplate sheets from the Indian Central government. Without this allocation, Dad's business would have folded early. The

173 Ibid., 311-312.
174 Ibid., 313-315.

requisite government agency that handled these allocation matters was located in New Delhi; so, twice a year, Dad made the trip to New Delhi to obtain his quota. I tagged along on one of these trips and my recollection of this encounter remains crystal clear to this day. True to British bureaucratic and procedural traditions, a lot of preliminary paperwork had to be filled out, usually in triplicate. Anyone producing and selling carbon paper in India at that time must have made a fortune. The agency required a bewildering array of forms, including forms to apply to make a request, forms to quantify the amount of tinplate required, forms to justify need, forms to establish the company's financial bona fides, forms to justify a strategic need in the context of India's shortage of available foreign exchange, and testimonials regarding the character of the applicant. In the last two cases, thankfully, the argument for strategic need had already been made, and Mr. Chatterjee was able to provide the flowery, wordy testimonials about Dad in glowing, golden English with liberal sprinklings of "esteemed," "dynamic," "impeccable character," "good citizen," and "important provider of labour."

At the government agency, the first barrier was always the acceptance desk where our application competed against literally hundreds of others. The height of the files that surrounded the accepting clerk could be measured in feet. I remember thinking that if these piles of paper ever overbalanced and fell on the clerk, he would have suffocated. So, strategically, it was very important to get an edge, namely, bypass the mounting stacks of files, get the requisite acceptance stamp, and move past this crucial first stage. Otherwise, it would take weeks to move the form from his desk to the next processing stage. The magic ingredient was the seduction of the acceptance clerk via an appropriate inducement. At this level, the inducement had to be very desirable, so Dad always brought with him three different sizes of Bata Ambassador shoes, beautiful black leather shoes, and placed them on the desk with the shoe description tag facing the clerk. In Calcutta, this form of petty bribery was known as buying "betel leaves and bidis" to influence matters. No words needed to be exchanged. The mutual understanding of this gesture was total and immediate and the clerk would pick his size. Then, Dad would hand over his bunch of papers. They would receive their date-stamp immediately and were entered into the accepting log. Now we could "walk" the application to the next stage immediately. This is what Dad referred to as "innocent seduction," in which the cost of a pair of Bata shoes sped up the process.

The next stage was more difficult and, of course, the inducements started to escalate in value. Some wanted the latest Pat Boone or Kingston Trio records, together with their Bata shoes. Sometimes these wishes were telegraphed to us well in advance and so we could buy the records prior to departure for Delhi from various clothes retail outlets near the Calcutta New Market. We required this advance warning because the retailers themselves needed to have time to smuggle these long-playing records (LPs) into the country from Singapore or Hong Kong. Dad was well acquainted with the Pat Boone LPs because my sister, Martina, was the President of the Indian Pat Boone Fan Club and served as the resident consultant on all things associated with Pat Boone. However, white shoes were difficult to get, since Bata did not have this style in its range of shoes yet. As the years passed, electronic technology advanced into our daily lives and transistor technology started to have its effect on consumer desires. At this point, the requirements became more discerning and included requests for little portable transistor radios. These, too, were available from the clothing retail outlets. The next stage in inducements for clerks and bureaucrats was cash in simple white envelopes. This development obviated the need for Dad to be present and so he hired an agent in New Delhi to handle such "money transfer" situations. I reflect on this period as relatively harmless; nevertheless, it was a vital necessity for the survival of the factory and it created a win-win situation: his bureaucratic contacts in Delhi were well shod in their Bata shoes, while they listened to popular music and Dad's need for a quota had been expedited.

The Art of Bureaucracy in Calcutta

Dealing with a new bureaucracy is a formidable task, the first of which is discovering the many different roles that contribute to a given process. A visit to the Calcutta Corporation building in 1961 to obtain a building permit for Dad's proposed new factory at Gobra revealed offices filled with rows and rows of desks each occupied by a *babu* (clerk). The pecking order of seniority or authority was never obvious to the casual observer, but each *babu* had a sacred duty: namely, to supply the applicant with a Form, perhaps WB-AC102, designed to indicate that we wished to apply for something. Filling out these forms was very time consuming. Returning the completed form was just the start.

The clerk would pick up a stamp from an impressive array that resided in a two-storey high stamp holder. Naturally, it took time to find the right one for this form. He then entered into the stamp pad ritual during which he would breathe onto the stamp's surface before he plunged it hard onto his inkpad. And now he had a moment of uncertainty. Had the ink actually been transferred to the stamp's surface? Logic dictated that it must be tested first and so he would pull out a blank sheet of paper for a trial run. He would press it onto the paper to verify that he had selected the right stamp. When satisfied about his choice, he would press it onto the form. All this ritual to obtain "Received" on your form itself. The end? Think again!

The *babu* still had to sign and date it. He would reach for his nib pen and open his inkwell. But the ink had dried up! A momentary panic ensued and alarmed words would pierce the air in Bengali or Hindi requesting Govinder to get some ink for his inkwell. Govinder, who had been allocated as the section's peon (the office gopher) sat near our industrious *babu*; when the call came, he would leap from his squatting position to attend to the needs of his clerk.

The clerk, without looking at Govinder, would just hand him the empty inkwell and tell him to fill it with ink. Govinder went away, with a clueless expression on his face, which seemed to say, "Where do I get ink?" In the meantime, the *babu* would look sheepishly at us, waggle his head from side to side a few times in a conciliatory manner and ask for patience and indulgence.

By this time, we may have wanted to wring his neck, but this man and this form were important to obtain what we wanted, so we would graciously respond, "Take your time."

A short time later, Govinder would return with some ink, fill the ink well and our *babu* then would dip his pen into it, add his signature, and dry it with blotting paper. Now the signature had to be date stamped. He would take out his date stamp, realize that it had the wrong date, look for a pencil, push the rollers to the right date and very carefully, with geometrical precision, make an impression under his signature. What would have been so difficult for him to sign and also add the date, with the same pen? But this was Calcutta. Finally, form WB-AC102 was complete and then the *babu* would ask for the application fee.

"Sir, that will be 7 rupees 50 paise."[175]

My father would reach for his wallet to pay the fee; the *babu* had to issue a chit for this amount that we had to take to the cashier together with Form WB-AC102. The cashier would then peruse Form WB-AC102, verify it with his name and signature and write across it "PAID." Where is his "PAID" stamp? Apparently lowly cashiers were not allowed stamps. My father would hand over a 10 rupee note which the cashier would hold up to the light to verify its authenticity. He would take out a loose piece of paper and calculate that he needed to come up with 2 rupees, 50 paise change. He would issue my father with the change and write, "PAID" across the chit. The applicant might be excused for thinking that perhaps progress had been made, and returned to the original clerk.

However, the *babu* had now started his lunch. He had his tiffin boxes laid out before him ready to enjoy their contents. After he had recovered from his lunch, he would slowly rise and go to the bathroom to freshen up while his peon cleaned up his desk. When he returned he would take a paper clip out of his drawer, and write on an attached sheet of paper in capital letters: "TO FORM PROCESSING SECTION 32, BUILDING 7, BLOCK 24A, NIMTOLLA. FOR ATTENTION: SRI BHIMEN CHATTERJEE, PROCESSING OFFICER CLASS 4B" for further processing and action.

The applicant might dare to ask, "How long will this take?"

"Oh, perhaps three or four months! You know, sir, there is very much backlog, and we are very much understaffed, but I will mark "URGENT" on your papers."

"Is that all?"

"Oh, no Sir! You must now proceed to my colleague at the next desk, as you need to fill out form EB–D173 version 3."

---

175 India changed to a decimal currency in 1957.

"Thank you." And it would start all over again. After having stood in countless queues and waited through the interminable tea and lunch breaks, the applicant would finally have filled out all the requisite forms, yet still hardly have moved an inch.

This was a Calcutta bureaucratic experience. But there was a plus side to all of this tedium. The city had provided the public with rows and rows of employed clerks, all very polite, all very presentable, in their white *dhotis* (loincloth) and short-sleeved pullovers. The *dhoti*-clad clerks enjoyed the same job status and engaged in cross-table banter. But, for appearances sake, they would periodically show that they had some authority by raising a hand and, without making eye contact with their peon, loudly say "*Pani dedho, jaldi, jaldi*" ("Quickly, quickly, bring me water). All work ceased until the water arrived.

After several of these encounters, I realized, that all this theatre of the absurd had some purpose: it supplied work to lots of people. If the process were actually efficient, or went any faster, the whole system would break down.

Dad's Driver

The convenience of a car was a kind of imprisonment. The distance from the apartment to the front gate of the factory was about two kilometers, similar to that of the bazaar and the New Market. In the early days, Dad had used a bicycle to make this trip. However, a car became an absolute necessity for Dad when he needed to get to *Burrabazar* (Large Bazaar) or other venues for business meetings with his dealers or the banks. Parking a car was extremely difficult and leaving it unattended was a recipe for disaster, since the car would have been stripped bare in no time if left unattended. Mum also needed the car to do her shopping and to go to the Swimming Club, at least once or twice a day. Dad therefore hired a driver who worked at least eight to nine hours a day, six days a week. He may only have done two or three hours of actual driving during this time; the rest of the time he waited and guarded the car, after having dropped Dad off at the doorstep and then gone to look for a suitable parking spot which, in Calcutta, could take a lot of time.

Our driver, Phul Mohammed, was a tall, good-looking man, lean, brown-skinned, a Muslim from a village about 60 miles from Calcutta near the East Bengal border. He wore a khaki uniform, preferring long pants to shorts, with a loose-fitting shirt. This outfit afforded him a small recognition of his status. Phul had a pleasant demeanour, very accommodating and helpful, not given to a lot of talk, but he knew his way around Calcutta. He drove the Citroen very carefully, and most importantly, he knew where all the best parking spots were to be found. He liked to read his local Urdu language newspaper over a cup of tea while he waited. He was paid about 100 rupees a month; and, with this amount, he supported not only himself but his whole family back home in his village.

Phul had a routine: every morning he would come up to the apartment and get his instructions from Dad and plan his day so that he could also meet Mum's needs. But his true value came when he had to drive Dad to those parts of Calcutta where it was difficult to park. He would drop Dad off close to where his appointment was scheduled and then disappear. Even though he had no watch, he arrived punctually early every morning. He had a knack of knowing when Dad's appointment would be over and he waited at the door to take him to the car. He stayed with us as our driver for over 20 years and, like our other servants, came to be seen as "family." Mum made a point of giving him two extra weeks *chuti* (holiday) as he only had an opportunity to visit his family once a year.

Burrabazar

The hurricane lanterns that were produced in Dad's factory were prepared for packaging in straw-filled wooden cases that held, and provided protection for, 24 lanterns including their globes. Dad had no distribution network of his own. But Calcutta had an enormous market at Burrabazar which provided the network of wholesale dealers needed to distribute these lanterns, not only in Calcutta, but also nationwide. The Burrabazar was at the centre of Calcutta's business district and occupied a whole neighbourhood to the north of Dalhousie, abutting the river Hooghly.

Burrabazar had quite a long history. Originally it was a market area for cloth and yarn; its origins can be traced back to the late 17th century. Burrabazar also included a market for gold or other products of interest to the British East India Company. The market gained economic prominence mainly through the commercial dealings of the Marwaris, who started trading there from the late 19th century onwards. In fact, they bought up so much of the land that then, and also today, it is predominantly the domain of the Marwaris.

Burrabazar covered over 26,000 square feet. It has been said that, in Burrabazar, everything from a pin to an elephant could be found. Primarily because of the wealth of the Marwaris, Burrabazar had many imposing buildings. Today, many of these have become somewhat dilapidated. But, even in the 1950s and 60s, the Rajasthani architectural influence and the wonderful residences were lost in a labyrinth of narrow alleys and lanes where even a rickshaw puller had difficulty. A few main thoroughfares surrounded the area; many were badly pot-holed, but cars and taxis still operated on them, with their car horns permanently activated. Everywhere, there were crowded trams running on questionable steel tracks, over-filled buses, hand-pulled carts, and the ever-present surge of people spilling out from the pavement onto the main road where they competed with each other for the space to move. Entering an alleyway on foot was, in many cases, the only means of forward progress. It was total mayhem: a throng of busy people who bumped into one another incessantly would swallow up the hapless adventurer immediately.

Any rickshaw driver stupid enough to try and make progress in these alleyways would get jostled from side to side. And, if the pedestrian were not careful, he might find the front end of a rickshaw jammed into his back. People who acted as sales agents for various storefronts would grab the arm of anyone passing by; even though they had no clue about the person's business, they would still try to manoeuvre him into their store!

Stores of every size and description filled the alleyways. The shops that sold saris had to be seen to be believed. They were the showplace for the rest of India; the varieties offered were too numerous to count. I remember one of Dad's dealers taking me on a guided tour. I have never forgotten his comment that over 500 different shades of colour could be found in these saris.

But Burrabazar represented much more than just a wholesale and retail shopping area. It had also become a thriving quasi-banking system accessible to the many clients of the Marwaris. This banking system had no shop front but resided with every Marwari dealer in Burrabazar. Each provided the finance - directly or indirectly - for projects and also lent money. This all operated outside the recognized banking system. The Marwari system worked through the use of contacts who provided current information by word of mouth about who had available capital, the terms of lending, whom they could work with, whom they could trust, and who would keep a promise, along with an intimate knowledge of the type of people that they wanted to deal with. It also had another feature that Dad learnt very quickly. The Marwaris, who had been schooled early in the world of money and business, knew instinctively when their sons were ready to transition into the family business world. Dad thought that banking was in their blood.

This informal "banking system" operated on trust and verbal commitments sealed with a handshake. Dad found that the Marwaris had a reputation for straightforward honesty in all their dealings; they aspired to establish a close relationship with their clients, as it helped make business that much easier for them. If ever this trust were compromised or betrayed, the informal banking system would shut the client out completely and he might as well close down his business or seek alternate forms of financing or trading.

In the early days of Dad's company, he always needed more tinplate than the Indian government licence would allow. The government tinplate quota kept the factory going for a maximum of six to seven months. The remaining quantity had to be acquired elsewhere. So, he proceeded to Bentinck Street in Burrabazar, just off Lal Bazaar St., where his driver Phul Mohammed would park the car. From there, Dad would make his way on foot to the wholesale metal and tinplate merchants to see whether he could buy some tinplate from other manufacturers with excess to sell, or acquire the tinplate on the openly-operating, black market. Naturally, Dad had to pay a small premium, but the cost of shutting down the factory far outweighed this additional amount. I went with him there quite a few times and I still remember going to a major dealer called Jhunjhunwalla (How could you ever forget a name like that?) and also a metal merchant called Baja and Sons. Dad did all the talking and the office staff ensured that I got the obligatory bottle of Coke with "pipe." In Jhunjhunwalla's shop, Jhunjhunwalla senior sat towards the back end, in a central position so that he could cast a watchful eye over the entire shop and the entrance. He sat on a slightly elevated chair (I believe that they called this position the *gaddi* seat). The cash box rested in front of him at the table, together with two or three telephones. From his *gaddi,* he entered all transactions into an array of books and ledgers so that they could keep track of their business dealings but, most importantly, all their cash and credit transactions.

The distributors of Dad's hurricane lanterns were located in another part of Burrabazar. This was the central hub of Dad's dealer network. Cases containing the hurricane lanterns would be delivered here, mostly by hand-pulled carts, as the carts could be easily manoeuvred in the narrow lanes. They would then be stored in larger *godowns* (warehouses) for distribution into the wider city and eventually to other parts of India. The dealers would first open each case to ensure that the lanterns were in order and that the glass globes had not been broken. Any broken globes would be replaced and then full responsibility for the shipment would be transferred to the dealer. Dealers would pay for the consignment in cash and the money deposited at a Dutch bank, the Nederlands Trading Bank, which was managed by Dad's friend, Gerrit van der Griendt.

Dad soon acquired a reputation of being trustworthy amongst the various Marwaris that he had dealings with, something that I admired greatly about my father. This reputation was also an asset for him as his business grew. On numerous occasions, he needed to tap into the liquid capital "available" amongst his dealer friends in Burrabazar. He had to pay his worker's wages every two weeks in cash[176]; if these were not paid, he would have had a riot on his hands in the factory. But sometimes, he had a cash flow problem and he would be short on the payroll. The Nederlands Trading Bank could meet the shortfall but the overdraft charges were quite high; so, he would turn to his Marwari friends in Burrabazar. They always had ready cash on hand and would help him make up the shortfall. They never imposed any additional financial demands like an interest charge

---

176 Initially, Dad used to pay his workers' wages every week. As this arrangement became onerous, he arranged to pay the wages every two weeks after agreement with all the relevant trade unions.

or a strict timetable for repayment. The quid pro quo usually included a commitment to provide some more cases of hurricane lanterns over and above any agreed amounts and Dad obliged happily. A handshake sealed and secured the agreement because, in this business world, a handshake was your bond and significantly more important than any signed contract.

Gherao

A crowd gathers. One of the many lessons learnt by the Mahatma Gandhi passive resistance movement was the power that large numbers of people in a small space could exert on an individual or a group of individuals. The refinement of this tactic in the context of the business world, though not practised by Gandhi, came to be known as the *gherao*.

Over time, workers developed, practised and exploited the *gherao* on management and senior supervisory staff as a form of industrial, rather than political, action. In its simplest terms, if a manager or supervisor refused to negotiate, listen, or submit to the demands of workers, the workers would find an opportunity to surround the manager or supervisor in such a way that he had very little room to move. He would have no means of getting away from the crowd. It did not really matter where the targeted individual stood at the time. The target could be in an office at his desk, or on the factory floor, or even crossing the courtyard, or trying to access his car or even be in the toilet; the protesters would envelop him by sheer force of numbers. A very important informal rule existed: the workers would not attempt to touch or push the individual, but they would heckle and jeer at him to their hearts' content. If the individual wished to move, he had to get the permission of the crowd. If someone had contacted the police, then the individual had to wait until the police arrived. You can imagine the impact that this tactic had on people who had been trapped outside in the blazing sun. No one was spared. In Calcutta, this included managers, supervisors, university professors and teachers, and even judges.

The stupidest thing a Westerner could do would be to try to exert some force by pushing, kicking or using his fists or briefcase or any other implement in order to escape from this throng of people. If he tried to escape, this became a tacit signal to whoever had surrounded him to initiate some retaliatory violence. Social status meant nothing. If a Westerner were in an accident and had hit somebody, or worse still a cow, he would find that a group of people would rapidly emerge and surround him. If the person knocked down had been seriously injured, the Westerner possibly invited a serious beating, even to death. In such a scenario, abandoning his car and taking flight from the scene of the accident was his best option for preservation of life and limb.

From the mid-1950s into the early 60s, the police were able to take unilateral action to free individuals from the *gherao*. However, after the Communists gained the ascendancy in government and, especially after 1967, the authority of the police to take a unilateral decision was removed. Instead, all instances of the *gherao* had to be referred to the West Bengal Labour Minister. If he deemed that people might be harmed, he would order the police to intervene.

Later on during this period, the incidence of *gheraos* increased dramatically and the reasons for them widened to encompass demands for bonus payments, increased percentage payouts on bonuses, recruitment of more staff, reinstatement of sacked staff, and any other reason that the unions felt was needed to protect and improve their interests.

The *gherao* now started to lengthen in time, from two to three hours in the 1950s to full days in the 60s, which was perhaps the most disturbing development. *Gheraos* became quite serious when agitators barricaded management in their offices with no access to water, food, or the lavatory. In addition, strikers would remove any means of communicating with the outside world, by either ripping out the phone or commandeering the switchboard.

July 1954 Strike

Strikes were generally a commonplace in Calcutta but, until 1954, they had not affected production at Dad's factory. The reason was simple. Dad still had a relatively small work force and the Communists had exerted little prior influence. But all this was soon to change. As the Communist Party started to enjoy electoral success for reasons previously outlined, their influence amongst labour started to grow. Concurrent with these political developments, the factory had grown quite rapidly so that, by about 1954/55, it employed between 250 and 300 people. The religious composition of the workforce to this date had been about 60 percent Muslim and 40 percent Hindu. Generally, the Muslims worked in the machine tool shop and the assembly plant area whilst the Hindu workers worked in the paint shop and in the factory operating the hydraulic presses. This mix, the division of labour, and also the geographic separation of the two groups across a courtyard, had proved to be a fairly harmonious one and any small tensions between this ethnic-religious divide had been quite minor up to the mid 50s.

After Shahadat Khan, Dad's partner and foreman, left for Dacca in 1950, he was replaced by Mr. Singh, who was responsible for managing the work force and the day-to-day running of the factory. Mr. Singh was a very competent man but he also appreciated his position as a Sikh sandwiched between this Muslim-Hindu workforce. He had learnt how to tread very cautiously when problems arose and in this difficult task he succeeded. Both Hindu and Muslim workers were now unionized. Soon Mr. Singh and Dad had to contend with union unrest. This had been happening in a lot of industries, as the Communists had started to identify potential union leaders. Systematically, these leaders began to organize their workers and form many unions in factories.

Management had another problem to confront, namely that many of these unions had been created and organized along different criteria. It therefore made it difficult for management to deal with several unions in the same shop, each with its own agenda. In consequence, daily production was halted quite regularly at Dad's factory whenever the union called on their workers to attend stop-work meetings or even to go on strike for periods ranging from a few hours to a day. Many of the stop-work or strike reasons were quite trivial: for instance, to down tools and march in sympathy and solidarity with the latest strike demonstration or procession wending its way down Chowringhee Road or elsewhere in Calcutta. They also insisted on arranging their stop work meetings inside the factory premises even though it had been made clear that they were expressly forbidden to do so.

The union leaders approached Dad and enquired whether they could have a stop-work meeting in the courtyard to discuss the latest call to strike by the various Bengali political leaders. Dad replied that he could not stop them from holding their meeting but it had to take place off the factory premises and any work stoppage that led to a cessation of production would be reflected in their wages. They did not like this news and went back to report to their members. The outcome of this directive was to conduct a *gherao* when Dad happened to be in the courtyard walking towards the tool shop. All of a sudden 50 people completely surrounded him, making it impossible for him to move, and they proceeded to shout their demands and slogans in Hindi directly at him. One of the factory union leaders then confronted him with their requests again and Dad repeated that they could meet as much as they wanted to, but not on the factory premises and not in normal working hours. If his wishes were ignored, he would dock the pay of any important production group that produced nothing or created a bottleneck. He also made it clear that he would not discriminate between participants and non-participants as it had become exceedingly difficult for him to identify everybody who was taking action against the factory's production interests. Fortunately for Dad, he decided to stand still and not react. After he was subjected to this agitprop demonstration for about two hours, the workers then dispersed. The message had got around to many of the non-participants in this mini-*gherao*; they came out and confronted their union leaders about not wanting their pay cut. Then, the workers returned to their workplaces and eventually Dad made his way back to the office.

But this incident shook him up and he realized that he needed someone who could assist him on labour-related issues. Mum suggested that Mr. Chatterjee could be that person, as he had been a lawyer and had all the necessary experience in the area of labour legislation and issues. Mr. Chatterjee, who had been retired for many years, said he would entertain the opportunity to earn additional income to supplement his pension. During this period of incessant strikes and disruptions to production and consequent effect on the company's labour costs, Mr. Chatterjee spoke out and advised Dad on numerous occasions about the benefits - if they could be called benefits - of a lockout. The factory had many unions and there existed virtually no co-ordination between them. So, it became quite common that a production line of 10-12 workers could be represented by 2-3 unions. If one union on a production line called a work stoppage, the non-striking workers would be precluded from doing any meaningful work, especially if they were dependent on the production output of the striking workers. In these circumstances, he suggested that Dad could declare a lock-out, whereby management would physically "lock out" the workers from the factory premises. In effect, the company went on strike and, in these circumstances, the company had no obligation to pay any wages if production were lost. The workers did not like this new development at all but it served to temper the headlong rush into strikes and industrial disruption. But this tactic also had a limited shelf life, as unions found ways to work around the lock-out by self-imposed slowdowns or short temporary work stoppages which got resolved as soon as a lock-out loomed. But I do remember that, over the coming years, Dad called quite a few lock-outs at the factory.

Dad's Racing Cars

Barackpore was situated about 13 or 14 miles from the centre of Calcutta. There had been a small airfield there and, during the War, the British and Americans used it as a base for their operations against the Japanese. After the War, and I am not sure about the years, Barrackpore ceased to be used as an airfield, so the local motor racing club organized a few car races - it was called a car-racing gymkhana - on the runways. Dad used to take us there on weekends. In fact, the Citroen that he later bought from his friend, Sasha Kahan, used to race there, together with other normal production cars. The available mix of cars made the racing quite interesting; however, the pursuit of speed was an illusion in the minds of the drivers - to call it an event for speed freaks or petrol heads would be stretching the point. But families came out and some even chose to dress up in racing gear with leather skullcaps and goggles. Safety had never been a concern but, in retrospect, the races generated their quota of tyre squeals and spin-outs a few times during each race. For most people, the gymkhana represented a family outing.

The reason I mention Dad's interest in racing is that I believe these car races at Barrackpore Airport were an outlet for Dad's frustration during industrial strife. In fact, I think that they influenced Dad's decision to try and build a roadster from scratch. The basic parts came from an old truck, which yielded parts of the chassis, axle, radiator, and V-8 engine. No blueprint or plans existed, and the development of the car was done on the "fly" in Dad's mind. The welders at the factory provided the tubular frame and a local panel beater provided the exterior shell of the racer. Problems of design and integration were solved as they arose. I remember that the full integration with the chassis and engine took some time. The electrical components came from the spare parts departments of local car dealerships; the pièce de résistance was the "eyeball" style headlights. Dad's racing car creation must have taken him well over a year to build and finally he got it ready to go to the painters. Dad chose an off-white colour for the car and the seats were done in red leather. His creation was a long car that exuded brutish power; it ran very low to the ground. Dad used to delight in showing how low it was by touching the road surface with his fingers whilst seated in the driver's seat.

Unfortunately, Dad did not allow me to drive this beauty, as I still wore short pants and knee socks. In any case, I think that the gearshift required more strength than I could offer at the time and then there was the pesky issue of age. *Quelle dommage!* But I loved going for a spin with him. We went down Park Street, crossed Chowringhee Road and then made for the Red Road, a wonderful, straight highway just near Fort William, where hardly any traffic existed and he could get up to some speed so that the wind coursed through our hair. Then, at the end of Red Road, came a sweeping left-hander and soon we entered Diamond Harbour Road, where he again opened the throttle and we enjoyed our 60 or 65 mph speed. This was considered high velocity for Calcutta at the time.

Well, whenever we went to the Barrackpore races, Dad's car stood out from the rest. No one at the meet could work out from which car manufacturer the car originated and they were totally surprised when they found out that Dad had assembled it from scratch. He entered it in a few races and handsomely defeated the assortment of production cars that competed against him. In fact, it was a no-contest event when four-cylinder family sedans competed against this long, elegant, white bullet. Come to think of it, "White Bullet" would have been an apt name for the car.

However, Dad's car-building adventures did not end with this first endeavour. He now started to think seriously about the next creation! After he had achieved and enjoyed all that he could out of his "White Bullet," he sold the car to a Marwari for a handsome amount. This vehicle had serious rarity value, being a one-off. In mid-1957, he started construction on another two-seater racing car; only this time, he built it after taking into consideration all that he had learnt from his first foray into car-building. For a start, he wanted this car to be shorter than the original. He wanted to enclose the wheels inside the body. He also wanted to incorporate body-styling elements from European sports cars. Again, there were no written plans or engineering drawings to fall back on when he started to build the second car, something that I found to be the most remarkable aspect of this new undertaking. It appeared at times that an artist had sculpted the new car, working in metal with only his imagination and an innate skill that guided the assembly of the vehicle. There were many stops and starts, and changes all the time during the construction phase.

I remember the problems that he encountered when he tried to get the elements of the bodywork together. The body panels had to be similar and, as these had been hand-extruded by hammering out the shape from metals, many reworks took place. He also wanted to reproduce an interior that resembled a normal production-line car. Like the first car, the engine, gearbox, axle and differential came from trucks. I remember that he became intrigued by a new suspension system that had been increasingly used by many manufacturers in Europe, namely, the wishbone suspension system. He had no original plans or anything substantive to work from, but he imagined what such a wishbone suspension should be like and created his own version. After all, he had a tool room and all the necessary equipment and skilled machinists who could shape his vision into auto hardware and so this new car of his had a wishbone suspension system.

When he finally finished his car, it was so far ahead of anything being driven in Calcutta that it became a sensation when it finally took to the roads. And the best part of all this was that I now had my West Bengal driving licence and I got to drive it, initially accompanied by Dad, but later all by myself! I had so much fun in this car. I remember the first time that I went with this beauty towards Diamond Harbour, about 30 miles outside the city, an empty road shared with the odd truck and bullock cart; here I got to enjoy a new sensation of speed. These two cars were a remarkable achievement for someone who had no automotive training at all, but had an idea, a creative spirit and the drive and energy to produce such gems. In many ways, these two cars were a metaphor for the drive and creative ability that Dad possessed in his persona and that ensured the success of his business.

The Mercedes Benz

From May to early July 1959, Dad took the rest of the family to Europe for a holiday. I did not join them as I was attending school at Stonyhurst College in England. But this was a holiday with a twist, namely a driving holiday. When we had gone to Austria for skiing holidays with the whole family in 1952 and 1953, we had become very friendly with a somewhat elderly German couple, Paul and Edith Gebser, who lived in Hamburg. Mr. Gebser was semi-retired but working part-time in the real estate business; he specialized in the sale and resale of large country properties with a few acres attached. This proved to be a lucrative sideline for him and did not interfere with his retirement plans of regular travel to sunnier climes further south in Europe. Mr. Gebser also happened to have been a racing driver in his younger days; he used to race on the famous Avus circuit in Berlin, and still maintained some contacts within the auto industry, in particular, the Mercedes Benz dealership in Hamburg. Anyway, in late 1958, Dad wanted to buy a car, with the assistance of Mr. Gebser; an order was soon placed to buy Dad's first Mercedes. He planned to pick it up in Hamburg when he came to Europe in late May. The car he chose was a beautiful two-tone 180-D diesel; he took great pride in this car. He planned to drive around various countries in Europe with the family and then return to Hamburg and ship the car off to Calcutta.

In mid-1959, after picking up this car, Dad met up with Mum, Martina, and Charley in Zurich and they travelled around Europe. They started their visit in Switzerland; I have often wondered why the starting point to their trips always appeared to be Bahnhofstrasse in Zurich. I am sure that their interest did not lie with Swiss chocolates, bratwurst sausages, Swiss watches, cuckoo clocks, or ornamental cowbells. From Zurich, they travelled through Austria, Czechoslovakia, and Italy. This trip had all the hallmarks of a last fling in Europe; in the late 1950s, Dad was making preparations for the family to move to Australia at some point. I think they realised that, from now on, these visits to Czechoslovakia were going to be few and far between. While the family was enjoying this wonderful holiday, I was coming to terms with the idea of starting my studies at Sydney University. I had given up a place at the London School of Economics so that I could finally be with them, but Sydney was a long way from England, where I had been at school for five years.

Their holiday was progressing with no trouble until they arrived at the crossing at Mikulov on the Czechoslovakian/Austrian border. On the Czech side of the border, Uncle Noris and Aunt Boženka were waiting to greet them. At this border crossing, the Czech Communist border police harassed them. Mum and Dad had to answer all sorts of questions. "Why are you coming here?" "Because we are visiting our Czech families." "Why did you leave Czechoslovakia and where did you go to?" "We left Czechoslovakia before the start of the war and went to work in India for Bata." There was a momentary pause as the guards went into a huddle, double-checking the passports, flicking through the pages, and looking frequently over their shoulders at Mum and Dad. One officer detached himself from the group and went to his captain to discuss something. Time passed and he returned with the captain. "Who are you planning to visit?" "Our Czech families, of course." "Don't be smart with us. I asked who in particular you are going to visit." Mum and Dad gave them a long list of names and locations, but still they persisted. "Why so many clothes and gifts?" "Because we like to help our family." On and on it went. It was quite obvious that Mum and Dad were now on the radar of the Security Police of the Czech Communist Party. Finally, they were cleared to pass at the border and drove off, closely followed by Noris. But they noticed that a black Škoda from the Security Police tailed their car. During this visit to Czechoslovakia, they made an effort to visit with both sides of their extended family. They departed via Mikulov again to Austria but this time they were not followed.

Toward the end of this holiday and prior to returning to India, Dad got word from Mr. Gebser that an opening on a shipping line had become available that could transport his car to India. At the time, the family was in Italy. Dad drove all the way from southern Italy non-stop to catch this sailing to Calcutta in something like 24 hours. Legend has it from the family that he did not even want to "waste time" with rest breaks and comfort stops, much to the chagrin of everyone else.

Mullick Bazaar

There is a well-known market in Calcutta known as Mullick Bazaar. In the 1950s, it sold a variety of "things" and miscellaneous bric-a-brac, but it is best known throughout India as one of the country's most famous scrap metal markets. It is also recognized as one of the largest in Asia and obtained its vast inventory of scrap metal from all over the world. Large amounts of money exchanged hands every day. But Mullick Bazaar also had another reputation that went with its fame. It was home to a large criminal element ranging from small-time operators to the more serious criminals who had an "understanding" with both the local police and politicians. It was here that money laundering took place. But, the market's *raison d'être* was wheeling and dealing in anything metallic.

Mullick Bazaar had a further claim to fame. It dealt in stolen goods and, in particular, new and used car parts. It enjoyed the popular monicker of *"chor bazaar"* (the thieves' market). If you had a new car, or better still, a foreign car, then you needed to make sure that, whenever you parked in Calcutta, you immediately engaged security or ensured that your driver was "tied" to the vehicle. You ran the risk that, if you left your car unguarded, it would be stripped of all four wheels and all easily disman-tlable parts. If you happened to leave it parked in the open overnight, you might return to a car without an engine or even a suspension.

In Mullick Bazaar, a lane existed with shops on both sides that were filled with stolen car parts from vehicles all over Calcutta. You could get everything here from electrical distributors, to spark plugs, suspension systems, headlights, radiators, grilles, engine blocks, transmissions, wheels, hub caps, axles and chassis from all types and makes of cars, trucks and even buses. All car owners in Calcutta knew about Mullick Bazaar. In fact, Dad had acquired many of the parts for his sports cars from dealers there. Later on, as his Citroen started to show its age and parts failed or had become rusted or could no longer be acquired, he started to buy spare parts from other carmakers' models to keep his car going.

Dad's Mercedes had hardly been two months in Calcutta when his hubcaps and the Mercedes Star emblem from the front of the car went missing. He was utterly devastated but then he thought that he would try Mullick Bazaar on the odd chance that he would find his parts there. And, sure enough, after some rummaging through the assortment of shops, he found his own hubcaps and the Mercedes emblem, paid the requisite amount, and made a promise not to report anything to the police; otherwise, he would never have seen his emblem again. He then had the parts refitted to his car. But his car was now known to the spare parts dealers and, in all likelihood, would be targeted again. Sure enough, within three months, his hubcaps and Mercedes emblem disappeared once more and, like clockwork, he went back to Mullick Bazaar. He found his own car parts again, but this time he entered into an agreement with all the stolen car part dealers that, for a monthly payment of 250 rupees, they would not target his car again. The dealers appeared happy with this arrangement and guaranteed him that, as far as Mullick Bazaar was concerned, his hubcaps, the Mercedes emblem and, indeed, his Mercedes car would be off bounds! Peace reigned and he never had any more problems with stolen parts!

1959 - Calcutta Visit after Stonyhurst

I returned to India in August 1959 after finally finishing my schooling at Stonyhurst. I had decided that I wanted to spend some time in Calcutta with Dad prior to going to Australia and university. We did quite a few things together for a change. It was on this trip that I tried to finally complete just one game of golf with him, with success. We spoke a lot of the factory, how he managed it, what his problems were, and what it had been like to keep it running. By this time, about 400 people worked in the factory and I came to appreciate what his responsibilities to his workers were. I could see that one of his biggest challenges was meeting the payroll every two weeks. With any delayed payment there would have been trouble and, from the perspective of the workers, families that were not fed. Some days, I accompanied him on his errands, visiting his dealer network in Burrabazar and meeting all his contacts there. It was during this trip that I learned first-hand the high regard in which his dealer network held him. I saw how they were only too happy to help him with any payroll problems and how the "deal" was always sealed with a handshake. No paper, no contracts, no lawyers, no signatures. Just a firm handshake, that's all.

But there were some surprises in store for me during this stay. One day, Dad asked me whether I would like to do some work at the factory. At first, I was taken aback, since he knew that my stay in Calcutta would be limited. But I think that he wanted to size me up in case I showed any inclination to work with him in the future. To be honest, it had not even entered my mind. And I do not believe that Dad had any thoughts about leaving India immediately. I did not have very much to do during my interlude in Calcutta, so Dad and I agreed that I should start in the office assisting Mr. Banerjee. This was, effectively, my first job. Mr. Banerjee was responsible for the company accounts, which were all hand-compiled. Working with them meant poring over small mountains of creditor invoices and sales receipts, all of which had to be entered into various ledgers. All very tedious, but I persevered.

In addition, Dad asked me to respond to unsolicited letters requesting employment, which came to the factory three or four times a week. I prepared a type-written reply and subsequently these were signed by someone in the office. These letters were something else to read. I often admired the initiative and courage of the writers. Some obviously could not write English, so they had engaged the services of the street scribes with their travelling typewriters. The thoughts of the person seeking a job were transcribed into some of the most flowery prose. They contained spelling fantasies where the scribe did know how to spell a word, but could say it, so he would spell it according to how it sounded.

The applications came in all shapes and sizes. We received some that were hand-written on a piece of notepaper, from people obviously wishing to save on postage by directly handing the document to the *durwan* (gatekeeper) at the front gate. These applicants would tell the *durwan* that, if there were work available, the applicant could be reached at a relative's address. The next category of applicant boldly stated that he was 21 years old and the breadth of his experience encompassed everything from production, purchasing and sales, accounting, auditing, typing, book-keeping and personnel management: basically, any position anywhere in the factory. I would puzzle over how to respond to this type of application. So much experience gained in such a short time! Then there were the applicants who asked for a position and included all their report cards and examination results from the year dot. This applicant obviously had an organised mind, because all this support material was referenced by section number and clause. Another category of applicant obviously did not believe in the paper route and turned up directly at the office soliciting work, probably thinking that he could bypass any interview process and start immediately. But my favourite application came from a man, using a street scribe, which was so fulsome in praise that I had to take pause when I read it.

Calcutta, October 19

> *Greetings and glory to illustrious and respected Manage Director, Shri Hruska, of Universal Lamp Mfg Co. Ltd.*

> *I am wishing to apply for esteemed position in your venerable company in any capacity that is available. My name is Dhibendra Das Gupta. I am 23 years of age, married with 1 child. I am a matriculate of Sri Aurobindo Bhattacharyo Primary School. I am also attendee at Calcutta University in BA program (failed 2 times). I am hearing much of your venerable establishment and offer myself to your goodself for work opportunity. I have very much energy and passion in my work and can offer twice working capability compare other workers. If I gain employment in your venerable company, I can promise total dedication to my work and your company.*

> *So, esteemed Sir, I am hoping that you will consider this application for work with much kindness. My contact details are below. I am going on holiday for three weeks with my family and look forward to your favourable reply on my return. I wishing to your goodself in advance many Good Mornings and Good Afternoons.*

> *Signed (D. Das Gupta)*

PS 1st time: I am a very good left arm spin bowler and will bring a bonus to your company cricket team.

PS 2nd time: I am also very good badminton player and could also benefit your company sports activities.

What to do with such a sincere pleading letter. The admission of "failed 2 times" was actually a positive message indicating at least that he could read and write, having attended university; this was a bonus to any prospective employer. The admission of going on holiday was a bad move. The various honorifics – illustrious, respected, esteemed, venerable - were normal. The mention of sporting prowess was totally useless, as my father did not understand, let alone follow, cricket or badminton and the company had no sporting aspirations or sponsored sport at all. However, many companies did and these skills would have been important there. I then very politely notified him that there were no current positions available, but due note of his application and his details would be placed on file; if a vacancy appeared, then notice would be posted to him. The next day, another similar letter would drop onto my desk. This time, instead, the applicant might be a good soccer player, hockey player, or even a *gilli-danda* player.

After about two weeks in the office, Dad suggested that I try and do a stint in the tool room and so he placed me under the care of Rafiq, the top tool-maker at the time. Among other skills, I learnt how to file, how to operate a drill, and set up a lathe. But this did not last very long, as one day Dad decided that I had had enough work experience. My stint at the factory came abruptly to a halt. I never found out why this happened. Perhaps he did not see me as factory material.

1959 - Start of Building at Castlecrag, Sydney

Dad told me that he wanted to start building a home at Castlecrag and had been in contact with John Brogan, an architect in Sydney who had been recommended by Dick Forbes. Dad and Brogan had agreed on the plans, the contract terms, and also the price for the structure and fittings. Dick

Forbes was the Manager of the Commonwealth Bank at Milson's Point in Sydney. Dad kept his funds at this bank and, over the years, the Forbes family had become friends with Mum and Dad. Dick had been the "go-to" person for advice and help in Sydney. He had also become my "de facto" guardian in Sydney. Dad wanted me to be his proxy and asked Dick Forbes to assist me in the execution of the contract. He helped me to get a Power of Attorney to represent my father and the authority to operate on the family account.

Well, I was totally non-plussed at this development. I was all of eighteen years old and did not have the slightest experience nor the confidence in managing a building contract, let alone overseeing the quality of the workmanship. But Dad had also added another dimension to these plans, namely that I would push the building plans through council and get all the pre-requisite planning approvals. I was not very happy at this news as it could seriously interfere with my studies. But there was no one else in Sydney to represent the family, so I had to find the time to get all the right plans submitted to Sydney's Willoughby Council, obtain all the planning permissions, and have building approvals signed off. John Brogan helped me fill out the applications, I signed the cheque, and presented all the plans and applications, together with the cheque, to the Council. After I submitted the application, I waited about a month for Council to approve the plans and get building work started. I had to attend progress meetings with John Brogan as part of my commitment. Brogan would take me through whatever progress had been made in the last fortnight; I then had to approve them and make numerous cash progress payments as they fell due. From my perspective, everything seemed to be going swimmingly, but who was I to pass a really critical eye on the work.

I remember being rather surprised when I saw the scale of the house as it started to take shape. When I looked at the architect's drawings, I did not have a feel for the size. This only happened when I actually saw bricks and mortar growing out of the architect's vision. Initially, building progress had been slow, as the builders had to excavate and remove a lot of hard rock. The full scale of the foundations amazed me. I thought at the time that they resembled the foundations of a fortress, since they were made to blend with the surrounding rock. This work seemed to last forever;

but soon the outer building shell started to rise and a discernible picture of a future dwelling began to take shape. After the swimming pool had been added as an integral part at the side of the house, the whole structure appeared to be suspended in the air.

During the first twelve months attending university, I lived with Dick and Athalie Forbes who owned a small house at the lower end of Edinburgh Road in Castlecrag. This suited me for the moment, as their eldest son, Peter, had a car and I often got transport to the bus stop situated at the top of the hill. The close proximity to our house meant that I saw and sometimes could review, daily progress on my way to and from university.

May 1961, India: The Silchar Incident

In Calcutta, my father was having to deal with increasingly dangerous working conditions, often caused by events elsewhere in India. Silchar (previously known as Sylhet in undivided Bengal) was the location of an incident with ramifications for many other places in Bengal.[177] The problem was about which language should be used in Silchar, a small town in the southern part of Assam, in north-east India. An ill-advised attempt to impose the Assamese language on the predominantly Bengali-speaking people resulted in violent protest in which 11 people were killed at the Silchar Railway Station. After this incident, the Assam Government allowed the Bengali language to be officially spoken in three or four districts.

Now what has this to do with Calcutta? The Communist led and influenced opposition felt that this assault on their language, coupled with their strong nationalistic feelings, warranted a robust protest throughout West Bengal. And so, once again, parts of Calcutta ground to a halt as workers from all sorts of industries were called out on strike, including the workers at Dad's Universal Lamp Manufacturing Company. Details of the strike are sketchy, namely, which workers opted to strike and which production work areas were affected by the strikers. But what I do know is that Dad attempted to initiate a lock-out when the threat of a strike became

177 A detailed description of the Bengal Language Movement and the incident at the Silchar Railway Station can be found on the following website: https://ipfs.io/ipfs/ QmXoypizjW3WknFiJnKLwHCnL72vedxjQkDDP1mXWo6uco/wiki/Bengali_ Language_Movement_(Barak_Valley).html

imminent. He hoped to force his workers back to work by putting pressure on them. However, the attempt at ordering a lock-out was poorly timed since the workers were still *inside* the factory premises. The whole strike scene inside the factory started to get ugly and soon Dad and many of his office staff were surrounded and "guided" back into their office by the combined pressure of many pressing bodies. They then became subject, for a second time, to a *gherao*. The trade-off for lifting the *gherao* was to be an agreement to pay the strikers while they continued their "in sympathy" strike.

At first, Dad did not realize that the strikers had ripped out the telephones, thereby eliminating the possibility of calling for any assistance. Five people were now locked up in an office that measured only about 25 by 16 ft.; half of that space was occupied by furniture and cupboards. And, of course, no one had made any arrangements for additional food and water, the toilet was not co-located, and the strikers had shut the door on them. The hours dragged on and still Dad could not contact anyone to come to the factory to free them all from the office. Mr. Singh had been isolated in a separate part of the factory and the workers would not let him get access to a phone. Eventually Mum realized that something was amiss, since she could not call Dad on the phone. She immediately got in touch with Mr. Chatterjee and asked if he would go to the factory to see what was happening. After he had done that, he contacted Mum to tell her that Dad was involved in a *gherao*. One must realize that, in this situation, where the political will lay more on the side of labour, there was absolutely no imperative or even desire on the part of the police to intervene; the strikers knew this.

Mr. Chatterjee decided to call on some of his old friends in the West Bengal police force and ascertain whether he still had any influence to initiate some action. I believe that he called in some favours still owing him and, after about 11 hours of *gherao*, the police sent a small detachment of officers, armed with *lathis* (a medium-sized truncheon) to clear a path to the office door and release those trapped inside in the early hours of the morning. They managed to do this; but, when they finally got the door open, they found that the old bookkeeper, Mr. Banerjee, was near collapse from dehydration and exhaustion. They had to call an ambulance to get him some medical help. But the *gherao* had been broken and, when the police had cleared the workers outside the factory gates, Dad ordered a lock-out. After about a week, some of the trade unions started to talk again with the factory management, including Mr. Chatterjee, and they agreed to some immediate demands from management as pre-conditions to returning to work.

Aftermath of the *Gherao*

The events leading up to the *gherao* now certainly accelerated Dad's thinking that the family needed to leave India as soon as he could manage it. Coming to this decision was difficult for him because, even though the labour and political situation in Calcutta was changing rapidly, he wanted to stay in India. He still ran a profitable business and he wanted to retire in the normal way. Despite the continual labour unrest, he had saved enough to enable him to re-establish himself later in Australia if need be.

But he also had major challenges, and his recent experience with the *gherao* made him realize that he had to reconsider the composition of the workforce in the factory. He initiated a hiring policy through which, from now on, he would give preference to Hindus and Bengalis rather than Muslims. While the Muslim workers had generally been the more skilled workers, they had a tendency to be the prime leaders of strike action whenever a dispute loomed. In consequence, the mix of ethnic and religious groups in his workforce changed markedly over the ensuing years. In Calcutta, the labour scene went from bad to worse: the strikes appeared to be interminable and in such a poisoned industrial climate, it was better to shut down the factory for long periods of time. These strikes had a significant effect on Dad. Any progress that could have been made at Gobra proceeded at a snail's pace and the availability of skilled workmen soon dried up. From 1962-1969, the factory was closed for long periods of time. The general situation became so bad that the National Government placed Bengal under President's rule for short periods in 1962 and again in 1968 and 1972.

I remember one such period between June and October 1962 when the factory remained shut for over 4 months. During these shutdowns, Dad took the opportunity to visit Europe with Mum, Martina, and Charley.

While there, they visited Czechoslovakia to see his mother as well as Mum's family.

The South Indian Option

Dad had a very good friend, Josef Nejedly, who had left Bata at about the same time as Dad. Nejedly had eventually found his way to South India and started a business making buttons. He lived and worked at Coimbatore about 300 miles west of Madras. Coimbatore proved to be an ideal location for the button business, as it was situated close to both the Bay of Bengal and the Indian Ocean. These two bodies of water were a source of shells, a prime ingredient for the manufacture of buttons. Later, as the plastics industry developed in India, he started to make his buttons from plastic. During the many interminable strikes in Calcutta when the factory shut down, Dad started to visit Nejedly. These visits, in 1963 and 1964, were like a holiday for him and an opportunity to get away from the chaos in Calcutta. Nejedly had prospered in his business, had married an English lady named Audrey and, together, they had built for themselves a beautiful, elegant, English-style home in Coonoor, approximately 5 miles from Ootacamund (affectionately known as Ooty).

Ooty is located in the Nilgiri Hills, about 90 miles from Coimbatore and is probably the best-known relic of the British hill station in India. Ooty became for South India what Darjeeling was to Bengal, or Simla to the north of Delhi. It is situated at a height of 7,500 feet. The countryside around Ooty feels like a transplant from England. Scattered around are beautiful bungalows, with their quaint English names like Windamere, Squire's Retreat, and The Pynes. At that time, each was surrounded by manicured lawns and flower beds that exploded with colour. In Ooty, the streets had English names like Dougherty's Lane, Woodcock Road, and even Charing Cross!

The surrounding area in Ooty reminded the British so much of home that it became a much sought-after destination. This nostalgia was the catalyst for starting a club in 1841. In the early 1960s, anyone who visited the Ooty Club walked into a time warp going back over 100 years. In the clubhouse, the visitor walked past photographs of past members resplendent in their uniform and medals, groomed to perfection, with moustaches well-trimmed; some even had a monocle that seemed to make direct eye contact with anyone entering those portals. Some photographs portrayed club events and notable visiting dignitaries. Other photographs captured the result of a successful hunt of tigers or wild buffalo. Indeed, when the guest entered the giant ballroom, it felt as though he had come upon the domain of a prosperous taxidermist. The walls were festooned with all sorts of hunting trophies. Animal skins lay everywhere on the floor and were even attached to the walls.

The floors of the Ooty Club had an exquisite parquetry design and the walls were panelled, probably with rosewood. Leather-clad, rosewood furniture was scattered throughout the building. In its prime, it had been in every sense a Club and beloved watering hole of the Raj. Here and there was the odd photo of Queen Victoria placed between paintings of famous horses that had been owned and raced by the Club's elaborately-mustachioed huntsmen. In the 1960s, the Club still had a billiards room, but it had obviously seen better days. The billiard cues had bent over time, as they dried up. The billiard room enjoyed one bit of notoriety, as Sir Neville Chamberlain (yes, the same Neville Chamberlain who returned to England after his meeting with Adolf Hitler, clutching a piece of paper and telling all and sundry that "Peace is at hand,") had defined the rules that dictated behaviour in the billiards room. When I visited there with Dad, we had to observe a strict dress code in the dining room. If required, the headwaiter could provide the visitor with a jacket and tie from their available stock. As visitors, we sensed the silent tradition that lay engrained within the walls of the Club and that was still proudly upheld by the members.

The Nejedlys used to go to Ooty practically every weekend to get away from the heat of the plains; it also served as a market town for the vegetable farms - potatoes, carrots, cabbages, and cauliflowers - and orchards of the surrounding area, and for the dairy farmers. In addition, Ooty had a charming cottage industry making and selling chocolates and pickles. To top it off, the surrounding area was known for the growing of fine teas.

Whenever they stayed at Coonoor, Dad and Nejedly played golf most mornings, when the weather was cool. They would then meet up with Audrey at the Ooty Club for lunch. The dining room at Ooty had an excellent reputation for its interesting South Indian cuisine. During these visits,

Nejedly talked to Dad about the business climate prevailing in Coimbatore, and especially about the South Indian work force. He noted that they had a reputation for being very smart and for having the best work ethic in India. Dad listened attentively to this information and very soon a seed took root in his brain. He began to wonder if he could relocate the factory to South India. He still had a lot of homework to do in looking at the logistics of it all, especially what the relocation costs would be. He considered the idea worth pursuing. For now, all he wanted was to enjoy this break away from Calcutta and so he played golf, enjoyed the tea gardens and the charming hill station with its quaint club, all of it a physical reminder of the better days of the Raj.

Eventually, Dad realized that the dream of relocating the factory to South India was unrealistic. When he put together what such a move would entail in time and money, it just made no sense to him. Perhaps, if he had entertained the idea ten years earlier, he might have realized this plan. In the future, South India would be nothing more than his escape from Calcutta, a place where he could forget his problems in the beauty of the Nilgiris, Nejedly's lovely English house at Coonoor, golf, and the club at Ooty.

Dad Gets the Factory Ready for Sale

The next major decision that Dad confronted was preparing the factory for sale at the earliest opportunity. However, when he put the word around his dealer network and other possible interested parties that he would consider offers for the factory, few emerged. The main reason for this disinclination to buy the factory had to do with the zoning of the land. When he had established the factory at 93B Ripon Street, there had been no zoning for the area at all. Furthermore, he had established the factory there in the aftermath of the War and so the origins of this business had come in under the zoning radar. Within a few years of the factory becoming an operational entity, with about 250-300 workmen earning their livelihood there, the Calcutta Municipal Corporation re-zoned the area as "Residential," with an exemption that related to the factory. This new classification definitely affected the sale price.

As a result, Dad decided that he needed to relocate the factory to an area already zoned "For Industrial use only." He purchased a block of land at a place called Gobra in the late 1960s as the first step in this new plan. Mr. Chatterjee had made Dad aware that a large parcel of industrial land had come available there. And, it was no coincidence that Mr. Chatterjee's house was also in that neighbourhood! The land had a small water tank, which happened to be stocked with some fish. After Dad bought the land, he had all sorts of ambitious plans to erect a large new building to accommodate the machinery from the tool shop and the presses from the factory under one roof. He wanted to get work underway as soon as possible, so he engaged an architect and, with help from Mr. Chatterjee, had all the necessary paperwork prepared for submission to the Calcutta Municipal Corporation Planning Department for the necessary approvals. Dad should have known better. This was Calcutta. Days drifted into weeks, weeks into months; progress was extremely slow. After about six months, he did manage to get an approval to finally clear the land and get it leveled prior to construction.

The decision to sell had been made and Dad had taken the first steps to transfer the factory to Gobra. From his perspective, it now just seemed a matter of time until all of these plans could be wrapped up and the family could be together in Sydney. But things were not going as well as Dad had hoped. He had not done his homework properly. Although he had purchased the land and planned to do all the things that he could understand, like constructing a new factory building, transferring the equipment, and setting up production on the new site, he was stalled by one very serious problem: how to get money from the sale of the factory out of India.

At the time, the Reserve Bank of India had a stipulation, mainly because of its ongoing foreign exchange problems, that the major portion of the sale proceeds would have to remain in India and only a very small portion - I believe that it had been set at about 5% or thereabouts - could be expatriated to another country. Dad would have had access to the money in India but again he could use only a small portion per annum and this money would have to be spent in India. Even if he allowed himself the most extravagant holidays and purchases of art and Persian carpets, he would have had trouble spending the sale proceeds within his lifetime. He now had to think of how to get his money out. That is, if he could sell the factory at all; as it turned out, this would take him another ten years.

1960 - Sydney University

In early March, I enrolled in Sydney University to study Electrical Engineering. This was to be a four-year course, but I had the option to break the Engineering course in Year 3 and do a Science degree, an option that I exercised later. After a year with the Forbes family, I decided to live on campus and board at St. John's College, conveniently located within the grounds of the University and within easy walking distance of the School of Engineering. I managed to get a Commonwealth Scholarship that paid for the tuition fees and part of the living costs; Mum and Dad made up the remaining amount, together with a small living allowance.

Being the only Hruska on the ground in Sydney, I opened up an account at Dick Forbes' branch of the Commonwealth Bank at Milson's Point; Dad periodically transferred funds into this account to pay, not only for the building of the house, but also for part of my residency in St. Johns College. 1960 passed uneventfully. Mum and Dad remained in contact with me primarily through letters, passing on all the family news and describing their plans and their comings and goings in Calcutta. Towards the end of the year in November, I sat for the examinations and passed all my subjects much to the delight of my parents. That year, I did not return to India for the end of year holidays but decided to spend it in Sydney. It was when we had to vacate college for the summer vacation that I went to live with Ralph and Edna Begbie until the new term started in March of the new year. The Begbies had migrated to Australia much earlier than we had. I believe that Dad had helped them with the transfer of their funds to Sydney.

I had by now got to be quite independent after all the years in North Point, Darjeeling, and then Stonyhurst. I enjoyed the opportunity to spend the holiday break visiting the beach, working on my tan, and worshipping sloth! I had to make periodic visits to the house in Castlecrag for inspections, progress reports, and to assemble enough information so that I could write a letter to Mum and Dad in Calcutta about the construction progress. Towards the end of December, the construction of the house was completed to the lock-up stage and, although progress payments were still being made to the architect, I was still uncomfortable with my role. Every time that I signed off a completed parcel of work and made a payment, it meant that I had approved what had been built against the plan and the quality of the associated work, something that I was not completely sure about. At the end of 1961, water and electricity were finally connected to the house so at least there would be access to the utilities if the family decided to move in.

1961 - Mum, Dad and Charley Visit Sydney from June to the end of October

In June of 1961, Mum, Dad, and Charley came to Sydney for a short visit. Martina didn't come because she was still being "finished" at her finishing school in Switzerland. Their main purpose in visiting Sydney had been to inspect the house, which by now was structurally complete, including the connection of water and electricity. They then would gauge what else the house needed and ascertain whether furniture should be built in Calcutta and sent to Sydney or whether they should furnish it locally. Building furniture in India was viewed as the cheaper option.

During the short semester breaks at the University, I stayed with the Forbes or the Begbies. In late November or early December, Dad picked up his newly-ordered, black Mercedes 220S in Stuttgart, Germany and made a short visit to Czechoslovakia. This second Mercedes Benz was shipped from Hamburg and finally arrived in Sydney in early 1962; I went to pick up the car from Customs, successfully completing all the import entry formalities. The bonus for me was that I now had wheels to move about in Sydney. But Dad gave me a long list of dos and don'ts about my use of the car. In any event, with my small allowance, I could not really afford to undertake any major excursions. For the 1962 end of year summer break, I bought a blow-up mattress and moved into the house, which was empty, apart from a small table in the kitchen. During my stay there, I gravitated between two rooms. The swimming pool could be used and my only chore was to keep it clean. I lived in the pool during the hot summer days in Sydney. The house provided Dad's Mercedes with a pretty secure parking place, absolute nirvana, and I could move around in Sydney as I wished.

Cooking was a problem, since we still had not purchased a fridge, so I started to buy whatever I could consume in the next two or three days and lived like a gypsy. Probably my distaste for pizza originated during this period. I now visited regularly with friends, the Rosenblums at Watson's Bay (a beautiful harbour suburb of Sydney) or the Begbies in Manly, locations that took an eternity to reach with public transport.

1963 - Mum Living at Castlecrag

By April 1963, when Mum, Martina, and Charley finally moved to Sydney, I had been living there alone since 1959, and the house had been finished and standing empty for one year. Martina had come back from Switzerland with all sorts of qualifications and skills related to fashion design and dress-making after completing her sojourn at École Martini in Lausanne. My sister could probably have had an illustrious career in fashion in Europe but she was already dating Ivan, her long-time boyfriend from Calcutta; he now lived in Sydney studying architecture at Sydney University. I had moved back into the house from college at some stage during the year and, for the first time since the age of six, was part of the family, actually living under one roof with them for a duration longer than school holidays. This was an opportunity to get to know Mum. I saw her in the morning prior to going to university and in the evening when I returned. But even though we now shared the same roof for extended periods of time, I came to realise that we had very little in common. My years away at boarding school had made us strangers; we were very much disengaged from one other. Initially she was housebound, as she still had not got a licence to drive. However, Dad's Mercedes was in the garage; so, on weekends, I took her quite often for a drive up to Palm Beach and Watson's Bay to visit our friends or just to enjoy Sydney's wonderful natural landscapes.

I acted as Mum's chauffeur as we visited the various furniture stores to buy items that would suit the many rooms in the house and, in this, she showed her impeccable taste. One room, however, presented quite a challenge and that was our library. One end of this room had a semi-circular form and finding suitable furniture to follow the curve of the room was difficult. Mum, however, had her vision of what she wanted and engaged a skilled carpenter to build bookshelves that would fit. This was, in my opinion, the signature room of the house. When the shelves were populated with our books and a superb painting of a Nepali girl was secured in the frame of a cupboard door, it became the room to which most of us gravitated. The far end of the library had a sliding door that opened out onto a very large terrace, affording an absolutely stunning view of Middle Harbour and, in the distance, beyond the Spit Bridge, the Tasman Sea. This terrace was the focal point for our family gatherings and entertainment, especially in summer; and a few steps down to the swimming pool took us to the "cooling off" location.

Dad's dream had been realized; but, from a family perspective, the house remained an empty shell where we came and went as we individually pursued our separate dreams. Martina thought only of getting married; Charley was still going to school, but spent most of his time dreaming about fishing; and I was completing my university degree. Unfortunately, Mum's dream of being with her husband and children was not realized, since Dad remained stuck in Calcutta running a business while also trying to dispose of it.

It soon became quite obvious that the separation from Dad had begun to take its toll. My eight-year-old brother Charley had just started school at Castlecrag Primary; neither he, nor Martina, nor I could provide the emotional support that Mum required. It was very hard for her. My spare time was consumed with study. I was in my final year of a Science degree and could not discuss Quantum Physics and Pure Mathematics with her. Each day after school, Charley disappeared with his fishing gear to Ice Cream Rock below the house to pursue what would become a life-long passion. I cannot quite remember what we did for Christmas in 1963; but at least Mum, Charley, Martina and I were able to sit around the same table and enjoy Christmas dinner. It seems to me now that the routine expectations of the annual calendar became the driving force in the house: birthdays celebrated throughout the year, Easter, and then the grand finale of Christmas. Any celebrations for the New Year were muted.

1963 - Mum's Entrepreneurial Spirit

Mum needed to provide some mental stimulation for herself. If she had not done this, and with all of us involved with our own lives, living in this big house would have felt like being in a prison, or even a tomb. I am not sure exactly how she came to do what she did next, but she developed her own niche that kept her busy and also proved to be quite profitable. While attending Sydney University, I started to play rugby for the first team. I had become quite friendly with law student, Rupert Rosenblum, who was a team-mate. Through Rupert, I got to know his father Myer Rosenblum (Rosie to his friends); eventually our family also became quite good friends with Rosie and his delightful wife Leila. They lived in a harbourside home, practically on the water in the beautiful Sydney suburb of Watson's Bay. As the friendship between the Rosenblums and the Hruskas grew closer, Rosie also became the family lawyer. Initially, even though he later represented us as our lawyer, all our dealings with Rosie were in the investment field. Rosie had been the anchor-man in assembling money to lend to property developers. These monies were basically loans that were provided to builders or developers to enable them to undertake a project and the loans were secured against bricks and mortar. The interest terms were quite attractive when compared with those offered by the banks. Investing at the Commonwealth Bank had never been very appealing and, anyway, property loans had similar risk profiles, since the banks were also using investor money to lend to home buyers. This was normal investment practice in Sydney, but you needed to have adequate capital to get started.

Late in 1963, Rosie suggested to Mum that she might want to become a developer herself, not by actually doing the physical work, but by providing a share of the required capital, in conjunction with others, to buy a suitable house that the partnership would renovate and place back on the market within a three- or four-month period. The part-owners would divide any realised profit according to the amount invested. I believe at the time there was no capital gains tax in effect. Rosie was the focal point for raising the capital and, soon after talking it over with Mum and other investors, they bought their first investment property in Avoca Street, Randwick, in the eastern suburbs of Sydney. The price for this three-bedroom house was about 15,000 pounds. They got a builder to do all the improvements and repairs needed. Mum's share totalled about 5,000 pounds; when the house was finally sold, she managed a profit of about 1,200 pounds after deducting her costs. But what was important was that Mum finally had something to do based on her growing knowledge of the residential housing market. She enjoyed the experience. So, the income from these first mortgage funds helped our family. By going out on house inspections, she also managed to get out of the house. She engaged in this "buying and selling a house" enterprise with Rosie at least two or three times and each time she made a profit. Their partnership had concentrated on the Randwick area.

Unfortunately, when Dad got wind of what she had been doing, he was quite annoyed and very promptly put a stop to this entrepreneurship. I am not sure what led to his objections, but I believe that the underlying reason may have been that he could not accept or even cope with the obvious success that Mum had in these ventures. He might also have felt that Mum's success challenged his role as "the family provider." Or he might have feared that it could encourage more independent thinking and action. In this very short time, we had witnessed a flowering of Mum's entrepreneurial talent but equally rapidly we saw its withering. This was a real tragedy, as it curtailed any other interests that Mum might have had. I believe that it contributed substantially to her deteriorating state of mind and health.

Mum's entrepreneurial exercise did not end without a spirited riposte from her. She had enjoyed this little moment of independence. She had also earned about 3,500 pounds profit, which she decided to spend on purchasing her own car that she would learn to drive. Her goal was to be independent of me for transport. She decided on a two-seater sports car. She set herself a budget and we went to Parramatta Road to look for a car; this was the street where all the new and used car dealerships were located. She was particularly taken by the looks of the Sunbeam Alpine. Looks were the important criterion in her car selection. For her, it did not matter whether it had 2 cylinders or 24 cylinders. The price met her budget but there was something missing. In the back of her mind there had always been a particular car, but it had not yet made it to the Australian market. Then, one day, after visiting a friend at Watson's Bay, we were returning home via William Street, another street in Sydney with car dealerships. Mum beckoned me to stop as we passed Continental Motors. Yes, she had seen her dream car in the show window.

Mum loved watching the British actor Roger Moore in the TV crime drama series called *The Saint*. I do not think that the plots held any great interest for her, but the show did have the immaculately dressed, very English and suave Roger Moore, who had a wry smile and a voice that would melt butter. Mum adored *The Saint* and never missed a show. Part of the attraction was that Roger Moore drove a Volvo P1800 sports car. Mum loved this car and, now, Continental Motors had an announcement in its show window that the Volvo P1800 had arrived In Australia. After stopping, we waltzed into the showroom and she enjoyed an "ooh and aah" session with the cream Volvo. She did not even blink at the quoted price and soon a test drive was arranged. Even though she did not have her licence, she agreed and so I got to take the test drive with Mum in the passenger seat. She loved every minute of this adventure in the red upholstered interior of the Volvo.

At home, she started to waiver with the usual, "Should I, or shouldn't I?", "What will Mirek say?", or "Should I get a Morris Minor instead, something more practical and reasonable?" But we managed to talk her into getting the Volvo P1800 sports car and so it took up residence in our garage. She then made arrangements to get her driver's licence and soon she was ready to take the car for her maiden drive. However, our house had quite a steep driveway leading down to the street. I had the pleasant task of backing the Volvo down the driveway into our street on Linden Way and Mum would then get in and take over from there. Initially, she made short excursions with the car, up to the local shopping centre and back; but, as her confidence grew, she drove it to a nearby suburb, Castle Cove; with each trip, her driving range increased. Soon she was driving to Narrabeen Lagoon and the northern beaches area. This route was her comfort zone. The furthest that she drove alone was to see her friend Alice Gange, whom she had befriended at the Rosenblums, and who lived at Whale Beach.

1963 - Calcutta Factory Sale Delays

In Calcutta during that year, all sorts of delays plagued Dad with his plans, not only to get construction moving at Gobra, but also to sell the factory. He still had one serious issue that he sought a solution for. Dad needed to find how to transfer the entire proceeds of the sale overseas despite the Reserve Bank of India rules.

Dad had already moved the family to Sydney but, in hindsight, he had not thought through all the hurdles he had to overcome in selling the factory. Being a very headstrong man and over-confident in his own judgement, he had initiated the building of the house in Sydney and sent Mum there, coupled with vague promises that he would soon follow. His periodic visits to Sydney were not the solution. And I believe that the prolonged separation and living in a large, lifeless, and practically empty house was the prime catalyst for the depression that Mum started to suffer. In hindsight, it would have been far better for both of them had she stayed in Calcutta where they could have supported each other, instead of being split like this over an ill-conceived plan.

1963 - President Kennedy Assassination

Our family life in 1963 drifted on. There was still no news from India regarding the sale of the factory. I had my annual examinations in November and I spent a lot of time in my room studying. In Sydney, on November 23rd at about 3 or 4 in the morning, I put the books down and went upstairs to the kitchen to make myself some coffee. As I approached the kitchen, I noticed Mum sitting at the head of the kitchen table, cigarette in hand, radio tuned to the Australian Broadcasting Commission (ABC) with only the light near the stove turned on. I asked her whether she was feeling alright or if she had troubles sleeping. She looked at me with a blank stare that I could honestly call a 1,000-yard stare and said calmly, "I just heard on the news that Kennedy has been shot." At first, I did not know what she was talking about, trying hard to reference her comment to the Australian context. She repeated, "President Kennedy has been shot." We looked at each other like stunned mullets in total silence. I made myself some coffee, sat down next to her and, for quite some time, we looked at each other trying to digest this awful news. Slowly, but ever so slowly, her first words tumbled out.

"What is wrong with this world when a good man, a father and a husband is killed, and for what?"

I could not respond in a coherent manner, but Mum was obviously quite upset by the news and we both cried. It was a wonderfully human response to this awful tragedy and, for me at least, for the first time, I felt a connection to an emotional side of my mother that I do not think I had ever experienced before. We continued to sit there in the dim light and talked and talked about so many personal things; together, we watched the sun rise until it was time to pick up the daily routine of our lives. But this moment has been etched into my memory, a personal moment that came to life out of a tragedy. Like everyone else who lived through this sad day, I know exactly where we were and what we were doing when President Kennedy was assassinated.

1964 - Mum's Health Problems

After the births of Martina, Charley, and me, Mum had developed severe varicose veins in her legs that were very noticeable. They manifested themselves as permanently enlarged veins located near the skin surface. They were coloured and had quite a knotted and lumpy appearance. In Mum's case, they were probably hereditary, as her sisters also had a history of varicose veins. This is not a life-threatening condition, but it can become serious with advancing age. In Mum's case, there were potentially much more serious complications including dermatitis, phlebitis, blood clots, hemorrhage, and non-healing venous leg ulcers. She had suffered serious blood circulation problems and this could have been life threatening. She had been to a hospital and for a while there was a realistic chance of amputation of her right leg. But the doctors managed to rectify her circulation problems and, in due course, she was discharged from hospital and returned to Castlecrag. This was just one of a stream of health problems that now began to plague her.

1965 Visit to Nejedlys with Dad

After I graduated from Sydney University, I did what most young Australians of my generation did and went OS (the popular abbreviation for "overseas"). I wanted to have a short holiday before I came back to Australia to look for a job. Dad still lived in Calcutta and that became the obvious starting point. In mid-February, I flew to Calcutta and settled into the flat with Dad. Dandia was still there and life was familiar and comfortable. Most of my friends had either got married, or moved away, and many of my Armenian friends had emigrated to Australia, with most having settled in Sydney. In the morning, Dad and I played golf at the Royal

Calcutta Golf Club, but unfortunately these rounds never ended very satisfactorily. I viewed the game as a form of relaxation; whereas, for Dad, it represented competition and his perpetual search for golf perfection. Dad subjected me to a non-stop golfing lesson after each shot, even after my shot ended up in the middle of the fairway. For the first two weeks of my stay, I don't believe that I finished more than six holes with him before I just packed it in and went back to the club and waited for him to finish.

Finally, I had to confront this situation and told him my point of view. I said to him, "Look, I play golf to enjoy the round, irrespective of whether I hit a bad shot or not. I enjoy the walk, I enjoy the scenery and I want to relax with you. After all, we have not had much time together, so let us just play and stop the constant tutoring."

He said "But it is important that you learn to have the right swing; otherwise you won't improve."

I replied, "I do not care. I do not care if I have an air swing or if the ball flies to the left after an almighty hook or to the right with an almighty slice or even if it goes into water. We are playing with a large entourage of people, who will always find the ball. We have 8 pairs of eyes walking with us, two *chokras* (young kids) patrolling the first 100 yards, two more *chokras* patrolling the 150-yard point on the fairway and two *aghe wallahs* (far distance golf ball lookouts) patrolling the 200-yard point. In addition, we have two *pani chokras* (water boys) in case the ball ends up in the water. So, I feel confident that, with every shot I take, there is a very high likelihood that the ball will be found and I will not get upset and I will just drop the ball at my feet and continue to play."

I could see that he was unhappy with this response and he said, "But that is not the point of the game. If you learn how to hit the ball correctly, you will not get so frustrated and will enjoy the game much more. I can show you how you can hit every ball down the middle of the fairway."

I could see that he was becoming more agitated and this is why for the first five or six games we never finished six holes together before I downed tools and just walked off the course. Eventually he got the message, he kept quiet and we started to enjoy our golf. There were some memorable moments during these golf outings. I remember one particular morning when we had been having a peaceful game, Dad sliced his shot into the scrub running adjacent to the hole and all the ball-seeking *aghe wallahs* dived into the scrub to look for the ball. Within 20 seconds, this highly-motivated, energetic, ball-seeking workforce ran out of the scrub and we noticed that they were visibly shaken and pointing into the vegetation. When we approached, they whispered to us, "*Sahib, Sahib, burra Kobara Sampa* (large Cobra snake)." Dad slowly ventured in to see what had happened and saw a large hooded cobra coiled around the golf ball; he very calmly came out and asked his golf bag *wallah* to hand him a Sand Wedge; then he went in and very calmly lifted the cobra off the ball and deposited it some yards away, picked up his ball and declared, "I am taking a free drop as I could not and still cannot play the ball for safety reasons." No ifs, no buts, but he obviously knew or claimed to know local club rules relating to cobras.

A week later, he suggested that we go to South India to visit the Nejedlys and do some sightseeing, as there was not much to do at the factory. We started off in Madras and there we met up with some friends who took us to visit the early 7th century temple complex at Mahabillipuram, which comprised seven temples and was located right on the fringe of the seashore overlooking the Bay of Bengal. It was quite remarkable; these Hindu temples were some of the oldest in South India. They had been constructed in the Dravidian style. The whole setting - the temples, the location near the sea shore and the ocean backdrop - was quite stunning. Over the years, the temple surfaces were weathered by the sea spray, rain, and wind. Near the temple complex, there were rock formations into which had been carved a row of stylized bulls and other religious motifs.

After Madras, we travelled on to Coimbatore and the Nejedlys. Dad had been asked by Nejedly if he would be interested in a joint business venture making bulletproof helmets for the Indian Army. In the 1962 war between India and China, the traditional Indian army issue helmets had been found wanting in that regard. They apparently did not give much protection to the Indian troops and Nejedly wanted to bid for the contract. He needed Dad's expertise with the whole extrusion process, whereby the helmet would be pressed out in a single step and subsequently would be reinforced and finished. Dad declined the opportunity as he wanted to sell up and move to Australia, but he said he would provide whatever "know-how" Nejedly needed. From Coimbatore, we drove to Nejedly's retreat in Coonoor and here we had a wonderful time exploring Ooty, the Nilgiri tea plantations, the Ooty Club, and the Coonoor Golf Club. We also took the opportunity to visit the Toda people, who lived at Ooty.

The Todas are rather tall and have an erect posture; they live in *munds,* a structure that is oval in shape, resembling half a barrel, about 10 ft. high, 15 ft. long and about 9 ft. wide; they have a smallish entrance door, about 5 ft. by 5 ft. in the front through which a person has to stoop to enter. This small entrance apparently offers them some protection from wild animals. The Todas are polyandrous, which means that one woman can have many husbands. But the puzzle still being asked is where they came from. In stature, appearance, bearing, and dress they are, generally speaking, so different from the South Indian people. The women's hair is prepared in long ringlets and their features seem very Jewish. Many theories about their origins circulate. Some believe that they are members of one of the Lost Tribes of Israel, a theory probably driven by the ringlet hairstyles of the women. Some think that they are the remnants of the Macedonian army of Alexander the Great, who invaded India in 326 BC. Today, they are a very small community and seem destined to die out. All we know is that many scholars have linked their language to Tamil, but their true origins remain in the realm of speculation.[178]

Nejedly suggested that we visit the western seaboard of India and he lent us his car. We descended to the coastal plain from Coonoor via a dangerous but spectacular road. I think that our driver had never driven on a downhill serpentine road before and he rode the brakes the whole way, so much that Dad had to tell him to "gear down"; otherwise, his brakes would have burned out. We visited the Mudumalai Game Reserve on a day trip, as it was only about 25 miles from Ooty at the very extreme end of the western borders of Tamil Nadu. In the game reserve, we moved around in a secure howdah fastened high onto the back of an elephant. Many parts of the game reserve were covered with large tracts of tall elephant grasses and thorny scrub, so sitting on the back of an elephant with shorts was not a

---

178 Recent linguistic scholarship has placed Toda into a grouping known as the non-literary South Dravidian languages, A more detailed discussion can be found at: https://www.britannica.com/topic/Dravidian-languages

very smart idea. But the elephant was the only way to make any progress to the many water holes in the region. There is a tiger sanctuary to the north of the game reserve at Bandipur and naturally we hoped that we might catch a glimpse of a tiger. This did not happen, but we saw many other animals: some wild Indian elephants, striped hyena, Gaur (Indian Bison), Indian Langur and Macaque monkeys, Chitrals (spotted deer), a rare sighting of the four-horned antelope, and an Indian Pangolin. In the trees, we quite often saw the Indian giant squirrel and an extraordinary array of birdlife, including wagtails and bulbuls. After we returned to Ooty, Dad and I visited Kerala via Coimbatore. Our first stop had been Trivandrum and from there we went, on Nejedly's recommendation, to Kovalam Beach. Well, what a recommendation and what a place to visit! Kovalam Beach was totally unspoiled at that time. The beach had one Circuit House where we could stay and it was situated right on the promontory overlooking the beach.

The Beach had not yet been discovered at that time by tourists, especially the Hippies, probably because beach life and rock music were alien to the locals. We shared this wonderful beach with the local fishermen. In the early morning, Dad and I went down to the beach for a swim. The fishermen put their nets out to within 150 feet of the shore; then two sets of fishermen took hold of the nets at opposite ends and slowly started to haul the nets in to the land. We would tag onto one end and help them bring the nets in. After these had been hauled onto the beach, Dad and I were curious to see how many fish they had caught. The pickings were slim indeed and for about 40 minutes of hard toil they had been lucky to pull out of the ocean between 30 and 40 fish. The women of the small village community came down to the shore with their wicker baskets and soon the sharing of the catch commenced. It gave us a very small insight into the daily lives of these hard-working people; later on, at the Circuit House, when we related our experiences, our host told us that there were also many good days when they caught a fine harvest of fish. This news made us feel better. I still remember the stay at Kovalam as a happy time that I shared with Dad.

From Kovalam, we travelled on to Trivandrum and visited the magnificent, old, wooden palace of the Travancore Rajas - 1550 to 1750 AD - at

Padmanabhapuram. The palace is best known for its stunning architecture, delicate rosewood carvings, sculptured décor, murals and paintings. There is one part of the palace complex that is called the Nataksala (Hall of Performance) that is noted for its bold, solid granite pillars and the most amazing, polished black floor that resembles marble. This spectacular floor was apparently made of burnt coconut, charcoal, river sand, jaggery (unrefined sugarcane), lime, and egg white. The Hall was the centre of the performing arts, ranging from concerts of the Karnatic music of the region to the famous classical dance form of *Kathakali*. The final stage of our exploration took us to Cape Comorin, or *Kanya Kumari,* as it is now known. Cape Comorin was the southern-most tip of India. This place was also an important pilgrimage site and, as the name *Kumari* implies, there was a temple overlooking the shore that was dedicated to the goddess *Kumari*, the virgin.

Three great bodies of water come together at Cape Comorin: the Bay of Bengal, the Indian Ocean, and the Arabian Sea. But, what could have been a pleasant visitors' destination was now surrounded by a lot of kitschy and garish buildings. As we stood at the southernmost tip and gazed out at the confluence of three major bodies of water, we could see nothing but water as far as the horizon. Nevertheless, the Indian Government had seen fit to put up a prominent sign which proclaimed to all and sundry: "For security reasons absolutely NO photography!" and a reference to the associated statute, i.e. DOD (Department of Defence) Statute 23f, section 3, sub-section 14f, para 5 and all associated amendments. We wondered about the object of the security for the only thing visible, as far as the eye could see, was water!

From here we made our way back to Coimbatore. Dad had to return to Calcutta, while I stayed in the south a further week, visiting Goa and Madurai to see the famous Meenakshi Temple and then on to Thanjavur and Madras and back to Calcutta. Dad had been very relaxed on this trip and we had therefore got on very well indeed. But I detected that he was not looking forward to returning home to Calcutta and all its concomitant labour problems, strikes, and the lack of progress on the sale of the factory.

Victoria Memorial

Howrah Bridge

Low-cost Bamboo Scaffolding

Trade Book Fair

City of Protest Posters

Garbage Services

Alipore Retirement Home for Cows

Drying Cow Dung for fuel

Traffic Breakdown. An Abandoned Load.

Refugees Living on Street near Howrah Bridge

Cow Enjoying a Break

Paan Shop

Street Home

Family Life on the Streets

Family Street Shelter

A Calcutta Slum

Street Hair Dresser

Dhobi (Laundry Man)

Mobile Cha Wallah (Tea vendor)

Street Shoe Repairs

Street Food Vendor

Grains Food Vendor

Street Fruit Vendor

Vegetable Street Vendor

Food Vendor

Outdoor Bathing Facilities

Monument to the Telephone that Never Worked

External Stock Exchange Brokers

New Market Egg Vendor

CHAPTER 10

Life in Australia and the Final Sale

The Early Years - Some Aspects of Sydney Life

Gradually, the family settled in. The University was my focus and I concentrated mainly on getting through my final years and passing my examinations. I had not even stopped to think about the post-university years, what I wanted to do, where I wanted to work, whether I would first travel and then work, or vice versa. My immediate thought was to pass my exams. Martina had finally got herself a job. Charley had moved on from Castlecrag Primary to a boarding school near Hunters Hill. Charley had a simple life. At the weekend, he came home and, more often than not, he would pack up his fishing gear and head for Ice Cream Rock in Middle Harbour.

Watson's Bay and Mr. Havlicek

Many Czechs from the Bata operation in Calcutta had already emigrated to Sydney, bought homes, and settled down with their children. Some of them retired and a few chose to continue to work. So, when Mum finally moved to Sydney, she resumed contact with a few of these Czechs families, albeit sporadically. Mr. Havlicek, a friend of hers, owned and operated a small restaurant franchise on the second floor of Dunbar House in the suburb of Watson's Bay. The restaurant was located close to the harbour foreshore and had a spacious balcony. Havlicek offered his guests a limited luncheon menu comprising fried chicken, wiener schnitzels, and a choice of potato, cucumber, and other fresh salads. In the afternoon, he served coffee, tea, and home-made Czech cakes. Mr. Havlicek was a good cook and he made great cakes and other Czech specialties, many with poppy seeds and cottage cheese.

Mr. Havlicek had a personal love affair with food and was therefore quite a large man. He was short in stature and I estimate that he weighed over 300 pounds. He lived in his kitchen; food was his constant companion and, often, when we arrived on Sundays to visit him, he would be seated at the kitchen table with a large bowl of chicken wings in front of him. He did not serve the wings: one by one, he would strip these little wings bare with great relish and an audible sound of satisfaction and pleasure. Mum joined him at the kitchen table and they caught up on all the local news. Havlicek was the central hub for the Czech community and he disseminated his information freely to all his fellow country men and women.

Watson's Bay and the Sydney Game Fishing Club

While Mum visited Havlicek at Dunbar House, we children went down to the pier at Watson's Bay a short distance away. A small clubhouse, home to the Sydney Game Fishing Club, occupied the far end of the pier. This club had been in existence since 1952. People were drawn to the large gantry and weigh station used for weighing the game fish brought in by the larger fishing boats. Every Sunday, people gathered around the large weigh scale and waited in anticipation for all the game fishing boats to return from their fishing forays. Experienced eyes searched each boat's mast to see which small triangular flags the boat had hoisted. The flags indicated that they had made a catch and more importantly what type of fish they had caught. A red flag with a shark symbol indicated a shark; a blue flag indicated a marlin. When a boat rounding the headland at Sydney's South Head was sighted with a red flag on its mast, word spread quickly around to the people in the vicinity of the pier and soon a crowd gathered to witness the weighing of the game fish. After the boat had tied to the pier, the operators swung the gantry around and the boat crew would attach the rope around the tail of the fish and attach the ends of the rope to the gantry hook. The signal was then given to hoist the shark or marlin out of the water, the little electric motor started to whirr, and the fish emerged ever so slowly out of the water. The hoisting of a shark seemed to last forever, but the water that had been collected in its mouth needed to drain out. The shark soon cleared the pier sufficiently for its tail end to be attached to the scales. A club official would climb up the ladder to read the scale for an official weight. I still remember the day when they pulled a large tiger shark out of the water. When the shark hung from the scales, it just cleared the water surface by about 6 feet. It must have been well over 12 ft. in length and weighed close to 1,700 pounds. It was so heavy that gravity caused the insides of the shark to fall out of its mouth. But first we managed to see the spectacular row of sharp, cloudy, white teeth.

Watson's Bay and the Rosenblums

Watson's Bay became a regular visit for our family on Sundays, starting first with a visit to the Rosenblums and then Havlicek. Mum enjoyed visiting Rosie and his wife Leila, who came from New Zealand. Often on Sundays, we were invited to their house for lunch. We loved going there. Leila always cooked up a storm that was both sumptuous and welcoming. But what made these visits memorable were the wide and eclectic range of friends that came to Rosie and Leila's house. We shared their home with opera singers, writers, Rosie's friends from Sydney's legal circles, musicians, actors and actresses and other equally interesting people. Rosie would hold court with all of them and there would be discussions on every conceivable subject, only interrupted by lunch. Leila might play the piano, accompanied by a visiting singer, and the assembled guests would then enjoy a musical interlude. Often, visiting singers currently appearing in operas being presented either in Sydney's theatres and later at the Sydney Opera House would join us and we would hear numerous solo or duet operatic arias. These were magical afternoons that my parents and I looked forward to. At other times, a writer might give us a private reading from his latest book.

Rosie was an amazing man. He could speak Italian and read French. He had read widely and absolutely devoured books. He had a library pass for Sydney University's Fisher Library where he had already worked his way through all the French and Italian classics, books that he loved to read in their original language. Most of the time, these Sunday lunches were Rosie's stage. He kept us in awe when he would utter something like, "What you just said reminds me of Voltaire's famous ruminations in his novel, *Zadig, ou la Destinée.*" He then would quote in French and, for the benefit of us non-cognoscenti, translated the comment into English.

These Sundays were a big part of the life of our family. On his visits to Australia, after he got to know the Rosenblums, Dad, of course, added another dimension to these visits. He had a wealth of life experiences from his early days in Czechoslovakia and his life in India; and he had always been a natural-born raconteur. When Dad started on his stories, he held the floor. At times, when he talked about his mountaineering exploits, he brought these expeditions to life in such a way that we went away feeling that we were in the presence of Himalayan royalty, a true pioneer who had moved into the unknown. At these luncheons, when he spoke about Calcutta and of doing business there, even Rosie had to stop and listen: Dad's tales of dealing with Indian bureaucracy and corruption were so vivid.

The Sydney Harbour Bridge Affair

One memorable incident during this time with my father has remained with me. In many ways, it exemplified his personality. As a meticulous and confident person, he trusted his judgement to the extent that he expected perfection in everything he did, whether in his technical or business dealings, or even with his family. I am sure that every one of us could recount an experience where we did something that met with his disapproval. When he saw what we had done and if it had not met his expectations, we could expect an expletive directed at us. Usually, he cursed under his breath, but we could understand words such as *hňup*, or *blázen*, or *trouba*. Then, he would show us how things *should* be done. He was a true, self-made man and his continued success in business only reinforced this strong belief in himself and his own judgement. But, sometimes this part of his personality led to ridiculous situations that demanded a practical solution. Such an occasion arose on a balmy Sunday when Mum, Dad and I were invited to Rosenblum's in Watson's Bay to meet Edward Ricardo Braithwaite or Ricky Braithwaite, as he was better known. Ricky was a writer from British Guyana, now known as Guyana. Jobs had been difficult to come by in post-war England, so he had finally taken a teaching job at a school in East London. As a result of his experiences as a black schoolteacher at this school, he wrote a semi-autobiographical book called, "To Sir, With Love," in 1959. This book dealt with the prevalent racial and other social issues in England. In 1967, it was made into a film starring Sidney Poitier. Somehow, Rosie had got to know Ricky and planned a luncheon where he was to be the guest of honour.

We departed in Dad's Mercedes. Dad wore what I used to jokingly call his German national costume, namely grey flannel trousers and a blue blazer. Mum and I were also attired in semi-formal clothes. Just as we reached the tollbooth on Sydney Harbour Bridge, a sudden torrential downpour happened. It rained cats and dogs. We paid the bridge car toll and drove in the single, outer left lane in the direction of the city. About half way across the bridge, Dad suddenly stopped the car in his lane and the cars following him also came to an abrupt stop.

I asked, "What has happened?"

He replied, "I have just noticed that the Mercedes star emblem at the front of the car is crooked and lying on its side. Please get out and straighten it."

I responded, "Can't we do this when we get to Rosenblums? It is raining quite heavily outside. I will get soaked." But no. He replied, "I am not moving until the Mercedes star is righted. The emblem on a Mercedes must be erect." I looked at him with a look that said, "Are you crazy!" I became quite furious but I could not do very much. Mum touched me on the shoulder as if to say, "Humour him!" And so, I got out of the car, got soaked, and straightened his Mercedes star and got back into the car, and we resumed the journey. Needless to say, I was in a foul mood and indicated at every possible opportunity that I was thoroughly annoyed with him. But to Dad, the incident had no import. It was water off a duck's back. For him, the Mercedes star had to be erect before he started to drive. No further comment needed. I learnt a lesson that day that logic sometimes did not enter into the equation with Dad and it was better just to move on.

1964 - Babi Pays a Visit to Sydney

The news out of Calcutta dampened our hopes, as the factory sale was further delayed. The city had again been gripped by strikes and the factory closed for extensive periods. In this scenario, nobody would be interested in buying a business that was shut and non-operational for long stretches of time. In Sydney, the ever-increasing period of separation for Mum and Dad was becoming more noticeable. As I watched Mum, it seemed that a spark in her life had been extinguished. But, a decision had been made, probably by Dad, to bring her mother, "Babi," to Sydney to keep Mum company. In Czechoslovakia, Babi considered this offer at length and, after she had got over all her concerns, she agreed to come. One must remember that Babi had been the central focus of her family in Loučka and she had been rightly concerned about what could happen to her daughters Hanka and Marketa, who were very dependent on her, during difficult periods in their lives. But my uncles Ota and Noris managed to talk her around and reassure her that Hanka and Marketa would be all right. Babi's other fear related to travel. She had never been further than Zlin, about 60 miles south of where she lived. I don't believe that she had ever visited Prague and the prospect of a 30-hour plane trip to Sydney filled her with trepidation. In addition, she had no travel documents and we did not even know if the Communists would let her leave. New fears soon surfaced; Babi started to worry that, once having left Czechoslovakia, she would not be allowed to return home. One by one, all her fears were allayed and she applied for a passport; once this had been obtained, Dad made all the arrangements through Uncle Noris to buy her an airline ticket with the help of Tuzex certificates.

Finally, the big day arrived; Uncle Noris and Aunt Boženka took her to *Ruzyně* Airport in Prague and put her on the plane to Sydney. The flight went via Singapore and, early one morning, the whole family drove to Sydney Mascot Airport to greet her. After a long wait, the doors finally swung open and Babi emerged. And, yes, she was wearing her favourite *tepláky* (track suit). Babi was quite a simple person and she came with few clothes; apart from her *tepláky*, the only other item of clothing that she had brought along for the trip was a simple long smock. On the way home to Castlecrag, we travelled in silence, as she took in all the new sights and sounds. We left her to enjoy her new experiences; but, from her reaction, it became evident that she felt she had landed on another planet. Later on, we found out that she could not comprehend the enormity of the change from a little village to a large metropolis and it took some time for her to digest this and adjust. At home, we got her settled in her room. But, old habits, like the lure of the kitchen table, were strong. So, Mum and Babi made themselves at home in the kitchen, as they caught up on all the news from Loučka. For all of us, this became a familiar scene.

After Babi had settled in, we took her on short excursions to the beaches and to the various koala parks that surrounded Sydney. Babi enjoyed feeding the kangaroos and emus and did not mind the pecking of the emus as they picked food from her outstretched palm. This was an enjoyable time for Mum and, with Babi around, the problems associated with the sale of the factory in Calcutta soon dissolved into the background. They went for drives in her Volvo sports car to the northern beaches. On many occasions, they went to Whale Beach to visit Mum's friend, Alice Gange. Alice had a beautiful beach-side home and Mum and Babi loved to sit on the terrace while Alice served tea and scones à l'anglaise. She really enjoyed this new experience and loved being served tea out of fine china and eating the strawberry jam served with the scones. And when Alice asked if all met with her approval, Babi replied "*Ja, děkuji. Jsou velmi chutné*" (Yes, thank you. It is very tasty).

At home, Babi helped Mum with the cooking and together they managed to create a wonderful apple strudel. Mum would prepare the pastry, Babi would prepare the apples and they would then create their strudel. Strudel became a staple in the fridge. Babi told us, "It's nice to have strudel in the fridge in case guests come." Things went well so long as they coordinated their actions together. But, on one memorable occasion, Mum had prepared the pastry and left it in the fridge to be used at a later date. In fact, the Rosenblums had been invited to visit for afternoon tea and Mum planned to serve her strudel. The evening before, they had made cabbage for dinner and the leftover cabbage had also been placed in the fridge. Babi, in her usual fashion, decided to help make the strudel. She took out the pastry, rolled it out to the required thinness and then, without thinking about what she was doing, took out the cabbage - which could resemble poached or stewed apples - and filled the pastry with it. Then she sprinkled some cinnamon and raisins onto the surface and rolled it up ready to be warmed up prior to serving.

The Rosenblums arrived and Mum offered them coffee and tea and the newly prepared strudel. We all sat down and Babi came out of the kitchen with the strudel; she started to cut slices and served everybody. I only realised that something was seriously wrong after taking my first bite into the strudel. Ordinarily, I love my strudel but this one had the most unusual taste. Even the cinnamon and icing sugar could not disguise the fact that this strudel had missed the mark. I looked at Mum as she tasted a piece and made a grimacing look at the strudel to indicate that it was "off colour." The Rosenblums, however, were a picture of politeness and said nothing, even though it became obvious that they felt uneasy. Mum took another bite and soon realised what had happened. She leapt out of her seat and quickly removed the strudel from the Rosenblums amid a torrent of Czech "polite" invective directed at Babi telling her what she had done. Babi had a legendary fighting spirit and a cutting tongue and responded in another equally potent response to Mum. Mum apologised to the Rosenblums about their cabbage-filled strudel. It all eventually ended amicably and we had a good laugh except for Babi who remained quite upset and went to sulk in the kitchen. Thus, ended the saga of the "cabbage" strudel. Babi stayed out of the kitchen when Mum prepared food after that until all personal temperatures had abated.

However, it was becoming obvious that Babi was feeling quite restless and homesick; we started hearing requests from her about wanting to return to Loučka. So, a visit that had been meant to last six months came to an end after only four months and she had a safe uneventful trip back to her village. Afterwards, we heard from Uncle Noris and Aunt Boženka that the strudel story had made the rounds in Loučka and Otrokovice. In some ways, Babi's visit had been successful, as it afforded Mum the opportunity to spend some time with her mother and show Babi a bit of her life in Australia. But, on reflection, I felt that Babi never really managed to come to terms with the contrasts that she encountered between the slow pace of life in a Czech village and the faster pace of a big city like Sydney. In the end, she had been happy to get home. But her visit had been a welcome one for us and we were sorry to see her go so soon.

End 1964 - Graduation and Departure for Europe

At the end of 1964, I finally completed my studies at Sydney University and planned to take a short holiday in Europe. Little did I know at the time that the short holiday would extend to four years and that I would eventually return to Sydney with a wife. On my way to Europe, I planned to stop over in India and spend some time with Dad. My graduation ceremony was scheduled for May 1965, but I did not want to wait that long in Sydney. So, I departed for Calcutta in mid-January. Mum now had a huge house to herself with only Martina and Charley to share it with. In 1964, Charley had started attending Hunter's Hill Primary School as a day boarder. The following year, he enrolled in St. Aloysius College in Kirribilli, again as a day boarder. This school was closer to home, so it made the travelling more palatable for him. Mum made a brave attempt to keep herself busy by visiting her Czech friends whenever she could, but her sense of life within a family context was obviously missing. I believe that this period also signalled the start of a steady withdrawal into herself. I think that she had been emotionally traumatized by having to leave Calcutta. Then, having to live alone, away from her husband, further fuelled her depression. She started to spend longer periods of time in that huge house gravitating between her bedroom, TV room/library and kitchen, making infrequent outings to Chatswood, a Sydney suburb, on inconsequential shopping excursions. Although we did not recognise it at the time, she had once again started to show all the symptoms of a clinical depression. And so, the weeks slipped into months and the months slid into years and the prospect of Dad coming finally to Sydney seemed even more remote.

In mid-1965, Mum went to Czechoslovakia to see her family for the last time. I believe that she wanted to go because she felt that, with the state of her health, opportunities to travel in the future would be few and far between.

So, now the family was truly scattered. After India, I flew on to Europe and spent some time in the Italian part of Switzerland with my girlfriend Josette Flury at their family home in Locarno in the centre of Tessin. In late October, I moved to Hamburg looking for work, which I eventually found at the Philips Central Laboratories as an engineer. Martina put all her new newly acquired fashion knowledge and skills to use in her job in Sydney. In her spare time, she actively pursued her increasingly close relationship with Ivan Valenta. When Mum returned from Czechoslovakia, she again became the cohesive link that kept the Sydney end of the family together.

1965 Indo-Pakistan War

From August to September 1965, in the State of Kashmir, in the northern part of India, a small "war" of attrition was being waged with numerous cross-border skirmishes between India and Pakistan. Pakistan tried to infiltrate their army into Jammu and Kashmir by stealth and hoped to start an uprising, but India retaliated without a formal declaration of war. The "war" lasted approximately from 5 August to 22 September, 1965, and was prosecuted on land, sea and air. After five weeks of these skirmishes in the high passes in Kashmir, the two countries agreed to a cease-fire organized by the United Nations.[179]

This war also affected West Bengal as it shared a common frontier with East Pakistan. Although there had been no actual open conflict, there had been religious riots reported on both sides of the border, and refugees started to move again between the two countries. Once again, this exacerbated problems in Calcutta and led to more riots and eventually more unrest in the city. The current West Bengal government had been progressively losing control of the situation. With this new increasingly large number of displaced people, the West Bengal Communist Party again had a ready audience for its message, namely that support for their party would lead to work and improved concessions. In consequence, the labour unrest continued, only this time the number of strikes, work to rule and lockouts increased. 1966 was a complete disaster for any sort

---

179 A very good summary of this war can be found in Ramchandra Guha, *India After Gandhi: The History of the World's Largest Democracy*, 398-403.

of meaningful production in the factory. It was completely shut down for over half a year. Without a working factory for prospective buyers to assess any potential, sale of the factory looked even bleaker. Very little money had been earned through production, and it had become very difficult to finance any further factory construction at Gobra.

September 1966 - Kashmir Holiday

As a means of escaping this stressful situation and as a way of bringing the family together, Dad came up with the idea that I should return to Calcutta for a holiday; he would bring Mum and Charley to Calcutta from Sydney and we would all go to Kashmir for three weeks. I had been working in Hamburg for about a year and was planning a holiday to see Mum and Dad in any event. At the time, I was not quite sure where or when that would be but I had four weeks at my disposal. Dad's idea seemed to be the perfect solution. He said that he wanted to combine this trip with a visit to see his friend Bobal in Pathankhot. We all assembled in Calcutta in September and flew up to Srinagar and were soon comfortably settled in our houseboat, "Lighthouse," on Dal Lake in the Vale of Kashmir. Kashmir, and especially the area around Srinagar, is covered with a large expanse of legendary lakes that are woven and interlinked with an intricate network of canals and backwaters.

Kashmir is one of the great jewels located in the north-west of India. It is, however, to this day a contested territory between India and Pakistan. The scenery of Kashmir is punctuated by gloriously beautiful valleys and lakes; and it is bordered on most sides by mountains, including the westernmost Himalayan range, highlighted by the majestic peak of Nanga Parbat that is visible from Gulmarg. Srinagar is also the gateway into other impressive areas like Ladakh, Gilgit and Hunza. The people in Kashmir are mainly Muslim and their religious focus is towards Mecca and Pakistan but there also exists a sizeable community of Buddhist Ladakhis and Tibetans, whose focus is towards Lhasa in Tibet. In fact, this Ladakhi connection to its large eastern neighbour has earned the area the name of "Little Tibet."

On our visit, the houseboats were moored in such a way that we over-looked Dal Lake; in the background were the mountains. We entered into this Persian-carpeted domain by stepping out of our *shikara* water taxi up three or four wooden steps and entering a little world of domestic cosiness. Many houseboats came complete with a seated balcony on the roof and a sun deck. There were windows all around the living area so that we felt the cooling breezes coming off the lake's surface while we enjoyed the view of the gentle hills that made up the Vale of Kashmir. Beyond them were the 16,400 ft. peaks of the Himalayan mountain range. At night, the gently lapping waters of the lake against the side of the houseboat made it easy to fall asleep. In the afternoon and evening, we experienced a veil of serenity over the lake as the sun set. These were truly magical moments that we were able to enjoy together as a family.

In the morning, the first *shikara* jostling for space at the entry steps was the vegetable seller with all his produce laid out along the full length of his boat. The fruit seller *shikara* was tethered on one side, while on the other side was the flower boat. Another brought live chickens and eggs. Each *shikara* boat owner knew when his turn came; he would very politely move over so that the next vendor could get his turn. Every morning we had this fresh produce delivered to our front door, all very civilised and satisfying. The day's plans were discussed over breakfast. Why not a visit to Srinagar's famous, landscaped gardens that were a paradise for nature lovers? The gardens had been laid out by the Mughals. The three main gardens, Chashmashahi Garden, Nishat Garden and Shalimar Garden had some of the rarest flowers in the world. We might also decide to visit the mosques and the old town of Srinagar, or perhaps take a day trip to Sonamarg and Pahalgam, or just spend a lazy day on the houseboat reading. The houseboat veranda provided enough of an excuse to stay on board, especially in the evening as the sun set behind the fort on Hari Parbat Hill to the west of the lotus-strewn Dal Lake.

Our houseboat had a well-equipped kitchen; all our meals were cooked on board. Since Kashmir had a predominantly Moslem population, the daily menu rotated between fish and chicken. After dinner, we often hired a *shikara* and reclined like decadent Romans on the heavily carpeted and cushioned front part while our gondolier poled his way through the labyrinth of canals that were connected to Nagin and Wular lakes. All along these canals, we glided past Kashmiri wooden homes, many three or four storeys high. As we were poled past these houses, we had the opportunity to witness at first hand daily life on the water.

The abundance of water everywhere was not lost on Charley. In the background, he could see the mountain ranges and valleys that, for him, also meant fast-flowing, mountain streams. For Charley, this signified a fundamental law of nature: all this water meant fish. So, the plaintive cry went out, "Can we go fishing, Dad?" Bobal advised that we needed a fishing licence and he offered to get the fishing rods. We went to the Kashmir Department of Fisheries and bought a fishing licence for two rods, which cost 50 rupees.[180] But the real surprise of this small fee came when we also got exclusive fishing rights to a three mile stretch of river with two fishing guides and a cook thrown in. A few days later, our large fishing party made its way up one of the valleys leading to some unnamed high mountain peak. When we reached our allotted patch of river, Charley and I waded in while Mum and Dad rested on the banks near where the cook had set up to make lunch. We all laughed in vain, as there was absolutely no way we could tell our guides to let us play the trout after it had taken the hook. As soon as a trout took the lure, our guides and the cook jumped into the river, grabbed the line, removed the trout and threw it to the river bank. This must have been local trout fishing tradition since the Raj, or even before. I have long since forgotten how many trout we caught that day but I do remember that it was a bountiful day's fishing on a river running between two high mountain ranges with not another person or car anywhere in sight. The real bonus for us was that we were all happy, relaxed and enjoying the moment. Dad forgot about the factory and the strikes, and we all forgot about the separation between Hamburg, Sydney and Calcutta. We just enjoyed a family occasion as though we were all living in Sydney. That evening, Charley selected the fish that he wanted to eat and gave the rest away to Bobal and the houseboat crew.

As we said goodbye to our days in Srinagar, we made preparations to move onto Gulmarg and the famous Nedou's Hotel. My abiding image of this car trip is of driving past many rice fields and small villages and long avenues of poplar trees. As the road wound up into the hills on our way to

180   The conversion for 50 Indian Rupees is about $2.00 Canadian or Australian.

the hotel, the vegetation changed to fir trees and the road emerged into a beautiful, bowl-shaped meadow covered in flowers.

We checked in at the hotel's reception, with Dad presenting his confirmation telegram that reserved two huts, one for himself and Mum and the other for Charley and me. It soon became obvious from the glances exchanged behind the reception desk that no booking had been entered in Dad's name. In the next five minutes, I think that I counted 33 "regrets" that passed their lips and soon the "regrets" morphed into "regretting." Dad, bless his soul, did not erupt in anger; he just kept pointing to the telegram that had come from Nedou's office, but which obviously had not made its way into the Booking Journal. The reception staff huddled together, and the conversation subsided into a hush. We had been totally ignored and forgotten. Dad exhibited a lot of patience, something alien for him, as they sought to find a solution. Their problem was that they had three huts, but two were already occupied. Consequently, they were trying to solve the eternal conundrum of how to fit 2 into 1. On another level, we had to wonder what the force of telegrams was in India. Telegrams represented a sense of urgency, but here its message had taken on an air of mystery. Glances were cast towards us and staff offered us helpful comments like, "Sorry for the delay but we are sorting this out." The solution was obvious: they should offer us the remaining hut and a room in the main hotel. But, in India, we had learned that the solution had to come from them. There was absolutely no point in demanding our rights whilst showing any displeasure or anger, when in fact we were powerless.

Finally, Dad politely asked if there was a problem and suggested that he could assist in finding a solution. A person from the back office finally appeared and approached Dad, saying, "Sorry, Sir, there has been a misunderstanding and we apologize with most profuseness and shame for causing this uncertainty. But will Sir be accepting, if we can offer one hut and one room in the main hotel building?"

"That will be very acceptable, thank you. My sons can stay in the hotel and we will move into the hut, as it has a beautiful fireplace. Can you arrange for the luggage to be moved?" And so, we agreed on a solution and went away happy knowing that, in India, these things can take time and patience. After we settled in, we met on the lawn for a drink and a chance to finally enjoy Gulmarg. The scenery was breathtaking and Dad lost no time in pointing out the Aparbhat range behind us where he had won his Ski Championship title. He left us with absolutely no doubt that he meant to take us over every blade of grass on the downhill course and give us a blow by blow commentary on how he had won. Dad obviously enjoyed telling us about his ski title. During the coming week, we went for long horse rides through the Strawberry and Leopard Valleys. Why they were thus called I have no idea.

Getting to the slopes of Dad's triumphs was quite an exercise. He had arranged for four mountain ponies to transport us up to the top of the range. Mountains ponies are stocky and shorter than the average horse. When you sit in the saddle and let your legs dangle out of the stirrups, they practically touch the ground. These ponies are sure-footed but we were not to know this as we started off. Stones were strewn over the trail; it became quite narrow and at times when we looked to the right, the mountain-side disappeared rapidly as it fell steeply away into the valley below. The mountain pony guides kept us going forward and we learnt to trust them completely, as they carried us safely to the top of the plateau. Here, Dad took over. Yes, he indicated to us where the finishing line had been situated and how he had to ski through this group of trees and make a sharp turn here and jump over this bump. He told us that he nearly fell there but, by a deft shift in his balance, had managed to stay upright, regain control of his skis, and cross the finishing line the fastest. This was definitely his big moment and he obviously enjoyed reliving that occasion. We mere mortals could only add a few supportive comments like "Really!" or "My, that was fantastic!" or "What an incredibly difficult course and you conquered it!" In addition to hearing this blow by blow account, we had the bonus of seeing in the distance, the whole Himalayan mountain range stretching from horizon to horizon, with Nanga Parbat prominently in view.

We enjoyed our stay in Gulmarg as much as the stay in Srinagar. But I couldn't help but think that, if we could all be together like this in Sydney, we really had something to look forward to. We talked freely and openly; we talked like adults to each other; we respected all our different points of view and I could not help hoping that Dad would be successful in selling the factory sooner rather than later. After we left Kashmir, we all went in different directions. I returned to Hamburg, Mum and Charley left for Sydney and Dad back to Calcutta and we started again at square one.

1967 State Elections in West Bengal

In the 1967 elections, the ruling Congress Party, with no answers to the problems of the city, had become extremely unpopular. There had also been a sort of schism within the Congress Party with a breakaway group forming a new political party. Many splinter groups had now emerged on the political scene. They attacked each other with charges and counter-charges to everything. Their disagreements spilled over into bloody confrontations in the streets. The noise from slogan-shouting grew louder as each party laid claim to being the only true representative of the people. As expected, the election results were fairly predictable and no one party emerged as a clear winner; so now, the jockeying for a coalition started. An unlikely alliance emerged between the breakaway Bangla Party and the Communist Party led by Shri Jyoti Basu, a famous West Bengal politician. However, this was not a political marriage made in heaven and soon they slept in separate beds. The Communists continued to pursue their agenda, namely the spread of the Maoist version of Communism throughout West Bengal. A policy vacuum emerged in the important areas of good state governance, law and order, and finance.[181]

In these political conditions, another orgy of public protests and demonstrations ensued, anti-industry posters shot up all over the city on every available space, and the number of strikes and work stoppages erupted everywhere like fast growing mushrooms. The Communists controlled labour completely and the wage demands became outrageous. Some political parties had their own little private gangs of thugs and people were killed when these opposing gangs met in the street. As if living with this level of political turmoil and unrest were not enough, news filtered through of a small peasant uprising, some might have called it a rebellion, in May 1967, at Naxalbari, a small village situated close to Darjeeling.[182] The ramifications of this uprising swept through Bengal like a typhoon. The rebellion of

---

181   Ibid., 425.
182   Ibid., 423-425.

these peasants against the tea plantation owners, the landlords and police was much admired by the educated young people and students in Calcutta. Even China viewed this uprising as a people's revolution in Bengal.[183] This rebellion spawned a movement amongst young, idealistic students, some of whom came from well-off families. Their objective was to overthrow the government. Slowly, the violence of the countryside permeated the city such that, by about 1968, bomb blasts, murders, robbery, the beating-up of police, businessmen, civil servants, government officials, teachers and ordinary people slowly overtook Calcutta. The *gherao* tactic had now become a popular form of weapon against selected persons. Some public buildings, cinemas and shops were torched. Soon rebel attention turned to the foreign community. The violent mayhem persisted for some time. This Naxalite violence was a wake-up call for many people and businesses in Calcutta, and the city experienced a subsequent decline as even more capital fled to other parts of India. These were dark times in Calcutta and produced a fertile field for further Communist inroads into the city and state. Hammer and Sickle graffiti took over empty wall spaces and street lamp posts.

1967 - Martina and Ivan Get Married

After a courtship that had practically started from the cradle and that had been pursued over three continents, Martina and Ivan finally got married in Sydney on 14 January, 1967. Dad came from India to give the bride away. Unfortunately, I could not attend because I was still working in Germany. In late November, Mum and Dad became grandparents for the first time with the arrival of Vincent on the 25 November 1967, followed closely the next year on 30 December 1968, by the arrival of little Ivan.

1967/1968 Visits to Europe

Early in 1967, Dad visited Czechoslovakia to attend his mother's funeral. She died at 93. He had received an urgent call from Uncle Noris that his

---

183 In June 1967, Radio Peking declared, "A phase of peasant's armed struggle led by the revolutionaries of the Indian Communist Party has been set in the countryside of Darjeeling….." Guha, *India After Gandhi: The History of the World's Largest Democracy*, 424.

mother was dying and made every effort to see her, but unfortunately arrived in Buchlov 24 hours too late. Those who had been keeping a vigil at his mother's bedside said she hoped to see him before she died. She kept asking, "Is Mirek coming?" Dad was utterly devastated at not seeing his mother one last time, but at least he managed to attend her funeral. He then visited the rest of the family before returning to India.

In July 1968, there had been another *gherao* at the factory. Fortunately, Dad escaped being trapped in his office, but the office staff and Mr. Josef Kintr were not so lucky. Mr. Kintr, a fellow Czech, had joined Dad a few years earlier and helped in the office with bookkeeping and general administration. Mr. Kintr was one of the men who, like my father, had left Bata. Unfortunately, he had very little money saved; but he was a friend of Dad's and so Dad gave him a job. This actually turned out to be a good decision because it allowed Dad to be absent from the factory during strikes and when he wanted to travel to Australia and Czechoslovakia. Alongside his obvious management skills, Mr. Kintr had other talents. He understood the bureaucratic English used in Calcutta and so the drafting and composition of formal letters to the various West Bengal government departments was always left to him.

1968 - Hamburg Visit and Miki's Marriage

In August 1968, Mum and Dad visited me in Hamburg; I had left Philips Research Laboratories and was thinking of returning to Sydney in the very near future. While I was living in Hamburg, I had met Bronja (known affectionately to all her friends as Muschi) and our relationship had progressed from casual to serious. I had a small BMW 1600, so Mum, Dad, and I decided to have a little holiday in Europe before their return to Sydney via India. Mum and Dad especially wanted to visit Czechoslovakia. We first drove to Berlin and, during our stay there, managed to visit East Berlin via the famous Checkpoint Charlie entry point. We walked along the magnificent *allée* called *Unter den Linden* and noted that this previously busy thoroughfare was now practically deserted. We visited the famous Pergamon Museum in East Berlin, with its impressive collections of classical antiquities, artefacts from the Ancient Near East, and a beautiful collection of Islamic Art. Nearby was the East German government building, which was reminiscent of Soviet monolithic architecture. But where were all the people? Dad noted that if he had wanted to have a pee here in the middle of the road, he could have done his business in complete privacy without fear of being interrupted; but, thankfully, he behaved appropriately - otherwise we might have had to endure a diet of bread and water somewhere in the East German Communist hinterland.

While in Germany, we took the opportunity to visit Bayreuth, home of the Bayreuth *Festspielhaus*, an opera house dedicated solely to the performance of Wagnerian opera. During our visit, we managed to see the rehearsals for an upcoming presentation of *Tannhäuser*. From Bayreuth, we entered Czechoslovakia from the west at the Hof border crossing, which we had negotiated this time without any trouble from the Czech border guards. We drove straight across the country, bypassing Prague totally, heading straight for Otrokovice where most of the family lived. While in Czechoslovakia, I informed Mum and Dad that I wanted to marry Muschi. My problem was that I had not as yet asked her; so, I decided to return to Hamburg at the end of our trip to find out one way or another if she would accept my marriage offer. Fortunately, Mum and Dad could extend their stay and came back with me to Hamburg. During the last week that we had left prior to our return to Hamburg, we decided to drive back via the *Schwarzwald*, up the Rhine valley, and on to Hamburg.

After our return, I asked Muschi to marry me and she accepted on the proviso that I make my intentions clear to her parents, Jackie and Christoph Kessler. For me, this was a harrowing experience. The thought of having to ask my prospective parents-in-law for permission to marry their daughter was a huge hurdle. I had to outline to them what I believed my future prospects were. After I passed this gauntlet, the two families met and we had a celebratory dinner as Christoph's guests in a well-known Hamburg restaurant. The dinner presented one embarrassing incident. Naturally, Christoph wanted to impress Mum and Dad and ordered a fine German wine, making sure, after tasting it, that Mum received the first pouring. Then all the others had their glasses filled and his intent had been that they would toast Muschi and me. Unfortunately, before Christoph could invite everyone to raise their glasses in a toast, Dad had already emptied his glass of wine and asked if he could have a beer! There was a moment of stunned silence and eyebrows were raised; but Dad did not read this awkward situation. He was totally oblivious to all the unease and repeated his request for a beer. Christoph and Jackie took this in their stride and were fantastic. It was their first glimpse into my side of the family, but fortunately both families got on fine after that incident. Shortly after, Dad and Mum left Hamburg to return to Calcutta and Sydney respectively. Dad returned to Hamburg in late November to attend my wedding on a cold snowy night in the evangelical Lutheran, St. John's Church, located in the Hamburg district of Eppendorf. Directly opposite the church was a quaint old German restaurant called Brahmskeller, where Muschi and I had enjoyed many an evening together prior to our marriage and which indirectly led to the choice of the church.

Dad left us and returned to a city that had practically ground to a halt, partly because of the Naxalite uprising, but also because of the violence in the streets. Business activity had effectively ceased. Many companies had by now closed down their Calcutta operations and re-established their businesses in more stable parts of India. The situation was so drastic that the Central Government of India again stepped in and dissolved the West Bengal Assembly, imposing President's Rule on the State. When President's Rule was finally lifted, elections for the next assembly were called.

1969 West Bengal Elections

In the assembly election in 1969, the Maoist West Bengal Communist Party (CPI(M)), with Jyoti Basu now Chief Minister, emerged as the single largest party and formed a governing coalition with other similar parties. But it would be a stretch of one's imagination to think that, with all of Calcutta's problems, there would be some abatement in the political extremism in the city. Guerilla labour tactics grew unabated and increased in acrimony; gone were the days when participating in an afternoon's protest march represented a pleasant few hours away from work.[184]

At the factory, Dad often had to confront picket lines; he could not get his goods to market. In the city, many normal commercial and government services necessary for the on-going running of his business had ceased to

---

184   Guha, *India After Gandhi: The History of the World's Largest Democracy*, 425.

function. He ordered a complete shut down at the factory, keeping only a skeleton staff to protect the machinery and the facilities from vandalism and sabotage. At this point, he was so desperate that he considered closing the factory for good and having a fire sale of the presses and other related machinery. When Mum and Dad came to Europe in late 1968 for a visit, he had opened up to both of us about his feelings and frustrations. I found out later that Mum had talked him out of this proposed action. She apparently suggested that she return to India to be there to support him. But he rejected this suggestion, since he was unsure what to do with the house in Castlecrag. Mom believed that the situation in Calcutta would improve, which would create the right conditions for the sale of the factory.

1969 Muschi and Miki visit India

In late February, 1969, Muschi and I arrived in India after stopovers in Arosa, Switzerland, for some skiing, then on to a freezing Istanbul - where we arrived the day after an enormous snowstorm - and where we had booked into a hotel that had been taken over by a football team from the Balkans. The footballers made as much noise as possible and we were relieved when we finally left for Teheran; after a week's visit there, we ended up in Bombay. Dad had given us, as a wedding present, a paid trip from Bombay to Calcutta via Udaipur, Jaipur, Delhi, Agra and Benares. When we arrived at Bombay, we discovered that Dad's instructions for all the bookings had not been acted on and so, after the initial disappointment, we flew directly to Calcutta. There, we settled into a daily routine with Dad. When he was busy at the factory, we went out and saw the "sights" of Calcutta and caught up with him much later in the day. We enjoyed a relaxed and pleasant stay with him in Calcutta; he was extremely generous with his time and things that we did together. He welcomed our company, but it was obvious that he was extremely frustrated that he could not sell the factory. Dad made travel arrangements for us from Calcutta and soon we were off again, but this time we went to Agra, Jaipur, and Benares. And, instead of going to the west of India, we went to visit Kathmandu instead. In early April, we finally left Calcutta and flew on to Sydney via Cambodia (where we visited the great temple complex at Angkor Wat), Singapore, Hong Kong and Japan, where Muschi and I stopped in Osaka to visit her old Kurashiki Rayon Japanese boss from Hamburg. And so, finally, after all this travelling, we arrived in Sydney to stay with Mum at Castlecrag. After three months "on the road," we were broke and I needed to find work soon, so that we could afford a place of our own.

Impact of Separation on Mum

While at Castlecrag, we saw first-hand the effect that the continued separation from Dad was having on Mum. She was suffering from total despair that the situation in Calcutta had not changed at all nor shown any signs of changing. It was now nearly ten years since the house had been built and six years since she had moved to Australia. The sporadic visits by Dad to Sydney each year had not been enough to help her break out of her frustration about living alone in this big house. In many ways, it seemed that the house was the problem, since Dad was very reluctant to rent or sell it. The solution lay there; he should have asked Mum to join him in Calcutta until the factory was sold. Then they could have moved to Sydney together. But, I believe that Dad's main concern was more about who would live in the house and look after it. One thing for sure: neither Martina nor I intended to live there. We were both married and raising young families; neither of us wanted to live in such a large house. Dad steadfastly refused to part with it as it represented, in a very tangible way, his reward for all the years of struggle, sacrifice and hard work that he had had in Calcutta. Castlecrag was always the place where he wanted to retire and enjoy whatever Sydney had to offer.

Mum's Mental Breakdown

By late 1970, Muschi and I had moved out of Castlecrag and were living in an apartment in the nearby suburb of Wollstonecraft. Muschi was pregnant and, on 30 November 1970, gave birth to our son Doug. Mum and Dad had become grandparents for the third time. Dad was in Sydney then and, when he found out that Muschi had delivered a boy, he offered us his congratulations. Then, he surprised me by saying in Czech, "I am so happy that the name Hruska will survive through Doug." My thoughts had been more about the well-being of mother and son, but his were about dynasty! Nevertheless, he seemed genuinely happy about Doug's arrival.

At the time, we had no idea what afflicted Mum. It became clearer only much later, when we started to understand her symptoms and when depression was in the public eye. In hindsight, I believe that she showed all the symptoms of clinical depression. She no longer took any interest in her own personal appearance. She lost all interest in life. She was not able to function as she had in the past. She no longer wanted to do the things that previously had given her enjoyment, like going for a drive or visiting with her friends. She seemed to gravitate between the bedroom and the kitchen in this gigantic cavern of a house. Even the opportunity to spend time on the large terrace enjoying the sun or the beautiful surroundings was too much for her. The long bouts of separation and loneliness continued to seriously affect her health, moods, thoughts, behaviour, and eating habits. It was increasingly noticeable that she was physically more frail. She did not seem to have any desire to "pull herself together" and seek medical help.

Today, I realize that it was the depression that prevented her from seeking help. Then, on 1 October, 1970, Mum suffered a serious stroke and was admitted to the local hospital in Castlecrag. She was in a coma, not expected to live, and received the last rites of the Catholic Church. But she did recover and remained there under observation for about three weeks before release to return home to Castlecrag. After this Mum suffered from recurring fits of epilepsy and cramping in her left arm and right leg. After Dad got news about Mum's stroke, he flew to Sydney for a short visit and stayed with Mum while she convalesced at home. But after three or four weeks, he returned to Calcutta and Mum resumed her "status quo" existence in her Castlecrag "prison."

During this time, two more grandchildren were added to our extended family. My daughter, Toni, was born on 6 June, 1973, and my sister's daughter, Gaby, was born on 3 May, 1975.

As the situation with Mum's health and demeanour became more apparent, I believe that Dad felt he should try again to do something. His answer to the problem was to invite Uncle Noris to Sydney so that they could celebrate their 40th wedding anniversary in May. Uncle Noris still worked in Otrokovice and, as he had no children, was able to take an extended leave of absence. He came for a seven week visit to Sydney starting 10 April, 1976. Again, for a while, Mum's spirits lifted. With Uncle Noris around, she made an effort to get out of the house and do all sorts of activities with her brother. Martina, Ivan, Muschi, and I played chauffeur on numerous occasions, taking Mum and Noris around Sydney and the surrounding area. Dad arrived from Calcutta, but his stay was not long. My recollection of this visit was that, for a moment, Mum's mood changed. She obviously enjoyed being with her eldest brother and they spent a lot of time chatting about Czechoslovakia and the family. But the visit was all too short and Uncle Noris went back home.

1971 India-Pakistan War and Formation of Bangladesh

In 1971, India and Pakistan again went to war, which eventually led to the creation of Bangladesh. Among the reasons for this war was the asinine decision by Pakistan to impose Urdu as the *lingua franca* in a region where the Muslim population predominantly spoke Bengali, not realizing that Bangladesh literally means "the Bengali-speaking people." The government of East Pakistan, which became Bangladesh, felt that it had been excluded from the political decision-making on the other side of the sub-continent 1,400 miles away in West Pakistan. They also felt that they had been especially neglected in West Pakistan economic policy-making and that they had been discriminated against, both ethnically and linguistically. Calcutta once more found itself to be the destination of choice as this war unleashed another massive exodus from Bangladesh of about seven million refugees. Needless to say, this huge influx further exacerbated Calcutta's housing and other infrastructure problems. These refugee streams into the city presented a pitiful sight. In many cases, people were carrying the total contents of their home wrapped in paper or cloth bundles on their heads or held in hand.[185]

The new wave of refugee migration effectively turned Calcutta into a living nightmare, as slums proliferated, poverty became endemic and the

---

185 An excellent synopsis of the tensions between West Pakistan and East Pakistan, West Pakistan and India, India and China, and finally between West Pakistan and Russia that led to the gradual slide into war in December 1971 can be found in Ramchandra Guha, *India After Gandhi: The History of the World's Largest Democracy*, 449-465.

city's infrastructure, already strained, totally collapsed. Eight or ten people were often crammed into decrepit one-room shacks, assembled from discarded bricks or plywood, corrugated metal sheets, torn bits of tarpaulin, wood off-cuts, packing cases and cardboard. These tenuous shelters were held together by heavy stones, metal piping, or ropes on the makeshift roof. Somewhere an entrance existed. Most had no light, poor ventilation, no water, no toilet facilities - the outside street serving that purpose. Approximately 11 million such people temporarily called Calcutta home at that time, a number equal to half the population of Canada in that year.[186] I believe that the city has never really recovered from this particular surge in population. With the increasing mass labour agitation and lawlessness in the city, the central government once again imposed President's Rule, this time from 28 June 1971, to 19 March 1972.

For the next two or three years, West Bengal once more had to cope with increasing poverty and various other social disturbances caused by natural calamities such as droughts and floods. This led to more and more agitation in the city and further fueled the ranks of the Communist parties in the state. At times, it seemed that all this industrial agitation was part of some imaginary board game played by the moronic fringe of the Communist parties. Other times, I think that the Bengali brand of Communism, conducted by the intellectual elite, was aimed to poke continuously at the side of the Congress Party of India. Certainly, by the 1970s, apart from the shell and some outward forms of civility, the Calcutta I knew and grew up in no longer existed. The landscape had changed. Commercially, Calcutta had become a fossil but, in Dad's case, the bulk of his market still existed outside Calcutta and thus he still had a reason to manufacture and sell hurricane lanterns. However, there was no escaping the situation and Dad didn't know what to do; he felt trapped and even desperate and again seriously considered a sacrifice sale of the factory.

---

186 Sukanta Chaudhuri, ed., *Calcutta, the Living City. Vol II" The Present and Future*, 95-96.

1976-1977 Sale of the Factory

Finally, in late 1975 or early 1976, some Marwaris from Burrabazar started to show some interest in the factory. The group of potential buyers represented a consortium of dealers involved in the distribution of the hurricane lanterns throughout India. They obviously had the financial wherewithal to buy the factory, but naturally the stumbling block was the price. The Government of India banking regulations still remained extremely tight and Dad had no way to repatriate 100% of the proceeds from the factory sale. In essence, Dad had to negotiate some sort of creative, multilayered, sales package with them. There would have to be an official price to satisfy the government, vis-à-vis banking regulations and taxation. There would also have to be an unofficial component that would be paid out in rupees and that would give Dad the opportunity to make a few private arrangements in Calcutta. Dad also pressed for a third component, namely, part-payment to be made in foreign currency outside of India. Dad knew that many Indians had accounts overseas and that the Marwaris would have offshore foreign currency accounts. I no longer know the details of the final agreement, but it certainly must have been a formula that addressed all three conditions. Finally, after the Marwaris had done their due diligence and checked all the accounts of the company, they paid special attention to whether the transfer of title to another company would be possible, since the building code for the land had changed after Dad built the factory. It now stipulated that no more heavy engineering could be pursued in the area. Satisfied that they could continue to manufacture on Ripon Street, the buyers signed an agreement with Dad and he was finally free to move to Australia.

Final Six Months in India

With the sale of the factory, most of the 500 people on the work floor found employment with the new owners. However, many fine people saw their working careers come to a close. There had been the office staff who had stuck with Dad through a lot of industrial disruption and most probably would not be able to find another job. Dad helped them to top up their Provident Fund which, in India, was the financial vehicle to provide them with their pension. He also did the same for Mr. Singh and helped him move back to the Punjab. Dad's right-hand man in the factory was Mr. Josef Kintr (affectionately known as Joschko). Dad mentioned to me that, when he sold the factory, Joschko Kintr decided to move to Coimbatore, in South India. Dad helped Joshko buy a modest house there and also bought him a pension. All the funds for the final settlement to his staff came out of the proceeds that went officially to the bank. Dad also gave some money to Phul Mohammed, his driver, since Phul planned to return to his village.

But Dad had a dilemma about what to do with Dandia. As luck would have it, the Czech Consulate in Calcutta just happened to be looking for a reliable cook at the time. Dad managed to get Dandia the job of cooking for them. And so, with the placement of Dandia, an "untouchable," who had transformed himself into a fine cook of Czech food, but who also knew enough Czech that he could understand the names of many dishes, the final act of making preparations to leave Calcutta could be achieved. Dandia's placement was, for me, the ultimate triumph in all these arrangements, in which someone from the lowest caste of Hindu society, was able to improve his knowledge, better his skills, and finally overcome his lowly state. Mum was indeed very happy for him. This had been another valuable lesson, namely the infinite capacity of people to respond to encouragement and then strive to improve themselves and grasp their opportunities, if only given a chance. Dad made further financial arrangements with Fr. Gabric and Mother Teresa to get additional money out of India, booked his ticket to Sydney, and finally flew out of Calcutta. With his departure, a chapter that had started in 1939 and ended in 1977 (38 years) came to an end.

Dad's Final Move to Sydney

News reached us in June that the factory had finally been sold and that Dad was in the process of completing all the contractual matters; he advised that he hoped to be in Sydney within a few months. In July or August 1977, Dad arrived in Sydney, but none of us had any idea about his future plans or what he wanted to do. He had always been a very active man and it soon became apparent that he had no intention of sitting on the terrace in his deck chair, sunning himself. He immediately made all the rounds of visits to his Czech friends and let everybody know that he had no intention of returning to India. That chapter of his life was closed for good. He felt unburdened and wanted to go out and socialize. Right away, he encountered an obstacle. Mum was cognisant of her poor state of health and told him that she had no real desire to go out and socialize, nor even the strength to indulge him. She made the odd exception here and there when the invitations came from close friends or from people that she felt an affinity with. Soon Dad started to go out on his own and the distance between them deepened. It became obvious that he needed something that would engage his mind, through problem solving, or tapping into his creative spirit. After he had attended to all the myriad little repairs around the house, he had one of his little "A-ha" moments. It occurred in January of 1978 or 1979 and entailed building a bar just opposite the entrance to the garage.

"The Czech Tavern"

A door inside the garage allowed direct access to the interior of the house via a small hallway. Opposite this door in the hallway there was an area, accessed by a door, that literally spilled directly onto the dirt and rock foundations of the house. Dad was intrigued by this large space. It had no windows and Dad thought that it had all the makings of a "*české hospody*" (Czech tavern). He envisioned a few small tables with chairs in the body of the room. A small bar with a counter at one end and the walls, wooden of course, would be decorated with his collection of Czech mementoes and pictures. I think he even wanted to display framed newspaper clippings of his sporting exploits. When Dad got an idea into his head, he went at it full speed. Nothing was too difficult and soon the little passageway opposite the doorway became a building site. He arranged for the electrical connections to be made and he procured lengths of lumber and stored them here. He had some preliminary clearing to do on the soil and preparations for water drainage.

Soon we could hear the sound of sawing and hammering and slowly a wooden base and flooring emerged. The walls began to fill out with wooden panels. The wooden structure started to take shape. The bar had an overhead beam from which he hung a few samples of his hurricane lanterns. After about four months of work, he was ready to install the carpet. All his little trinkets and mementoes found their place in this "bar." His *české hospody* was nearing completion. However, when we all went in to help him celebrate the end of his project, we noticed that there was something seriously wrong. The floor had a slope in it, an eight inch difference in elevation from the bar end to the opposite wall! You walked very noticeably uphill or downhill, whichever was the case. This did not appear to faze him at all; he was very proud of his tavern. I asked him about the slope and he just dismissed me saying that it had a more rustic look this way. I then told him that he had a resident architect, namely his son-in-law Ivan, at hand and why had he not consulted with him on how to level the floor. I also added that there would have been no consultation charges. I do not think that this comment even registered with him. Thus, the house acquired this additional furnished room. I cannot recall it ever being used or that anybody spent any time there drinking *pivo* (beer) and eating *klobáski* (sausages). I think it later became a storage room; but, Dad had at least used some of his creative energy in implementing this project, and he was home!

The Mountain Lodge Affair

In 1980, Dad went skiing at Perisher Valley in the Snowy Mountains area of the Australian Alps and there he befriended a Czech family, the Homolkas. I am not certain whether Dad knew the Homolkas from India. I don't believe so, but they owned and operated a ski lodge in Perisher. We stayed there once and it was a true family run affair. In any case, Dad enjoyed the company of the Homolkas and from somewhere, I do not know the origins of the idea, he got extremely interested in the notion of owning and operating a ski chalet in Perisher Valley. I often wondered if the idea stemmed from his failed dream to own and operate a ski Bed and Breakfast pension in St. Anton, Austria. He spoke about this new idea often and, right from the start, I forcibly made it quite clear that the idea was not a good one. My objections to the idea remained strong, namely, that he saw this as a family run enterprise with roles for everyone. Mum would be responsible for the kitchen, Martina would look after the guest's rooms as the chief chambermaid, my role would be probably some sort of office help/accountant/taxi driver/waiter and Charley would assist in a somewhat similar role.

My father, of course, would be working at the reception, greeting the guests in his blue blazer and grey trousers (this had by now become my father's favourite clothing combination). In the evenings, he would be the local bon vivant and raconteur; after all, his life had a certain caché, having spent much of it in India and Europe. As the owner of a ski chalet, he would have been able to trade on his history as a prominent sportsman in Czechoslovakia and as a ski champion from India. Of all the roles that he envisaged for the rest of us, his own role was the best defined and best suited to his personality. His mind was made up and he ignored our objections even though Mom was ill, Martina and Ivan already had their own family and life, and I had a full-time job, my own home, and two children. Charley, that great outdoorsman, was probably the only one who may have found some enthusiasm for this grand scheme. For a while, it seemed that Dad would bulldoze his vision forward but other family issues emerged; and so, after about a year, the idea gradually evaporated. But there was absolutely no doubt in my mind, that he was restless and wanted to start something, be it a small project or a business opportunity.

Dad the Venture Capitalist

With the increasingly deteriorating condition of Mum's mental health and physical wellbeing, it was unfortunate that Dad did not appreciate or understand how serious the situation had become. My own feeling about this is that no one in this era, least of all Dad, knew anything about depression, and certainly nothing about its effects on people. I believe that my father saw everything through the lens of his own needs and plans; he was not capable of seeing life through another person's eyes. Therefore, he could not come to terms with Mum's total disinterest in his schemes. I think his response was that, if she remained married to him, he would have to go it alone. Gradually, ever since Dad's arrival, they had started to live their own lives and both progressed down different forks in the road. Dad met with his friends more frequently, some of them old ones and some new. The vast majority of them were Czechs. He knew few Australians and the only regular friends that I knew he still socialized with were the Gartleys, whom he knew from India, where Mr. Gartley had flown as a pilot for commercial airlines. They were now retired and living in Sydney.

Dad's favourite port of call became the Cosmopolitan Café in Double Bay, an eastern suburb of Sydney where much of the city's Jewish community lived. The Cosmopolitan had a very "European" feel about it and was a popular meeting place for affluent émigrés who had arrived from Europe after the War. The Cosmopolitan also had a band that played the sort of music that appealed to this old country European community. There may have been a Czech ring-in in the band because, whenever Dad arrived, he would call out, "*Ej Od Buchlova*" and they would play the famous Czech folk song, which originated in Buchlov, the village where Dad was born. Whenever Dad heard this beautiful, old Moravian folk song, tears would well up in his eyes and he would sing along. I personally think that the words are particularly beautiful.

Ej, od Buchlova větr věje	Behold, the wind is blowing from Buchlov,
už tej Kačence pentle bere	blowing Kačenka´s ribbons away.
Dneska nevěsta, zajtra žena,	Bride today, tomorrow woman,
dnes večer budeš začepená	Today in the evening you will be wed
Ty si Kačenko bílá růža	You Kačenka are a white rose,
tobě nebylo třeba muža	you didn´t need a man.
Tys mohla chodit po slobodě,	You could have swum freely,
jak ta rybička v bystrej vodě	like a fish in a brook.
Ty si Martine strom zelený	You Martin are a green tree,
tobě nebylo třeba ženy	you didn´t need a woman.
Tys mohl chodit po galánkách,	You could have met many sweethearts,
jak ten holúbek po hambálkách	like a pigeon on a roof.

After some time, I found out that Dad was socialising more and more with some of his new Czech friends and that he planned to become financially involved with a group that had started to promote a radically new technical process. Unfortunately, I cannot remember the details but, supposedly, when the prototype had been fully tested and developed, it would be an industry game changer. The promise was that this process had the potential to return the investors serious profits. The group's main stumbling block, naturally, was the lack of finance to complete the prototype and conduct the operational trials. The unfortunate thing was that Dad's experience in India had not prepared him for a totally different way of conducting business in Sydney. I believe that he trusted this group because they were Czech and because they all appeared to be reliable people. And so, rather stupidly, he became their financier and lent them some money on the basis of this "Cosmopolitan Café" camaraderie, without ever understanding the technology involved. Even worse, he did not conduct any due diligence on these men, nor did he enter into a simple contract that would, as a minimum, have spelled out the rules for his involvement and his "exit," should things go off the rails. As a result of this venture, they took him for a ride and he lost quite a lot of money that he could ill afford. This was a salutary lesson for him, and it also put paid to any plans for building and owning a ski chalet in Perisher Valley. No amount of playing "Ej, Od Buchlova" at the Cosmopolitan Café could ever ease the pain and hurt.

The Final Parting Between Mum and Dad

While they continued to live under the same roof, serious tensions had arisen between my parents. Dad made it quite clear that he had no intention of closeting himself at home. Now that he was free from the daily responsibilities of running a business, he wanted to enjoy life and was not interested in changing his ways. His argument was that his social activities encompassed visits to people at their homes, or meeting them at a restaurant or café, and that Mum always had the option of accompanying him when he went out. Mum's position was more home-centric, arguing that he had a family and a home and that he should spend more time with her at home and perhaps help with her medical issues. The latter suggestion, unfortunately, had no resonance with Dad, since he had no real appreciation of the nature of depression. Perhaps things may have been different for the two of them if awareness of the condition and appropriate medication had been available to treat the depression. But, in the 1970s, this was not the case. Dad assumed that she had no interest in his life and interests and, after several decades in India, there was no way that he wanted to spend the twilight of his years sitting in the kitchen making "small talk." In many ways, both laid blame for the situation on the other, hence finger-pointing seemed the easy option. The sad result for the extended family was that our parents had no strong emotional ties with their children or grandchildren, now numbering five: they were just too caught up in their own situation. Even small family celebrations like birthdays or other important family events were few and far between.

Dad possessed a loud voice, possibly a by-product of having to talk over the clatter of machinery in the factory. When he spoke or wished to make a point, it sounded like he was shouting. He could not help it and no matter how hard he tried to keep his voice down, it was quite loud and could be intimidating. At the very least, it heightened the tensions between him and Mum. Unfortunately, she could not accommodate it. I remember that I had to intervene a few times and ask him to tone it down, but with limited success. Obviously another solution for this impasse between them had to be found. He had a singular point of view that he considered to be correct. His reaction to any discussion or argument that ran counter to information he had acquired from the magazines he read or from television in Sydney was to just clam up and that ended the argument. Arguing with him was a totally futile exercise. I remember Mum taking me aside after one of these verbal jousts and saying, "Mikuško, if your father tells you that something is black and you know it is white, just tell him that it is black. We sidestep any potential disagreements and we all move on."

Eventually my parents agreed to live separately. None of us were involved in this decision. They simply agreed to sell the house and go their separate ways. So, in 1980, they put the house on the market and it sold about a month later. After the legal formalities, they split the monies from the sale and parted company. Mum already had her ideas about where she wanted to go. Over the years, when Mum experienced her problems, Martina had devoted a lot of time to her care. Martina had ceased to work full-time, although she still had the odd work engagements here and there. But, in the end, she had the time to attend to Mum. Ivan, her husband, worked as an architect and they lived quite close to the original family home. Mum agreed to use a portion of her proceeds from the sale to build a one-bedroom annex attached to their existing home. Her annex had its own front door entrance, private toilet and kitchen niche. There was also a small living room area with enough room for a sofa, small table, and a television set. And so, eventually, after the Annex was completed, Mum moved in and this became her home until the end of her days. Dad knew a family in the Sydney suburb of Turramurra who had a large basement-like area under the house. It was not a subterranean space but, as the house was built on a slope, it had its own natural entrance from the driveway. This is where Dad went to live the rest of his life. In the separation agreement, they had also decided that they would not get divorced. I do not think that either of them wanted to take this final step. They still had emotional attachments to each other and, besides, divorce had no place in their belief system.

What is ironic is that, after they separated and were no longer living under the same roof, they started to really develop a more civilised relationship with each other. They no longer had to justify themselves to the other and were now free to make their own decisions without feeling any pressure. Dad drove over to see Mum almost daily so that he could check to see how she was, do any shopping for her, or other little chores. Their interactions became quite tender. The only difference now was that they no longer lived under the same roof. It was quite touching. Dad continued to do the things that he always had, albeit at a much slower pace. He played chess with an old friend of his, Mr. Vohralik, and I remember him telling me how exasperated he was with their chess encounters. They both loved the game, but Dad's chess style meant using a lot of "fast" moves; whereas, Mr. Vohralik played at a measured pace that would have served him well at the chess world championships. This irritated Dad to no end. But they continued to play. I remember telling Dad that this might have been a tactic adopted by Vohralik precisely to irritate him and put him off his game; but he just shrugged that observation off.

Over the coming year, Dad slowed down noticeably and I do not recall that he went to the mountains to ski again, even though he loved to ski. Remarkably, during this time, my own relationship with him improved. To my surprise, when we met, he would listen sympathetically to my issues or problems and either offer advice or try to help. It was during this period that I finally got to spend time with him and talk extensively about many aspects of his life in Calcutta, including all the challenges that he had had to face. For probably the first time, I came away with the feeling that he cared. However, he never did admit to me, from the benefit of hindsight, that he regretted sending me away to boarding school. In his view, he had discharged one of his great responsibilities to me, Martina and Charley, in that he had given us the best education that he could afford. The emotional price that we had all had to pay was high, especially for me.

Although he did indicate that he had reflected on his personal life, in one respect he never changed. He hated Communists with a passion and this antipathy manifested itself in bizarre ways. He had a pathological hatred of the colour red. At one point, Muschi and I owned a red car; my father steadfastly refused to sit in it, so we were forever making alternate travel arrangements. If we had planned an outing together, and either Muschi or I turned up in clothes with any "red" in them, he would just say, "I am not going out with you." But I understood that his view had been shaped by his history and experiences with Communist regimes both in Czechoslovakia and West Bengal, and I came to respect this quirk of his personality.

While living in the Annex, Mum had become less and less well; she was now totally dependent on Martina. She hardly moved out of her place and even had to be coaxed to pay a visit to see some of her friends. Her few remaining Czech friends still invited her to their gatherings, but she generally went under duress and it was plain for all that she felt uncomfortable. Martina had taken over the management of her daily affairs and ensured that all her needs were met. I usually visited her on Sundays, when we sat down and tried to make some intelligent conversation. But, most of the time, our chats were just gossip or small talk. It was hard to see my mother in this state. But every now and again, there were flashes of comic relief when some episode in the past was resurrected. These were usually associated with Dad. When telling these stories, she would embellish and draw the story to a humorous conclusion. Sometimes when we met, she impressed on me her own words of wisdom. The one that I still remember and follow passionately is, "Remember, Miki, that life is not a dress rehearsal!" The other little pearl of wisdom given to me by Mum and which I do not always take heed of is, "God gave you two ears and one mouth; you should use them in that proportion." I admit to often transposing the two! When I think about it, she seemed to come to life when she told her stories, usually about Dad. Deep down, I believe that she never stopped loving him, but the scars of the past years could not be ignored and there appeared to be no way forward. It was truly sad to experience.

Dad's Visit to Breckenridge March/April 1983

In late 1982, Dad renewed contact with his American friends from the Second World War. He made plans with them for a reunion in America in March or April, 1983, in Breckenridge, Colorado, where Pat Gould lived. This was a well-known ski resort, so it was natural for them to meet there, reminisce, and spend some time skiing together. Mum was in no condition to travel, so she remained in Sydney. By all accounts, the skiing reunion was successful. Phil Seeling joined them, but unfortunately Frank Schuster could not get away from his farm in Texas. The newspaper, *The Summit Daily News*, reported the following:

> When the "war to end all wars" ended, the two Americans came home, and Hruska continued his business in Calcutta for some 33 years. "We kept up a torrid correspondence. One year I'd write, the next year they would answer," recalled Seeling.

> Looking back, Hruska quipped, "We were young and pretty then. Now we are only pretty." This re-union became their last.

Dad's Passing

After his trip to the US to catch with his friends, Dad's life became very simple; he spent it mostly visiting his friends in Sydney and in Melbourne. He still called on Mum most days at Castlecrag. On Sunday, 15 June 1987, I got a call from Ivan that Dad had suffered a massive heart attack while lying in bed watching the Australian TV program, *4 Corners*, and had been moved to Hornsby Hospital. This program had been one of his favourites and, to this day, I wonder which stories had been shown that night and if any of them had upset him enough to cause the heart attack. When I finally got to see him at the hospital, he had already passed away; my brother

Charley and I kept a short vigil over his body. Even though we had had a distant relationship for most of our lives, I found that, in his later years, we grew closer. That has been, and always will be, my endearing memory of him: that, at the end, he became the father that I had never really had. At the same time, when I saw him at the hospital, I could not help but reflect on his amazing life and the cards that had been dealt him as he negotiated the major historical events of the time. He certainly made an indelible mark on all of us. And, although we each had our own personal memories, he left one legacy to all the young men in his family - Charley, Ivan, Vincent, young Ivan and me - an appreciation of the gift that India had given us, a love of our Czech heritage and an insatiable love of the outdoors, in particular, the mountains.

Dad was cremated and, in 1990, a friend subsequently took his ashes to Czechoslovakia where they now lie alongside his beloved mother in Buchlov cemetery. And with this, his story came to an end, in a full circle from the country of his birth to India, to Australia, and finally back to the Czech Republic. I like to think that he would love to know that, at least when he returned home, that the *"zatracený komunisti"* (bloody Communists) were no longer there!

Mum's Stroke

A month after Dad's passing, on 14 July, Mum suffered a mild stroke which left her paralysed on one side of her body and with limited use of her arm. She was admitted to the Emergency Ward at the North Shore Hospital, where she was treated to stabilise the condition. After this immediate treatment at the hospital, she started to recover some partial mobility in her body and arms. However, she was still too weak to move and, after two weeks, was sent to the North Ryde Psychiatric Center for rehabilitation. In Mum's time, this facility offered specialized mental health care, but it also provided extended care and rehabilitation for adults who were recovering from strokes. Initially, because of a shortage of beds in the extended care ward, she was placed in the serious mental case ward where the hospital staff exercised strong security at all ingress and egress points. I visited her once in this secure area and came face to face with the reality of life for mental patients, something that absolutely horrified me. Very soon, we managed to get her transferred to the much more benign extended care ward, where she spent about a month until she recovered sufficiently to return home to Castlecrag.

Mum's Passing

About a year before Mum's death, I noticed that, on my visits to her, she came alive only when she reminisced at length about her life with her parents, her early life with Dad, and the happy years in Calcutta. At times, she even seemed to reflect on some of the major decisions that affected her life. During these meetings with Mum, I learned many of the stories that I have recounted in this book. In particular, she relentlessly questioned why it had been necessary to leave Calcutta just for the sake of a huge house. She would very much have preferred to stay in the city until the factory was sold and then move to Sydney. Unfortunately, she had little or no voice in the decisions that affected our family. I sometimes believe that she was a victim of the times, a product of a generation where women did not question decisions made by the male head of the family. Certainly, independent thought was not nurtured. And it became even less possible the more successful my father became in business. On 11 February, 1988, she got news that her eldest brother Noris had passed away; this hit her quite hard, as he had really been the link to her past, something that they had kept active through their letters. By now, she was totally house bound and was finally released from her suffering, on 4 October, 1990.

My brother-in-law, Ivan, bless his heart, later took her ashes to Otrokovice where she is buried in the family columbarium[187] in the little cemetery in Otrokovice. Today, her urn rests next to her mother, Uncle Noris, and other members of her family.

When I reflect now on both their lives, it is clear to me that their passage in life from the "West" to the "East" and back again would have happened much earlier but for the Second World War and the subsequent Communist takeover of Czechoslovakia. And ours would have been a very different family story. This was a true case of "No Way Back Home."

And with the telling of their story, we can now leave their tent……..

---

187 A columbarium is a place where the urns holding the cremated remains of family can be stored.

CHAPTER 11

Consequences

It is not often that we have a chance to reflect on how the circumstances and decisions of many decades have affected the lives of our families. Writing this book has allowed me the time, not only to put together the stories and memories of my parents, but to try and make sense of it all.

My Reflections on the Decision to Leave Czechoslovakia

Without doubt the pivotal event of my parents' Czech years was their recognition that war was coming to Europe and the related decision to take up friend Tomik Bata's suggestion that they leave Zlin for Calcutta, where they could start a new life. They were lucky to have known Tomáš Bata. Had they stayed in Czechoslovakia, the questions that immediately come to mind, aside from whether they would even have survived the war, are these: "Would it have been any different for them as a couple if they had stayed behind and the children had been born in Czechoslovakia? Would our parents have been different people?" The answer for me, anyway, is definitely in the affirmative. The great leveller for their personal relationship would have been work and the presence of a supportive extended family. They would both have worked together for Bata; my father would likely never have started his own factory because the entrepreneurial opportunities under the Communists would have been nil. I think the integrity of the family unit would have survived, as both Mum and Dad would have been equal contributors in its well-being. History shows that their extended family in Czechoslovakia, their brothers and sisters, had much more stable family relationships, despite the oppressive nature of Communism. Family history indicates that *they* were survivors.

Departure from Czechoslovakia

Mum and Dad were neither economic migrants, nor political exiles, but a strange combination of the two. The twist here was that their decision to leave was heavily influenced by the prospect of war in Europe. There was a strong possibility that the factory where they worked would be shut down. Their world was still affected by the Depression and there were not many other jobs to go to. They had the opportunity to begin a new life in India where a job would be waiting, and they took it. Obviously, they had no idea what was actually going to happen in Czechoslovakia. In fact, I hesitate to use the word "migrant" with reference to my parents because it implies that they had no desire to return to their country of origin. I do not believe that this was the case with them. At the outset, I think that they saw their departure for India as a short-term measure; and, frankly, it was a great adventure. But I think they fully intended to return to Czechoslovakia after the War was over (if, indeed, a war came at all). But, with the Communist takeover in 1948, any opportunity to return evaporated; at this point, they could definitely have been described as political migrants.

The Bata and Metal Box Years

I am convinced that Dad's early working years in Bata were pivotal to his future business success in Calcutta. On his arrival at Batanagar, he soon realised that the Bata expatriate community was a closed society, with its cliques and informal pecking order. Later arrivals like my father found themselves on the outside looking in; they would never be able to access the levels of power and acceptance that were reserved for the "first" families. This gulf between early and late arrivals manifested itself, for instance, in the way houses were allocated and in the way the company handled its internal problems and disputes. This unofficial code of preferment led to bitter internal tensions. For a strong personality like Dad's, his departure from Bata must have been a relief on the one hand, just as much as it was a welcome challenge on the other. Fortunately for our family, Dad was able to secure work in a very short time with Metal Box.

Even though he had a young family and there were few jobs, Dad's implicit belief in himself carried him through uncertainty and adversity. To begin with, leaving Batanagar meant that Mum and Dad had to learn English quickly. Reflecting later on these events, Mum would say that, although times were tough, they were happy years. They felt they were building something together. It was at Metal Box that Dad learnt his trade in the machine shop. Although he had no formal qualifications in engineering, he brought to Metal Box a wealth of practical experience which, in the early days, provided some job security. At Metal Box, he also encountered and had to solve many of the problems of making the machine shop environment work; this experience, in addition to the technical skills he was acquiring, would serve him well when he eventually left that company.

The management skills Dad had acquired at Bata, and the technical skills learned at Metal Box were the building blocks for establishing his own company. Was it perhaps happenstance that they came to live at 53 Chowringhee Road and that Mr. Cargnelli lived on the next floor above? This congruence led to the idea of producing the hurricane lantern and developing the means to mass produce and sell it. It was the foundation of his future success in India. This achievement also provided him the financial and other tangible means to support not only the families back home, but to help those most in need in Calcutta, through his close friendship with Fr. Gabric.

In a sense, Mum and Dad were used to being outsiders by the time they moved from Batanagar to Calcutta, so they were well prepared for their treatment there by the British. Not only were my parents not British, they were not Western Europeans, which meant that Dad's British bosses at Metal Box treated Mum and Dad as second-class citizens. They had to swallow their pride on many occasions when confronted by this insular attitude. It was at this point that their resourcefulness came into play. Mum and Dad simply made friends with Indians and with other members of the non-British, European community and were well accepted and received for who they were as people. This was their real moment of creating a home in a foreign land.

Dad had an engaging personality; in many ways he was the heat source in any room, with his commanding presence and loud voice. He was a proud man and extremely confident in his own judgement. I still have a vivid picture of this human furnace in social situations. He was absolutely magnetic. All eyes turned to him. He was loud, proud, imperious, and intractable. He had that gift of the exaggerated forcefulness of an ambitious man in a new country. With increasing business success, Dad's personality traits were magnified. He became more and more inflexible. His message was, "My way, or the highway." His views were very black and white.

Blending into Calcutta and India

Within some émigré communities, the migrants blend into the new society and interest in their ancestral country gradually wanes. With the passing years, the bonds are weakened and the children lose all family contact as well as their ancestral culture and language. But the Czechs, including Mum and Dad, blended into the prevailing Indian cultures in an adaptive way. For many years after their arrival, they still planned to return to Czechoslovakia, so they retained their culture and language. But they had to fit into colonial India for practical reasons. They had to make a choice about which culture they developed a closer affinity to. As the contrast between British and Indian culture was quite large, it seemed easier to transition toward British culture. And, as a practical consideration, British culture was still where the power lay. So, my parents learned English, became familiar with British customs and club life, and watched very closely the ways in which British parents viewed parenting and education.

Some Aspects of British Colonial Culture in Calcutta

Calcutta in the years prior to 1947 was very much a man's world. Men generally made decisions that affected them first before family considerations came in to play. This is why, in this British colonial culture, club life was dominant. The clubs provided sporting outlets for golf, tennis, swimming, horse-riding, and shooting; and the men gravitated to these quite readily. The lives of British women, on the other hand, revolved around tea clubs, bridge parties, horse-riding and occasionally other sports like tennis or swimming. Dad adapted easily into this cultural mindset and, although he was not a party animal or even a club-going aficionado, he was very much of the mold that saw the man as the fount of all wisdom as regards family decisions. Most of these decisions radiated outward from him first, then to Mum, and to the children after that. The result, for example, was his unilateral decision to go alone for a skiing holiday in Kashmir during the War while Mum stayed behind in Calcutta to look after the family. Mum did not have a strong enough personality to put her foot down and say something. With business success, this sense of personal entitlement regarding family decisions amplified. Later on, in post-independence India, he decided that he needed to go on three separate mountaineering expeditions to Sikkim and Nepal. Naturally this decision was grounded in his love for mountains. But I believe that the truth lies more in the old male ethos leftover from the Raj - for my father, it was still a man's world, so he had a right to indulge in adventure. Again, Mum was left to fend for herself, but now she had two children to look after. In my own case, Dad decided to go trekking during the very months that I was back in Calcutta for the school holidays, thus depriving me of his company for three of the years that I was in boarding school.

I believe that, if circumstances had been different and, if the family had made a life for itself in Czechoslovakia, even under a Communist state, this type of behaviour might not have happened, or would have been severely curtailed. For a start, Mum would have been working and contributing to the household and she would have had the support of her immediate family in responding to my father's schemes. My father would not have had such a range of opportunities for indulging himself at the expense of his family. Czech parenting models would have been available to him on a daily basis. And pressure from extended family would have curbed any tendencies he might have had to colour outside the lines. In short, I think that their parenting would have been different because it would have been modeled on their own culture. As it was, they fell under the sway of a foreign mindset. I also believe that the difficult relationships between my father and his children as well as the future estrangement between him and my mother had their genesis in these early years living under the influence of the Raj.

Effects of British Culture on Raising Children

Most British families in India sent their children to boarding schools in England, where they had families who could assume guardianship of the children over the summer months. This practice effectively cut parents and children off from one another for years. The Czechs in India did not come from this type of educational tradition. In Czechoslovakia, children attended day schools close to where they lived. In fact, Mum was fairly typical of others in the Czech community in the pre-war era, in that she had a very limited schooling experience in Moravia, being forced to leave early in order to support her siblings. But, even in such difficult circumstances, Czech families were able to stay together. In India, following British tradition, the best schools for expatriate children were English-style boarding schools. So, for my parents and their friends in the Czech community, who were in the unique situation of being able to provide something for their own children that they themselves had never had (that is, a good education), the only real option was to send their children away to school. Someone had even done the homework for the community by identifying target schools, namely North Point in Darjeeling for boys and Loreto House for girls. One of the best choices in England for Catholic colonials from India was Stonyhurst.

Consequences of the Schooling Decision

Of the three of us, I was the only child to spend his entire school life as a boarder far away from home. Martina was originally sent to Loreto in Darjeeling, but quite soon refused to be there and was returned to Calcutta to attend a day school. Charley also spent most of his school life in day schools, but in Sydney, not Calcutta. As for me, I learned to be independent at a very early age, as I stumbled through the boarding school filter, from being a tender six-year-old and emerging on the other side as a young man. What the experience taught me was to rely on my own wits and judgment. But the price I paid was heavy. Looking back after all these years, I can honestly say that I never really knew my parents or siblings, nor they me. I never experienced the daily involvement of a mother and father in my growing up. And I never learned the lessons of family life that most would consider both normal and necessary in today's world. Mum and Dad paid all the bills, but this was never the ideal parenting model, nor an example for their children to follow when raising their own families. I often ask myself why they followed a path that was so counterintuitive to what they had grown up with.

How much different our lives could have been had our parents been involved in our growing up and helped us make good decisions, we shall never know. It is easy to be judgmental in hindsight, but this is definitely one of the most dramatic early consequences that India had on our family.

The Humanitarian Behaviour of these "Trapped Exiles"

In many respects, the Batamen and their families were trapped in India by world events. First the War and then the Communist takeover in Czechoslovakia meant that they really couldn't go home. So, they set about making a home in India, whether within the precincts of Batanagar, or in Calcutta. In my father's case, once he had established himself in business, he began to do what he could for others. Partly because of the influence of Fr. Gabric, Dad found a practical outlet for his natural generosity. It is hard to prove, but my feeling is that Mum and Dad were grateful for their success and wished to help in whatever way they could. Thus, Dad made himself freely available to people like Fr. Gabric, Mother Teresa, the Tibetan refugees and others, with both material and labour (access to plumbers, electricians, carpenters, brick layers, general handymen, etc.) and financial help. With the advent of Communism in Czechoslovakia and the devastating effects that regime had on people's lives, he went to quite extraordinary lengths to support both his and Mum's families. And, when I think about this aspect of my parents' incredible generosity, I believe that the Indian side of life in a British colony changed their values to thinking more about the less fortunate.

Business World

When I started to write this book, and as I assembled the timeline of our family's history, I finally became aware of all the travel my Dad paid for. As Dad's business prospered, he and Mum started to travel more and more to and from Europe. And there were my trips to and from boarding school in England. Then came my sister Martina's travels to and from Switzerland and, when I started to think about all this air travel in an age when there were no discounts or budget airlines, I began to realise that my father must have been making very good money from the factory in Calcutta. Money was not something that was ever mentioned in our family, so I literally had never thought about it until I began to piece our history together. As I sifted through documents and recalled stories, I also came to appreciate the fact that he supported the Czech "family" not only with actual money but with tangible goods: cars, pharmaceuticals, clothing, etc. In addition, there were the numerous holidays that he took in Europe with the whole family, sometimes associated with the purchase of an expensive car. And finally, there were his invitations for some members of the Czech family to visit us in Sydney. The evidence kept mounting. I have no idea how much money I brought into Switzerland as my father's "bag man," but these proceeds partly financed my sister at her finishing school in Lausanne. Then he bought the land in Sydney and built a huge house on it with a swimming pool. It gradually dawned on me that he had indeed been extremely successful in his business in India, despite the latter years of strikes and labour unrest.

But there was another aspect of Dad's business world that needs to be mentioned. He was operating in a business community with some of the shrewdest businessmen, namely the Marwaris, whom one could hope to meet and he had earned their respect. This was a business world where your word was your bond; your very survival depended on it. And it cut both ways. When the Marwaris made a request for more lanterns to sell, Dad moved heaven and earth to meet the need. When they advised that there would be a delay in payment, it usually would be for a short period of time, but this was a community that met its obligations. Likewise, when wages were to be paid in the factory and Dad had a temporary cash flow problem in meeting the deadline, he knew that he could rely on his

Marwari business contacts in Burrabazar to advance him the shortfall. The remarkable aspect of all this mutual trust is that there was never any need for contracts or IOUs or lawyers to establish any mutual obligation.

I am sure that there were other countries that had such business ethics; indeed, I think that, in many rural communities around the world to this day, this is still the way that business works. I admired this aspect of Dad's dealings immensely, but it was precisely this experience of the way it was done in Calcutta that later proved to be his undoing. He came to Sydney with a naïve belief that business would be conducted this way in Australia as well. But, it wasn't and he was taken for a ride by his Sydney business partners and lost quite a lot of money. To be sure, there were other contributing factors, such as his blind trust in his own decision-making ability and refusal to listen to good advice that contributed to this bad experience. I think it is sad that, in the West today, we appear to have lost this sense of personal responsibility in business. A man's word is no longer his bond. Now, we have to resort to paper and a battery of lawyers to prescribe and protect every step of the way through a commercial transaction.

Mum and Dad's Views of their Experience

But the important question is what Mum and Dad themselves would have said at the start and then at the end of their life journey. At the start they would probably have expressed relief that they had not experienced the War first hand. They might have referred to the prospect of an exciting adventure in India. They would probably have believed that they could return to Czechoslovakia. They certainly would not have anticipated that they would spend the next forty years in Calcutta let alone end up in Australia.

What would be their view of living in Calcutta? I think that Dad would acknowledge that Calcutta both made him and broke him. It gave him opportunities that he grasped with both hands. But the developing political situation in Bengal, the growing acceptance of Communism there and the labour unrest, proved to be his undoing.

Dad would probably have been very satisfied with his business success. He would also acknowledge that he did not anticipate how difficult it would be to sell the factory and move to Australia. He might also concede that, if he had known how difficult it was to disengage from Calcutta, he would have deferred the decision to build in Sydney and send Mum there to an empty house. I am also confident that he never really understood the impact of this forced separation on Mum's health and their marriage. I think, on the other hand, that Dad would feel he had done what was expected of him as a father. He cared and provided for his family, he gave us the best education that he could afford; and he allowed us to enjoy a comfortable life in India and Australia.

Mum, on the other hand, admitted to me in later life that she grew to love Calcutta, as she got to understand its rhythms and flows much better than Dad. She loved the people in Calcutta and their humanity and she was truly sad to have to leave it behind. This life was taken from her by the decisions Dad had taken on behalf of everyone. For me, this was the real tragedy for Mum. The flame that had nurtured her spirit and life was well and truly extinguished in Sydney.

What are my Conclusions?

So why do I still regard Calcutta with so much affection? In the first place, it is the city of my birth and I still view it as the home that gave me my values in life. My attitude to Calcutta can be summed up in an observation once made by the historian Herodotus in the fifth century BC. He wrote that "Egypt is the gift of the Nile," because Egyptian civilization depended and throve on the Nile. In many ways, I see a parallel for our family with Calcutta and India. My parent's lives were "the gift of India." It gave them a home after they left Czechoslovakia; it provided them with safe haven; it offered them an opportunity to prosper; and it afforded them a chance to live in a free and democratic country, no matter how flawed that democracy might have seemed at times. But its greatest gift was that it taught them important human values that sustained them in their later lives, whether it was in ethical business practice or a spirit of caring for people who were less fortunate than they.

Our relationship with Calcutta was, in many ways, a physical one. Mum and Dad lived there, pursued their daily lives there, raised their family there and, even though they were not children of India, they became attached to the country in many other tangible ways. While living in Sydney, Mum often expressed a strong nostalgia for Calcutta and India, a form of "home-sickness"; the bonds between her and Calcutta were deep indeed.

As for the Hruska children, I believe that our Calcutta experience equipped us for life: the city was a catalyst for the love of observation, for both the written and spoken word, and for the history of our environs. In such a rich stew of humankind, what better place to teach us about the human condition? In later years, when living in the West, I always had the Calcutta experience against which to question western values. For instance, in Calcutta as children, we had to come to terms with the impact of poverty. We could not avoid it. I learnt very early on to accept that poverty was a fact of life and to look for the humanity that surrounded us everywhere. I developed a profound respect for the daily struggle of the poor and to appreciate the grace and kindness that often came from those in this condition. And I thank Mum and Dad for the lesson never to take for granted or misuse my privileged position in society. The Calcutta experience also taught me something about the use and abuse of power. Anyone living there at the time was frustrated by the ineptitude of those leaders who had the ways and means to rectify many of the city's problems, but who did nothing.

Indeed, although the city was often overwhelmed by natural disasters and human catastrophes, its political leaders and civil servants concentrated more on games of political opportunism, or plain neglect, than on trying to address its very real problems. As an example, less time and energy could have been spent on the endless committees involved in renaming streets and more time in solving such problems as providing adequate housing, safe drinking water, and proper disposal of sewage. Other aspects of religious intolerance and religious snobbery certainly played their part.

But this book is not about tragedy, it is about the human endeavour that survives in the midst of misfortune; it's about those people who make the world a better place in spite of all the odds.

And so, I end with a reminder from Stephen Hawking, a scientific thinker whom I admire:

> *Remember to look up at the stars and not down at your feet. Try*
> *to make sense of what you see and wonder about what makes the*

universe exist. Be curious. And however difficult life may seem, there is always something you can do and succeed at. It matters that you don't just give up.[188]

Mum and Dad's life started with so much promise when they left Czechoslovakia. They lived a largely happy life in India, a place that challenged them to develop their skills and broaden their thinking. Slowly, Calcutta accepted them into community life. And these good times over a period of four decades sustained them later when the family disintegrated and scattered. Would it have been any different had they stayed in Czechoslovakia? I think so. The pervasive hand of Communism would most likely have destroyed my father's spirit as it did for so many who either had little education or were unwilling to surrender to the ideals of the Party. The family, most probably, would have remained together as a unit but any personal development of inherent potential would have been limited.

When my brother and sister and I think about our growing up, we are always brought back to the city itself, a human place, filled with enigmas and contradictions. It taught us to appreciate what life sends us. Yes, our family's journey had its own tragedy shaped by individual personalities and by the history and politics of the times but, despite this, we retain our love and affection for our benighted parents and for Mother India.

188 Accessed at Goodreads: https://www.goodreads.com/quotes/490245-remember -to-look-up-at-the-stars-and-not-down

GLOSSARY

Bhangis the sweepers and scavengers, outcasts even among outcasts

bidi a poor man's cigarette, usually with some tobacco grounds wrapped and rolled up in a tendu leaf and fastened with a thread

bishti mobile water seller

bukha hungry

burra big

Burrabazar large bazaar

burra khana a big meal or feast

burra Kobara Sampa large cobra

bustee slum

chapatti wheat pancake

chai tea

chakra a thunderbolt

chana street snack

chappal sandal

chata umbrella

chawal rice

chhurpi processed, Tibetan, yak milk cheese

chini sugar

chokras young kids

choli type of woman's blouse

chor bazaar thieves' market

chota small

chowkidar caretaker

Chu river

Chula a small, portable, cow dung, charcoal or wood-burning oven. The interior and exterior of the chula frame is plastered with a mud-brick mixture and has a smooth finish. At the bottom is an opening where the fuel is fed in. The covering may be a grill top, but is usually open so that the cook can rest a pot, pan, or even a skewer there. The chula can also be used as a heater.

chuti holiday

dacoit robber or armed bandit

dhal a dish based on red or brown lentils

dharma a set of natural universal codes of living and conduct prescribed in the Hindu scriptures, the observance of which allows adherents to live happy and contented lives and provides spiritual discipline

dhobi person who washes clothes

dhoti-kurta traditional men's dress consisting of a roll of cloth about 12-15 ft. long, wrapped around the waist, and secured by passing the end between the legs and tucking it into the waist

gaddi seat

ghar house

gilli danda a game played with a long wooden stick (the danda) and a roundish piece of wood (the gilli). The object of the game is to hit the gilli up into the air with the danda from a fulcrum and, while it is in the air, hit it as far as you can and then run to an agreed place before your opponent retries the gilli.

ghora gharrie horse-drawn carriage

golgappa street snack

godown warehouse

goonda violent troublemaker

harijan Indian who belonged to the lowest social stratum in India's caste system.

hartals strike actions that usually involved the shut-down of a workplace or public disruption through protest rallies, processions, and general civil disobedience

Hum kya cahate haim What do we want?

Jai Hind Jindabad Long live India

Jhall Muri spiced puffed wheat

juta unclean, unwashed after use

katcha poor, or inferior

kameez shirt

Kala chai, khoi dudh ne manta, merwan only black tea, no milk, please

karma a belief that anything that we say or do has a cause and effect. A good deed performed will earn a future good deed, and vice versa for bad deeds. Karma is like a balance sheet that keeps track of all rewards and punishments earned from a person's past conduct. If a person has good karma, that person can be freed from her current station to another in her reincarnation on death.

khana food

Kisan farmer

kulhar the little clay cups from which tea is drunk

kurta a loose shirt falling either just above or somewhere below the knees of the wearer

lathi a medium sized truncheon

mali gardener

marwa a local brew made from fermented millet seeds

Memsahib a European woman in colonial India

Mera nam Baswant hai My name is Baswant

masala muri street snack

mochi shoe and sandal repairer

moja sock

monkey wallah a travelling showman who uses monkeys to put on a show

Muni-ma, pani pampa kholem Muni, open up the water pump!

nai barber, hairdresser, beauty parlour worker

Nawab semi-independent Muslim ruler of an Indian state

nikalo take down

paan a dry betel leaf which is folded into a triangular shape and filled with finely crushed areca nut, cardamom, grated coconut, and small amounts of crushed candy and held together with slaked lime paste and chewed with much relish

pani chokra water boy

paisa money

pandal marquee

panka ceiling fan

pani chokras water boys

Pani dedho, jaldi, jaldi Quickly, quickly, bring me water!

Puja festival

pukka perfect

Rabindra Sangeet literally, Songs of Rabindra: a performance of songs written and composed by Rabindranath Tagore

rasogolla a divine, extremely sweet, Indian sweetmeat

sabzi wallah the vegetable seller

sadhu holy man

Sahib mister, sir

Sahib, sahib, khana manta Sir, Sir, I want some food!

Sari a garment worn by women consisting of a fold of cloth, typically 6 to 9 yards long. It is assembled by wrapping around the waist, with one end finally draped over the shoulder, baring the midriff. The sari is worn with different styles of fitted bodice commonly called a *choli*.

shikara a distinctive gondolier type of water taxi seen in Srinagar

sirdar leader

suttee this was a traditional practice where a Hindu widow would cremate herself on her husband's funeral pyre in order to fulfill her true role as wife

tamasha goings-on

tandoor a bell-shaped clay oven

Tawaif female singers and dancers and their accompanying musicians: stringed and tabla drum players

Teli Bhaja a crisp, salty fritter, usually made with potato, onion, or a vegetable such as brinjal that is coated in gram-floured batter and deep-fried in mustard oil

Thora chini dedho Give me some sugar.

tola a very traditional Indian unit of mass equal to about half an ounce

Topee/topi a pith helmet to protect the wearer from the sun

unda wallah egg seller

CZECH

ahoj Czech greeting

anděl a winged angel

babička an affectionate Czech word for grandmother

blázen fool or idiot

bramborová polévka potato soup

bratr filozof brother philosopher

buchty cakes

katolický hovada a paraziti Catholic rubbish and parasites!

čert a horned devil

česká hospoda Czech tavern

česneková polévka garlic soup

Co Čech, to muzikant Whoever is Czech is a musician.

Děkuji Thank you.

detektivky detective books

do prdele literally means "up yours!"

důlkové koláčky jam-filled thumbprint cookies

důstojný pán Reverend Father

frťan (dát si frťana) snort of Slivovitz

hajzl bog

hergot sakrament God Sacrament

hospoda tavern or pub

hovězí guláš s knedlíkem Beef goulash stew with dumplings

hovorová čeština spoken Czech

hňup half-wit

hrad castle

Jo, děkuji. Jsou velmi chutné. Yes, thank you. It is very tasty.

Ježíš Maria Jósefe Jesus Mary and Joseph

Ježíšek Baby Jesus

Katolický odpadky a paraziti Catholic rubbish and parasites

Kostel svatého Martin Church of the Holy Martin

Karlův most Charles Bridge

Kde domov můj Where is my country?

Kde máte záchod? Where is your bathroom?

klobásky sausages

knedlíky dumplings

koláče cakes

Kralická Bible the Kralice Bible

Kronika Trojánská Trojan Chronicle

krucifix crucifix

krucinál damn

kuchyňská čeština Kitchen Czech

Ruzyně Airport in Prague

Má Vlast My Country

magor retard

Malá Strana Lesser Town

máslové pečivo buttered bread

Měla babka v kapse brabce, brabec babce v kapse píp. Zmáčkla babka brabce v kapse, brabec babce v kapse chcíp. Grandma had a sparrow in her pocket and the sparrow made a sound. Grandma pressed the sparrow and it died.

Mikuláš Festival of St. Nicholas

Musím jít srát! Kde je záchod? I need to have a crap! Where is your bathroom?

Národní obrození National Revival

Nazdar Greetings

Nazdar důstojný pane (Greetings, Reverend Father.)

Nový svět New World

obchodní dům Department Store

Obecná čeština Common Czech

Ovocné knedlíky fruit dumplings

Palác Knih Palace of Books

Palačinky pancakes

pálenka slivovitz, a fairly potent transparent liquid with a slightly oily texture but with the kick of a mule and which could double up as paint stripper

papuče slippers

pivo beer

polib mi prdel lick my rear

potok little stream

sakra blast it or hell

Škoda lásky a popular Czech folk song also known in English as "Roll out the Barrel"

Slav/ Sláv nebo Slovan A term that refers to ethnically related groups whose origins can be traced to the western fringes of the Eurasian Steppes. These Slavic groups include the Czechs, Slovaks, Poles, Ruthenes (Ukrainians), Russians, Slovenians, Serbs, and also the Bulgarians.

Spisovná čeština Literary Czech

Staré město Old Town

Staroměstské náměstí Old Town Square

Štědrý večer Christmas eve or evening

Strč prst skrz krk Stick your finger through your throat!

Sudetenland a compound word where "land" means country and "Sudeten" is the German name of the Sudetes Mountains, which run along the northern Czech border and Lower Silesia in Poland. However, Sudetenland included areas well beyond those mountains.

Svatý Václave Good King Wenceslas

tepláky track suit

Třistatřiatřicet stříbrných křepelek přeletělo přes třistatřiatřicet stříbrných střech Three hundred and thirty-three silver quails flew over three hundred and thirty-three silver roofs.

trouba nitwit

trouba hloupá stupid nitwit

Utopenci pickled sausages

Už té mám az po krk I've had it up to here with you!

Václavské náměsti Wenceslas Square

vanilkové rohlíčky vanilla crescents rolled in confectioners' sugar

vánočka a braided Christmas bread

vánoční cukroví Christmas baking

Zatraceně damn

zatracený katolický zloději Bloody Catholic thieves!

zatracený komunisti Bloody Communists!

zelí pickled cabbage

Zemský sněm the name of the Parliament in Brno

FRENCH

allée avenue

foie gras goose liver

tableaux morts visions of death

GERMAN

Arbeitszeugnis work certificate
Bahnhofstrasse Station Street
bratwurst mit senf pork, veal, or beef sausage with mustard
Empiresaal Empire Salon
Gasthof guest house
Haydnsaal Haydn Salon
Platz place
realpolitik literally, pragmatic politics based on practical rather than ideological or moral principles
Schloss castle
Schwarzwald Black Forest

HUNGARIAN

Csárdás a traditional Hungarian folk song
friss fresh
puszta a large tract of Hungarian grasslands where there is extensive cattle-raising
Szegedinsky Guláš goulash from Szeged in Hungary

SPANISH

El Pescador the Fisherman

OTHER

lingua franca a language that is adopted as a common language between speakers whose native languages are different
mofussil a term widely used in India and Bangladesh referring to the regions of India outside the three British East India Company capitals of Bombay, Calcutta and Madras; hence, parts of a country outside an urban centre; the regions, rural areas.

BIBLIOGRAPHY

Agnew, Hugh. *The Czechs and the Lands of the Bohemian Crown.* Stanford, CA: Hoover Institution Press, 2004.

Allen, Charles. *Kipling Sahib: India and the Making of Rudyard Kipling.* New York: Pegasus Books, 2009.

Baros, Jan. *The First Decade of Batanagar.* Batanagar: Club for the Graduates of Bata School, 1945.

Beneš, Edvard. *Mnichovské Dny. Pameti.* Prague: Svoboda Press, 1968.

Bourke-White, Margaret. *Halfway to Freedom: A Report on the New India.* New York: Simon and Schuster, 1949.

Chaudhuri, Nirad C. *The Autobiography of an Unknown Indian.* Bombay: Jaico Publishing House, 1951.

-----------------------. *The East is East and the West is West.* Calcutta: Mitra and Ghosh, 1996.

-----------------------. *Thy Hand, Great Anarch! India 1921-1952.* London: Chatto & Windus, 1987.

Chaudhuri, Sukanta, ed. *Calcutta, the Living City. Volume 1: The Past.* Oxford: Oxford University Press, 1990.

-----------------------. *Calcutta, the Living City. Volume 2: The Present and the Future.* Oxford: Oxford University Press, 1990.

Clark, Christopher. *The Sleepwalkers: How Europe went to War in 1914.* London: Penguin Books, 2012.

Cohen, Leonard. "Suzanne." *Parasites of Heaven.* Toronto: McClelland and Stewart, 1966.

Cowasjee, Saros and K.S Duggal, eds. *Orphans of the Storm: Stories on the Partition of India.* Kolkata: Publishers' Distributors, 1995.

Dalrymple, William. *City of Djinns.* London: Harper Collins, 1993.

Das, Durga. *India From Curzon to Nehru and After.* NY: John Day Co., 1970.

Das, Suranjan. *Communal Riots in Bengal, 1905-1947.* Oxford: Oxford University Press, 1991.

Das, Soumitra. *A Jaywalkers Guide to Calcutta.* Mumbai: Eminence Designs, 2007.

de Riencourt, Amaury. *The Soul of India.* London: Jonathan Cape, 1961.

Demetz, Peter. *Prague in Black and Gold: Scenes from the Life of the City.* New York: Farrar, Strauss and Giroux, 1997.

Frater, Alexander. *Chasing the Monsoon.* London: Penguin Books, 1990.

Gandhi Heritage Portal, *Harijan,* 1.1 (11 Feb. 1933) https://www.gandhi-heritageportal.org/journals-by-gandhiji/harijan.

Guha, Ramchandra, ed. *Makers of Modern India.* Cambridge, MA: Harvard University Press, 2011.

Guha, Ramchandra. *India after Gandhi: The History of the World's Largest Democracy.* New York: Harper Collins, 2008.

Hajari, Nisid. *Midnight's Furies: The Deadly Legacy of India's Partition.* New York: Houghton Mifflin Harcourt, 2015.

Herman, Arthur. *Gandhi and Churchill: The Epic Rivalry that Destroyed an Empire and Forged our Age.* New York: Random House, 2008.

Ivanov, Miroslav. *Sága o životé Jana Bati a jejo bratra Tomáše.* Nakladatelství XYZ, s.r.o., 2008.

Kamra, Sukeshi. *Bearing Witness: Partition, Independence, End of the Raj.* Calgary: University of Calgary Press, 2002.

Keneally, Tom. *Three Famines Sydney.* Australia: Random House, 2010.

Khan, Yasmin. *The Great Partition: The Makings of India and Pakistan.* New Delhi: Viking, 2007.

------------------. *The Raj at War: A People's History of India's Second World War.* London: The Bodley Head, 2015.

Kipling, Rudyard. "A Tale of Two Cities." In *Verse Inclusive Edition, 1885-1918*. London: Hodder and Stoughton, n.d. 86-88.

Kouba, Karel. "Bata's Zlin in Czechoslovakia, 1918-1938: A Model of a High Modernist City." Paper presented at the Midwest Slavic Conference, Columbus, OH. March 3-5, 2005.

Kumar, Chandra and Mohinder Puri. *Mahatma Gandhi: His Life and Influence*. London: William Heinemann 1982.

Lelyveld, Joseph. *Great Soul: Mahatma Gandhi and His Struggle with India*. New York: Random House, 2012.

Longfellow, Henry Wadsworth. "Sunrise on the Hills." *Longfellow's Poetical Works*. London: Routledge, 1891.

Markovits, Claude. "The Calcutta Riots of 1946." *The Encyclopedia of Mass Violence*. 5th November, 2007.

Marquez, Gabriel Garcia. *Living to Tell the Tale*. Tr. Edith Grossman. New York: Vintage, 2004.

Merchey, Jason A., *Building a Life of Value: Timeless Wisdom to Inspire and Empower Us*. Little Moose Press, 2005.

Moorhouse, Geoffrey. *Calcutta*. London: Weidenfeld and Nicholson, 1971.

------------------------. *India Britannica*. London: William Collins, 1983.

Mountbatten, Pamela. *India Remembered*. London: Pavilion Books, 2007.

Mukerjee, Madushree. *Churchill's Secret War: The British Empire and the Ravaging of India During World War II*. New York: Perseus Books, 2010.

Panek, Jaroslav, Oldrich Tůma, et al. *A History of the Czech Lands*. Prague: Karolinum Press, 2009.

Panigrahi, D.N. *India's Partition: The Story of Imperialism in Retreat*. London: Routledge, 2004.

Peissel, Michel. *Tiger for Breakfast: The Story of Boris of Kathmandu*. Dutton, 1966.

Pokluda, Zdeněk, ed. *Bata: Ze Zlína do Světa, Příběh Tomáše Bati*. Zlin: Bata Foundation, 2009.

-------------------. *Zlin*. Praha: Paseka Press, 2008.

Pyarelal. *Mahatma Gandhi. Volume 1: The Early Phase*. Ahmedabad: Navajivan Publishing House, 1965.

Raghavan, Srinath. *India's War. World War II and the Making of Modern South Asia*. New York: Basic Books, 2016.

Sahni, Bhisham. *Tamas*. New Delhi: Penguin Books, 1988.

Salkeld, Audrey. "The Mad Yorkshireman Gilman." In Peter Gilman, ed. *Everest: The Best Writing and Pictures from Seventy Years of Human Endeavour*. Boston: Little Brown and Company, 1993. 47-48.

Sarila, Narendra Singh. *The Shadow of the Great Game: The Untold Story of India's Partition*. Basic Books, 2006.

Sayer, Derek. *The Coasts of Bohemia: A Czech History*. Princeton, NJ: Princeton University Press, 1998.

Singh, Khushwant. *Train to Pakistan*. Hyderabad, India: Orient Longman, 2005.

Sinha, Dinesh Chandra and Ashok Das Gupta. *1946: The Great Calcutta Killings and Noakhali Genocide: A Historical Study*. Kolkata: Sri Humansu Maity, 2011.

Stern, Robert W. *Changing India*. Cambridge: Cambridge University Press, 1993.

Szulc, Tad. *Czechoslovakia Since World War II*. New York: Grosset & Dunlap, 1971.

Suraiya, Jug. *Rickshaw Ragtime: Calcutta Remembered*. Penguin, 1993.

Tagore, Rabindranath. "Come oh come ye tea-thirsty restless ones -- the kettle." https://www.quotetab.com/quote/by-rabindranath-tagore/come-oh-come-ye-tea-thirsty-restless-ones-the-kettle-boils-bubbles-and-sings#xktvB7HIa9EedSRE.97

Tagore, Rabindranath. *My Reminiscences*. Chapter 15. Project Gutenberg. http://www.gutenberg.org/files/22217/22217-h/22217-h.htm#Page_89

Tharoor, Shashi. *Inglorious Empire: What the British Did to India*. Brunswick, Vic: Scribe Publications, 2017.

The Insia Paper: One Volume Edition of Rudyard Kipling's Verse. Inclusive Edition 1885 – 1918. London: Hodder and Stoughton, n.d.

Tuker, Sir Francis. "While Memory Serves." https://www.sanipanhwar.com/1950 While Memory Serves by Tuker.pdf

Tully, Mark. *No Full Stops in India*. New Delhi: Penguin Books India, 2000.

Twain, Mark (Samuel Clemens). *Following the Equator*. Chapter 54. Project Gutenberg http://www.gutenberg.org/files/5813/5813-h/5813-h.htm#ch54.

von Tunzelmann, Alex. *Indian Summer: The Secret History of the End of Empire.* London: Simon and Schuster, 2008.

Wilson, Jon. *The Chaos of Empire: The British Raj and the Conquest of India.* New York: Perseus Books, 2016.

Wolpert, Stanley. *Shameful Flight – The Last Years of the British Empire in India.* Oxford: Oxford University Press, 2009.

ABOUT THE AUTHOR

Miki Hruska was born and raised in Calcutta, India. Although trained as an engineer, he later took a history degree. He spent many hours researching post-war politics and living conditions of Czechoslovakia and India, which finally answered the questions he always had about why his parents chose to move in 1938. He lives in Edmonton, Alberta, Canada, with his wife, Evelyn Ellerman.